CHILD LANGUAGE

CHILD LANGUAGE

A Reader

Edited by

MARGERY B. FRANKLIN

and

SYBIL S. BARTEN

New York   Oxford
OXFORD UNIVERSITY PRESS
1988

Oxford University Press

Oxford   New York   Toronto
Delhi   Bombay   Calcutta   Madras   Karachi
Petaling Jaya   Singapore   Hong Kong   Tokyo
Nairobi   Dar es Salaam   Cape Town
Melbourne   Auckland

and associated companies in
Beirut   Berlin   Ibadan   Nicosia

Copyright © 1988 by Oxford University Press, Inc.

Published by Oxford University Press, Inc.
200 Madison Avenue, New York, New York 10016

Oxford is a registered trademark of Oxford University Press

Library of Congress Cataloging-in-Publication Data
Child language.
Bibliography: p.   Includes index.
1. Language acquisition. I. Franklin, Margery B., 1933–
II. Barten, Sybil S., 1933–
P118.C455   1988   401'.9   87-13992
ISBN 0-19-504332-4
ISBN 0-19-504333-2 (pbk.)

Preface

This anthology came into being because, over the years, we have become increasingly convinced that students should be introduced to the field of child language through primary sources. The writings collected here are drawn from the work of leading researchers and theoreticians, many of whom have played a critical role in establishing the lines of inquiry that define the field. In reading these selections, students will gain access to the way that questions are posed, investigations framed, and findings evaluated in the research enterprise. They will, at the same time, become acquainted with some of the major theoretical controversies and richest phenomena in child language.

The field of child language is varied and continually expanding. Rather than attempting to present a view of this diversity by providing a few examples of work on each of many topics, we focus on five areas that are considered significant in the field and in which there is ongoing theoretical controversy and productive research. Thus, we seek to acquaint the student with the recent history of the field and to provide an organized view of contemporary work. With very few exceptions, the articles and chapters reprinted here were originally published within the past fifteen years. In selecting articles, we have been guided by several ideas. The collection reflects our interest in the emergence and development of the child's uses of language; it also includes a number of papers specifically addressed to the acquisition and development of language as a formal system. Intent on communicating the excitement of the research enterprise, we have given emphasis to empirical studies. At the same time, we have made certain that theoretical issues are not given short shrift. Most of the empirical studies included in the collection review other research in the field and frame their specific questions or hypotheses in terms of basic theoretical issues; several of the selections in the book are primarily theoretical in orientation. The introductions to each part are designed to bring to the fore major issues that structure inquiry in given areas.

The reader will see that the book's five parts are arranged in some correspondence to a developmental sequence—from consideration of precursors and first phases of language, through acquisition and consolidation of basic language forms and uses, to metaphor and metalinguistic processes. The first part of the book, *Beginnings: From Vocalization to First Words*, is concerned with communicative and referential activity in the transition to language, and with the child's acquisition and use of words in the early phases. The last two papers in this section go beyond first words, focusing on contexts of early lexical development and significant changes in how words mean. *Form and Meaning in Early Language*, the second part of the book, begins with a classic paper that examines phenomena and theoretical conceptualization of the child's earliest word combinations. Specific aspects of grammatical development are taken up in other papers, which focus on interrelations between syntax, semantic relations, and lexicalization patterns in the child's language. Some relations between acquisition of word meaning and formation of concepts are also dealt with in this section. Controversial issues concerning the bases of language learning, and relations between conceptual development and language acquisition, are raised in several of the papers included. In the third section, *Social and Private Speech*, the focus shifts to the functions of language, especially self-directing and communicative uses. Debate in this area centers on the evolution of a social orientation and of communicative skills in young children's language. Part IV, *Discourse: Conversation and Narrative*, includes studies in the rapidly growing area of children's use of language in conversation and storytelling. Investigators in this area have attempted to conceptualize the rules for initiating, sequencing, and terminating conversation and narrative, and the shared knowledge of scripts and story grammars that underlies such uses of language. The first three chapters in the final part of the book, *Metaphor and Metalinguistic Processes*, are concerned with another area of great current interest: children's understanding and use of figurative language. Questions about relationships among the production, comprehension, and explanation of metaphor permeate research in the field. Explaining the bases of metaphor involves the ability to reflect on, and examine, language itself. Such abilities enter into the kinds of metalinguistic performances dealt with in the final papers on jokes, word-object relationships, and verbal definition.

It should be recognized that some topics are taken up in more than one section of the book. For example: (1) aspects of *word meaning* are systematically considered in some papers in parts I, II, and V; (2) the acquisition and use of language as a *communicative medium* is specifically dealt with in papers in parts I, III, and IV; (3) the *rule-governed* nature of language as a formal system and as a communicative medium is given explicit consideration in papers in parts II and IV, and runs as a theme throughout the volume. The teacher will readily discern other overarching topics that are considered in several sections of the book and that can serve as organizing themes in a course on child language.

A range of methodologies is exemplified by the research studies in this collection. Some studies rest on analysis of a single case, while others use a fairly large number of subjects. Situations for gathering observations range from the naturalistic setting of home or classroom to the use of structured tasks in laboratory settings. It will be seen that qualitative analyses of findings are prominent in some studies, while others give more emphasis to quantitative analyses with statistical treatment of data.

This anthology can stand on its own as a set of readings or can be used in coordination with other textbooks. The extensive bibliography at the end of the book is a compilation of references from all of the selections and introductions. It is a very rich resource for further reading. The index will guide the student (as well as the teacher) to specific topics, some of which are dealt with in more than one part of the book. Many of the research articles included are sufficiently accessible to be used as the basis for student research projects. In some cases, this would involve replicating the study in whole or in part; in other cases, the selection could serve as the starting point for designing an original study.

To compile an anthology that covers a group of significant areas in child language and represents research in each area, we felt it was necessary to have a substantial number of articles in the book. Constraints on length led to the very difficult decision to abridge many of the articles—some of them quite considerably. All deletions are indicated in the text, and the original source is cited at the beginning of each selection.

We are deeply appreciative of the authors' agreement to having their articles included in this volume. We take this opportunity also to express our appreciation to a number of individuals who have contributed to the work on this book. We thank librarians at our respective institutions, particularly Paula Hane and Esther Williams at the State University of New York, Purchase, and William Haines, Judith Kicinski and Stephanie Pfaff at Sarah Lawrence College. Evan London worked on compiling the bibliography; Susan Grossman and Cathy Tice helped to construct the indexes. Mary Giuseffi provided secretarial assistance and S. Patrick Larvie assisted with proofreading. Susan Meigs, the editor in charge of production for this book, has been extremely helpful at various stages. We are particularly grateful to Shelley Reinhardt, our editor at Oxford University Press, who has been a source of support and very thoughtful advice throughout the entire process of work on this book, from initial idea to completion.

August 1987   M.B.F.
                                                          S.S.B.

Contents

CHILD LANGUAGE

I

BEGINNINGS:
FROM VOCALIZATION TO
FIRST WORDS

Long before the study of child language became a formal discipline, students of human behavior sought to understand relations between the infant's prelinguistic vocalization and gesture and the emergence of language. Darwin (1877), among others, kept a diary of his child's progress from early cries to the appearance of first words. From the time of these early inquiries to the present day, investigators have provided accounts of the sequence of occurrences that constitutes this evolution. It should be understood that charting such a sequence is not simply a matter of objectively describing what occurs. How the sequence is constructed and, in fact, whether a line of evolution is discerned at all depend on how language is characterized and how the process of language development is seen.

Some psycholinguists, impressed by the unique character of human language, see little direct connection between prelinguistic activity in the child and the beginnings of language proper. These same theorists tend to be highly skeptical of supposed similarities between the communication systems of the higher apes and human language. At the other extreme, certain psychologists—generally endorsing one or another version of behaviorist learning theory—have argued that linguistic behavior is gradually shaped from prelinguistic behavior under the influence of environmental input. In recent years, such simplified forms of "discontinuity" and "continuity" views have given way to more differentiated perspectives that generate questions focused on specific aspects of language and their possible origins in prelinguistic phases of development.

Contemporary research on relations between prelinguistic behavior and the beginnings of language tends to reflect one or both of two major theoretical perspectives. The first perspective emphasizes the referential or representational use of language and the close relations between language development and cognitive growth. Investigators taking this perspective seek to identify origins of reference and conceptual grouping in prelinguistic activity, and to identify sources—within

3

the organism and in the environment—that contribute to the emergence and subsequent development of the child's understanding and use of language as a medium for representing ideas and feelings. The second major perspective stresses the social origins and communicative nature of language. This emphasis has led investigators to examine patterns of prelinguistic interaction—involving eye-contact, gesture, and vocalization—between mothers and infants, and to consider the emergence and development of communicative intent (see Bullowa, 1977).

Werner and Kaplan see language primarily as a referential/symbolizing medium through which meanings are created as well as expressed. In their view, as in Piaget's (Piaget, 1962), the emergence of language is inherently linked to the development of symbolizing capacities that occurs as part of early cognitive development. At the same time, language is seen as a communicative medium that has its origins in the interpersonal matrix of mother-child interaction. In the excerpt from *Symbol Formation* (1983) included here, the beginnings of referential activity are located in the "primordial sharing situation" in which infant and mother together contemplate and indicate—typically through pointing—an object in the outside world. This early situation is conceptualized within the framework of a communicative paradigm involving addressor, addressee, symbolic vehicle, and referent. **Dore, Franklin, Miller and Ramer** focus on the transition from prelinguistic vocalization to first words. Working with data on several children, they suggest that this crucial transition is marked by the use of "phonetically consistent forms" which lie on the borderline between babbling and true words. It is proposed that these vocal expressions serve several discriminable functions; some are primarily affective or instrumental, while others prefigure genuine reference and conceptual grouping.

As many investigators emphasize, a significant portion of prelinguistic gesture and vocalization occurs in interaction situations, appears to be inherently "social," and lends itself to description in terms of conversation. Describing these interaction situations, and attempting to ascertain their significance for language acquisition, have become important research foci in the past 10 years. In her article, **Snow** considers data on two mother-infant dyads in relation to alternative hypotheses about mothers' talk to their babies. Examining the patterning and content of mother-child exchanges from early infancy to the middle of the second year, Snow suggests that long before the beginnings of language, mothers treat their babies as conversational partners—seemingly attributing intentions to them—and that a significant change occurs when the mother perceives the baby as a more active partner in nonverbal exchange, at about 5–7 months. It may be that mothers' interpretations of their infants' vocal and gestural expressions as intentional contribute to progress toward communicational competence. Emphasis on the mother's contribution to the acquisition process, and on dialogue as the basic format within which learning occurs, is also central to **Ninio and Bruner's** study of a mother-child dyad. These authors argue that much early naming occurs without "discernible utilitarian purpose" (such as demand for an object). They propose that the "scaffolding" of dialogic exchange, established early on by the mother, provides a format within which the child moves from prelinguistic referential activity to first mastery of explicit verbal reference—a mastery that involves some grasp of the nature of talk as communication as well as of word-thing relationships (see Bruner, 1983).

Children begin to say their first words between 10 and 15 months, often acquiring a working vocabulary of some size prior to producing their first combinatorial utterances. The interpretation of what is going on during this period has been a matter of interest and controversy since the early part of this century (see, for example, Stern and Stern, 1928; Bühler, 1934). Among phenomena noted by early investigators are three singled out by **Nelson**: the vocabulary spurt that occurs in many children in the middle of the second year; the prevalence of underextensions, overextensions, and overlappings of meaning in the application of early terms, and the disparity between comprehension and production in the period of single-word use. Nelson discusses these phenomena in relation to several fundamental questions that pervade the field: What are the conditions governing the learning of first words? What must we assume, and what can we infer, about the relation between children's nonlinguistic, conceptual structuring of experience at this point in development and their acquisition of words? What underlies the widely noted discrepancy between comprehension and production in the early phases? These questions arise in the context of considering early words as lexical items in the child's developing store of semantic knowledge, that is, as "names" for things or events.

Another perspective on early words is provided by **Gopnik and Meltzoff** in their study of the child's use of relational terms, such as "there," "no," and "more." They point out that there has been an ongoing controversy about whether early use of these terms should be interpreted as social-communicative in character (the "pragmatic" perspective) or as based on encodings of sensorimotor schemes of the kinds described by Piaget (the "cognitive" perspective). Data from several of the studies of Gopnik and Meltzoff lend support to their thesis that, in fact, there is a "shift of function" in the early use of these terms—from social to planning to object-indicating—and that this shift goes along with distinct changes in cognitive functioning, such as the ability to solve certain means–ends problems.

Contemporary investigators emphasize that significant qualitative change takes place within the period of single word speech (see Barrett, 1985). Nelson points to marked changes in the child's use of single words as names. Gopnik and Meltzoff analyze shifts in the meaning of relational terms. It has also been suggested that there is a progression from the use of single words as names to the use of single words as "holophrases" or "predicative syntagms" (Dore, 1985), that is, as one-word expressions for more complex underlying thoughts that, in the next period, will be expressed through two-word combinatorial utterances and, finally, in full sentences.

1

Heinz Werner and Bernard Kaplan

On Developmental Changes in the Symbolic Process

In this chapter, we present an overview of some of the major developmental changes in symbol situations, that is, changes which—in accord with the "orthogenetic principle"—occur in the direction of an increasing differentiation of the components of symbol situations and of increasing integrative systematization (autonomization) of symbolic forms. In the following, then, we focus predominantly on the aspect of differentiation utilizing the developmental notion of "distancing" or "polarization," and shall only briefly touch in this chapter on the correlative developmental aspects of "autonomization."

The situation in which symbolic activity occurs may basically be viewed in terms of four principal (generic) components: two persons—an *addressor* and an *addressee*, the object of reference or the *referent*, and the *symbolic vehicle* employed in referential representation. In the course of development, each of these principal components comprising symbol situations undergoes change, e.g., the *addressor* matures, the *addressees* change from parents to peers to generalized others, the *referents* become increasingly complex and abstract, and the *symbolic vehicles* are of an increasingly conventional and communal nature. Concurrently, the components become related to each other in different ways. Initially, they are more or less fused with each other; they then become progressively differentiated from each other and at the same time linked or integrated with each other in various ways. For a reasonably full account of the development of symbolization, one must consider conjointly both the changes within the components and the changes between components.

For the designation of the process of differentiation in the domains of object

From *Symbol Formation* (pp. 40–44) by H. Werner and B. Kaplan, 1983, Hillsdale, NJ: Lawrence Erlbaum Associates. Copyright 1983 by Lawrence Erlbaum Associates. Reprinted by permission of publisher and Bernard Kaplan. (Originally published, 1963).

formation and symbolization, we shall employ the concept of *distancing* or *polarization*. Here, then, we shall indicate how, in the course of development, there is a progressive distancing or polarization between person and object of reference, between person and symbolic vehicle, between symbolic vehicle and object, and between the persons in the communication situation, that is, addressor and addressee.*

The Primordial "Sharing Situation"

The increasing distancing or polarization of the four components in interpersonal commerce emerges slowly in ontogenesis from early forms of interaction, which have the character of "sharing" experiences *with* the Other rather than of "communicating" messages *to* the Other. The primordial sharing situation (see Fig. 1) may be described as one in which the distancing between the components has hardly begun to form; it is a presymbolic situation in which there is little differentiation in the child's experience between himself, the Other (typically the mother), and the referential object.

Initially, interindividual interaction occurs in purely sensorimotor-affective terms. Sooner or later, however, a novel and typically human relationship emerges, that of "sharing" experiences, which probably has its clearest early paradigm in the nonreflexive smile of the infant in response to the mother's smile (see Kaila, 1932; Spitz and Wolf, 1946). This sharing attitude in its true sense then becomes manifest when the infant begins to share contemplated objects with the Other.

It is worthy of note that within this primordial sharing situation there arises *reference* in its initial, nonrepresentational form: Child and mother are now beginning to contemplate objects together—however slightly these objects are detached from the child's self. Thus, the act of reference emerges not as an individual act, but as a social one: by exchanging things with the Other, by touching things, and by looking at them with the Other. Eventually, a special gestural device is formed, *pointing* at an object, by which the infant invites the Other to contemplate an object as he does himself. . . .

In a primordial sharing situation, what is shared is the concrete object, perceived by both persons but not explicitly delineated; referring to an object by touching, looking, or pointing entails mainly an invitation to the other person to "look at that thing over there!" with the expectation by the person who is pointing that the other person will perceptually articulate this object in a way similar to his own. But sooner or later a higher stage is reached at which sharing in contemplated objects is achieved through *symbols*, particularly through verbal symbols or *names*. The constitutive mark of a symbol, as we have indicated, is its representational function: A symbol represents a referent. Thus, whereas pointing entails

* Figure omitted. [Eds.]

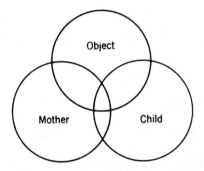

Fig. 1-1. *Diagram of primordial sharing situation.* ·

only reference, the indication or denotation of a concretely present object, symbolization involves differentiation and integration of two aspects: reference to an object and representation of that object. In reference by pointing, the referent (the object) remains "stuck" in the concrete situation; in reference by symbolization, the characteristic features of the object (its connotations) are lifted out, so to speak, and are realized in another material medium (an auditory, visual, gestural one, etc.). From this early situation, in which symbolic vehicles (names) are intimately bound to the concrete situation and shared by persons intimately linked to each other, there ensues in the course of ontogenesis an increasing distance between the four components of the symbolizing activity.

2

John Dore, Margery B. Franklin, Robert T. Miller, and Andrya L. H. Ramer

Transitional Phenomena in Early Language Acquisition

Virtually every investigator of early child language for the past century has identified three major periods of development: the prelinguistic, the one-word stage, and the multiple-word stage. In the past some investigators have considered all three periods in their characterization of language development, while others have focused primarily on one or another of these "stages." The history of the field indicates that at different times one or another of these periods has been the principal area of interest—depending upon the influential theories or crucial issues of the time (Stern, 1928; Bühler, 1934; Lewis, 1936; Brown and Fraser, 1963). Currently attention has centred on the cognitive and semantic aspects of language acquisition (Bloom, 1970; Brown, 1973), and still more recently there has been a marked resurgence of interest in the one-word stage (Bloom, 1973; Clark, 1973b; Dore, 1975; Greenfield and Smith, 1976; Nelson, 1973).

Despite the strong and persistent interest in early child language, little attention has been given to developmental phenomena occurring between (or apart from) the three major periods. This relative neglect appears to be the result of several related factors: lack of theoretical interest, tendencies to assimilate transitory (borderline) phenomena to well-established nodal points, and, until recently, the absence of or insufficient use of audiovisual technology. We believe that the transitions between the developmental milestones are extremely important for at least two reasons: (1) their delineation is essential to a complete description of language development, and (2) they bear directly on basic theoretical issues concerning developmental progression.

The existence of transitional phenomena has not gone entirely unnoticed in

Abridged from "Transitional phenomena in early language acquisition" by J. Dore, M.B. Franklin, R.T. Miller, and A.L.H. Ramer, 1976, *Journal of Child Language*, 3, 13–29. Copyright 1976 by Cambridge University Press. Reprinted by permission of publisher and author.

the literature. Concerning the acquisition of words, Lewis (1936) observed that his son used stabilized sound patterns in certain situations and he suggested that while these are not words, they cannot properly be considered simply as comfort or discomfort sounds or as babbling. Similarly, Leopold (1939) found that his daughter produced clusters of consistent sounds that were not like conventional words but were distinct from babbling in that they had a "constancy of meaning." Piaget (1962) argued that the first word-like utterances of his children were not genuine words but "semiverbal signs" that were often idiosyncratic in form, closely linked to action, and in many respects more like the symbols of early play than like words in a language system. Finally, referring to the diary literature and to the work of H. Tischler in 1957, Werner and Kaplan (1963) demarcated a category of "vocables"—utterances that lie on the borderline between babbling and conventional words.

Regarding the transition from one-word utterances to multiple-word speech, isolated observations have been made. Leopold (1949), for example, found that late in his daughter's one-word stage she began to utter strings of single words. He argued that each word was essentially a separate utterance because, taken together, the string of words could not be analyzed in terms of adult syntactic patterns. Bloom (1973) elaborated upon Leopold's insight in two important ways. First, she videotaped many successive single-word utterances produced by her own daughter, formally distinguishing these from syntactic utterances by pointing out that their word order was not constrained and that each word had its own intonation pattern (typically, each word received a primary stress and had a falling terminal contour). Second, Bloom found a significant related phenomenon—occurrences of single words accompanied by an "empty form" (phonemically/widə/), both produced within a single prosodic envelope. It seems clear that "successive single-word utterances" and this "/widə/ phenomenon" are on the one hand something more than one-word speech and on the other something less than syntax. Still another kind of utterance that appears to be transitional between one-word and patterned speech is the child's "playing" with the sounds of phrases and sentences whose meaning he apparently does not know. This has often been observed, although not satisfactorily explained, in the language development literature (Jakobson, 1968; Weir, 1962).

In this paper we describe two kinds of transitional phenomena and propose a theoretical framework for interpreting these phenomena and for explaining their relations to the milestones of language development. Our approach offers a more systematic treatment of these above-mentioned phenomena than has been previously provided. The data were collected as part of a larger study of the child's second year of development. Each of four children (three boys and one girl), all from middle-class backgrounds, were videotaped in 1-hour sessions once a month. The child's mother and a nursery school teacher were with the child during the sessions that centered on free play in a familiar setting. The children's utterances were independently transcribed by two of the authors, and a third author settled initial disagreements. In addition, the child's actions and the relevant features of the context were recorded. Further specification of all nonverbal material, in particular detailed behavioral descriptions of the children's affective states, was made independently by another of the authors. The children ranged in age from 0;11 to 1;4 at their initial session and were observed over an 8-month period. Only two of the children progressed beyond single-word utterance productions. The observations we report below provide illustrative examples of the transitional categories we postulate.

Phonetically Consistent Forms

In the early stages of the investigation we observed that the children produced phonetically consistent forms (PCF) that appeared to be intermediate between prelinguistic babbling and words. These forms are characterized as follows: (1) PCFs are readily isolatable units, which are bounded by pauses (unlike babbling); (2) they occur repeatedly as items in a child's repertoire of sounds; (3) PCFs can be partly correlated with specifiable, recurring conditions—thus, their production is neither random in the sense ascribed to babbling nor do they conform to rules governing words; and (4) they exhibit what might be described as a "protophonemic" structure in so far as their phonetic elements are more stable than in babbling although less stable than in words.

The first step in our procedure was to identify phonetically similar forms that occurred more than five times in a single session. Judgments of phonetic similarity were based upon three criteria: identity of syllabic structure, consonantal similarity concerning manner and place of articulation, and vocalic similarity concerning tongue placement and height. Second, we examined phonetically similar forms for consistencies in conditions of usage. On this basis, four function categories for PCFs were identified.

1. *Affect expressions* are stabilized around specific affects such as joy, satisfaction, anger, or protest; they are expressions of mood or attitude. The judgment of the child's affective state rests upon the interpretation of nonvocal cues such as facial expression, posture, and body movement. These utterances do not appear to be directed toward any person or any aspect of the surroundings. For example, one child uttered [æːː] in a variety of contexts: looking at a puppet while holding up a bottle, playing with hats, rocking on a horse, walking around the room with a cup in her mouth. On all these occasions pleasurable affect was evident. The same child said [iːːː] in varying circumstances, invariably as an expression of protest at her mother's intrusion into an ongoing activity. Another child used [gaga], [gægi], [gagi], and [əgagi] at different times when pleasurable affect was apparent: while chewing on crayons, while being dressed, while idly handling a toy. The same child said [eːːː] on varying occasions involving completion of a circumscribed action, apparently as an expression of satisfaction.

2. *Instrumental expressions* occur in contexts in which there are grounds for inferring that the child wants an object and/or seeks to engage an adult in a

specific activity (thus this category subsumes utterances traditionally called "conative" in function). The particular objects or activities vary greatly, the common condition being the child's orientation toward obtaining something. The primary cues for identifying such a goal-directed orientation are the child's gestures of reaching, grasping for, or in some cases a more global bodily "straining toward." The appeal to an adult, which is almost always involved, is evidenced by a shift in directed gaze from object to adult or vice versa or by body movement. One child uttered [m:::] as she walked to her mother and reached for a coffee cup, as she reached her mother's purse, and as she reached for her bottle. Another child said [ʌ] and [ʌː] on different occasions when he entered the kitchen, apparently seeking the food located there which was almost always given to him. Here we may note that Lewis (1936) cites his son's utterance of 'e-e-e' ($14\frac{1}{2}$ to 16 months), accompanied by directed reaching, in situations in which he desired objects beyond his grasp.

3. *Indicating expressions* occur in conjunction with the child's taking note of, or indicating to another, some aspect of the environment. The characteristic nonvocal behavior that provides the basis for interpretation here is pointing accompanied by directed gaze. In contrast to instrumental expressions, these utterances most often occur in the absence of any manifest desire to obtain anything or to engage in action with another—the child does not reach for or strain toward an object, and does not become dissatisfied if nothing happens as the result of his vocalization. For example, one child used [bæ] and [dæ] alternately in such situations: as she turned on a play horse and looked out the window, as she looked back at the bathroom after leaving it, as she looked at herself in the mirror, and when she looked at a ring of plastic beads in the sink. Each time the utterance was produced with an abrupt rising-falling intonation pattern. A month later, the child produced [ʌh], accompanied by pointing. Another child uttered [dədi] with the same intonation when pointing in the direction of the door or upon hearing footsteps, and the form [didi] when pointing to various pictures in a book, or pointing to his mother. The forms [dæ] and [idædæ] also occur in conjunction with pointing to certain objects and pictures.

Bloom (1973, p. 71) remarks that her daughter used a "deictic form" [ə ↑], accompanied by pointing, with great frequency for about a month (1;1 to 1;2) and she notes that this may have been preceded by a "primitive demonstrative that was phonetically variable." Leopold (1939, p. 61) describes his daughter's use of [da] at 1 year and [a] slightly later, both involving pointing. Although forms like [dæ] and [da] appear similar to the adult *that*, they are so variable in form and function as to be totally unlike the adult word upon closer analysis.

4. *Grouping expressions* appear to reflect an interaction between subjective state and attention to object properties (or other aspects of the external situation), but the organizing factor seems to be affect. Two generic types of grouping expressions can be distinguished. In one type different utterance forms are associated with the same group of objects, depending upon the child's affective state. For example, one child used [ubiba] (and [ubibu], [upibu], [əbiba]) in relation to

a peg, a crayon, a puppet, and a jack-in-a-box, along with the expression of mild frustration; the same group of objects was associated with [ədæ] (and [dæ]) at other times, along with the expression of relative contentment. That these utterances are not simply affect expressions is indicated by the fact that they did not occur in other conditions of mild frustration or relative contentment, but only when one of these objects was present. In the second type of grouping expression the child uses one form in conjunction with two very different objects that evidently have similar affective import for him. For example, a child uttered [babi] repeatedly with respect to his bottle, and he used the same form in relation to a favorite doll. Thus, he applied the same PCF to two very different objects on the basis of a subjective commonality: these were the two objects he apparently used for emotional reassurance.

Our data clearly indicate that different children use different forms for different functions, which suggests that the "selection" of forms is not biologically determined (as in expressive cries) nor governed by social convention. Also, utterances here have been characterized in terms of *dominant* function; however, even stabilized forms in a child's repertoire serve more than one function (Halliday, 1973), particularly since intentions are not highly differentiated at this point. Further, there is undoubtedly a complex interaction between the stabilization of the phonemic patterns of words and the development of intonation patterns that serve the expression of intentions apart from the expression of lexical content (cf. Dore, 1974).

PCFs and First Words: The Emergence of Reference

The problem of identifying first words (involving a distinction between prelinguistic vocalization and genuine speech, and the relation between the two) has been a persistent one on both practical and theoretical levels (cf. Jakobson, 1968; Kaplan and Kaplan, 1971). Investigators have employed one or both of two general criteria for identifying a child's initial word (Darley and Winitz, 1961): (1) the approximation of phonetic form to forms of the adult language, and (2) consistencies of usage with regard to objects or situations. Both criteria allow wide latitude for operationalization. The second, involving inferences about function, is clearly more problematic; nonetheless, it is most often central. Thus, most investigators accept as "words" some forms that do not at all resemble items in adult speech. More importantly, the second criterion typically involves some notion of reference, often left unspecified.

The PCFs we isolated do not for the most part approximate adult word forms and thus fail to meet the first criterion for "word." Here we shall argue that, in addition, these utterances cannot be said to refer in the conventional sense, although two *uses* of PCFs—the indicative and grouping expressions—probably contain germs of reference.

The status of reference in earliest speech has been a matter of some dispute.

Some have argued that even highly idiosyncratic forms can be interpreted as referential in the sense that objects or situations "named" by a given term share criterial attributes and so constitute a primitive class. Thus, Clark (1973b) has argued that the range of application (overextension) of earliest terms is based on saliency of perceptual attributes in the external situation (size, movement, shape, etc.). Bloom (1973, p. 75) takes issue with such interpretations, suggesting that prior to the time when overextension occurs in terms of criterial features distinguishing classes of objects, there are overinclusions that represent "a loose and shifting association of figurative, functional or affective features of otherwise diverse objects and events." She discusses an example from Guillaume: the use of his child's *nénin* at 11 to 12 months to "ask for the breast; in reference to the red button on a piece of clothing; the point of a bare elbow; an eye in a picture; his mother's face in a photograph" (1973, p. 73). Bloom appears to take the position that *what* these early terms refer to may differ dramatically from what later terms refer to, but she does not seem to seriously question *that* they refer. More fundamentally, Nelson (1974) criticizes Clark's "semantic feature" theory of word acquisition for not being able to distinguish between "perceptual" and "semantic" features, for not allowing for conceptual meaning independent of lexical items, and for the fact that much recent data on earliest words do not support the theory. Nelson argues instead that many perceptual features are secondary in importance for word acquisition: "the outstanding characteristic of children's first words is their basis in dynamic or functional relations . . . they refer to things that move or change in some way or that the child can act upon" (p. 279).

Nelson's view is similar in some ways to that developed by Werner and Kaplan (1963) and Piaget (1962), who draw a distinction between early forms (vocables; semiverbal signs) and later word usage. They emphasize the distinction not in terms of range or type of reference, but in terms of the fusion of the subjective and objective, thus highlighting the problematic status of referring in earliest speech. The application of a given term is governed only in part by attention to properties of objects and events; it is also governed by subjective factors—the child's stance (emotional and/or physical) *vis à vis* the diverse objects or situations in question. For example, *tch-tch* was used by Piaget's daughter J. at 1;1 in relation to a train passing below the window; shortly thereafter it was uttered in relation to cars, carriages, and a man walking (seen from another window) and also in a disappearing game played with her father (1951, p. 216). Piaget suggests that his daughter's use of *tch-tch* does not reflect designation of objects or the recurrent pattern of movement *per se*, although this is one aspect in its application. Rather, *tch-tch* (and other utterances he cites) are said as accompaniment to situations that have a subjective commonality (in this case having to do with the physical position from which the child views given events).

We propose that referential utterances must meet two criteria: (1) they must *indicate* in the sense that an act of indication serves to point to some thing or event, often singling it out in a larger field and so calling attention to it (Searle, 1969; pp. 26–27), and (2) their use must provide some differentiation among alternatives (Olson, 1970), which results in the use of the same form for members of a given group and the use of different forms for different groups of entities. In other words, term A refers if it is used consistently to indicate any member of the set (X,Y,Z) whose members have something identifiable in common, and is *not* used to indicate any member of the set (Q,R,S). To this may be added the more stringent criterion that a term A may be said to refer only if there is another term B that is used consistently to indicate a member of (Q,R,S) but is not used to indicate a member of (L,M,N). If the second condition is applied, a child with a one-term vocabulary cannot be using that term referentially.

Given this characterization of reference, neither indicative PCFs nor grouping PCFs are genuinely referential. Indicative PCFs meet the first criterion, at least in part, but do not in any way reflect the partitioning of alternatives inherent in genuine reference. Grouping expressions are indeterminate with respect to the first criterion and, since their application is only semiconsistent, they do not fully meet the second criterion either.

We suggest, however, that indicative and grouping PCFs contain germs of reference. At the entrée to speech, the child "knows" something about indication-in-general (as evidenced in pointing) and develops the hypothesis that sound segments, like gestures, can be used to perform acts of indication. But given only this hypothesis he does not use vocalization to indicate *discriminatively*—thus the same form is used in relation to widely divergent objects or events that are not in any sense organized cognitively as a group [not even through associative chaining, as in Vygotsky's (1962) "chain complex"]. In this regard we suggest that the forms *uh oh* and *there* by Bloom's daughter do not "encode relations" (i.e., refer to commonalities in events) but are simply indicative expressions since they were used interchangeably to "point out objects or people that were noticed or found" (1973, p. 87). Grouping PCFs appear to reflect a relation—however tenuous—between utterances of a given form and some primitive experiential groupings. That is, in contrast to indicative PCFs, these utterances are used across objects or situations that are loosely organized in terms of a subjective commonality.

Whereas Piaget has stressed the importance of primitive cognitive organizers (sensorimotor schemas), our data suggest that attention must also be paid to affect-governed organizations. We propose that the child's use of affect-related PCFs reflects a hypothesis distinct from the one that underlies purely indicative utterances: namely, the same sound-form is to be produced in relation to various but similar situations (i.e., primitive experiential groupings). In that these utterances evidence the use of a given vocalization in relation to events presumably grouped in terms of experienced commonalities, they could prefigure the partitioning of alternatives inherent in genuine reference. In our view, then, productive linguistic reference results, in part at least, from the confluence of two hypotheses operative in the transitional phase: that a segmental sound pattern can serve the indicative function, and that other sound patterns can relate globally to sets of objects or events that are linked together in terms of experienced commonalities.

In a similar vein, it might be suggested that affective and instrumental PCFs are precursors for the emergence of words that do *not* primarily encode the representation of objects, events, properties, or relations in the environment. We have in mind here terms such as exclamations of surprise, highly circumscribed utterances in games like "peekaboo," greetings and leavetakings, ritualistic and rote forms, and many other of the child's early words that have no well-defined, stable referents. Such words apparently serve to express emotion or to negotiate interpersonal relations, and in this sense they are probably the late linguistic developments of affect and instrumental PCFs.

Presyntactic Devices

Syntax has been defined as the system of rules for the combination of words in grammatical relation to each other. In dealing with the developing rather than the mature system, the need to differentiate between successive single-word utterances and utterances that have a true combinatorial output is clear. Prosodic features constitute a succinct way of making this distinction. In this paper syntactic utterances are considered to be those in which two or more words are produced forming one intonational pattern and in which the relation among the words is one of the factors determining the meaning of the utterance.

Examination of the corpora revealed that there were certain multiple-item utterances that did not meet the above criteria and thus were not truly syntactic. However, since these utterances were composed of more than a single word, neither could they be considered one-word utterances. We identified several distinct kinds of utterances transitional between one-word productions and syntactic combinations, and we labeled them *presyntactic devices* (these phenomena were first described in Ramer 1974). For some types, more than a single word is produced, but lexical content is lacking for one of the forms; in other cases, the productions involve rote forms in which the individual elements do not appear in combination with other elements. . . .*

Summary and Discussion†

The sequence of development we postulate is summarized in Table 2-1, which also provides contrastive definitions of the transitional phases we describe. The table outlines the child's development from meaningless, phonologically undifferentiated babbling to utterances with two or more words within a single intonation pattern bounded by pauses and having one primary stress.

Virtually all linguistic theories have recognized that the fundamental crite-

*The following section on presyntactic devices is omitted. [Eds.]

† Report of quantitative findings and two tables are omitted. [Eds.]

Table 2-1. *Summary of Classificatory Criteria for Types of Utterances*

Types of utterance (in sequence of emergence)	Criteria	
	Sound	Meaning
Prelinguistic babbling	Prosodically unisolatable units and nonphonemic	No meaning
Prelinguistic jargon	Prosodically isolatable patterns and nonphonemic	No meaning
Phonetically consistent forms	Prosodically isolatable, but nonphonemic units	Loose associative or expressive relation to conditions of usage
Words	Conventional phonemic units	Differentiated reference
Presyntactic devices	Word plus "empty" phonetic forms in single prosodic pattern	Differentiated reference
Successive single-word utterances	Chained conventional phonemic units forming separate intonation patterns	Differentiated reference
Patterned speech (syntagmas)	Prosodically complex patterns	Combinational (or structural) meaning

ria by which the linguistic status of any utterance must be measured are sound and meaning and the relation between the two. Indeed, language has been defined by Chafe (1970, p. 15) as "a system which mediates, in a highly complex way, between the universe of meaning and the universe of sound." Our data on language development indicate some of the ways in which the child accomplishes his central task of coordinating sounds with meanings. We would argue, furthermore, that the way the child accomplishes this coordination differs from the explanations proposed by recent grammatical approaches to the acquisition problem.

Whereas most investigators have claimed that children acquire syntactic and/or semantic categories *directly*, we suggest that what the child acquires are *syntagmas*. Kozhevnikov and Chistovich (1965) define the syntagma as the structural unit that correlates sounds with meanings in the *process* of speaking. McNeill (1974) claims that unlike one-word productions, the child's earliest multiple-word utterances are organized as syntagmas that represent conceptual schemas in terms of phonetic strings. In this paper we have of course been concerned with the earliest development of syntagmas, that is, with how the child comes to coordinate a conceptual meaning (and combinations of meanings) with linear sequences of phonetic elements in articulation.

The existence of successive single-word utterances and presyntactic devices provides evidence that the child is acquiring syntagmas as opposed to learning formal grammatical categories directly: successive single-word utterances express two separate referring items in two separate intonation patterns; presyntactic devices express one referential item and a nonreferential item within a single intonation pattern. These two transitional phenomena are best viewed as complementary failures to produce integrated syntagmas, the first lacking prosodic integration and the second lacking referential integration. Both of course lack a relational component. Thus, in so far as syntagmas are organizational schemas for relating meanings to phonetic outputs in the speech process, they appear to be conceptual developments that do not require the specifically syntactic or semantic knowledge described by formal linguistic theories.

Our analysis suggests, then, that sound and meaning develop partly independently and that the child must learn to put the two together. In other words, the process of forming sound-meaning correlations seems to be central to the child's learning of language. Both in the acquisition of reference and the acquisition of syntagmas, the child must bring his knowledge of meaning into line with his knowledge of sounds: in reference he coordinates single conceptual representations with phonemic strings; in syntagmas he coordinates conceptual relations with prosodic patterns. The transitional phases we have described as immediately preceding these linguistic acquisitions clearly provide the child with the necessary preliminary content to make operative this process of sound-meaning correlation.

We suggest, further, that this progression in sound-meaning correlation involves a bridging process. This refers to the child's ability to acquire *part* of a major acquisition prior to his mastery of other parts and the subsequent integration of parts in the whole. The applicability of this notion to language development seems particularly à *propos* when we consider how often it has been reported that children "practice" various aspects of language separately at different points in development. Babbling, for example, appears to serve the function of limiting productive sounds to the phonological system the child is exposed to. Similarly, "jargon" has often been considered to serve the function of practising prosodic patterns of the model language. In the case of PCFs the child is acquiring stabilized phonemic forms, without attempting the kind of systematic coordination with conceptual representations that is requisite for conventional word usage. And in the case of the PSDs we described, the bridging process allows the child to acquire complex intonation patterns without having yet acquired structural meanings. The child can then insert lexical items into these intonation frames as he learns new words and as he constructs new conceptual relations.

If the above views of the child's development are correct, then what begins to emerge is a conceptual-pragmatic explanation of early language that contradicts the grammatical theories that have dominated the field for the past decade. Although we agree that the child must acquire grammatical competence in his language, we suggest that such learning occurs later in development than is currently supposed. Simply because the child's earliest utterances have been *described* in purely grammatical terms does not constitute evidence that the child in fact "knows a grammar." And, in fact, we propose that conceptual syntagmas provide an adequate basis for acquiring grammatical categories.

3

Catherine E. Snow

The Development of Conversation
between Mothers and Babies

Studies performed over the past 5 years have offered evidence that the speech
addressed to children of language-learning age is simpler and more redundant
than speech to older children and adults. The simplicity is reflected in such
measures of syntactic complexity as mean length of utterance (MLU) and incidence of subordinate clauses, both of which are very low in speech to young
children (Phillips, 1973; Snow, 1972). Redundancy, as reflected in type-token
ratios (Phillips, 1973) and in incidence of repetition of utterance constituents or
entire utterances (Snow, 1972), is very high. A more complete review of simplicity and redundancy features in speech to young children is given in Snow (1977).

In addition to these modifications, speech to young children is different
from speech to adults in several other ways. Pitch of the voice is higher and
prosodic contours are exaggerated (Garnica, 1977; Remick, 1975). A special
lexicon of baby-talk words is used, which shows predictable phonological simplification and deviation from the adult words (Ferguson, 1977). A remarkably high
incidence of interrogatives is also typical in speech to young children; as many as
50% of the utterances were found to be interrogatives in one study (Sachs, Brown
and Salerno, 1972). The question arises why these modifications occur, and why
the same modifications have been observed in all the languages and social class
groups studied, regardless of the sex of the child addressed or the sex or maternal
status of the speaker (these findings are reviewed in Snow, 1977). Even children
as young as 4;0 produce many of these same modifications when addressing 2
year olds (Sachs and Devin, 1976; Shatz and Gelman, 1973). . . .

A crucial prediction of the view that the child listener's attention and comprehension are responsible for the features typical of speech to children is that these features will not appear until the addressee is 1;0–1;2 and able to respond to adult speech differentially. Syntactic simplification would not be expected until the addressee is old enough to process the syntactic form of the speech addressed to him (at about 1;3–1;4, if we make the unwarranted assumption that receptive control of syntax precedes expressive control by about 2 months). Large amounts of repetition would not be expected before the addressee is old enough to distinguish redundancy levels in speech (about 1;2 according to Friedlander's 1968 findings). Phillips (1973) found that speech addressed to children of 0;8 showed a greater variability in utterance length, ratio of function to content words, number of verbs per utterance, type-token ratio, and percentage of weak verbs than speech addressed to those of 1;6 or 2;4. Phillips interpreted her findings as supporting the notion that mothers adjust their speech to their children's linguistic level, and that no adjustment is therefore called for before the child has any language. Similarly, under the assumption that mothers repeat words, phrases, and entire sentences because their children do not fully comprehend the original utterance, one would hardly expect to find such repetition to very young children who could not be expected to understand in any case. Although no fully adequate description has been given of the functions of questions in mothers' speech to children, it has been reported that many of these questions are tutorial (e.g., 'What is it?,' 'What color is it?,' Snow et al., 1976), and that others function as requests for action (Newport, Gleitman and Gleitman, 1977) or for clarification of preceding child utterances. One would expect that all these various question types would start to appear only after children had started talking and understanding. Similarly one would expect that the high proportion of imperatives in mothers' speech would not appear until an age when compliance could reasonably be expected.

The present study was originally carried out to test the prediction that the central characteristics of mothers' speech to children would be introduced at 1;0–1;2 or later, and thus to evaluate the explanation that these characteristics are produced in response to cues of inattention and poor comprehension from the child. Since an explanation in terms of attention and comprehension seemed unable to explain the findings, an alternative hypothesis about the mechanism determining the characteristics of mothers' speech to children is presented.

Quantitative Analysis

The speech of two mothers to their babies at several ages between 0;3 and 1;8 was analyzed. The last two points analyzed for each mother can be seen as providing overlap with the studies of mothers' speech cited above. The earlier ages, well before the babies could talk or respond to syntactic features in their mothers' speech, provide the crucial test of the attention and comprehension hypothesis.

Ann and Mary were normal, first-born daughters of middle-class English parents whose mothers volunteered to participate in a study on the development of intention. In connection with that study, vidio and audiotapes were made in the home at 2- to 3-week intervals from the time the babies were 0;3 until they were 1;0. Starting at about 1;6, audiotapes were made at approximately 6-week intervals. The transcription of some of these tapes provided the basis for the analysis presented here. Tapes made when Ann was 12, 29, 49, 79, and 87 weeks old and when Mary was 13, 22, 29, 38, 44, 52, 75, and 81 weeks old have been analyzed for the relevant mothers' speech features. Each tape contains 20 consecutive minutes, including a feeding session and the immediately preceding or following play session.

The number of maternal utterances and the amount of time devoted to feeding and play in each session are presented in Table 3-1. It is striking that the MLU, the most-used index of syntactic complexity, showed almost no change over the 15-month period. The mothers' speech to Ann and Mary at 0;3 was as simple as at 1;6. All the MLU values fall well within the range found in the other studies.

Though Ann's mother's longest utterances were as short at 0;3 as at 1;6, Mary's mother's MLU10L was quite high until Mary's first birthday. She produced a small proportion of relatively long utterances, which were faster and lower pitched than most of her utterances, and which gave the impression that she was "talking to herself out loud." These had disappeared by 1;6. This small proportion of utterances not directed at the child at the earlier ages may be what Phillips (1973) was tapping with her finding of greater variability in various mothers' speech features at 0;8. . . .*

Data from MLU and interrogatives have been discussed in some detail because these are two often-cited characteristics of the mothers' speech register for which considerable data were also available from other studies. Other measures calculated for Ann and Mary include the percentage of declaratives, imperatives, and "contentless" utterances (utterances consisting of verses, songs, sound-play, imitations of the babies' babbles, etc.), and the temporal reference of the mothers' utterances.† For these measures, as for MLU and interrogatives, there is no indication whatsoever that the characteristics of the mothers' speech change abruptly at 0;10 to 1;2, in response to the children's growing linguistic abilities. Changes that did occur started about 0;7, if not earlier. This suggests strongly that explanations of the mothers' speech register purely as a response to cues of attention and comprehension from the child have been simplistic and incorrect. Another explanation must be sought for why mothers' speech is the way it is.

The speech of Ann's and Mary's mothers did change strikingly between 0;3 and 1;6 in terms of what they were talking about. If each maternal utterance (except the contentless utterances and exhortations such as *come on*) is classified in terms of whether it refers to the child, to the mother, to entities or actions in

---

*Data pertaining to mothers' use of interrogatives are omitted. [Eds.]

†Two tables omitted.

Table 3-1. Amount of Time Spent and Number of Maternal Utterances Produced in the Feeding and Play Portions of the Sessions Analyzed

	Ann (age in weeks)					Mary (age in weeks)							
	12	29	49	79	87	13	22	29	38	44	52	75	81
Minutes of feeding	17.50	8.50	3.50	10.00	5.50	9.10	10.50	12.20	15.40	9.00	5.45	7.40	10.00
Minutes of play	3.45	13.00	16.20	10.00	14.10	12.20	10.30	9.10	5.40	12.30	15.45	12.20	10.00
Utterances, feeding	133	66	23	139	90	45	80	56	127	65	53	123	109
Utterances, play	100	150	231	130	280	157	149	112	69	148	235	276	198
Utterances, total	233	216	254	269	370	202	229	168	196	213	288	399	307

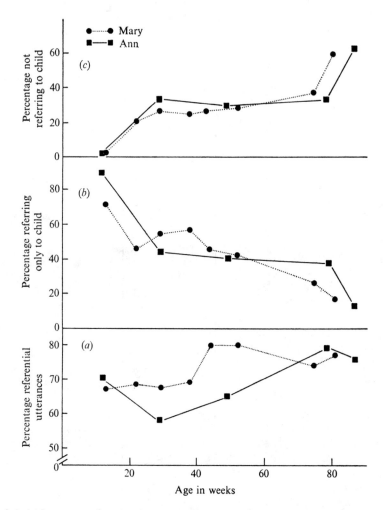

Fig. 3-1. *(a) Percentage of maternal utterances that were referential. (b) Decline with age in the percentage of referential utterances that referred only to the child. (c) Steady increase with age in the percentage of referential utterances that did not refer to the child at all.*

the world, or to combinations of these, then a steady decline is seen in the references to the child alone, and a steady increase in utterances containing references to the world (see Fig. 3-1). At the earliest age, the mothers were talking a great deal about the children's feelings and experiences (their being tired, hungry, bored, what they were looking at, etc.), and at later ages about their activities and about objects and events in the immediate environment. The mothers were attuning their speech to their children's growing interest in objects and activities outside themselves, and their need for information about those objects and activities. This attunement began, however, well before the children could realistically be said to have needed it or to have been actively eliciting it. The change started by 0;5 for Mary and by 0;7 for Ann. Thus, for this measure of the maternal speech, like the others, one must reject the hypothesis that the characteristics of the mothers' speech register appear as responses to the child's need for or attempts to elicit appropriately simplified, redundant, and semantically relevant speech.

Conversational Model

What, then, is the explanation for these adjustments in the mothers' speech? And what changes occur in the mother-infant interaction at 5–7 months that could explain the changes in mothers' speech style that takes place then? Answering these questions requires looking more specifically at the functional aspects of the maternal utterances, and especially at the nature of the interaction the mothers were engaging in with their babies. I would suggest that the interactions between these mothers and babies can best be described as conversational in nature, and that the changes in the maternal speech result from the development of the baby's ability to take her turns in the conversation. In order to support this contention, I will cite some examples of interactional sequences that occurred between Ann and her mother (similar sequences from the transcripts of Mary and her mother could also be quoted) and analyze them using the conversational model presented by Sacks, Schegloff and Jefferson (1974).

The hypothesis that the mothers were using a conversational model in interacting with their children rests on two crucial assumptions: that they were trying to communicate specific information to the babies, and that they were receiving (or trying to receive) specific information from them. The conversational mode differs from other communicational modes precisely in that it is *reciprocal*—information is exchanged between the partners in both directions. It is thus of special interest that the mothers would choose this reciprocal system for interacting with babies still so young that their ability to communicate was very limited. If the mothers' only purpose was to keep the babies quiet and contented or attentive by talking to them, then they could have chosen any of several other modes of interaction—telling stories, singing songs, reciting poems, talking nonsense, or thinking aloud. In fact, the mothers made almost no use of a monologue mode; even when they did sing songs or recite nursery rhymes they did so as part of a game in which the baby also played a role, e.g., the Ride-a-cock-horse game described by Bruner (1975b). Essentially, all of the mothers' speech was related in content to the baby or the baby's activities and direction of attention, and much of it was directed toward eliciting responses from the baby. It is for these reasons that it seems appropriate to describe the mothers as operating within the conversational mode in interacting with their babies.

Sacks et al. (1974) proposed a two-part system for the organization of turn-taking in conversation: a *turn-constructional* component, which produces the unit types that make up a speaker's turn; and a *turn-allocational* component, which operates through a set of rules to determine who will speak next. The turn-allocational component operates only at transition-relevant places, which are determined by the end of the unit type selected by the current speaker. Unit types may be words, phrases, or clauses; they are, in fact, equivalent to the units traditionally called utterances. The end of an utterance is a transition-relevant place, i.e., a place at which a new speaker may be selected or may select himself, or where the current speaker may continue with another unit type. The most common technique for self-selection as the next speaker is by starting to talk first. The means by which the current speaker selects the next speaker include the "adjacency-pairs," i.e., utterances that by their nature demand a reply from a specific person, such as a question addressed specifically, a compliment, an insult, or a greeting. The rules proposed by Sacks et al. are designed to account for turn-taking in multiparticipant conversations. The mother-child interactions studied here were simpler, in that only two potential participants were present. They also differed in that, whereas getting one's turn is a major goal in adult conversations (Sacks et al. suggest that it is a motivation to go on listening carefully), getting the child to take her turn seemed to be the primary goal of the mothers studied. Nonetheless, much of the mechanism suggested by Sacks et al., especially the notion of speaker selection by the use of adjacency-pairs, seems very useful in describing the mother-infant interactions discussed here and in accounting for many of the characteristics of the mothers' speech.

THREE MONTHS

Before discussing the evidence supporting the conversational interpretation of mothers' speech to young babies, it is perhaps instructive to cite an example of a very typical exchange at 0;3:

(1)	Mother	Ann
		(smiles)
	Oh what a nice little smile!	
	Yes, isn't that nice?	
	There.	
	There's a nice little smile.	(burps)
	What a nice wind as well!	
	Yes, that's better, isn't it?	
	Yes.	
	Yes.	(vocalizes)
	Yes!	
	There's a nice noise.	

This sequence demonstrates several points. First of all, it gives an example of the short, simple, baby-centered utterances typical of the mothers' speech at this time. Second, it includes three cases of specific maternal responses to infant behaviors. These are typical of many more instances; at 0;3 in fact, 100% of both Ann's and Mary's burps, yawns, sneezes, coughs, coo-vocalizations, smiles, and laughs were responded to by maternal vocalizations, suggesting that under conditions of reasonable proximity such responses were almost obligatory for these mothers. Third, it exemplifies the nature of maternal responses to the class of infant behaviors in question: the behavior is referred to specifically, either by naming, as above, or by using a relatively stereotyped content-related response, such as *That's better* or *Pardon you* to a burp, and *What's so funny?* or *Do you think that's nice?* to a smile. Such specific, content-related and predictable responses on the mothers' part have been taken as the criterion for referring to infant behaviors as unit types within the Sacksian model, i.e., as the units that constitute a turn. Using this criterion of maternal responsiveness, it is possible to identify a fairly restricted class of infant behaviors that at 0;3 qualify as unit types: smiles, laughs, burps, yawns, sneezes, coughs, coo-vocalizations, and looking attentively at something. These behaviors do not satisfy the normal adult criterion for a unit type, that it be intentional and communicative. However, they do all have in common that they are directly interpretable, i.e., that they can be responded to as if they were intended to communicate something specific. Infant behaviors that do not have this quality of signalling something unambiguous about the infant's state of mind, e.g., arm or leg waving, bouncing, head movements, or crying, do not seem to function as infant unit types in conversational interactions.

Responding, even responding consistently and reliably, to this class of infant unit types does not provide the basis for very extensive turn-taking, partly because the babies did not emit such behaviors very often. The mothers devoted a much greater proportion of their utterances to trying to elicit specific responses, most often coos or smiles, from the babies. That these utterances had the very specific function for the mother of trying to elicit turns from the baby, thus justifying our referring to them as first-pair parts of adjacency-pairs, is evidenced by the fact that the topic of the maternal utterances was shifted as soon as the elicitation was successful. Ann's mother at 0;3 devoted 124 consecutive utterances to the topic of burping, and shifted to the topic of what Ann was looking at as soon as Ann had indeed burped. The adjacency-pair nature of these turn sequences is, of course, apparent only to the mother. It is she who is imposing on the interaction the rules of conversation, of which her baby is still unaware (though it has been suggested that babies of this age are capable of elementary turn-taking; Jaffe, Stern & Perry, 1973). The mothers' attempts to maintain a conversation despite the inadequacies of their conversational partners account for the most striking characteristics of the maternal speech style—its repetitiveness, the high frequency of questions [especially tag questions and postcompleters such as *Hmm?*, which are described by Sacks et al. (1974) as devices for passing a turn on], and the frequency of sequences such as (2) and (3), in which the mother takes both parts:

(2)   Mother
Oh you are a funny little one,
aren't you, hmm?
Aren't you a funny little one?
Yes.

(3)   Mother
Where is it? (referring to the
baby's wind)
Come on, come on, come on.
You haven't got any.
I don't believe you.

The mother here repaired the breakdown in the conversational exchange by filling in for the baby, taking the turn for her. A further conversation-repair device used by the mothers at 0;3 consisted of phrasing questions so that a minimal response on the baby's part could be treated as a reply. In (4) the mother shifted topics as if the baby had said she was finished, whereas all she had in fact done was refrain from crying when the bottle was removed.

(4)   Mother
Are you finished?
Yes? (removing bottle)
Well, was that nice?

This sequence also exemplifies one of the most ubiquitous features of the mothers' speech at even the earliest age studied: the mothers constantly talked about the child's wishes, needs, and intentions. A crying baby was always offered specific comforts, as if the mother's task was to find out something the baby already knew. Persistent crying was referred to as "being stroppy," as if it reflected intentional naughtiness. The babies' behavior was never described as random, and only rarely as a function of physiological variables. It was seen, just as adult behavior is seen, as intended and intentional. This view of infant behavior is of course prerequisite to the attempts to communicate with the baby, and to interpret the baby's behavior as communicative, which have been described above . . . The tendency to report intentions and consequences instead of actual behavior is not peculiar to mother-infant interaction; it is simply more striking there because nonvoluntary behaviors such as burps are also interpreted as intentional and because the basis for assigning intention is so often unclear to the observer.

The mothers talked very little to the babies during bottle feeding while the bottle was in the mouth at 0;3 (see Table 3-1). Maternal utterances during the feeding sessions were restricted to the winding episodes, unless the baby did something special which elicited a response, such as ceasing to suck (eliciting

Table 3-2. *Frequency of Speaker-Switching and Mean Length of Maternal and Child Turns for Ann and Mary at 0;3, 0;7, 1;0 and 1;6*

	0;3		0;7		1;0		1;6	
	Ann	Mary	Ann	Mary	Ann	Mary	Ann	Mary
Frequency of speaker-switching	18	24	56	30	70	72	222	226
Mean length of maternal turns in utterances	23.50	15.54	7.45	10.50	7.06	7.78	2.42	2.98
Mean length of child turns in unit-types	1.00	1.00	1.04	1.07	1.03	1.00	1.19	1.08

What's the matter? or *Have you had enough?*) or staring at something in the room (eliciting *What are you looking at?* or *What can you see?*). The lack of maternal utterances during bottle feeding supports the contention that the mothers' speech was produced on the basis of a turn-taking model. The mother's aim was to engage in adult-style conversation with true turns, and she therefore refrained from talking when the baby was prevented from answering. A similar pattern emerged during spoon feeding, when maternal utterances were produced between spoonfuls, not when the baby's mouth was full.

Interestingly, crying on the part of the baby did not seem to act as the first half of an adjacency-pair in the same way as burping, smiling, laughing, etc. The mothers did, of course, respond to crying, but they did not respond in specific and predictable ways, perhaps because crying gives too little information about what the appropriate response would be.

SEVEN MONTHS

The most striking change between 0;3 and 0;7 was that the babies were at 0;7 considerably more active partners. This is reflected in the figures given in Table 3-2, which show that the mean length of a maternal turn (i.e., the mean number of maternal unit types that followed one another without intervention of a baby unit type) declined drastically between 0;3 and 0;7, and the frequency of speaker switching increased concomitantly. The increased participation of the infant in the interaction occurred in spite of the facts that the baby's repertoire of unit types had expanded only slightly, and that the mothers had become somewhat more demanding as to what kinds of vocalization they accepted as a unit type.

At 0;7 the baby could initiate an adjacency-pair by smiling, laughing, or burping, as at 0;3, and also by producing a kind of protest cry. This cry was observed when, for example, Ann's mother persisted in offering a spoonful of food that Ann had already refused, and when Ann's mother restrained her from moving out of camera range. It was more discrete than the crying at 0;3, and had much more the character of a signal which the mother had to respond to, e.g.

(6)	Mother	Ann
		(protest cry)
	Hey hey hey hey hey	(protest cry)
	Hey come on, lookit, look shh.	(looks at mother)
	There.	

The mother no longer responded to all child vocalizations, only to "high-quality" vocalizations, i.e., a vocalic or consonantal babble. These high-quality babbles were quite frequent and did elicit sure responses, often in the form of imitations. Elaborated and lengthy babbling sequences were responded to with *What was that all about?* or *Oh, really?* Responses to the baby's babbles accounted for 7.2% of Ann's and 4.4% of Mary's mother's utterances at 0;7. The turn-taking character of babble imitations is made especially clear in the transcript from Ann and her mother, because Ann's mother had introduced an imitation game, in which she set rules about the nature of the correct response. This is illustrated in (7):

(7)   Mother   Ann
    Ghhhhh ghhhhh ghhhhhh
    ghhhhhh
    Grrrrr grrrrr grrrrrr grrrrr   (protest cry)
    Oh, you don't feel like it, do   *aaaaa aaaaa aaaaa*
    you?
    No, I wasn't making that
    noise.
    I wasn't going aaaaa aaaaa.   *aaaaa aaaaa*
    Yes, that's right.

This imitation game was, in principle, symmetrical, with either partner privileged to imitate the other. In fact, as the quoted exchange indicates, Ann often failed to observe the rules, and her mother carried much of the structure of the game.

The babies had at 0;7 a somewhat larger repertoire of motor responses that could be recruited into the turn-sequences. Taking a bite of food was accepted by Ann's mother as a response to *Isn't it nice?*, looking about or reaching for an object as a response to *What's that?* or *Where's it gone?*, and looking at the mother as a response to the child's name. In example (8) Ann's mother refers to the object as *it* in her third utterance, as if Ann had named it, whereas all Ann had in fact done was to establish joint reference by looking at the object:

(8)   Mother   Ann
    Look, what's that?
    What's that?   (looks at object)
    Well you thought it'd gone
    away, didn't you?

In spite of the fact that the children were more active in taking their turns at 0;7 than at 0;3, they still very often failed to do so. Occurrences of maternal questions without answers and of such conversational repairs as mothers answering their own questions and simplifying their own questions were still frequent. *

TWELVE MONTHS

The turn-taking activities at 1;0 did not differ greatly from those at 0;7, although in general the babies were both responding more reliably to maternal utterances and were initiating more adjacency-pairs with their own activities. The nature of the mothers' responses to the infant vocalizations had changed. Rather than

---

* Here and subsequently, some examples are omitted. [Eds.]

simply producing imitations of the high-quality babbles, the mothers now sometimes expanded or explained the babble, implicitly accepting it as an attempt at a
word:

(9)   Mother   Ann
                                           abaabaa
    Baba.
    Yes, that's you, what you are.

Hiding and finding objects had become a favorite game for Ann, one which
ideally allows symmetrical turn-taking, but which was initiated only by the
mother at this stage:

(10)   Mother   Ann
        (rattling container) *What's in*
        there?
        What's in there?   (drops object out)
        There it is.

The following sequence was initiated by Ann, but she failed to take her second
turn, so her mother had to answer her own question:

(11)   Mother   Ann
                                          (straining to get out of mother's
                                          arms)
    Oh, where do you want to go
    then?
    Hey!
    Where do you want to go?
    Where do you want to go?
    You want to go exploring.

   Although the turn-taking activities did not change greatly in nature between
0;7 and 1;0, the number of and amount of time spent in shared activities increased steadily from 0;3 until 1;0. At 0;3 Ann and her mother had only two short
periods of shared social activity—an episode of mutual looking, and the protocon-
versational sequence partially quoted above. By 1;0 they shared several different
kinds of activities, some of which extended over several minutes, e.g., their
imitation game, hiding and finding an object, retrieving an object from inaccessible places, and looking at Ann in a shiny surface.

EIGHTEEN MONTHS

By the time she was 1;6, Ann was taking her turn quite often and most of her unit
types consisted of words. Her mother expected not only that she would take her
turn, but that she would provide appropriate responses, e.g.,

(12)	Mother	Ann
	Who's that?	*Daddy.*
	That's not daddy, that's	
	Dougall.	
	Say Dougall.	

(13)		*Hot.*
	Hot, hot.	*Tea.*
	No, it's not tea, it's coffee.	*Coffee.*
	? (incomprehensible	*Coffee.*
	utterance)	
	You're not having coffee	
	now, you're having dinner.	

Such sequences of response, correction, and corrected response, which occurred for pronunciation corrections as well as content corrections, formed an important part of the turn-taking at 1;6.

Almost any clearly articulated word from Ann seemed to function as the initiator of an adjacency-pair at 1;6, and her mother would even interrupt an ongoing conversation with the observer to respond to them. Example (14) shows how Ann's words initiated new conversational topics:

(14)	Mother	Ann
		(blowing noises)
	That's a bit rude.	*Mouth.*
	Mouth, that's right.	
	Face, yes, mouth is in your	*Face.*
	face.	
	What else have you got in	*Face.* (closing eyes)
	your face?	
	You're making a face, aren't	
	you?	

Even if the mother had nothing to say about the new topic, she never failed to respond by at least repeating the word. This mother's insistence on politeness formulas and her consistency in responding to them provided another turn-taking situation, e.g.,

(15)	Mother	Ann
	(giving Ann a biscuit) *What*	
	do you say?	
	What do you say?	
	No, you don't put it straight	
	in your mouth.	
	What do you say?	*Thank you.*
	There's a good girl.	

and numerous cases of (16):

(16)   Mother   Ann
                         Please.
       Please what?

Ann's mother continued to use the question-reformulation technique to make it easier for Ann to take her turn:

(17)   Mother   Ann
       What else have you got in
       your face?
       Where's your nose?
       Where's your nose?
       Ann's nose?

(18)   *Where's Titus?*
       He went out, didn't he?

However, in spite of the imperfect turn-taking, the interaction at 1;6 gave the strong impression of being a real conversation, both in terms of the frequency of speaker switching and in terms of the apparent effectiveness of the communication. This impression was dependent on the mother's willingness to follow up on any conversational opening given by the child, and to fill in for the child whenever necessary. Ann still clearly violated some of the rules of turn-taking— for example, by interrupting a conversation going on between mother and observer, by introducing new topics before current topics were exhausted, and by failing to complete many adjacency-pairs introduced by the mother. The mother very effectively kept the conversation going, in spite of these inadequacies on the part of her conversational partner, by her constant willingness to cede a turn to the child, to accept any reasonable attempt at a word as a first pair part, to follow the child's shifts in conversational topic, to fill in for the child when she missed her turn, and to change the form of her own first pair parts until they did elicit a response.

Discussion

The hypothesis that mothers operate on the basis of a conversational model in interacting with their babies helps to explain some of the striking aspects of mother-infant interaction and some otherwise puzzling aspects of the mothers' speech register as well. This hypothesis accounts for the fact that mothers talk to young babies at all, and explains why they talk to them most while in a face-to-face position or sharing activities, and least while feeding. Furthermore, it accounts for the very high frequency of questions in speech to babies: questions, especially tag questions and other postcompleters such as *Hmmm?*, are devices for passing the turn to the partner, which is precisely what the mothers are trying hardest to do. Another adjacency-pair used by mothers in much the same way is greetings; an analysis is currently under way of the situations in which mothers greet their infants, but preliminary observations confirm that mothers greet infants after only very short absences or separations, situations in which greeting an adult would be quite abnormal. Both questions and greetings enable the mother operating within the conversational mode to treat any response on the part of her child as a communicative response, because the mothers' conversational rules dictate that the unit types that follow questions or greetings be responses. Very often, of course, the question or greeting was not followed by any behavior that could be interpreted as communicative, and then the mother was forced into conversational repair procedures such as repetition or taking the baby's turn.

The nature of adults' speech to 2-year-old children can also be better understood if it is recognized that such speech occurs within conversations and is largely directed toward keeping the conversation going (Lieven, 1978). For example, the mothers studied used turn-passing devices frequently, but never used turn-grabbing or turn-keeping devices (prestarters such as *Well . . .* and *But . . .*, and pause fillers), which are quite frequent in adult-adult conversation. This fact may help to explain the absence of inappropriate pausing, segmentation ambiguities, and false starts in mothers' speech to 2 year olds. Mothers' desire to communicate reciprocally with their children, which underlies their use of the conversational mode, may well be a crucial factor in limiting the topics discussed and thus the semantic and syntactic complexity in mothers' speech. The question-reformulation sequences and similar sequences with imperatives may account for much of the utterance and constituent repetition in mothers' speech to 2 year olds, as it does in mothers' speech to babies. Furthermore, recognition of the skill and insistence with which mothers introduce the conversational mode into their interactions with their children may help to explain how children acquire turn-taking skills, both in conversation and in other types of interaction, so early (Escalona, 1973; Keenan, 1974).

The way in which mothers talk to their babies is one reflection of their belief that the babies are capable of reciprocal communication. Their choice of the conversational mode not only reflects this belief, but also provides opportunities for reinforcing it by giving meaning within the rules of conversational turn-taking to the infant behaviors that occur. . . . Maternal expectations about infants' abilities both arise from and are tested by the nature of the interaction mothers establish with their babies. An important question for future research is the extent to which the nature of the interaction established between mothers and infants in the first year of life contributes to the speed and the nature of later language acquisition.

4

Anat Ninio and Jerome Bruner
The Achievement and Antecedents of Labeling

One of the first uses a child makes of his emerging language is to *name* people and objects (Greenfield and Smith, 1976; Leopold, 1949; Werner and Kaplan, 1963). *Nominals* comprise up to 64% of a child's 50-word vocabulary (Nelson, 1973), while in terms of frequency of occurrence in his speech they appear in the majority of utterances in the first months of speech production (Greenfield and Smith, 1976). Analyses of the contexts in which naming occurs indicate that a substantial amount of it occurs without a discernible utilitarian purpose, such as a demand for an object. The child appears to name objects and people for the sake of naming itself, and seems, moreover, to take great delight in doing so.

A number of investigators, puzzled by the apparent sophistication displayed in the early use of nominals, have questioned whether the function of early nominals is the same as that of adult naming, i.e., informing another that an object has a specified name. Atkinson (1974) has pointed out that early naming is stimulus bound and fulfils principally an attention-getting or attention-directing function, while Halliday (1975) regards naming either as "interactional" (i.e., a means of getting another's attention), or as "practice" (all examples of which he excluded from the language-corpus analyzed in his book). Bruner (1975b), following Harrison (1972), has suggested that it is a technique for bringing another's attention to one of a set of alternative environmental objects or events. Brown (1973) pointed out that early nomination occurs in a setting where it serves either to call attention to the presence of a referent or to demonstrate that the child is able to match the name and referent, e.g., a teaching-learning situation.

An added perspective is offered by Werner and Kaplan (1963). These authors propose that reference emerges as a concomitant to a new mode of treating the world, as "objects-of-contemplation" rather than "things-of-action." But Werner and Kaplan offer no explanation for the shift to the contemplative attitude, apart from the general psychodynamic development of the child, which enables him at this age gradually to "separate" himself more from the world. In their view, the mother's role in the emergent new behavioral pattern is solely to provide the interpersonal context in which the child "shares" his experiences with her, rather than "communicating" messages to her (1963, p.79).

The present paper reports the results of a longitudinal study of a single mother-infant pair in the process of mastering the use of standard lexical labels from the eighth to the eighteenth month of the infant's life.

The fashionable assertion that language is learned but not taught, a hyperbole nurtured by a decade of "strong" nativism in the 1960s, is nowhere less true than in the child's acquisition of a lexicon. Indeed, there is some reason to believe (Nelson, 1973; Lieven, 1978; Cromer, 1976) that there is more than one form of pedagogy among mothers and possibly several routes to acquisition.

At the outset of any bout of language acquisition—whether it be pointing, labeling, or making comments on shared topics—the mother has possession of a skill that the child either lacks completely or "has" only in some primitive sense, as when he has mastered pointing but is unable to use labeling as a linguistic device. It is almost invariably the case, as Snow (1976) reminds us, that the child, for all his ineptness, is *seen* by the mother as having the intention to carry out the function that will later be realized by the linguistic form she is trying to teach him. As Ryan (1974) proposed, the mother's pedagogy might consist of supplying the appropriate form to what she guesses the child is intending to express. In consequence, as Holzman suggested (1972, p.312), "the child finds out by the responses of adults what he is assumed to mean by what he is saying."

All this contributes to the construction of a kind of "scaffolding dialogue" between mother and child. The origin of this dialogue obviously precedes the emergence of labeling. Indeed, it now appears as if even the earlier exchanges between mother and infant have a contingent pattern, with the mother responding selectively and even imitatively to the child's gesturing and vocalization, and the child then responding to the mother's response. Trevarthen's work (e.g. 1974) certainly suggests this early origin, as do the precise studies by Daniel Stern (1975) on turn-taking in early vocal and gestural exchanges. In time, the dialogue increases in complexity and serves as a "carrier wave" for new communicative functions—for signaling and responding to demands, for directing attention, and so on.

In the study to which we now turn, we have used book reading as a principal source of data—the mother and child looking at pictures in a book. We have chosen to concentrate on book reading since it appeared to be the major activity in which labeling occurred. Moreover, we were particularly eager to study the continuity between labeling and earlier forms of ostension, e.g., pure pointing.

When Richard, our subject, first achieved pure pointing for indicating objects (at around 0;10) it was most likely to occur with a referent that could not be manipulated (Bruner, Caudill and Ninio, 1977). Many of these referents were pictures in picture books. This continuity of contexts seemed to be more than a coincidence and thus justified a closer investigation.

Method and Procedure

The data were drawn, as noted, from a longitudinal study of one mother-infant dyad between 0;8 and 1;6. The child was a first-born only child. His parents were white, English, and middle class, the mother having worked as a secretary before the child was born. The father was a schoolmaster.

Videorecorded observations were made in the home at 2- to 3-weekly intervals. Each session consisted of 30 minutes of normal play, routinely engaged in by mother and child. Two experimenters were present in these sessions, one filming. Most sessions were also audiotaped. Book reading occurred in the natural course of play and no special instructions were given about it.

The data tapes, marked in real time, were analyzed with a stopped-frame Sanyo VTR. All book-reading sessions were analyzed. Such sessions were defined as those interactions between mother and child that involved initiating, maintaining, executing, and stopping joint looking at picture books. In all, twelve filming sessions contained incidents of book reading, the first of these at 0;8.

Video data were first transcribed into a written protocol, note being taken of the duration of various behaviors. The following behaviors were recorded. For the mother:

1. the full content of all verbal utterances;
2. the occurrence of pointing to a picture;
3. laughing.

For the child:

1. the occurrence of all vocalizations, with the following additional information: (a) the content of obviously articulated or word-like vocalizations (i.e., possible lexical items) and (b) the apparent functional category of all other vocalizations, i.e., excitement, demand, fretting, and book reading, the last a "basket" category for every vocalization not categorized as excitement, demand or fretting;
2. gestures (toward the book), in the following categories: mouthing, manipulating, hitting, touching, reaching, scratching, pointing;
3. smiling;
4. direction of gaze: to book, to mother, to the experimenter, at other parts of the room, searching for specified objects in the room.

Transcribing was performed jointly by two recorders. In the event of disagreement a decision was arrived at by asking for a third opinion.

Examination of the timing of the mother's and child's behaviors indicated an almost complete alternation pattern, i.e., the two participants could be best described as taking turns in a conversation or dialogue. The next step in data analysis was, then, to identify discrete dialogue cycles (Stern, 1975; Garvey, 1974) in the continuous stream of mother-child interaction. Only cycles of book reading were analyzed in this way.

The *onset* of a reading cycle was defined as occurring if:

1. a book was open to a picture, within easy sight, *and*
2. mother *or* child was paying attention to a picture and was pointing, gesturing, or vocalizing in a fashion directed to the contents of the book. This excluded passive gazing at a book, calling for a book at a distance, simply turning pages without looking, etc.

The *offset* of a reading cycle was defined as occurring when any of the following occurred:

1. the book ceased being open to a picture within sight;
2. a new picture was introduced, i.e., the onset of a new cycle;
3. the child's attention was withdrawn from the picture as shown by manipulation of the book, leaving the scene, fretting, etc. A gaze at adults was not considered to end a reading cycle unless the child did not return to the picture within a few seconds, but lapsed into another activity;
4. mother's attention was turned away from book reading for more than a few seconds.

Concluding turns were excluded from the cycle (e.g., a fretting vocalization of the child's and the mother's response to it).

Discrete *turns* in a reading cycle were defined as follows. Two adjacent vocalizations or gestures by the same person were considered to belong to two different turns of a dialogue cycle if they were separated by a pronounced pause, whether the pauses were filled or unfilled by the other person. A set of such turns constituted a cycle if they met the requirements noted above for onset and offset.

Two independent recorders assigned the recorded behavior elements to cycles and turns. Interrater reliability was 96.4%, which is the percentage of all instances on which the two recorders agreed. All discrepancies were referred back to the videotape recordings and, in every case, an agreement was reached. In addition, every label uttered by the mother was recorded for nine complete half-hour sessions (from 0;10 to 1;6) whether the label occurred in book reading or not. Labels were defined as the stressed element in a demonstrative utterance, e.g., "It is (an) X," the X being a stressed nominal, verb, or modifier. The referents of these labels were categorized as to their position at the time of labeling—whether they were manipulated by the child, at a distance from him, or were pictorial referents.

Results and Discussion

To begin with, we may inquire whether labeling occurs in particular contexts—recalling that we had noted earlier that its precursor, pointing, was limited to situations in which grasping and manipulation were not present. Pointing, of course, is under the control of the child. Does the mother conform to the same rule? An analysis was made of the circumstances under which Richard's mother labels objects, based on nine full 30-minute sessions from 0;9.27 to 1;5.21. Of the specified objects 7.2% were being manipulated by the child as they were labeled, 17.2% were at a distance from him, and 75.6% consisted of a picture. This distancing of objects for labeling probably serves to ensure that the child's attention is free and therefore more easily directed to the names of objects, rather than to their manipulative characteristics.

The choice of pictures as the preferred vehicle for vocabulary teaching is significant by itself. Pictures, being two-dimensional representations of three-dimensional objects, have special visual properties: they can be perceived both as a two-dimensional object *and* as representing a three-dimensional visual scene. This poses a conflict for a child, which he solves increasingly by assigning a privileged, autonomous status to pictures as visual objects. There is steadily less evidence of the child trying to manipulate, grasp, or scratch pictured objects on a page. This process might be one of the stepping stones to grasping arbitrary symbolic representation in language, since visual representations are themselves arbitrary in the sense that a crucial object property, i.e., graspability, is missing.

The most striking characteristic of labeling activity is that it takes place in a structured interactional sequence that has the texture of a dialogue. Here we find ourselves in agreement with Stern (1975) and Snow (1976), both of whom note the early appearance of patterned turn-taking in rule-governed situations involving gestures, eye contact, and vocalizations.

The early forms of "dialogue" observed in the present study and others conducted along similar lines (Bruner, 1975b) are mostly thing-oriented and involve the use of a concrete object that serves as the topic of the exchange. This might take the form of a game of give-and-take in which an object is passed from child to mother or from mother to child and back again. This game exhibits the basic characteristics of dialogue, in that it ascribes roles, turn-taking, initiating, and responding to another. Once book reading starts, the child uses his already established skills for dialogue to engage in a structured exchange on nonconcrete topics. It is not surprising, then, that joint book reading by mother and child very early and very strongly conforms to the turn-taking structure of conversation. Indeed, turn-taking in book reading is nearly perfect from the start, with only about 1% of the two participants' phrases occurring simultaneously rather than alternately.

During the investigated period, principally between 0;11 and 1;6, reading dialogue cycles were highly constant on a number of structural characteristics.

The mean number of turns per cycle (average of 11 sessions) was 3.9 (*sd* 1.3), the mean duration of a cycle was 5.8 seconds (*sd* 2.2), and the mean duration of a turn was 1.49 seconds (*sd* .25). Spearman rank correlations failed to reveal a significant age trend in any of these measures ($r = -0.255$, -0.316, and -0.144, all > -0.535, $p > 0.05$, 11 *df*, for turns per cycle, time per cycle, and time per turn, respectively). These constancies in the dialogue are quite remarkable if one considers that during the same period the child's linguistic performance undergoes profound changes, including the appearance of standard lexical words in his communicative repertoire. In the following we shall attempt to identify some of the factors contributing to these formal constancies, and to assess their significance to the child's acquisition process.

To begin with, the variety of the mother's utterances in book reading is very limited: she makes repeated use of four key utterance types. These are the *attentional vocative Look*, the *query What's that?*, the *label It's an* X, and the *feedback utterance Yes*. They are illustrated below by an example from the session at 1;1.1.

> Mother: Look! (*attentional vocative*)
> Child: (Touches picture)
> M: What are those? (*query*)
> C: (Vocalizes and smiles)
> M: Yes, they are rabbits. (*feedback and label*)
> C: (Vocalizes, smiles, and looks up at mother)
> M: (Laughs) Yes, rabbit. (*feedback and label*)
> C: (Vocalizes, smiles)
> M: Yes (Laughs) (*feedback*)

All dialogue cycles defined by our rules (see above) contain at least *one* of these utterance types by the mother, although each type might take some slightly different token form. Table 4-1 presents the distribution of the tokens found for each major type.

These key utterances by the mother account for virtually all of her utterances in reading cycles during the whole of the period studied. Moreover, it should be noted that the wording and intonation of these utterances are indistinguishable between the early and the late sessions. The key utterance types have strict privileges of occurrence and ordering. Every book-reading cycle initiated by the mother begins with one of the *Look*, *What's that?* or *It's a (label)* type of sentence. Within a given cycle, the order of these sentences is almost always constant: *Look* precedes *What* (in 94.7% of the cases, $n = 19$, $p < 0.001$, binominal test), *Look* precedes a label (in 92.9% of the cases, $n = 28$, $z = 3.97$, $p < 0.01$); and *What* precedes a label (94.3%, $n = 35$, $z = 4.73$, $p < 0.01$). A feedback type of utterance that either confirms or corrects the child's contribution nearly always occurs in a later position than either *Look* or *What* (92.9%, $n = 28$, $z = 3.97$, $p < 0.01$; 97.6%, $n = 41$, $z = 5.78$, $p < 0.01$). It always follows a phrase of the child's. Since feedback utterances often occur with label, the

Table 4-1. *Distribution of Utterances Classified as Tokens of the Four Major Types of Maternal Speech*

Type/tokens	Frequency	Type/tokens	Frequency
I. Look	65	III. (cont.)	
Look!	61	More X	3
Look at that	4	They are X	3
		These are the X	3
II. What question	85	The X	2
What's that?	57	You can see the X	1
What are those?	8	That one is X	1
What are they doing?	6	Look at the X	1
What is it?	5	It says: X	1
What are they?	1	We'll call it an X	1
What's on that page?	1	Kind of X	1
What have we got here?	1		
What's the next one?	1	IV. Feedback	80
What's over here?	1	Yes	50
What else can you see there?	1	Yes I know	8
What does that do?	1	It is not X	5
What do you see there?	1	That's it!	3
What can you see?	1	Isn't it	2
		Not X	2
III. Label	216	No, it's not X	2
X(=a stressed label)	91	Yes, it is	1
It's a (an) X	34	That's charming	1
That's a (an) X	28	You are right	1
There is a (an) X	12	No, it's an X, not a Y	1
A (an) X	12	No, it's an X	1
That's X	6	Yes, they are	1
There is X	6	Yes, very good!	1
Lots of X	5	That's not an X	1
They are X-ing . . .(e.g., going to bed)	5		

position of the two is not ordered, given that sentences such as *Yes, it is an* X are common. When feedback and label utterances appear together in a pair of separate sentences, the latter almost invariably follows the former.

These privileges of occurrence suggest that the mother uses the key utterances with due regard to accepted presuppositional structure. That is, *Look* presupposes that the other person is not attending to a shared focus of attention; it it not used once shared attention has been achieved. Conversely, *What's that?* presupposes that the referent of *that* has been established previously. Similarly, the occurrence of labeling after the query, rather than before it, is conventional. In this sense it is important to note that no gross modification of the adult's customary use of language is required to carrying out book reading. The mother is acting in a linguistically conventional manner.

There are, of course, fundamental differences between adult-to-adult conversation and that of a mother with a small infant. As Trevarthen (1974), Snow (1976), and others have reported, mothers are ready to accept an astonishing variety of responses on the baby's part as his turn in the conversation and to interpret anything he does as having a specific, intelligible content. The imputation of intent and content to the infant's signaling behavior probably constitutes an important part of the mechanism by which the child is advanced from more primitive to more adult-like communicative behaviors. This mechanism might be at its maximal efficiency when repeatedly and consistently applied in a standard action format (Bruner, 1975b). These are simple and recurrent joint action patterns (like playing peek-a-boo or putting on a pair of shoes), in which the participants seem to have worked out a mutually clear set of expectations and actions. Since the set of possible "meanings" in such a format is both restricted and shared, these might provide the referents to which more and more advanced communicative signals are attached.

The book-reading situation has the characteristics of such a standard action format, with the additional qualification that its language-teaching function is more central than in other formats. As we have seen, in its basic form it consists of just three ordered elements (the attentional vocative, the query, and the label). It is possible for the mother to go through the three-step routine by herself, with the child providing minimal participation by passively attending to her and to the book. But on the great majority of occasions the child takes his turn in the cycle in a more active way and this provides the mother with a signal that she then interprets as the child's taking over of one or more of the elements in the labeling routine.

The mother usually responds to the child's turns by a new turn of her own (72.3%) within the same cycle. This tendency to continue to discuss a particular picture if the child seems to be interested in it undergoes very little change as the child grows older (Spearman rank correlation $= -0.49 > -0.51$, 12 df, n.s.). The mother reciprocated equally to the child's response whether it was vocal or gestural (71.6% versus 75.5% reciprocity, $\chi^2_{(1)} = 1.44 < 3.84$, $p > 0.05$, n.s.). However, the mother was more likely to respond to a turn of the child's if it constituted the initiation of a new dialogue cycle (86.0%) than if it constituted a reciprocation of a previous maternal turn in an already started dialogue (68.5%, $\chi^2_{(1)} = 5.95 > 3.84$, $p < 0.05$).

The child's initiating turn, if it is recognized by the mother, is mostly interpreted by her as meaning both *Look!* and *What's that?*: in 78.7% of the cases she immediately labels the picture that the child is looking at. In the other 12.8% of the cases she asks a *what* question, and 8.5% of the time she utters a reinforcing comment. When the mother is responding to a turn of the child that is in mid-cycle, the distribution of her responses is different: there are more reinforcing comments (27.5%), fewer labels (57.3%), and about the same percentage of *what* questions (15.2%, $\chi^2_{(2)} = 7.44 > 5.99$, $p < 0.05$).

Guessing what is "on the child's mind" is obviously crucial to the teaching of a vocabulary. The use of pictures must surely narrow that guess. Once the mother has some reason to believe that the child knows the object presented in a picture, she can provide a label for it as the most likely candidate for reference.

There is, of course, the classical many-many mapping problem of reference, i.e., how to achieve a match between that *attribute* of the picture the child may be noticing and the attribute singled out by the mother's label. In our dyad, the problem was bluntly but probably effectively managed by the mother's concentrating most of her labeling upon *whole* objects or *whole* persons in the picture. Table 4-2 presents the distribution of the mother's labels according to their referential focus. The words considered as labels were, of course, the Xs in sentences such as *It is an X, An X, See X,* etc. All labels were stressed, sometimes in an exaggerated manner. Each label was counted only once per cycle, even if it was repeated in the cycle several times. In turn, the child used labels that in adult discourse conventionally stand for whole objects, as also indicated in Table 4-2.

Once mother and child step out of the labeling routine, the range of possible interpretations of the child's focus of attention opens up dramatically. When, for example, the mother reads a nursery rhyme aloud and the child vocalizes at the end of a line, there is no simple way for her to guess his intended meaning. Since she wishes to stay in a conversational framework, she responds, but can do so only with a "contentless" phrase, e.g., *Yes, I know, You are right, Yes, it is,* etc. In none of the dialogue cycles that started with a rhyme or a procedural comment of the mother was there ever a reply by the mother to the child's response in the form *Yes, it is a (label)*, while 37.5% of reading dialogues with a like reinforcing comment contained a label as well in the same turn ($\chi^2_{(1)} = 5.47 > 3.84$, $p < 0.05$). The comparison suggests why book reading is such an effective means of assuring significative convergence between mother and child.

Imputation by the mother of reference or of meaning in book reading seems to be anything but indiscriminate or self-delusory. On the contrary, it seems to be based on a constantly updated, detailed "inventory" of the child's past exposure to objects and events, of the words he has previously understood, and of the forms of expression he has achieved. The Richard corpus is abundant with evaluative utterances in which the mother expressed (perhaps partly for the experimenter's benefit) the reasons for her expectations that the child would or would not recognize a picture or utter a label. For instance: *You haven't seen one of those; that's a goose. You don't really know what those are, do you, they are mittens;*

Table 4-2. *Distribution of Mother's and Child's Labels by Referential Focus*

Type of referent	Mother's Labels (%)	Child's Labels (%)
1. Common nouns of whole objects	88.9	89.8
2. Common nouns of parts of objects	2.9	4.1
3. Proper names	4.1	4.1
4. Other (actions, attributes etc.)	4.1	2.0
Total (%)	100.0	100.0
Total number of labels	170	49

Table 4-3. *Proportion of Reading Cycles in Which the Child Emitted an Active Response, Proportion of Active Turns of the Child's Containing a Vocalization, and Proportion of Vocalizations Which Were Lexical Labels, by Age*

Age	Number of reading cycles	Cycles in which child emitted at least one active response (%)	Number of active turns by the child	Active turns containing a vocalization (%)	Vocalizations that are lexical labels (%)
0;8.14	2	50.0	4	0.0	0.0
0;11.7	9	55.6	17	35.3	0.0
1;0.25	7	71.4	10	90.0	0.0
1;1.7	6	83.3	13	76.9	0.0
1;1.22	40	37.5	17	41.2	0.0
1;2.7	26	43.8	18	38.9	28.6
1;3.13	36	86.1	60	93.3	50.0
1;3.21	18	88.9	22	95.4	61.9
1;4.14	35	77.1	50	92.0	54.3
1;5.8	19	84.2	32	100.0	28.1
1;5.22	4	100.0	5	100.0	20.0
1;6.1	7	100.0	12	100.0	50.0

wrong time of year for those. It's a dog; I know you know that one. We'll find you something you know very well. You don't know that one, do you? Come on, you've learned "bricks," etc. It was obviously impossible, in spite of its desirability, to account for every instance of imputation in terms of the underlying structure of maternal expectations. Nevertheless, it was possible to trace one gross adjustment of the imputing rules according to the child's changing abilities.

Table 4-3 presents information on changes in the rate and nature of the child's participation in book reading. An active response includes vocalization, gesture, smile, eye contact with mother and search for a specified object. Active participation, vocalization, and lexical utterances all increase steadily. Spearman rank correlation between age and proportion of active cycles was significant ($r = 0.740 > 0.712$, $p < 0.01$), as was the correlation between age and proportion of turns containing a vocalization ($r = 0.902 > 0.712$, $p < 0.01$).

The appearance of vocalizations that were recognizable approximations to lexical labels at 1;2 probably encouraged the mother to believe that the child now possessed a hypothesis about a relation between sound and meaning. She now began to act as if she believed that the child was capable of producing appropriate words rather than mere babbles. This modification in the mother's "theory of the child" might explain the changes that now occurred in her "imputation rules" with respect to the child's gestures and vocalizations. These changes are presented in Table 4-4.

Table 4-4 shows that, to begin with, the mother is ready to accept her child's lexical vocalizations as labels, never in twenty opportunities challenging him with *What's that?* after such an utterance. But more interesting still, she is, after the first appearance of lexical-like utterances, treating his babbling in a new way. Whereas before she responded by treating such utterances as if they were *attempts* at labeling, confirming them, and supplying a correct label, now she demands that he do better by responding with a *What's that?* query. The difference in response to such vocalizations before and after the turning point is highly significant ($z = 3.84 > 2.32$, $p < 0.01$). Note that the child's capacity to generate phonologically well-formed labels does not change her interpretation of his gestures: they are still treated as calling attention to an item and provoke about the same frequency of *What's that?* queries before and after 1;2. Such nonvocal behavior never falls into the category of labeling: it is treated by the mother as indicating demand for a label, with the mother insisting on the child's trying to provide it himself. Looking at these phenomena from a broader point of view, it is possible to regard the mother as coaxing the child to substitute, first, a vocalization for a nonvocal signal and later a well-formed word or word approximation for a babbled vocalization, using appropriate turns in the labeling routine to make her demands.

The book-reading dialogue seems, as we have noted, to be a format well suited to the teaching of labeling. It has few elements and strict ordering rules between them. It is flexible in the sense of accepting a great variety of responses by the child. It is highly repetitive. Not only do the fixed elements [*Look, What's that*, and *It's a (label)*] appear over and over again, with minimal changes in the wording, but the variable elements, the labels themselves, appear repeatedly as

Table 4-4. *Mother's Response to the Child's Gestures, Vocalizations, and Labels, before and after Occurrence of First Lexical Labeling by the Child*

	Child's action		
Mother's response	Before labeling (0;8.14–1;1.22)	After onset of labeling (1;2.7–1;6.1)	Total
A. Nonvocal gesture			
Yes, it is an X[a]	3	1	4
What's that?	6	9	15
Total	9	10	19
B. Nonlexical vocalization			
Yes, it is an X[a]	6	3	9
What's that?	0	17	17
Total	6	20	26
C. Lexical vocalization			
Yes, it is an X[a]	0	20	20
What's that?	0	0	0
Total	0	0	20

[a]Including "No, it is not an X."

well. Disregarding repetitions within cycles, the mean recurrence rate of specific labels was 2.4 (*sd* 2.3), namely each label appeared in a mean of 2.4 different cycles, the maximum recurrence being 15 cycles for one label. And since our mother-child pair engaged in joint book reading outside the recorded half-hour sessions as well, using the same limited set of children's books, the true recurrence rate is probably very high indeed.

Another effective characteristic of the reading dialogue as a teaching device was its close-coupled feedback system. Once the child could produce easily recognizable words, the mother could and did respond to most of them quickly and appropriately. All eleven incorrect labels offered by the child were corrected by the mother. Corrections contained the following information:

Negation of child's label (e.g., *It is not a flower*): 2 cases.

Offer of correct label (e.g., *It is a dog*): 3 cases.

Both (e.g., *It is not a flower, it is a dog*): 6 cases.

The corrections seem to have had an immediately ensuing behavior effect, since only once in eleven opportunities did the child *repeat* a label that had been corrected, in the same cycle.

In all, the mother reinforced 81% of the child's "correct" labels at least once in the cycle in which they appeared. Positive feedback consisted of three elements, singly and in combination: (1) idealized imitation of the child's label, (2) *Yes*, and (3) laughter. These three formed a Guttman scale (in the above stated order),* which accounted for 81% of all observed combinations. The second best alternative scale order is *Yes*—imitation of labels—laughter, which accounted for only 50% of the combinations. Imitation was the most common response, occurring in 24 out of 31 (77.5%) of all instances of feedback.

Lest it should seem that the high incidence of imitation by the mother is the principal factor leading the child to utter labeling responses, the two following cautions should be stated. The first is that the likelihood of the child immediately *repeating* a label is not affected by the *nature* of the mother's positive feedback. The rate of repeating a label is 45.8% following the mother's imitation of it, but it is 42.9% following laughter or her merely saying *Yes*. Moreover, in the absence of *any* overt positive response, the child repeats the label 40.0% of the time. This suggests that it is not so much imitation as the dialogue structure and its reciprocity that is reinforcing the child. In all, a nonnegative response leads to a repetition of the label in 43.9% of instances, but a negative response (combining the three types mentioned earlier) suppresses repetition to 9% ($z = 2.21 > 1.65$, $p < 0.05$).

There has been a claim in the literature (Nelson, 1973) that correction causes words to disappear from the child's working vocabulary. To test this claim, we traced the later fate of words involved in a mismatch, and of words correctly

---

*A perfect Guttman scale of these elements in this order would mean that *Yes* appeared only if imitation did, but not vice versa, and that laughter appeared only if *Yes* did, but not vice versa.

applied. The latter reappeared in 60% of the cases, 83% of them correctly used. Misapplied labels, all of which were corrected by the mother, reappeared in 87.5% of the cases, of these 85% correctly applied. Although those words which the child *should* have uttered (but for which he substituted a wrong label) appeared later in the corpus only 25% of the time, all were used correctly. The difference in the fate of correctly and incorrectly *used* words is not significant ($z = 1.41 < 1.96$), the trend in any case being in favor of the misapplied words recurring more often. Correcting a misapplied word not only does not suppress its reappearance, it may increase its chances of being used again.

Does imitation play any notable part in the acquisition process at all? Does the child learn labels by immediate imitation? Take the probability of the child uttering a recognizable label. That probability is very dependent on the type of utterance that opened the cycle in which it occurs ($\chi^2_{(3)} = 12.48 > 11.34$, $p < 0.01$). It is greater if the cycle is initiated by the child (0.49) or by the mother uttering a *What's that?* question (0.37), than if it is initiated by the mother saying *Look* or offering a label (0.20 and 0.10). *What* questions, moreover, usually elicited a label from the child without further explicit prompting: 93.3% of the labels given in response to the mother's *What's that?* initiated cycles occurred before the mother offered a label in the cycle. In child-initiated cycles the same was true of 73.1% of the labels.

It would seem then that providing the child with a model to imitate actually depresses the probability that he will utter that word immediately, but if the mother provides the correct conversational setting for labeling (by asking *What* questions or letting the child initiate) it is more likely that the child will label on his own. On the other hand, there is reason to believe that the mother *starts* a cycle with a label *only* if she thinks that the child will not label the picture himself, either because he does not yet know the correct word, or because he is not attentive enough to make the effort at labeling. If circumstances seem more favorable for labeling to occur, she will usually start the cycle with a *What's that?* question. Some evidence for such a difference between cycles initiated by a label and by a *what* question comes from an analysis of labels occurring in such cycles. The two contain different words and different target objects to be labeled. Testing for cooccurrence of words in the two types of cycles, we find such cooccurrence is significantly less than would be expected by chance ($\chi^2_{(1)} = 8.66 > 6.64$, $p < 0.01$). But cycles initiated by the child tended to have the same words in them as those initiated by the mother's *What's that?* ($\chi^2_{(1)} = 1.83 < 2.71$, $p > 0.05$, trend for positive association) and differed from the label-initiated ones ($\chi^2_{(1)} = 8.06 > 6.64$, $p < 0.01$). The two classes of words could be categorized as the familiar-easy ones and the unfamiliar-hard ones, the latter being reserved by the mother for initial labeling. By adjusting her stimulus to the probability of the child's emission of a response, the mother helps the child to acquire a fundamental language skill: differential response rate to questions and statements.

Conclusion

One can properly conclude, we believe, that a central element in the achievement of labeling by the child is his mastery of the reciprocal dialogue rules that govern the exchanges between him and his mother into which labeling is inserted. Reference, then, is dependent not only upon mastering a relationship between sign and significate, but upon an understanding of social rules for achieving dialogue in which that relationship can be realized.

5

Katherine Nelson

Acquisition of Words by First Language Learners

The first step in learning any language is to learn a few words with which to begin making oneself understood. Unlike phonological development, syntactic development, or even reading and writing, this basic process continues throughout the life span. The process of word learning has, paradoxically, been considered both transparently simple and so complex as to defy the efforts of linguists, philosophers, and psychologists to understand it sufficiently to produce a coherent theory explaining it. In recent years, the developing vocabularies of very young children have been the focus of attention and the center of theoretical debates. Many issues have been drawn forth, such as the problem of overextension, underextension, and overlapping extensions of meaning, the conceptual structure of meaning, the disparity between comprehension and production, and individual differences in both process and product.

While I cannot hope to resolve all of these issues, I would like to examine them with an eye to (1) determining their importance at different stages in the development of a lexicon, (2) providing a preliminary map of those stages, (3) relating processes at work during these stages to conceptual and linguistic development, and (4) discovering the limitations on their applicability to second-language learning later in life.

To the extent that characteristics of word learning in a first language are related to the child's conceptual development, they are unlikely to characterize the older learner. It is important to bear in mind that the first-language learner begins the process as an infant, a child with no preestablished language skills and with

Abridged from "Acquisition of words by first language learners" by K. Nelson, 1981, in *Native Language and Foreign Language Acquisition* (H. Winitz, Ed.), *Annals of the New York Academy of Sciences*, 379, 148–159. Copyright 1981 by New York Academy of Sciences. Reprinted by permission of publisher and author.

cognitive abilities that are limited but undergoing rapid development. The period between 1 and 3 years is one of almost miraculous change in all areas of cognition, some no doubt the result of language, but some clearly independent of it. Thus the process by which a child begins to learn and progresses in the language may be dependent to an unknown degree on the limits of his or her ability to process information about both the world and the language describing it. We understand many of these limits and how they change, but by no means all.

On the other hand, to the extent that characteristics of word learning in a first language are general characteristics of mastering any new linguistic or symbolic system, then we would expect parallel processes to be the rule in learning a first and a second language. The lexicon forms an interface between the conceptual system and the semantic system, where language maps words onto meanings. It is difficult to talk about word meanings without talking about concepts, while the reverse is quite possible. Language develops into a system that relates to but is not isomorphic with the individual's conceptual system. The relation between these two at different points in development is the key to unraveling some of the controversial issues in this area.

Word-Learning Processes

Word learning most frequently has been viewed as a simple process, dependent primarily on the association of a word spoken by another person and an object to which the word refers. Hidden behind this description are difficult problems such as: How does the learner know what a word is (Peters, 1980)? How does the learner know to what the word refers, whether to an object, a quality, an action, or even *which* object, quality, or action (Quine, 1960)? What is an association? To solve these problems, it has been suggested that the learner is a hypothesis tester, testing his understanding of the reference of the word against the uses of others, and seeking confirmation of his own use in a novel situation (Brown, 1958). Assuming then that the reference has been established correctly, is the referent object now the meaning that is established for the word? That is, does the *extension* of the word (all of its identified referents) constitute its *intension* (its meaning components)? Is there such a thing as intension separately considered from extension (Rosch, 1978)? What about nonobject, abstract words? How are their meanings established?

Let us posit at the outset that learning word meanings is in general a process of *conceptual inference*. The limits that this sets on the system at any given point have to do with the state of development of the conceptual system in that concepts cannot be attached to words if such concepts lie beyond the current limitations of the developing system. In addition, there are limits to the inferential power of the cognitive system that are set by the stage of general cognitive development in addition to the availability of concepts and words to express them. However, it should be noted that making inferences about word meanings on the basis of their uses appears to be within the power of most children by the middle of the second year of life. The type of inference that is made, however, may shift with development.

There are two basic dimensions along which the learning process may vary. First, there may be more or less direct teaching by a tutor. Second, the context of use of the word may involve the nonverbal situation, the linguistic context, or a combination of both.

Consider the conditions of learning at the very outset of language acquisition, when the child is between 10 and 18 months old. Here, because of limited language understanding, whatever is learned must be derived from the situation of use, not from the verbal context. It is therefore the prototype of situationally determined word learning. Next, note that the child may be taught a word directly by having another person point to an object (or a picture) and repeat the word over and over until the child comes to repeat it reliably in the presence of the stimulus. If the tutor also applies the word to other objects from the same class, as when she may say "car" in the presence of the family car, cars in parking lots, cars in picture books, and so on, the child is faced with the problem of conceptual inference, of going from the word used by another to the formation of a *concept* to be attached to the diversity of uses of that word, in this case the concept of car suitably defined. In the process, the child may make inappropriate overextensions based on the experiences he has had with cars and the word car, or he may underextend the word because no one has yet pointed out unusual instances of cars, such as limousines. With sufficient exposure to the culture, however, the child's concept of car will come to match the uses of the word in the adult community.

On the other hand, the child may have a primitive concept of car already, one involving his experiences with the family car, toy cars, and cars seen on the street. At some point and for some as yet unfathomable reasons, he may hear his father say, Do you want to go in the car?, and conclude that "car" is the word that refers to his concept, even though he has not been taught the word specifically. In this case, the word maps onto the preestablished concept. Here the child's experience will be central to the meaning of the word because the concept, embedded in experience, was established before the word referring to it was known.

It is much later that the child comes to be able to learn a word from its linguistic context rather than from its situational context, whether directly taught or not. For example, a parent may say, A zebra is a kind of horse with stripes, and expect the child to set up a meaning on the basis of what he already knows about horses and stripes, even without an example to point to. This is definitional teaching, and it has definite limitations, as teachers can testify and as consulting a dictionary with an eye to learning a new word can demonstrate. Another kind of verbal contextual inference condition exists when the word to be learned is embedded in a verbal context but is not taught explicitly. For example a person may say to the child, That's not a long stick, it's short, and the child may infer that "short" is the opposite of "long," thereby learning a new lexical item for an already available concept. Note that this type of learning depends upon the prior existence of a concept space into which the word can fit.

Although there have been few direct studies, it has been claimed that the vast majority of words that are acquired during early to middle childhood must be acquired from either situational or verbal context, because the numbers acquired by the average child (about 20 new words per day) preclude the special teaching that would be required if this were not the case (Carey and Bartlett, 1978; Miller, 1977). In turn, this claim rests on the assumption that it is easier to make conceptual inferences from previously established knowledge than to learn new concepts to fit new words.

These different methods of learning and teaching have implications for development. First, learning from situational context is primary in the early stages of vocabulary building. However, such learning does not disappear as the child becomes more facile with language. Ostensive teaching proceeds throughout life, and the individual in a novel situation may form a concept (of a particular type of shellfish found on the beach, for example) before encountering the correct word (horseshoe crab) for it. Second, at all stages, attaching words to concepts or knowledge already acquired is far quicker and easier than forming a new concept to go with a novel word. Finally, the fact that learning from linguistic context becomes possible in the preschool period is an indication that a lexical *system*, a network of relationships, has been established, as Bowerman (1977) has demonstrated with independent evidence.

Thus far, nothing has been said about what the word meanings of concepts consist of, or how they are structured. Are they representations of the objects referred to? Are they features or relations? Are they conceptual or semantic components of a type not yet defined, general or specific? What relation do they bear to other words in a semantic domain? These are important and contentious questions of considerable theoretical significance. The evidence at the moment is not strongly favorable to any single position. I tend to lean toward a rather fuzzy conception of meaning as a complex of information that is closely or loosely attached to a concept and that changes—both contracting and expanding—as the conceptual system and the lexical system develop over time (Nelson, 1978a). Different semantic domains contain different complexes of information. This conception is similar to that set forth by Miller and Johnson-Laird (1976), but I am not staking anything on it here. The only point that I think is vital, and that also is indisputable, is that at some point in development (but not, I think, at first), relations between words become established in the lexicon such that a lexical network is set up that is independent of but interacts with the underlying conceptual network.

Some Typical Phenomena of Early Lexical Development

With these considerations in mind, let us consider three phenomena of early development that have presented some controversy and that may or may not be relevant to later learning. The first is the vocabulary spurt that has been observed to occur in the middle of the second year in a number of children. This spurt was identified by many early observers. Stern (1930) referred to it as the realization on the child's part that "everything has a name." Similarly, Dore (1978) has referred to the "designation hypothesis" and believes it marks the child's way into the language as a truly symbolic system. McShane (1979) makes a similar claim. The facts to be considered here are that the child usually has been speaking only a few words for a number of months (3 to 12) and within the space of a month or so—at around 17 to 20 months—accelerates the rate of acquisition of new words from a rate of around 3 or 4 per month to 30 to 50 per month (McCarthy, 1954; Nelson, 1973). (As noted earlier, this rate continues to increase, but the rate of acceleration becomes less dramatic.) Lest we rush to explanations of the phenomena too quickly, it must be pointed out that individual differences are the rule here, as they are in so many phenomena of early language. Some children spurt very early, at 13 or 14 months rather than 17 or 20. Some children do not spurt until 24 or 25 months. And some children never spurt at all, plugging away, adding a few words each week, and gradually increasing their rate of acceleration without ever seeming to go through a period in which the "designation hypothesis" drives them to learn the name of everything in sight.

However, considering the processes outlined above, what is the best or most probable explanation for the spurt in vocabulary development? I hypothesize that it indexes an important cognitive development, where the child becomes capable of making conceptual inferences, of leaping from word to concept and from concept to presented word. This development in turn appears to be the result of the establishment of a conceptual system in which individual concepts are disembedded from larger contexts and thereby become available for naming. The evidence for this development is too complex to elaborate here (Nelson, 1980). However, the important and interesting corollary is that words used prior to this time, that is, during most of the single-word period, are not conceptually based.

Consider next the common observation that children engage in underextensions, overextensions, and overlapping meanings in their first-language learning. The frequently discussed overextension of terms involves the application of a word to an object that does not belong to the class of objects that form the referent class for adult speakers. While this phenomenon is striking, as when a child calls a horse "doggie," it is not by any means a universal occurrence. A systematic study by Rescorla (1976) found that fewer than one-third of the words learned by children between 12 and 20 months ever were overextended. Moreover, she found that during this time period, there was no variation in overextending by age, that is, it did not seem to be a function of cognitive development during this period, as some authors had suggested. The basis for overextensions usually has been found to be perceptual, that is, an object receives a label because it looks like, sounds like, moves like, or feels like the "true" referent. Occasionally the extension can be identified as having a functional basis, as when a child puts a bucket on his head and says "hat" or throws an apple and says "ball."

The *function* of overextensions has been speculated by some to be attributable to the economical use of a small vocabulary in the effort to communicate. However, frequently young children do not seem to be attempting to communicate in these uses but simply to be labeling for the child's own sake; no acknowledgment or response seems to be expected. In some cases, what appear to be overextensions can be seen to be efforts to say something *about* an object, for example, "Daddy" in reference to Daddy's shoes. An extension of this explanation may be made to cases in which the child labels an object or a series of objects with a term from another semantic class entirely, as when the child says "clock" when she hears water dripping or labels crescent-shaped objects "grapefruit" (Rescorla, 1976; Bowerman, 1976). It does not seem too unreasonable to consider that in these cases the child is using one term to point out a similarity (or comparison) of its referent object to a feature of another, but not an identity of the two (Nelson et al., 1978). Indeed, some data from Winner (1979) on children's early analogies in language and action support this interpretation.

In sum, interpretations of the overextension phenomena fall into three categories. First, the linguistic interpretation claims that children need to learn what words refer to, that is, in the case of nouns, a referent class of objects, not the individual features that define those objects. A second explanation based on communicative needs is that children are trying to use their limited language in the most effective way and in so doing stretch its meaning. A third, conceptual explanation is that children are learning simultaneously about language and about object classes in the world—including their similarities and differences. In the course of doing so, they not only label objects that fit their preestablished concepts but also point out these characteristics and relationships (e.g., possession), using the only words at their limited command. I believe the latter explanation explains more of the data than do the first two, although clearly the second may have some validity and is the explanation most likely to be relevant to overextension in second-language learning. If, however, the third explanation is the correct one, the phenomenon of overextension should occur much less frequently among second-language learners since they no longer would be at the stage where object concepts are being basically built up, and perceptual similarities and differences are being compared.

It has been claimed that overextension occurs in the production of terms rather than in comprehension. Several studies (e.g., Thompson and Chapman, 1975) have shown that children will identify correctly the appropriate referents for a term that they mislabel with an overextended term in production. However, a recent study by Kay and Anglin (1982) has shown that when appropriately controlled tests are employed, 2-year-old children both overextend and underextend newly learned words in both production and comprehension. Since word learning in this task (and others like it) is essentially concept learning, this perhaps is not so surprising. It also supports the contention that the basic phenomenon of overextension (and underextension) is a cognitive one having to do with conceptual inference, not a specifically linguistic or communicative one.

Thus, as children pass through the stage of learning basic object concepts and then superordinate classes, these phenomena should be less apparent. Of course, anytime a novel class is acquired, some variability in the extension of its term can be expected.

The disparity between comprehension and production in first-language learning is another phenomenon to be considered. Most children learn to understand some language before they begin to produce it. As with production, they learn to respond in action situations and at first may know only one key word in a sentence, but will use that knowledge to respond with an appropriate action. For example, "where's" uttered by mother may send the child on a search for an object while "what's that?" may produce pointing behavior. An object term will direct the child to pick up or give the named object. In general, the acquisition of receptive vocabulary by children in the second year leads production by about 6 months (Benedict, 1979).

This lag in production may have two sources. First, the child may begin to understand language in specific situational contexts, as the above examples indicate and as Bruner's studies have shown (e.g., Bruner, 1975a). In this case the word may not indicate a concept at all but may only direct the child's action. When mother says Where's the ball?, the child understands the action response called for and the object referred to, but does not attach the word to his own concept of ball (if such exists) and has no reason to produce the word to trigger action on mother's part. Second, the child entering a first language has specific problems in mastering the articulatory and phonological systems that hinder production. Thus the great disparity between comprehension and production may be a phenomen unique to first-language learning.

Variations in Learning within and between Children

In making the argument that word learning primarily rests on the process of conceptual inference, I also pointed out that some types of language, in particular those used and understood early in the second year, need not have a conceptual base. It long has been conventional to distinguish contentive (or substantive) words from grammatical functors. The former include nouns, verbs, and modifiers and generally are the types of words produced first by young children, giving their early sentences a "telegraphic" look. Functors include articles, demonstratives, prepositions, and copular verbs among others. They are acquired later as the grammatical system is developed.

But recently a different category of speech productions has come to be recognized, which resists this type of classification because it consists of preformed units (or formulas) that are used to perform a pragmatic function in a specific situational context. A formula is a conventional construction that is learned and produced as an unanalyzed whole. Formulas range from simple greetings and polite forms (e.g., "hi," "thank you," "how are you?") to complex phrases used in ceremonies ("I pledge allegiance to the flag") and everyday life ("and that's the way it is"). There are two things that make these formulas important in language learning. First, they provide the language learner with a ready-made phrase that is useful in a recurrent context without necessarily being understood in terms of its component parts. Second, they may provide the learner with a repertoire that can be subjected to further analysis and thus serve as a foundation for language development.

However, formulaic speech also highlights a problem that pervades all of language learning, the problem of unitization (Peters, 1980). Unless pieces are specifically made salient by the teacher, language comes to the child in clumps that are not easily broken apart. Words are not separated neatly by pauses but run into each other. One of the significant problems for the learner then is to identify what *is* a word. Older speakers often help with this by embedding a significant word within one or more repeated formulas, e.g., "Where's the ball?" "Can you get the ball?" "Get the ball." Thus formulas and single substantive words play off against each other.

It is not surprising, given the difficulty of identifying substantive words and the usefulness of pragmatic formulas, that children tend to pick up formulas early in language learning. Indeed, such learning seems to constitute a normal early phase of language development for many children, and for some children formulas continue to play a large role in their speech production throughout the early years (Nelson, 1973, 1981). Recent studies have shown that second-language learners rely on such formulas even more than do first-language learners (Vihman, 1979).

Children usually begin around the end of the first year to understand a few words in a familiar, gamelike context and to produce a few forms that are identifiable as having conventional word targets. These first words usually are like formulas in that they perform a pragmatic function but do not have referential content. Examples are "byebye" said only in the context of someone's leaving, or "mama" used to request help or food, or "peekaboo" in the conventional game context (Benedict, 1979; Bruner, 1975a). As Grieve and Hoogenraad (1979) have put it, these terms enable the child to share experience but not to talk about it. This characterization fits the hypothesis that early words are not conceptually based. Two other early speech types also support this hypothesis.

Relational words have been described by Bloom (1973) and more recently by Nicolich (1980). These are terms—such as "all gone," "more," "here," "open," and "up"—that express general object relations of the type that are beginning to be understood by children toward the end of the infancy period. They tend to accompany the child's own actions, and they refer to *single* object relations, that is, disappearance, reappearance, direction of movement. Although these relations can be expressed by speakers at any stage, they tend to decline in the children's spontaneous speech as children get older. Thus, their importance in early vocabularies probably derives from their cognitive significance rather than from any specific linguistic stage or process.

In addition children may learn names for things early in the second year, particularly in the picture-naming game that mothers often engage in and that has been described by Ninio and Bruner (1978). However, these labels usually have a narrow situationally specific reference (like the early formulas) and are not used in the absence of the referent or extended to new instances. Or they may be conceptually unbounded and refer to a wide range of loosely related phenomena.

Thus there appear to be a number of different types of early speech, all of which are conceptually empty but situationally significant. However, late in the second year and into the third, the child begins to build a lexicon that is conceptually based. That is, each word appears to be attached to a concept in the child's growing conceptual system. Several hundred words may be acquired by the time the child is two—enough to provide names for everything in the child's limited conceptual space.

However, the power of the 2 year old's vocabulary is small indeed compared to that of the 5 or 6 year old who has learned many thousands of words. In order to account for this later achievement, it is necessary to posit the establishment of a lexical *system* that links words themselves (and not simply a word and the concept associated with it). The establishment of this system depends on finding similar meaning components that are shared by two or more words and thereby defining a semantic space occupied by words of similar but different meanings, that is, that share some meaning components but not others. Note that forming an independent lexical system requires the identification of semantic components, although simply learning words for things does not. That is, the analysis of meanings may take place after the meaning has been acquired.

Because of this evolving semantic network, the child becomes able to place new words into nodes that are already, in a sense, predefined but empty. For example, a child who knows the meaning of "big," "little," and "tall" will already have an empty slot to be filled by "short" and therefore will have no trouble in picking it up at the first opportunity. This seems to be the necessary implication of the work of Carey and Bartlett (1978) on the acquisition of a novel color word and it also fits Carey's (1978b) finding that, contrary to Donaldson's claim, "less never means more." That is, words are not confused in meaning with their opposites. Rather, the understanding of a word like "more" in its quantitative sense implies a contrasting position that "less" easily can fill. Much more work is needed on the development of these lexical systems in early childhood, but their existence seems reasonably well demonstrated.

While developing a lexical system is by definition a linguistic process, it also is a cognitive one. Once fully developed, the lexical system can operate pretty much autonomously; a new relation between language and thought is established. An older child or adult who already has such a system in a first language would be unlikely to go through the same process of development in learning a second language. Thus the postulation of such a system has implications for the relation between the two languages, depending on the age or stage at which the second is acquired.

In sum, I propose three major periods of lexical development. The first, a preconceptual stage, may begin late in the first year and last through the second year. It usually coincides with but is not coextensive with the period of single-word use. In this period, children use their language performatively, pragmatically, or ritually in situationally specific contexts. They are learning to use language but are not learning what language means.

The second stage usually begins around the middle of the second year but may begin earlier for some children and later for others. Here, substantive words are connected directly with concepts, and in the beginning, concepts are combined directly to form primitive sentences.

The third stage begins early in the preschool period and evolves over a number of years with the establishment of relations between words and eventually an autonomous lexical system. It makes possible the learning of new words from verbal as well as nonverbal contexts. . . .*

---

*Section on implications for second language acquisition is omitted. [Eds.]

6

Alison Gopnik and Andrew N. Meltzoff

From People, to Plans, to Objects: Changes in the Meaning of Early Words and Their Relation to Cognitive Development

There is an intriguing group of early words that is sometimes called *relational* words (Bloom, 1973). This group includes words such as "more," "gone," "there," "no," "uh-oh," and "down." These words are common in very early language in spite of the fact that in the adult language they have rather abstract and complex meanings and serve a variety of syntactic and semantic functions. This paper reports three studies investigating the meanings of these relational words for children and exploring why children use these words so frequently when they begin to talk.

Two kinds of accounts of relational words have been advanced in the literature. One group of authors has stressed the pragmatic qualities of these early words. They have described the ways children use these words to influence the behavior of other people and have emphasized the developmental continuity between these words and prelinguistic communication. Another group of authors has stressed the cognitive content of these words. They have proposed that these words encode concepts that are related to the child's cognitive concerns and claim that the emergence of these words is related to the significant cognitive advances that occur at about 18 months of age.

We will show that both these accounts are partially correct. Children do begin by using at least some relational words to encode social or interpersonal meanings. In this respect, these words are reminiscent of prelinguistic communication. However, during the one-word stage they also begin to use these words in nonsocial contexts. Rather than using these words exclusively to encode aspects of their interactions with other people, they begin to use relational words to refer to their own actions and plans, and later, to refer to events in the world. Furthermore, we will show that it is this shift in function, from social to referential uses of relational words, rather than the emergence of relational words themselves that is directly related to important cognitive developments.

Pragmatic Accounts of Relational Words

A number of writers have described particular relational words as primarily "social" or "expressive," rather than referential. Nelson (1975) argued that there were two types of early language learners. "Referential" children use names and use language primarily to refer to the world, while "expressive" children use relational words and use language primarily to express their own emotions and to influence the behavior of others.

Halliday (1975) provided a pragmatic account of many early relational words. For example, he described "more" as an instrumental term meaning "I want some more." Similarly, expressions like "dere" and "dat" were described as attempts to draw the attention of another person to an object, and an expression like "uh-oh" was glossed as "I'm sad, it's broken" (Halliday, 1975). Halliday argued that these words are part of a broader, nonverbal communicative system.

Bruner (1975a,b, 1983) has examined in great detail the continuity between prelinguistic communication and early words, including relational words. He describes the emergence of deictic terms like "that" and "there" and terms like "hereyare," "thank-you," and "bye-bye" in the context of shared routines between mothers and children—routines like book reading, give and take games, or peek-a-boo. Bruner proposes that the vocalizations and gestures that are produced during these games will eventually develop into early words.

The continuity between nonverbal communication and early relational words has also been noted by Carter (1975, 1979). She described the evolution of "more," "mine," "here," "there," and "gone" in the speech of one child. She argued that these words originate in nonlinguistic combinations of gestures and vocalizations with specific pragmatic functions. Thus, for example, "more" and "mine" appeared to develop from an early [m]-initial sound the child used to demand objects or action from other people.

Finally a number of authors, including Pea (1980), and Antinucci and Volterra (1979), have suggested that children begin by using the word "no" to refuse or reject suggestions made by others, and only later use "no" to negate propositions.

All these authors stress the role relational words play in the interactions between the child and other people. On this view, if we want to describe the meaning of these words we must talk about the relationships between the child and his interlocutors, rather than talk about relationships between the child and the world. According to these accounts, "there" means something like "Look at this!," "more" means "Give me some more!," and "no" means "I won't!"

Cognitive Accounts of Relational Words

Another group of authors has stressed the cognitive significance of early relational words. Bloom (1973) suggested that they encoded concepts that played a significant role in sensorimotor intelligence. This suggestion has also been made by by Sinclair (1970) and McCune-Nicolich (1981). These authors both suggest that the relational words encode the sort of sensorimotor schemes Piaget described in his account of infant development (Piaget, 1952). In particular, McCune-Nicolich has argued that these concepts are typical of what Piaget calls stage V of the sensorimotor period.

Gopnik (1981, 1982, 1984) has argued that relational words encode rather abstract relationships between children, their actions, and the objects around them, particularly relationships that involve plans. She suggests that children begin to understand these relationships at around 18 months, and that relational words encode what Piaget calls stage VI or *preoperational* concepts. She has also suggested that young children are especially motivated to encode these concepts linguistically because they are relevant to the cognitive problems they are trying to solve.

There is some empirical evidence that the acquisition of relational words is related to early cognitive developments. In particular, several recent studies have shown a relationship between the acquisition of the word "gone" and the development of object permanence problem-solving skills (Corrigan, 1978; Gopnik, 1984; Gopnik and Meltzoff, 1984; McCune-Nicolich, 1981; Tomasello and Farrar, 1984). Specifically, the data indicate that children begin to use "gone" only after they are able to solve object permanence problems involving "simple invisible displacements" (Piaget, 1952), but that they consistently use it before they reach the stage of solving "serial invisible displacements." These data suggest that children begin to use "gone" at about the same time that they develop what Piaget has labeled the stage VI concept of the object.

Gopnik and Meltzoff (1984) have recently reported a similar relationship between the development of means-ends skills and the development of words encoding success and failure, words like "there," "no," "more," and "uh-oh." Their data show that children acquire these words at about the same time that they begin to use "invention" and "insight", rather than trial and error, to succeed in certain problem-solving situations. These findings again suggest that there are interesting relationships between the child's developing cognitive system and the use of relational words.

The Problem of Early Relational Words

Which account of early relational words is correct? Are relational words primarily social devices, designed to affect the behavior of other people, and acquired because of their role in social interaction? Or do they encode abstract notions about transformations and relationships—concepts that play a central role in the child's cognitive development at about this stage?

In an effort to answer these questions we conducted three studies* using both longitudinal and cross-sectional designs. The findings suggest that the answer depends on which relational words you investigate and when in development you look at them. Some relational words, in particular "there," "no," and "more" are initially used in social ways and encode cognitively significant concepts by the end of the one-word stage. Other relational words retain their social meaning throughout the one-word stage. Still others are used in a referential way from the very beginning.

STUDY 1

Method

Study 1 included nine English-speaking children in a longitudinal design. The nine subjects consisted of three different groups. Three of the subjects were observed every 2 weeks from the time they were 12 months old. Audiotaping began from the time they produced their first words until they began to use two-word constructions. The three subjects were, respectively, 12, 19, and 17 months old when the audio recording began, and they were 27, 26, and 23 months old when the study ended. Three other children were videotaped in half-hour sessions once a month for 6 months starting from the time they were 15 months old. A final three children were videotaped in half-hour sessions once a month for 6 months starting from the time they were 18 months old. All the recording took place in the children's homes. All the children's utterances, along with the contexts in which the utterances occurred, were transcribed for subsequent analysis. For the purposes of this report we focus here on the subjects' uses of the relational words. Further details about the methods used to collect the corpus and the sample are provided elsewhere (Gopnik, 1981).

Results

"THERE." Children used "there" (usually pronounced as a [d]-initial expression) in three different types of contexts. They used it when they indicated an object, particularly when they pointed to it or held it up for other people to see. This deictic use (Bruner, 1975b, 1983) of "there" has a strongly social quality. It may be interpreted as an attempt to draw someone else's attention to an object, to indicate it to another.

However, at slightly older ages children began using "there" when they succeeded in completing a plan of action or achieved a goal. For example, children said "there" when they completed a jigsaw puzzle or finished building a

---

*Only the first study is included here. [Eds.]

tower of blocks. Children also used "there" when they changed the location of an object, for example, when they moved a toy doll from one place to another. This use of "there" did not have any clear social significance. In these contexts, the children simply commented on their own plans, rather than trying to influence the actions of others.

At still older ages, children used "there" to comment on the location of an object. Children said "there" when an object moved by itself or was moved by someone else, or (most frequently) when they pointed out the location of a stationary object. For example, one child said "up dere," pointing to a toy on a high shelf.

In the first deictic contexts, children seem to want to affect the behavior of other people. In the second contexts, when children comment on the success of their action or when they try to change the location of an object, they seem instead to comment on their own plans and goals. Finally, when children simply comment on the location of an object, they do not try to affect another person's behavior, and they also do not comment on their own plans. In this case they simply comment on an event or state of affairs in the world.

Thus we can classify these uses of "there" into three categories. The *social* category includes indicative uses of "there." The *plan* category includes uses of "there" to indicate success and uses of "there" in which the child changes the location of an object. The *object* category includes uses in which the child comments on the location of an object. A preliminary review of the transcripts revealed that 95% of the uses of "there" could be captured using these three categories.

Once the instances of "there" were classified using the above scheme, we analyzed the data to check for systematic developmental patterns in the use of the word. The results show that there was a clear ordering of development: children first used "there" in social contexts to indicate objects to others, next to mark the success of plans, and finally to denote the locations of objects. Only one subject violated this order of emergence. It is noteworthy that all of the children who used "there" to denote the location of an object did so only after they had already used "there" to indicate and to comment on plans; there were no violations of this developmental pattern. The overall developmental ordering—using "there" first socially, next for action, and finally to mark the location of objects—can be assessed statistically using a nonparametric trend test (Ferguson, 1966). The results are significant $(z = 3.69, p < 0.001)$.*

"NO." Children also used "no" in three different ways. They used it socially, to mark plans, and to denote relationships between objects.

There were several different social uses. Some children used "no" when they refused to perform an action suggested by someone else. For example, one child

---

*All tables omitted. [Eds.]

said "no" when his mother asked him to come inside. The children also used "no" when they protested the actions of other persons; for example, one child said "no" when his brother tried to take his teddy bear. Finally, some children also used "no" as an all-purpose answer to questions, whether or not this use was appropriate, apparently simply in order to maintain the conversation. When children use "no" in these ways, they seem to be reacting to the behavior of another person or trying to affect that behavior. All of these were classified as *social* uses.

The children also used "no" in ways that did not have this interpersonal or social quality. They frequently used "no" when they tried to do something and failed. For example, children would say "no" when a jigsaw puzzle piece did not fit or when a tower of blocks they were carefully building tipped over and fell down. Children also used "no" when they began to do something and then changed their minds. One child was shaking a container of dice and began to throw them. He then said, "no," stopped himself, and proceeded to shake the container some more. In both these cases the children do not appear to be trying to influence the actions of others. What they have in common is that the child seems to have a plan of action in mind that fails or is suddenly changed. "No" seems to encode this fact. All of these uses were classified as plan uses.

Finally, children sometimes used "no" to deny propositions. One child said "hat off no," looking at a picture of a man with his hat still on. This use of "no" is not of a pragmatic or social nature; instead, it is used to comment on the relationships between objects in the world. These uses were classified as *object* uses.

Ninety-eight percent of the different uses of "no" fell into one of these categories. The results reveal a systematic developmental ordering of the children's uses of the word "no." They first use "no" for interpersonal purposes, next to indicate the failure of a plan, and finally as a propositional negative, to comment on relationships between objects. There are no violations of this developmental pattern, although there are several instances of ties, viz. when the children first used the word in a social fashion in the same test session in which they first used it to indicate failure. It is noteworthy that all the children used "no" to negate propositions only after they had begun to use the word socially and to indicate failure; there were no violations of this pattern, (which supports similar findings by Pea, 1980). The developmental ordering was statistically assessed using a nonparametric trend analysis, and proved to be significant ($z = 3.36$, $p < 0.001$).

These changes in the meaning of "no" are similar to the changes in the meaning of "there." The very first uses of "no" have a social quality. Later, children begin to use "no" to comment on their own plans, and finally they use "no" to comment on relationships between objects in the world.

"MORE." Children also used "more" in social ways, to comment on plans, and to mark realtionships between objects. Regarding the social uses, children used "more" when they wanted to repeat an action on an object and needed someone else's help to do so. They used "more" to request assistance. For example, they said "more" when they wanted their mothers to give them another cookie, or to help them turn another somersault. These utterances of "more" were clearly designed to influence the behavior of other persons. They were classified as *social* uses.

However, in addition to using "more" when they wanted help from another person, children also used "more" when they simply announced that they were about to repeat an action leading to a particular result. One child put a peg in a tin, and then said "more" as she put in another peg. She also said "more" as she turned the page of a book, after she had turned the previous page. In these contexts the children did not need any help from others, and these utterances did not seem to be addressed to other people. The utterances were used instead to comment on the repetition of their own behavior. They were classified as *plan* uses.

Finally, children began to use "more" to comment on the similarity or quantity of objects independently of their own actions on them. For example, one child said "more" as she watched her mother add more newspapers to a pile of newspapers. These uses were classified as *object* uses.

Ninety-six percent of the children's uses of "more" could be classified in terms of these three categories. The results show a clear developmental progression in the use of the word "more." The children first used it socially, as a request. They next used it to indicate the repetition of a plan. Finally, they used it to denote the similarity between objects and events in the world. There was only one violation for this developmental pattern. This developmental ordering was significant ($z = 2.77$, $p < 0.01$). This progression from using the word first in a social sense, and then to comment on the child's own action or plans, and finally to refer to the relation between objects or events in the world is the same as found with the other relational words examined here.

Pragmatic Expressions that Do Not Shift Uses

The above data show that children change their uses of "there," "no," and "more." The data also show that another group of expressions retained their social quality throughout the one-word period. These expressions were produced only in particular social situations. For example, children commonly used "hello" and "bye-bye" when they greeted or took leave of other people. While some children occasionally extended these terms to objects as well as people, these uses were rather rare and often involved social objects such as dolls and puppets. Children also used "hereyare," "thank-you," and "please" when they exchanged objects with other people. Finally, they used "mine" when they wanted to claim possession of an object from another person, and often used "yes" as an all-purpose answer to questions when seeking to maintain the conversation. In sum, these words seemed to be used almost exclusively as responses to someone else's actions or as a way of influencing someone else's actions. They were not used to comment on the child's own plans or to comment on events or relationships in the world.

There were other relational expressions that had the opposite characteristics to those just described. These words were never used exclusively in social contexts. Words like "oh dear" and "uh-oh" were used from the very beginning to comment on the failure of the child's plans. Another group of words, including "up," "in," "on," and "off" was used from the very beginning to comment on the fact that the child moved an object; and words such as "find," "get," "do," and "finish" were used from the beginning to comment on plans. Finally, children used "gone" to comment on the relationships between their present perceptual experience and objects.

Many of the purely social words, for example, "hereyare," "byebye," and "thank-you," appeared at a very early stage. However, some of the referential relational words, particularly "uh-oh" and "gone," also appeared at an early stage. In this study, there was no clear evidence indicating that the words that were used in purely pragmatic ways ("hereyare," "bye") appeared before words that were used to refer exclusively to plans or objects ("uh-oh," "gone").

DISCUSSION

The results suggest that for at least some relational words there are important developmental changes in children's use of them. First, children use these expressions in social ways. These social uses are reminiscent of their prelinguistic gestures and vocalizations (Bates, Benigni, Bretherton, Camaioni, and Volterra, 1979; Bruner, 1975b, 1983). Later, they begin to use the expressions in more referential or cognitive ways. There are two especially interesting features of this transition. First, it takes place rather early in the one-word stage. Second, the shift in the use of these words is not a simple one-step process. Children do not move directly from using words to influence other people's behavior to using those words to comment on relationships between objects. Instead, there is an intermediate period in which children seem to use them to comment on their own actions and plans (Gopnik, 1982). . . .

General Discussion

The evidence presented here suggests that the meanings of at least some early words develop in a particular sequence. Moreover, the results show that this developmental progression is related to certain cognitive developments. Children begin by using the words "there," "no," and "more" in social contexts. Later, they use them to refer to their own plans and, finally, to refer to objects and events in the world. At least for "there" and "no," the first of these developments, the shift from using words in social contexts to using them to comment on the success and failure of plans, occurs at the same time as the development of the ability to use insight to solve difficult means-ends problems. These findings have several implications for studies of linguistic and cognitive development.

One important methodological consequence of these findings is that we must consider the particular meanings of early words when we try to relate early linguistic and cognitive development. General measures of linguistic development— such as the emergence of two-word strings, vocabulary size, or mean length of utterance (M. L. U.)—appear to have relatively little relationship to cognitive development (Corrigan, 1978; Harris, 1982). Even more fine-grained measures that take into account the occurrence of particular words, such as those employed by McCune-Nicolich (1981) and Tomasello and Farrar (1984), may not be sufficiently subtle. . . .

These findings also suggest several promising avenues of research. It is possible that the emergence of nonsocial uses of other relational words is directly related to certain cognitive developments. It would be interesting, for example, to study the emergence of the word "more" from this standpoint. Similarly, it is possible that purely social words (e.g., "hereyare," "byebye," "thank-you") emerge before sensorimotor stage VI, but that relational words that encode more abstract aspects of plans or objects emerge only after the child has entered stage VI. Our own previous studies support this latter idea by showing a relationship between the emergence of "gone" and the development of stage VI object permanence skills (Gopnik, 1984; Gopnik and Meltzoff, 1984). In addition, Tomasello and Farrar (1984) have recently reported that children used "byebye," "thank-you," "hi," and "stuck" (plausible candidates for purely social words) before they entered stage VI in the development of the object concept, but used "find," "another," and "gone" only after this development.

Finally, these findings have implications for general theories of the relationship between linguistic and cognitive development. It is important to emphasize that what we have called social uses of "no," "there," and "more" are not limited, stereotyped, or ritualized uses. They do not occur only in a particular *script* nor do they comment on particular action schemes, although it is possible that other early utterances do (Barrett, 1982; Bates et al., 1979). On the contrary, these words are used productively in a wide range of situations, and they have arbitrary and conventional meanings. They are analogous to constructions like "I promise" or the imperative in the adult language. The meaning of these adult constructions is fundamentally social; to understand these constructions one must consider the relationship between the speaker and an interlocutor (Austin, 1962; Searle, 1969). Nevertheless, these constructions are as productive and arbitrary as any other constructions in English.

This point is particularly important because our findings are not in accord with the strict Piagetian account of the emergence of language. For Piaget, the development of any kind of word at all, even a limited and context-bound word, requires stage VI symbolic abilities (Piaget, 1962). However, our findings, like the findings of Bates et al. (1979) and Tomasello and Farrar (1984), suggest that children may use some words *before* they reach stage VI. Our data further show that many of these very early words refer to relationships between the child and his/her interlocutors, rather than to his/her plans or to external objects and events.

These very early social words may well be related to the intentional gestures described by Bruner (1975a, 1983), Bates et al. (1979), Trevarthen and Hubley (1978), and Lock (1980), and which, according to Bates et al. (1979), emerge in conjunction with stage V means-ends skills. However, our findings also suggest that at around stage VI, children take the general linguistic skills and even the particular words they have developed for social purposes and begin to apply them to their cognitive problems. At this stage, many of the most crucial of these problems involve the relationships between actions and goals (Bruner, 1973; Piaget, 1952)—that is, they involve *plans*. Evidently, children begin to use words to talk about these problems at the same time that they develop a new understanding of the problem themselves. This raises the possibility that social, linguistic, and cognitive development may interact in interesting and significant ways during this very early period.

II

FORM AND MEANING IN EARLY LANGUAGE

The impact of Chomsky's theorizing on the field of child language can hardly be overestimated. Chomsky (1957, 1965) formulated a new approach to the analysis of language and, in addition, put forth a devastating critique of B.F. Skinner's behaviorist analysis of language and language acquisition (Chomsky, 1959)—a critique that had far-reaching implications for behavioristic formulations more generally and, in an important sense, cleared the ground for new ways of thinking about child language. Chomsky argues that it is the ability to comprehend and generate novel sentences that stands at the center of human language capacity, and that this ability resides in our grasp of fundamental rules of syntax. The question then becomes, what is the nature of these rules and how are they acquired? Brown led the field of developmental psycholinguistics by initiating a series of studies directed to analysis of syntactic rules underlying young children's spontaneous utterances (Brown and Bellugi, 1964; Bellugi and Brown, 1964). In the article included here, **Brown** points out that the first attempts to formulate rules for the child's combinatorial utterances employed standard syntactic categories of the adult language or novel syntactic categories designed to capture the particular form of very young children's speech. As Brown notes, Bloom's (1970) argument that such analyses overlook the kinds of meaning relations expressed in early utterances—relational semantic intentions such as possession and attribution—provided a strong impetus for new theorizing and research. Considering a range of evidence on semantic relations expressed by children in "Stage I" and "Stage II," Brown proposes that these semantic relations, as well as other expressions of meaning, emerge in an invariant order (see also Brown, 1973).

The articles in this section reflect several interrelated themes that have guided research in the 25 years since developmental psycholinguistics was delineated as a field of inquiry.

The first of these themes is the question of how different aspects of language

71

are coordinated in acquisition and development. How is learning syntactic structure coordinated with learning semantic relations, morphological rules, and
lexicalization patterns? In the article included here, **Bloom** focuses on the period
of 2 to 3 years of age during which children begin to combine clauses to form
complex sentences. She traces the course of acquisition of syntactic connectives
(e.g., "and," "because") during this period and shows how they are used to
encode semantic relations such as the temporal and causal. Although the semantic meaning relations emerge at different ages for the four children in the study,
the order of emergence is roughly constant—paralleling Brown's findings on
younger children. In her analysis, Bloom is able to show that there are relationships between specific semantic relations and different kinds of sentence structures, and between the expression of semantic relations and aspects of discourse
context.

Working with data on children 3 to 10 years of age, **Bowerman** focuses on
the child's growing knowledge of lexical, morphological, and syntactic options
for encoding particular meanings such as causality. The younger child seems to
operate on the hypothesis that there is only one form for expressing a given
meaning. Subsequently, as the child begins to understand that there are alternative ways to encode a particular meaning, she begins to make errors in the
selection of the correct form. Although Bowerman does not deal with the developmental course of this selection process, she proposes that there is a necessary stage
in which linguistic form and meaning are uncoupled, leading to the possibility of
choice among competing forms.

A second theme—clearly prominent in all the selections in this section—is
the rule-governed, creative nature of language. As we have seen, some researchers are primarily concerned with the development of rules governing the combination of words or phrases into sentences. Bowerman, Clark, and other investigators (e.g., Berko-Gleason, 1960) have considered the operation of rules in word
formation as well. In the article included here, **Clark** focuses on a class of
deviations that she terms "lexical innovations." She hypothesizes that children,
like adults, tend to invent terms when they do not have an appropriate word in
their vocabulary—that is, to fill a lexical gap. Clark draws an important distinction between innovations for which interpretation of meaning depends on knowledge of context, and those for which the meaning can be computed from known
meanings of the parts. Furthermore, in support of her view that lexical innovations are clearly rule governed, Clark formulates the constraints on innovation
that obtain between speakers.

The nature of the relationships between specific aspects of language and
conceptualization constitutes a third major theme in contemporary work on the
evolution of form and meaning in early language. In his study, **Kuczaj** examines
changes in the ability to use obligatory hypothetical forms, such as "would" and
"would have," in different kinds of contexts. The questions presented refer to past
and future situations and real and imaginary characters. It is hypothesized that
young children find it more difficult to use hypothetical forms correctly in

contexts involving both actual and hypothetical elements than in contexts in which such crossing of boundaries is not involved. Another approach to interrelations between early language and thought is exemplified in the article by **Markman and Hutchinson.** As they point out, there is considerable evidence that young children tend to experience the world in terms of contextual wholes (event structures, thematic relations) rather than categorical relations; yet children rapidly acquire words that are categorical terms. How do we account for this? Markman and Hutchinson take exception to the common view that category terms are learned through ostensive definition. Rather, they suggest, the young language learner operates with implicit hypotheses that function as constraints on possible kinds of word meaning. The proposal that young children are geared to seek categorical meaning when they hear a new word is explored in a series of studies: Children of preschool age are presented with a choice between categorical and thematic organizations of pictured objects under two conditions—with no name provided and with a novel name (such as "biv") provided. The findings that categorical responding is enhanced in the naming conditions not only supports Markman and Hutchinson's hypothesis, but raises the question of the extent to which the young child's tendency to interpret novel words as category names is either learned very early or is biologically preprogrammed.

This brings us to the fourth major theme: the role of biological dispositions and environmental input in the child's acquisition of language. **Gleitman** introduces her discussion of this topic with an analysis of the "language learning problem" as formulated by Chomsky and others (Pinker, 1982; Wexler and Culicover, 1980). Stated in general terms, the question is How does the young child, whose experience consists of hearing utterances in conjunction with observing situations, acquire not only word meanings but the syntactic structures that govern comprehension and production of sentences? What role should be ascribed to environmental factors and what role to biological predispositions in the acquisition of various aspects of language? Gleitman analyzes previous research bearing directly on these questions, and reports a series of studies in which she and her associates investigated the effects of variations in environmental input and of biological endowment. Their research involves sampling natural cases in which some components of the language learning situation are varied. Assessing the evidence presented, Gleitman argues that significant aspects of language learning are biologically preprogrammed; furthermore, in agreement with Chomsky, she argues that the language capacity is highly specific, and that the learning of language as a formal system is not a simple by-product of cognitive development more generally—as some developmental psychologists have argued. Questions concerning the interrelations of various aspects of language learning and cognitive development, and the ways that biological predispositions and specific environmental factors interact in the complex process of language acquisition, continue to structure theoretical debate and empirical research in the field.

7

Roger Brown

Development of a First Language in the Human Species

The fact that one dares set down the above title, with considerable exaggeration but not perhaps with more than is pardonable, reflects the most interesting development in the study of child speech in the past few years. All over the world the first sentences of small children are being as painstakingly taped, transcribed, and analyzed as if they were the last sayings of great sages. Which is a surprising fate for the likes of "That doggie," "No more milk," and "Hit ball." Reports already made, in progress or projected for the near future, sample development in children not only from many parts of the United States, England, Scotland, France, and Germany, but also in children learning Luo (central East Africa), Samoan, Finnish, Hebrew, Japanese, Korean, Serbo-Croatian, Swedish, Turkish, Cakchiquel (Mayan-Guatemala), Tzeltal (Mayan-Mexico), American Sign Language in the case of a deaf child, and many other languages. The count you make of the number of studies now available for comparative analysis depends on how much you require in terms of standardized procedure, the full report of data, explicit criteria of acquisition, and so on. Brown (1973), whose methods demand a good deal, finds he can use some 33 reports of 12 languages. Slobin (1971), less interested in proving a small number of generalizations than in setting down a large number of interesting hypotheses suggested by what is known, finds he can use many more studies of some 30 languages from 10 different language families. Of course, this is still only about a 1% sample of the world's languages, but in a field like psycholinguistics, in which "universals" sometimes have been postulated on the basis of one or two languages, 30 languages represents a notable empirical advance. The credit for inspiring this extensive field work on language development belongs chiefly to Slobin at Berkeley, whose vision of a universal developmental sequence has inspired research workers everywhere. The quite surprising degree to which results to date support this vision has sustained the researcher when he gets a bit tired of writing down Luo, Samoan, or Finnish equivalents of "That doggie" and "No more milk."

It has, of course, taken some years to accumulate data on a wide variety of languages and even now, as we shall see, the variety is limited largely to just the first period of sentence construction (called Stage I). However, the study of first-language development in the preschool years began to be appreciated as a central topic in psycholinguistics in the early 1960s. The initial impetus came fairly directly from Chomsky's (1957) *Syntactic Structures* and, really, from one particular emphasis in that book and in transformational, generative grammar generally. The emphasis is, to put it simply, that in acquiring a first language, one cannot possibly be said simply to acquire a repertoire of sentences, however large that repertoire is imagined to be, but must instead be said to acquire a rule system that makes it possible to generate a literally infinite variety of sentences, most of them never heard from anyone else. It is not a rare thing for a person to compose a new sentence that is understood within his community; rather, it is really a very ordinary linguistic event. Of course, *Syntactic Structures* was not the first book to picture first-language learning as a largely creative process; it may be doubted if any serious linguist has ever thought otherwise. It was the central role Chomsky gave to creativity that made the difference, plus, of course, the fact that he was able to put into explicit, unified notation a certain number of the basic rules of English.

In saying that a child acquires construction rules, one cannot of course mean that he acquires them in any explicit form; the preschool child cannot tell you any linguistic rules at all. And the chances are that his parents cannot tell you very many either, and they obviously do not attempt to teach the mother tongue by the formulation of rules of sentence construction. One must suppose that what happens is that the preschool child is able to extract from the speech he hears a set of construction rules, many of them exceedingly abstract, which neither he nor his parents know in explicit form. This is saying more than that the child generalizes or forms analogies insofar as the generalizations he manifests conform closely to rules that have been made explicit in linguistic science.

That something of the sort described goes on has always been obvious to everyone for languages like Finnish or Russian, which have elaborate rules of word formation, or morphology, that seem to cause children to make very numerous systematic errors of a kind that parents and casual observers notice. In English, morphology is fairly simple, and errors that parents notice are correspondingly less common. Nevertheless, they do exist, and it is precisely in these errors that one glimpses from time to time that largely hidden but presumably general process. Most American children learning English use the form *hisself* rather than *himself* when they are about 4 years old. How do they come by it? It actually has been in the language since Middle English and is still in use among some adults, although called, for no good reason, a "substandard" form. It can be shown, however, that children use it when they have never heard it from anyone else, and so presumably they make it up or construct it. Why do they invent something that is, from the standard adult point of view, a mistake? To answer that we must recall the set of words most similar to the reflexive pronoun *himself.* They are such other reflexive pronouns as *myself, yourself,* and *herself.* But all of these others, we see, are constructed by combining the possessive pronoun, *my, your* or *her* with *self.* The masculine possessive pronoun is *his* and, if the English language were consistent at this point, the reflexive would be *hisself.* As it happens, standard English is not consistent at this point but is, rather, irregular, as all languages are at some points, and the preferred form is *himself.* Children, by inventing *hisself* and often insisting on it for quite a period, "iron out" or correct the irregularity of the language. And, incidentally, they reveal to us the fact that what they are learning are general rules of construction—not just the words and phrases they hear.

Close examination of the speech of children learning English shows that it is often replete with errors of syntax or sentence construction as well as morphology (e.g., "Where Daddy went"). But for some reason, errors of word formation are noticed regularly by parents, whereas they are commonly quite unconscious of errors of syntax. And so it happens that even casual observers of languages with a well-developed morphology are aware of the creative construction process, whereas casual observers of English find it possible seriously to believe that language learning is simply a process of memorizing what has been heard.

The extraction of a finite structure with an infinite generative potential which furthermore is accomplished in large part, though not completely, by the beginning of the school years (see Chomsky, 1969, for certain exceptions and no doubt there are others), all without explicit tuition, was not something any learning theory was prepared to explain, though some were prepared to "handle" it, whatever "handle" means. And so it appeared that first-language acquisition was a major challenge to psychology.

While the first studies of language acquisition were inspired by transformational linguistics, nevertheless, they really were not approved of by the transformational linguists. This was because the studies took the child's spontaneous speech performance, taped and transcribed at home on some regular schedule, for their basic data, and undertook to follow the changes in these data with age. At about the same time in the early 1960s, three studies of, roughly, this sort were begun independently: Martin Braine's (1963) in Maryland, Roger Brown's (Brown and Bellugi, 1964) at Harvard with his associates Ursula Bellugi (now Bellugi-Klima) and Colin Fraser (Brown and Fraser, 1963), and Susan Ervin (now Ervin-Tripp) with Wick Miller (Miller and Ervin, 1964) at Berkeley. The attempt to discover constructional knowledge from "mere performance" seemed quite hopeless to the MIT linguists (e.g., Chomsky, 1964; Lees, 1964). It was at the opposite extreme from the linguist's own method, which was to present candidate-sentences to his own intuition for judgment as grammatical or not. In cases of extreme uncertainty, I suppose he may also have stepped next door to ask the opinion of a colleague.

In retrospect, I think they were partly right and partly wrong about our early methods. They were absolutely right in thinking that no sample of spontaneous speech, however large, would alone enable one to write a fully determinate set of construction rules. I learned that fact over a period of years in which I made the attempt 15 times, for three children at five points of development. There were always, and are always, many things the corpus alone cannot settle. The linguists were wrong, I think, in two ways. First, in supposing that because one cannot learn everything about a child's construction knowledge, one cannot learn anything. One can, in fact, learn quite a lot, and one of the discoveries of the past decade is the variety of ways in which spontaneous running discourse can be "milked" for knowledge of linguistic structure; a great deal of the best evidence lies not simply in the child's own sentences but in the exchanges with others on the level of discourse. I do not think that transformational linguists should have "pronounced" on all of this with such discouraging confidence since they had never, in fact, tried. The other way in which I think the linguists were wrong was in their gross exaggeration of the degree to which spontaneous speech is ungrammatical, a kind of hodgepodge of false starts, incomplete sentences, and so on. Except for talk at learned conferences, even adult speech, allowing for some simple rules of editing and ellipses, seems to be mostly quite grammatical (Labov, 1970). For children and for the speech of parents to children this is even more obviously the case.

The first empirical studies of the 1960s gave rise to various descriptive characterizations of which "telegraphic speech" (Brown and Fraser, 1963) and "Pivot Grammar" (Braine, 1963) are the best known. They did not lead anywhere very interesting, but they were unchallenged long enough to get into most introductory psychology textbooks where they probably will survive for a few years, even though their numerous inadequacies are now well established. Bloom (1970), Schlesinger (1971), and Bowerman (1970) made the most telling criticisms both theoretical and empirical, and Brown (1973) has put the whole, now overwhelmingly negative, case together. It seems to be clear enough to workers in this field that telegraphic speech and Pivot Grammar are false leads that we need not even bother to describe.

However, along with their attacks, especially on Pivot Grammar, Bloom (1970) and Schlesinger (1971) made a positive contribution that has turned out to be the second major impetus to the field. For reasons which must seem very strange to the outsider not immersed in the linguistics of the 1960s, the first analyses of child sentences in this period were in terms of pure syntax, in abstraction from semantics, with no real attention paid to what the children might intend to communicate. Lois Bloom added to her transcriptions of child speech a systematic running account of the nonlinguistic context. And in these contexts she found evidence that the child intends to express certain meanings with even his earliest sentences, meanings that go beyond the simple naming in succession of various aspects of a complex situation, and that actually assert the existence of, or request the creation of, particular relations.

The justification for attributing relational semantic intentions to very small children comprises a complex and not fully satisfying argument. At its strongest, it involves the following sort of experimental procedure. With toys that the child can name available to him he is, on one occasion, asked to "Make the truck hit the car," and on another occasion "Make the car hit the truck." Both sentences involve the same objects and action, but the contrast of word order in English indicates which object is to be in the role of agent (hitter) and which in the role of object (the thing hit). If the child acts out the two events in ways appropriate to the contrasting word orders, he may be said to understand the differences in the semantic relations involved. Similar kinds of contrasts can be set up for possessives ("Show me the Mommy's baby" versus "Show me the baby's Mommy") and prepositions ("Put the pencil on the matches" versus "Put the matches on the pencil"). The evidence to date, of which there is a fairly considerable amount collected in America and Britain (de Villiers and de Villiers, 1973a; Fraser, Bellugi, and Brown, 1963; Lovell and Dixon, 1965), indicates that, by late Stage I, children learning English can do these things correctly (experiments on the prepositions are still in a trial stage). By late Stage I, children learning English also are often producing what the nonlinguistic context suggests are intended as relations of possession, location, and agent-action-object. For noncontrastive word orders in English and for languages that do not utilize contrastive word order in these ways, the evidence for relational intentions is essentially the nonlinguistic context. Which context is also, of course, what parents use as an aid to figuring out what their children mean when they speak.

It is, I think, worth a paragraph of digression to point out that another experimental method, a method of judgment and correction of word sequence and so a method nearer that of the transformational linguist himself, yields a quite different outcome. Peter and Jill de Villiers (1972) asked children to observe a dragon puppet who sometimes spoke correctly with respect to word order (e.g., "Drive your car") and sometimes incorrectly (e.g., "Cup the fill"). A second dragon puppet responded to the first when the first spoke correctly by saying "right" and repeating the sentence. When the first puppet spoke incorrectly, the second, tutorial puppet, said "wrong," and corrected the sentence (e.g., "Fill the cup"). After observing a number of such sequences, the child was invited to play the role of the tutorial puppet, and new sentences, correct and incorrect, were supplied. In effect, this is a complicated way of asking the child to make judgments of syntactic well-formedness, supplying corrections as necessary. The instruction is not given easily in words, but by role-playing examples de Villiers and de Villiers found they could get the idea across. While there are many interesting results in their study, the most important is that the children did not make correct word-order judgments 50% of the time until after what we call Stage V, and only the most advanced child successfully corrected wrong orders over half the time. This small but important study suggests that construction rules do not emerge all at once on the levels of spontaneous use, discriminating response, and judgment. The last of these, the linguist's favorite, is, after all, not simply a pipeline to competence but a metalinguistic performance of considerable complexity.

In spite of the fact that the justification for attributing semantic intentions of a relational nature to the child when he first begins composing sentences is not fully satisfactory, the practice, often called the method of "rich interpretation," by contrast with the "lean" behavioral interpretation that preceded it, is by now well justified simply because it has helped expose remarkable developmental universals that formerly had gone unremarked. There are now I think three reasonably well-established developmental series in which constructions and the meanings they express appear in a nearly invariant order.

The first of these, and still the only one to have been shown to have validity for many different languages, concerns Stage I. Stage I has been defined rather arbitrarily as the period when the average length of the child's utterances in morphemes (mean length of utterance or MLU) first rises above 1.0—in short, the time when combinations of words or morphemes first occur at all—until the MLU is 2.0, at which time utterances occasionally will attain as great a length as 7 morphemes. The most obvious superficial fact about child sentences is that they grow longer as the child grows older. Leaning on this fact, modern investigators have devised a set of standard rules for calculating MLU, rules partially well motivated and partially arbitrary. Whether the rules are exactly the right ones, and it is already clear that they are not, is almost immaterial because their only function is a temporary one: to render children in one study and in different studies initially comparable in terms of some index superior to chronological age, and this MLU does. It has been shown (Brown, 1973) that while individual children vary enormously in rate of linguistic development, and so in what they know at a given chronological age, their constructional and semantic knowledge is fairly uniform at a given MLU. It is common, in the literature, to identify five stages, with those above Stage I defined by increments of .50 to the MLU.

By definition, then, Stage I children in any language are going to be producing sentences of from 1 to 7 morphemes long with the average steadily increasing across Stage I. What is not true by definition, but is true in fact for all of the languages so far studied, is that the constructions in Stage I are limited semantically to a single rather small set of relations and, furthermore, the complications that occur in the course of the Stage are also everywhere the same. Finally, in Stage I, the only syntactic or expressive devices employed are the combinations of the semantically related forms under one sentence contour and, where relevant in the model language, correct word order. It is important to recognize that there are many other things that *could* happen in Stage I, many ways of increasing MLU besides those actually used in Stage I. In Stage I, MLU goes up because simple two-term relations begin to be combined into three-term and four-term relations of the same type but occurring on one sentence. In later stages, MLU, always sensitive to increases of knowledge, rises in value for quite different reasons; for instance, originally missing obligatory function forms like inflections begin to be supplied, later on the embedding of two or more simple sentences begins, and eventually the coordination of simple sentences.

What are the semantic relations that seem universally to be the subject matter of Stage I speech? In brief, it may be said that they are either relations or propositions concerning the sensorimotor world, and seem to represent the linguistic expression of the sensorimotor intelligence which the work of the great developmental psychologist, Jean Piaget, has described as the principal acquisition of the first 18 months of life. The Stage I relations also correspond very closely with the set of "cases" that Charles Fillmore (1968) has postulated as the universal semantic deep structures of language. This is surprising since Fillmore did not set out to say anything at all about child speech but simply to provide a universal framework for adult grammar.

In actual fact, there is no absolutely fixed list of Stage I relations. A short list of 11 will account for about 75% of Stage I utterances in almost all language samples collected. A longer list of about 18 will come close to accounting for 100%. What are some of the relations? There is, in the first place, a closed semantic set having to do with reference. These include the nominative (e.g., "That ball"), expressions of recurrence (e.g., "More ball"), and expressions of disappearance or nonexistence (e.g., "All gone ball"). Then there is the possessive (e.g., "Daddy chair"), two sorts of locative (e.g., "Book table" and "Go store") and the attributive (e.g., "Big house"). Finally, there are two-term relations comprising portions of a major sort of declarative sentence: agent-action (e.g., "Daddy hit"), action-object (e.g., "Hit ball"); and, surprisingly from the point of view of the adult language, agent-object (e.g., "Daddy ball"). Less frequent relations, which do not appear in all samples but which one would want to add to a longer list, include experience-state (e.g., "I hear"), datives of indirect object (e.g., "Give Mommy"), comitatives (e.g., "Walk Mommy"), instrumentals (e.g., "Sweep broom"), and just a few others. From all of these constructions, it may be noticed that in English, and in all languages, "obligatory" functional morphemes like inflections, case endings, articles, and prepositions are missing in Stage I. This is, of course, the observation that gave rise to the still roughly accurate descriptive term *telegraphic speech*. The function forms are thought to be absent because of some combination of such variables as their slight phonetic substance and minimal stress, their varying but generally considerable grammatical complexity, and the subtlety of the semantic modulations they express (number, time, aspect, specificity of reference, exact spatial relations, etc.).

Stage I speech seems to be almost perfectly restricted to these two-term relations, expressed, at the least, by subordination to a single sentence contour and often by appropriate word order, until the MLU is about 1.50. From here on, complications which lengthen the utterance begin, but they are, remarkably enough, complications of just the same two types in all languages studied so far. The first type involves three-term relations, like agent-action-object, agent-action-locative, and action-object-locative which, in effect, combine sequentially two of the simple relations found before an MLU of 1.50 without repeating the term that would appear twice if the two-term relations simply were strung together. In other words, something like agent-action-object (e.g., "Adam hit ball") is made up *as if* the relations agent-action ("Adam hit") and action-object ("Hit ball") had been strung together in sequence with one redundant occurrence of the action ("hit") deleted.

The second type of complication involves the retention of the basic line of the two-term relation with one term, always a noun-phrase, "expanding" as a relation in its own right. Thus, there is development from such forms as "Sit chair" (action-locative) to "Sit Daddy chair" which is an action-locative, such that the locative itself is expanded as a possessive. The forms expanded in this kind of construction are, in all languages so far studied, the same three types: expressions of attribution, possession, and recurrence. Near the very end of Stage I, there are further complications into four-term relations of exactly the same two types described. All of this, of course, gives a very "biological" impression, almost as if semantic cells of a finite set of types were dividing and combining and then redividing and recombining in ways common to the species.

The remaining two best established invariances of order in acquisition have not been studied in a variety of languages but only for American children and, in one case, only for the three unacquainted children in Brown's longitudinal study—the children called, in the literature, Adam, Eve, and Sarah. The full results appear in Stage II of Brown (1973) and in Brown and Hanlon (1970). Stage II in Brown (1973) focuses on 14 functional morphemes including the English noun and verb inflections, the copula *be*, the progressive auxiliary *be*, the prepositions *in* and *on*, and the articles *a* and *the*. For just these forms in English it is possible to define a criterion that is considerably superior to the simple occurrence-or-not used in Stage I and to the semiarbitrary frequency levels used in the remaining sequence to be described. In very many sentence contexts, one or another of the 14 morphemes can be said to be "obligatory" from the point of view of the adult language. Thus in a nomination sentence accompanied by pointing, such as "That book," an article is obligatory; in a sentence like "Here two book," a plural inflection on the noun is obligatory; in "I running," the auxiliary *am* inflected for person, number, and tense is obligatory. It is possible to treat each such sentence frame as a kind of test item in which the obligatory form either appears or is omitted. Brown defined as his criterion of acquisition, presence in 90% of obligatory contexts in six consecutive sampling hours.

There are in the detailed report many surprising and suggestive outcomes. For instance, "acquisition" of these forms turns out never to be a sudden all-or-none affair such as categorical linguistic rules might suggest it should be. It is rather a matter of a slowly increasing probability of presence, varying in rate from morpheme to morpheme, but extending in some cases over several years. The most striking single outcome is that for these three children, with spontaneous speech scored in the fashion described, the order of acquisition of the morphemes approaches invariance, with rank-order correlations between pairs of children all at about 0.86. This does not say that acquisition of a morpheme is invariant with respect to chronological age: the variation of rate of development even among three children is tremendous. But the order, that is, which construction follows which, is almost constant, and Brown (1973) shows that it is not predicted by morpheme frequency in adult speech, but is well predicted by relative semantic and grammatical complexity. Of course, in languages other than English, the same universal sequence cannot possibly be found because grammatical and semantic differences are too great to yield commensurable data, as they are not with the fundamental relations or cases of Stage I. However, if the 14 particular morphemes are reconceived as particular conjunctions of perceptual salience and degrees of grammatical and semantic complexity, we may find laws of succession that have cross-linguistic validity (see Slobin, 1971).

Until the spring of 1972, Brown was the only researcher who had coded data in terms of presence in, or absence from, obligatory contexts, but then Jill and Peter de Villiers (1973a) did the job on a fairly large scale. They made a cross-sectional study from speech samples of 21 English-speaking American children aged between 16 and 40 months. The de Villiers scored the 14 morphemes Brown scored; they used his coding rules to identify obligatory contexts and calculated the children's individual MLU values according to his rules.

Two different criteria of morpheme acquisition were used in the analyses of data. Both constitute well-rationalized adaptations to a cross-sectional study of the 90% correct criterion used in Brown's longitudinal study; we will refer to the two orders here simply as 1 and 2. To compare with the de Villiers' two orders there is a single rank order (3) for the three children, Adam, Eve, and Sarah, which was obtained by averaging the orders of the three children.

There are then three rank orders for the same 14 morphemes scored in the same way and using closely similar criteria of acquisition. The degree of invariance is, even to one who expected a substantial similarity, amazing. The rank-order correlations are between 1 and 2, .84, between 2 and 3, .78, and between 1 and 3, .87. These relations are only very slightly below those among Adam, Eve, and Sarah themselves. Thanks to the de Villiers, it has been made clear that we have a developmental phenomenon of substantial generality.

There are numerous other interesting outcomes in the de Villiers' study. The rank-order correlation between age and Order 2 is .68, whereas that between MLU and the same order is .92, very close to perfect. So MLU is a better predictor than age in their study, as in ours of morpheme acquisition. In fact, with age partialed out, using a Kendall partial correlation procedure, the original figure of .92 is only reduced to .85, suggesting that age adds little or nothing to the predictive power of MLU.

The third sequence, demonstrated only for English by Brown and Hanlon (1970), takes advantage of the fact that what are called tag questions are in English very complex grammatically, though semantically they are rather simple. In many other languages tags are invariant in form (e.g., *n'est-ce pas*, French; *nicht wahr*, German), and so are grammatically simple; but in English, the form of the tag, and there are hundreds of forms, varies in a completely determinate way with the structure of the declarative sentence to which it is appended and for which it asks confirmation. Thus:

"John will be late, won't he?"
"Mary can't drive, can she?"

And so on. The little question at the end is short enough, as far as superficial length is concerned, to be produced by the end of Stage I. We know, furthermore, that the semantic of the tag, a request for confirmation, lies within the competence of the Stage I child since he occasionally produces such invariant and simple equivalents as "right?" or "huh?" Nevertheless, Brown and Hanlon (1970) have shown that the production of a full range of well-formed tags is not to be found until after Stage V, sometimes several years after. Until that time, there are, typically, no well-formed tags at all. What accounts for the long delay? Brown and Hanlon present evidence that it is the complexity of the grammatical knowledge that tags entail.

Consider such a declarative sentence as "His wife can drive." How might one develop from this the tag "can't she?" It is, in the first place, necessary to make a pronoun of the subject. The subject is *his wife*, and so the pronoun must be feminine, third person, and since it is a subject, the nominative case—in fact, *she*. Another step is to make the tag negative. In English this is done by adding *not* or the contraction *n't* to the auxiliary verb *can*; hence *can't*. Another step is to make the tag interrogative, since it is a question, and in English that is done by a permutation of order—placing the auxiliary verb ahead of the subject. Still another step is to delete all of the predicate of the base sentence, except the first member of the auxiliary, and that at last yields *can't she?* as a derivative of *His wife can drive*. While this description reads a little bit like a program simulating the process by which tags actually are produced by human beings, it is not intended as anything of the sort. The point is simply that there seems to be no way at all by which a human could produce the right tag for each declarative without *somehow* utilizing all of the grammatical knowledge described, just how no one knows. But memorization is excluded completely by the fact that, while tags themselves are numerous but not infinitely so, the problem is to fit the one right tag to each declarative, and declaratives are infinitely numerous.

In English all of the single constructions, and also all of the pairs, which entail the knowledge involved in tag creation, themselves exist as independent sentences in their own right, for example, interrogatives, negatives, ellipses, negative-ellipses, and so on. One can, therefore, make an ordering of constructions in terms of complexity of grammatical knowledge (in precise fact, only a partial ordering) and ask whether more complex forms are always preceded in child speech by less complex forms. This is what Brown and Hanlon (1970) did for Adam, Eve, and Sarah, and the result was resoundingly affirmative. In this study, then, we have evidence that grammatical complexity as such, when it can be disentangled, as it often cannot, from semantic complexity, is itself a determinant of order of acquisition.

Of course, the question about the mother tongue that we should really like answered is, How is it possible to learn a first language at all? On that question, which ultimately motivates the whole research enterprise, I have nothing to offer that is not negative. But perhaps it is worth while making these negatives explicit since they are still widely supposed to be affirmatives, and indeed to provide a large part of the answer to the question. What I have to say is not primarily addressed to the question, How does the child come to talk at all? since there seem to be fairly obvious utilities in saying a few words in order to express more exactly what he wants, does not want, wonders about, or wishes to share with others. The more exact question on which we have a little information that serves only to make the question more puzzling is, How does the child come to *improve* upon his language, moving steadily in the direction of the adult model? It probably seems surprising that there should be any mystery about the forces impelling improvement, since it is just this aspect of the process that most people imagine that they understand. Surely the improvement is a response to selective social pressures of various kinds; ill-formed or incomplete utterances must be less effective than well-formed and complete utterances in accomplishing the child's intent; parents probably approve of well-formed utterances and disapprove or correct the ill-formed. These ideas sound sensible and may be correct, but the still-scant evidence available does not support them.

At the end of Stage I, the child's constructions are characterized by, in addition to the things we have mentioned, a seemingly lawless oscillating omission of every sort of major constituent including sometimes subjects, objects, verbs, locatives, and so on. The important point about these oscillating omissions is that they seldom seem to impede communication; the other person, usually the mother, being in the same situation and familiar with the child's stock of knowledge, usually understands, so far as one can judge, even the incomplete utterance. Brown (1973) has suggested the Stage I child's speech is well adapted to his purpose, but that, as a speaker, he is very *narrowly* adapted. We may suppose that in speaking to strangers or of new experiences he will have to learn to express obligatory constituents if he wants to get his message across. And that may be the answer: The social pressures to communicate may chiefly operate outside the usual sampling situation, which is that of the child at home with family members.

In Stage II, Brown (1973) found that all of the 14 grammatical morphemes were at first missing, then occasionally present in obligatory contexts, and after varying and often long periods of time, always present in such contexts. What makes the probability of supplying the requisite morpheme rise with time? It is surprisingly difficult to find cases in which omission results in incomprehension or misunderstanding. With respect to the definite and nondefinite articles, it even looks as if listeners almost never really need them, and yet child speakers learn to operate with the exceedingly intricate rules governing their usage. Adult

Japanese, speaking English as a second language, do not seem to learn how to operate with the articles as we might expect they would if listeners needed them. Perhaps it is the case that the child automatically does this kind of learning but that adults do not. Second-language learning may be responsive to familiar sorts of learning variables, and first-language learning may not. The two, often thought to be similar processes, may be profoundly and ineradicably different.

Consider the Stage I child's invariably uninflected generic verbs. In Stage II, American parents regularly gloss these verbs in one of four ways: as imperatives, past tense forms, present progressives, or imminent-intentional futures. It is an interesting fact, of course, that these are just the four modulations of the verb that the child then goes on, first, to learn to express. For years we have thought it possible that glosses or expansions of this type might be a major force impelling the child to improve his speech. However, all the evidence available, both naturalistic and experimental (it is summarized in Brown, Cazden and Bellugi, 1969), offers no support at all for this notion. Cazden (1965), for instance, carried out an experiment testing for the effect on young children's speech of deliberately interpolated "expansions" (the supplying of obligatory functional morphemes), introduced for a period on every preschool day for 3 months. She obtained no significant effect whatever. It is possible, I think, that such an experiment done now, with the information Stage II makes available, and expanding only by providing morphemes of a complexity for which the child was "ready," rather than as in Cazden's original experiment expanding in all possible ways, would show an effect. But no such experiment has been done, and so no impelling effect of expansion has been demonstrated.

Suppose we look at the facts of the parental glossing of Stage I generic verbs not, as we have done above, as a possible tutorial device but rather, as Slobin (1971) has done, as evidence that the children already intended the meanings their parents attributed to them. In short, think of the parental glosses as veridical readings of the child's thought. From this point of view, the child has been understood correctly, even though his utterances are incomplete. In that case there is no selection pressure. Why does he learn to say more if what he already knows how to say works quite well?

To these observations of the seeming efficacy of the child's incomplete utterances, at least at home with the family, we should add the results of a study reported in Brown and Hanlon (1970). Here it was not primarily a question of the omission of obligatory forms but of the contrast between ill-formed primitive constructions and well-formed mature versions. For certain constructions, yes–no questions, tag questions, negatives, and wh-questions, Brown and Hanlon (1970) identified periods when Adam, Eve, and Sarah were producing both primitive and mature versions, sometimes the one, sometimes the other. The question was, Did the mature version communicate more successfully than the primitive version? They first identified all instances of primitive and mature versions, and then coded the adult responses for comprehending follow-up, calling comprehending responses "sequiturs" and uncomprehending or irrelevant responses "nonsequiturs." They found no evidence whatever of a difference in communicative efficacy, and so once again, no selection pressure. Why, one asks oneself, should the child learn the complex apparatus of tag questions when "right?" or "huh?" seems to do just the same job? Again one notes that adults learning English as a second language often do not learn tag questions, and the possibility again comes to mind that children operate on language in a way that adults do not.

Brown and Hanlon (1970) have done one other study that bears on the search for selection pressures. Once again it was syntactic well-formedness versus ill-formedness that was in question rather than completeness or incompleteness. This time Brown and Hanlon started with two kinds of adult responses to child utterances: "approval," directed at an antecedent child utterance, and "disapproval," directed at such an antecedent. The question then was, Did the two sets of antecedents differ in syntactic correctness? Approving and disapproving responses are, certainly, very reasonable candidates for the respective roles, "positive reinforcer" and "punishment." Of course, they do not necessarily qualify as such because reinforcers and punishments are defined by their effects on performance (Skinner, 1953); they have no necessary, independent, nonfunctional properties. Still, of course, they often are put forward as plausible determinants of performance and are thought, generally, to function as such. In order differentially to affect the child's syntax, approval and disapproval must, at a minimum, be governed selectively by correct and incorrect syntax. If they should be so governed, further data still would be needed to show that they affect performance. If they are not so governed, they cannot be a selective force working for correct speech. And Brown and Hanlon found that they are not. In general, the parents seemed to pay no attention to bad syntax nor did they even seem to be aware of it. They approved or disapproved an utterance usually on the grounds of the truth value of the proposition which the parents supposed the child intended to assert. This is a surprising outcome to most middle-class parents, since they are generally under the impression that they do correct the child's speech. From inquiry and observation I find that what parents generally correct is pronunciation, "naughty" words, and regularized irregular allomorphs like *digged* or *goed*. These facts of the child's speech seem to penetrate parental awareness. But syntax—the child saying, for instance, "Why the dog won't eat?" instead of "Why won't the dog eat?"—seems to be set right automatically in the parent's mind, with the mistake never registering as such.

In sum, then, we presently do not have evidence that there are selective social pressures of any kind operating on children to impel them to bring their speech into line with adult models. It is, however, entirely possible that such pressures do operate in situations unlike the situations we have sampled, for instance, away from home or with strangers. A radically different possibility is that children work out rules for the speech they hear, passing from levels of lesser to greater complexity, simply because the human species is programmed at a certain period of life to operate in this fashion on linguistic input. Linguistic input would be defined by the universal properties of language. And the period of progressive rule extraction would correspond to Lenneberg's (1967 and elsewhere) proposed "critical period." It may be chiefly adults who learn a new, a second, language in terms of selective social pressures. Comparison of the kinds of errors made by adult second-language learners of English with the kinds made by child first-language learners of English should be enlightening.

If automatic internal programs of structure extraction provide the generally correct sort of answer to how a first language is learned, then, of course, our inquiries into external communication pressures simply are misguided. They look for the answer in the wrong place. That, of course, does not mean that we are anywhere close to having the right answer. It only remains to specify the kinds of programs that would produce the result regularly obtained.

8

Lois Bloom, Margaret Lahey, Lois Hood, Karin Lifter, and Kathleen Fiess

Complex Sentences: Acquisition of Syntactic Connectives and the Semantic Relations They Encode

Children begin to combine simple sentences to form complex sentences in the period from 2 to 3 years of age, and development of complex sentences involves learning aspects of *form* (syntactic connectives and syntactic structures), *content* (semantic relations between propositions), and *use* (discourse cohesion). The focus of the study reported here was on the acquisition of connective forms that are used in complex sentences, both phrasal and sentential, that theoretically combine two simple sentences (or, more accurately, the structures that underlie them). Previous studies of the development of complex sentences have dealt most often with the forms of complex sentences (e.g., Limber, 1973; Menyuk, 1969). Few studies (e.g.,Clark, 1970) have dealt with the intersection of linguistic form with semantic content, and none has considered the intersection of linguistic form with content and use in discourse. Furthermore, most studies have described the language of children older than 3 years of age, who already have considerable knowledge of complex sentences (e.g.,Bates, 1976a; Clark, 1970, 1973a; Ferreiro and Sinclair, 1971).

In a preliminary study (Hood, Lahey, Lifter, and Bloom, 1978), the tentative developmental sequences, from 2 to 3 years of age, of syntactic connectives and the semantic relations between propositions were reported separately. The present study is·concerned with the developmental interactions between connective forms and meaning relations, and between these form/content interactions and the discourse environments in which they occurred. It was the purpose of this study to investigate the developmental interface among linguistic knowledge,

Abridged from "Complex sentences: acquisition of syntactic connectives and the semantic relations they encode" by L. Bloom, M. Lahey, L. Hood, K. Lifter, and K. Fiess, 1980, *Journal of Child Language*, 7, 235–261. Copyright 1980 by Cambridge University Press. Reprinted by permission of publisher and authors.

event knowledge, and discourse skills in the acquisition of complex sentences by 2-year-old children.

Methods

The subjects of the study were four first-born children, Eric, Gia, Kathryn, and Peter, whose language development in the period from about 1;7 to 3 years of age has been reported on elsewhere (e.g., Bloom, 1970; Bloom, Lightbown & Hood, 1975). The data base consisted of five observations of Eric, five of Gia, five of Kathryn, and seven of Peter, beginning with the first observation at which connectives were produced and using approximately every other observation until the child's third birthday. Information about the children's age and mean length of utterance (MLU) in these observations is presented in Table 8-1. The total number of utterances in these observations was 15,713 for Eric, 20,443 for Gia, 20,025 for Kathryn, and 19,024 for Peter. All child utterances that contained conjunctions, relative pronouns, and *wh* pronouns provided the corpus for further analysis.

Each utterance that included a connective was copied onto sorting cards from the transcription, along with relevant nonlinguistic context and preceding and subsequent utterances by both child and adult. Sentence relations that extended cohesion across utterance boundaries (either in the same speaker turn, for example, # *I carry this/ and you carry that* #, or in two or more turns of different speakers, for example, # *Your Mommy gave you a bottle?* # *yes* # *why?* # *because I'm a little baby* #), were included in the analysis if the child used a connective form(/indicates utterance boundary; # indicates turn boundary). All the speech events were examined and coded according to their (1) connective forms, (2) semantic relations, (3) syntactic structures, and (4) cohesion relations between connected clauses.

The procedures for identifying the connective forms and the discourse environments for cohesion relations were relatively straightforward because they de-

Table 8-1. *Summary Description of Speech Samples*[a]

Child	Age range (months, weeks)	Mean length of utterance		
		Range	Mean increment	*sd*
Eric	25;1–36;0	2;63–3;49	0.22	0.58
Gia	25;2–34;2	2;30–3;71	0.47	0.55
Kathryn	24;2–35;1	2;83–4;23	0.35	0.40
Peter	25;3–38;0	2;00–3;57	0.22	0.53

[a]The mean increment and the standard deviation were included in this table to indicate the variability of MLU in this development period.

pended upon identifying formal regularities in the data, that is, whether or not one or another connective was said, and whether or not two connected clauses extended across utterance boundaries. On the other hand, the identification of semantic relations between clauses was an inferential process of interpretation. The interpretation process was centred on the question: what is the meaning of two clauses in *relation* to each other, given

1. The meaning of a first clause,
   /maybe you can bend the man—
2. the meaning of the second clause,
   —he can sit/
3. the fact that the two clauses are connected by *so* in the sentence
   / maybe you can bend the man *so* he can sit / and
4. the fact that the child was trying to bend a wire figure that he subsequently put on a train car.

This process of interpreting the semantic relations between clauses in complex sentences is a continuation of the procedures used in earlier studies of the semantic relations between words in children's simple sentences. In early child language data, when MLU progresses from 1.0 to 2.0, the semantic relations between words in simple sentences can be inferred on the basis of information from the situational context. For example, *Mommy pigtail*, in which Mommy is combing the child's hair, can be interpreted as the semantic relation agent-object. The categories of semantic relations in early sentences, such as recurrence, possession, agent-object, action-object, etc. (described in Bloom, 1970, 1973; Schlesinger, 1971) were *derived* from the child language data in this way, on the basis of inferences from contextual cues, rather than being *imposed upon* the child language data on the basis of inferences from the adult model. Similarly, the semantic relations between connected clauses in complex sentences were interpreted, in the later child language data described in this study, on the basis of the relation between what was said and the situational context in which utterances occurred. After repeated passes through the data, certain meaning relations between clauses emerged as being more consistent or regular, and developmentally relevant, than others, and these categories of meaning relations form the major results of this study.

There was homogeneity among the categories of semantic relations with respect to the *criteria* that were used to identify relevant instances. The semantic categories were formed on the basis of the inferential process of interpretation, rather than according to the forms the children used (i.e., connectives or verbs) and their meanings in the adult model. Although certain semantic relations were expected in the data, for example, causality and temporal relations, in part because the children were using such connectives as *because* and *and then*, the meanings of these connectives were not always transparent. The meanings of the semantically more general connectives, i.e., *and, that, what*, were even less transparent. . . .

Ultimately, the reliability of judgments of interpretation was decided by consensus. Once the final semantic categorization was obtained (the eight semantic relations reported below), the reliability of coding was tested as follows. A sample of 100 utterances was drawn from each of two observations from each of the individual children, and coded independently by three of the investigators. The proportions of agreement between independent codings ranged between 0.80 and 0.90. . . .

Given these two qualifications on the interpretation of meaning relations (ambiguity and/or equivocal interpretation, and subcategorization) it was possible to identify the major semantic relations between clauses in an average of 0.87 of the children's complex sentences. The semantic relations that were either anomalous or otherwise uninterpretable comprised the remaining 0.13 of the data (range 0.08 to 0.18 for the several observations of the four children).

In order to establish that a form (i.e., a connective or syntactic structure), or a meaning relation, or a connective/meaning relation interaction was acquired, a criterion of productivity was set in advance: the occurrence of five or more different utterances in at least two successive observations of a particular child was counted as evidence of productivity for the child (see Bloom et al., 1975; Bloom and Lahey, 1978, for discussions of productivity and criterion-referenced descriptions of language acquisition, respectively).

Results

Connective forms were used primarily in three different ways. First, *nonconnective use* involved the use of certain forms, such as *what, where, that,* and *like* in nonconnective contexts, such as *what doing, where doggie, that my shoe,* and *like this.* Such forms were homonymous, having both connective and nonconnective functions. They were learned first in their nonconnective contexts, and with the exception of *what,* they were the last forms to be used as connectives. In contrast, other connective forms, such as *and, then,* and *because,* were nonhomonymous, and were the first forms used as connectives.

Second, *contextual use* involved the use of *and* to chain a child utterance to a nonlinguistic event that was either something the child did or saw in the context, for example:*

(1) Kathryn IV (K had opened a
box of figures and taken them
out; picking up box of furni-
ture)   *and* let's see dis

---

*Utterances on the right were spoken by the child. Material in parentheses on the left describes the situational context, and utterances from the adults are presented on the left without parentheses. The connective used as an illustration is italicized, to highlight it and differentiate it from other connectives in the same utterance not under immediate discussion.

(2) Eric VI (E picks up puppet,
    puts it in box with other
    puppets)   *and* I close them

The third use of connectives was the focus of the present study: the use of *syntactic* connectives to either connect two constituents within a sentence phrase (phrasal structures) or to connect two related clauses (sentential structures). Most frequently, the constituents in phrasal structures were the noun phrase of the predicate complement, for example:

(3) Gia VIII (Mother and Lois talk-
    ing about redecoration in Gia's
    home)   and Mommy's gonna get me
                                     chair *and* table

(4) Eric VI (pointing to train
    engine)
                                     I put the engine dere

    right/mhm
    (takes engine off)
                                     and take off

    yes
                                     and wash it/

The use of *and* in sentence subject phrases was relatively rare, for example:

(5) Gia VII (telling Lois about yes-
    terday's visit to Grandma's)   Uncle Paul *and* Grandma
                                     no there

The children began to use contextual *and* and syntactic *and* at the same time, except for Kathryn who used contextual *and* before using connectives syntactically. The syntactic use of connectives in phrasal and sentential structures is described in the results that follow. *

SYNTACTIC CONNECTIVES

The connective forms (conjunctions, *wh* pronouns, and relative pronouns) used most frequently by the four children combined were *and, because, what, when, so;* the less frequently used connective forms were *and then, but, if, that,* and *where* (see Hood et al., 1978). The sequence in which the connectives became productive for each child individually is presented in Fig. 8-1, according to age. The developmental sequence was rank ordered for each child. When two or more connectives became productive in the same sample, ranks were determined according to proportional use, and the ranks were split if a difference in proportion was ≤ 0.05. The rank orders were averaged across the four children, for only those connectives that were used productively for at least two of the chil-

*Some tables and figures omitted. [Eds.]

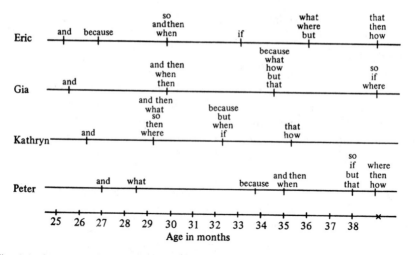

Fig. 8-1. *Sequence of emergence of syntactic connectives for individual children. (Those connectives listed above the X were not productive within the age period studied.)*

dren. . . . When a connective was not productive for a child, although it occurred, that connective was assigned a later rank than the forms that were productive for that child. Spearman rank order correlations were computed by comparing the rank orders of connective emergence for all combinations of pairs for the four children. In the six correlation coefficients that were computed (range 0.45 to 0.84) there was a significant correlation in only one comparison, which indicated variation among the children in the rank order of emergence (as seen in Fig. 8-1). For example, *then* was productive early for Kathryn and Gia and never became productive for Eric and Peter; *where* was productive early for Kathryn, late for Eric, and never became productive for Gia and Peter; *what* became productive very early for Peter and later for the other children. . . . There was considerably more variation in age of emergence than in rank order. *And* was the first connective to emerge, and the remaining connectives, by and large, emerged subsequently, although at different ages for different children.

SEMANTIC RELATIONS

There were eight major meaning relations observed;* these are described below, with examples. †

---

*One other semantic relation was observed that never became productive for any of the children: *Manner*, e.g., *I wanta do it like you did.*

†Here and subsequently, some examples are omitted. [Eds.]

Additive

In additive relations, two events and/or states were joined without an added dependency relation between them. Each clause was meaningful by itself; the combination of the two clauses did not create a meaning that was anything other than the meaning of each clause separately. Additive relations were expressed when the child carried out successive actions and chained each clause with each action.

(6) Eric VIII (looking at picture in
    book)

                  They're taking a vacuum cleaner
                  to wipe *and* puppy dog's
                  running

Temporal

In a temporal relation there was a dependency between events and/or states that involved temporal sequence or simultaneity. The utterance was not chained to successive actions as could be the case in additive sentences, that is, at least one of the events was not concurrent with the utterance.

(7) Kathryn IV (talking about visit
    to friend, Jocelyn)

                  Jocelyn's going home *and*
                  take her sweater off

(8) Kathryn VI (pushing car to
    hall)

                  I going this way to get the
                  groceries *then* come back

Causal

In a causal relation there was a dependency between two events and/or states which was most often intentional and/or motivational. One clause referred to an intended or ongoing action or state, and the other clause gave a reason or result (see Hood and Bloom, 1979).

(9) Kathryn VI (giving bendable
    man to Lois)

                  maybe you can bend him *so* he
                  can sit
                  get them *cause* I want it

(10) Peter XX (telling about a
     friend who hurt her foot)

                  She put a bandaid on her shoe
                  and it maked it feel better

Adversative

In this category the relation between two events and/or states was one of contrast. Most often the relation between the clauses was one of opposition, in which one clause negated or opposed the other, or of exception, in which one clause qualified or limited the other.

(11) Kathryn X (telling and demon-
      strating how she sleeps on the
      sofa)
                                        cause I was tired/*but* now
                                        I'm not tired

Object Specification

In this category the two clauses combined described an object or person mentioned in the first clause. The most common descriptions of the object or person concerned function, place, or activity.

(12) Gia XI (Gia using toy tele-
      phone)
      Mommy: Who'd you call?   the man *who* fixes the door
(13) Kathryn X (K comes into room
      with fishing pole)
      Lois: What's that?   it looks like a fishing thing
                                        and you fish with it

Epistemic

The dependency relation in utterances in this category involved certainty or uncertainty on the part of the person named in the first clause (the child most often), about a particular state of affairs named in the second clause.

(14) Eric XII (playing with family fig-
      ures)
      Lois: What do you think this   I don't know *what* her name is
      baby's name is?

Notice

Utterances in this category called attention to a state or event named in the second clause.

(15) Gia XI (showing Lois some   look *what* my Mommy got me
      candy)

Other

These were complements, other than epistemic and notice complements, with verbs of communication or the copula primarily.

(16) Eric XII (Eric had just awakened
      when Lois entered room)   tell Iris *that* I wet my bed

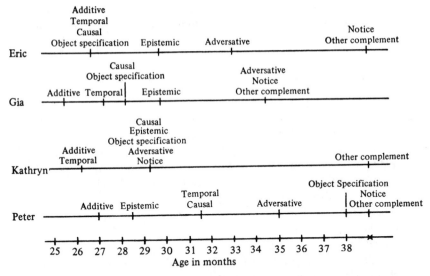

Fig. 8-2. *Sequence of emergence of semantic relations for individual children. (Those connectives listed above the X were not productive within the age period studied.)*

The sequence of emergence of the meaning relations is plotted for each child individually, according to age, in Fig. 8-2. The sequence in which the meaning relations first became productive was rank ordered for each child. When more than one relation was productive within a sample, rank order was decided according to relative proportion, and ranks were split if a difference in proportion was ≤ 0.05. The average order of acquisition for the four children was determined by averaging the individual rank orders for those categories that were productive for at least two of the children. . . . There was a sequential development of the meaning relations over the course of 10 months.

Although the acquisition order was based on the meaning relations that became productive for at least two of the children, all the meaning relations were observed (although they were not necessarily productive) in the speech samples for each child. When a category of relations was not productive for a child, that category was assigned a later rank than the productive categories for that child. Spearman rank order correlations were computed by comparing the rank order of emergence for all combinations of pairs for the four children. Six correlation coefficients were computed; they ranged from 0.75 to 0.95, with $p < 0.05$ for four of the six comparisons. The largest differences occurred in the rank order of the Epistemic relation; it emerged much earlier for Peter than for the other children. With Epistemic eliminated from the rank order, pairwise comparisons yielded correlation coefficients ranging from 0.87 to 0.95, with $p < 0.05$ for all six comparisons. Thus the children were quite similar to each other in terms of order of emergence of the meaning relations, although the meaning relations emerged at different ages for the different children. There was far more similarity in rank order of meaning relations than in rank order of connectives.

INTERSECTION OF CONNECTIVES AND SEMANTIC RELATIONS

There were 8 meaning relations expressed with 12 connectives that were productive in these complex sentences. Although it was statistically possible to have 96 intersections of content (the meaning relations between clauses) with form (the syntactic connectives used to connect clauses), only 45 intersections actually appeared in the data. However, only 10 of these intersections were productive for at least three of the children, and 15 were productive for at least two of the children. Two of the connectives, *where* and *how*, that were productive overall did not become productive with particular meaning relations.

The development of the intersection of connectives with semantic relations is presented in Fig. 8-3. The average ages of emergence of the connectives are displayed along the horizontal axis. The crossed lines indicate the productive intersection of connectives with semantic relations, and average age of intersection emergence is displayed along the vertical axis. *And*, which was the first and most frequent connective used, was also used with more different meaning relations than were the other connectives (e.g., Additive, Temporal, and Causal). With a less stringent criterion of productivity (i.e., productive for at least two rather than three of the children), *and* was observed with Object Specification

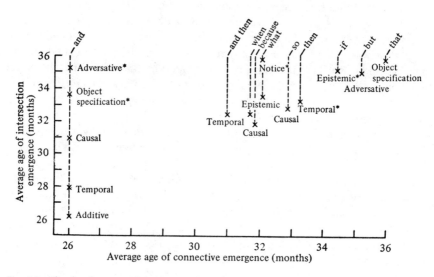

Fig. 8-3. *The development of the intersection of connectives with semantic relations. (Where and how did not become productive with any semantic relations.)*Intersections that were productive for only two out of the four children.*

and Adversative as well. Other connectives (e.g., *because, so, but, when,* etc.) appeared after *and* and were each used selectively with different meaning relations.

SYNTACTIC STRUCTURES

The children acquired complex sentences with connectives with three syntactic structures: conjunction, relativization, and complementation. There was a strong relationship between semantic relations and syntactic structures. Conjunction was used with the utterances that expressed Additive, Temporal, Causal, and Adversative relations. Conjunction was also used occasionally to express Object Specification. Complementation was used with utterances that expressed Epistemic and Notice relations, and occasionally for Object Specification. Relativization was used only to express Object Specification. The sequence of acquisition was, in general, conjunction < complementation < relativization. Conjunction developed first for all of the children, with three conjunction meanings in the order Additive < Temporal < Causal. The fourth conjunction meaning, Adversative, appeared 4 months later along with other, later-appearing structures.*

Complementation developed after conjunction in the order Epistemic < Notice < Other, except for Kathryn, who acquired Epistemic, Notice and complementation with Object Specification at the same time. Verb complements with syntactic connectives entailed *wh* pronominalization of a constituent (subject or object) in the complement sentence (e.g., *watch what I'm doing* and *look what my mommy got me*).

Relativization with *that,* or *wh* pronominalization of an antecedent noun, e.g., *the man who fixes the door,* was the last structure to appear, was always infrequent, and was used with only one meaning relation (Object Specification). The meaning relation Object Specification was encoded with all three of the structures by one or another of the four children: Gia and Peter used only relativization, Eric used conjunction first and then relativization, and Kathryn used all three in the order complementation < relativization < conjunction.

On another level of syntactic structure, within the structure conjunction, both phrasal structures (connected constituents within a phrase) and sentential structures (S = SVO + SVO) were distributed differentially across the four meanings of conjunction. Both phrasal and sentential structures were acquired at the same time, with Additive conjunction, for all the children except Gia, who acquired phrasal structures first. While the relative frequencies of phrasal and sentential structures in Additive conjunction remained essentially the same across time, there was a developmental increase in the proportion of sentential structure in Temporal conjunction. Sentential structures predominated at all times with all the children for Causal and Adversative conjunction.

---

*The terms used for the four meanings of conjunction have been changed from the terminology used in the earlier report (Hood et al., 1978) in an effort to conform with terminology suggested by Halliday and Hasan (1976).

COHESION RELATIONS IN DISCOURSE

While the syntactic connective was always part of a child utterance, the connective was sometimes used to connect relations that extended across utterance boundaries. When both parts of the relation occurred within one or across two consecutive child utterances, the cohesion was *child-child*. That is, both parts of the meaning relation, before and after the connective, were said by the child, e.g., *and there's my eye/and there's my feet*. For two of the conjunction meanings (Additive and Temporal), for Object Specification, and for complementation, cohesion was child-child 0.90 of the time, averaging across samples and across children.

When the two parts of the semantic relation before and after the connective occurred across two or more different speaker turns, the cohesion was either *adult-child* or *child-adult-child*, e.g., *#maybe he'll ride the horse#yeah, when he comes in#*. The only two meaning relations with cohesion that involved an adult utterance more than 0.20 of the time were Causality and Adversative. For all children, the first appearance of the Causality meaning relation occurred with child-child cohesion at least twice as often as with adult cohesion. The first appearance of the Adversative relation occurred with child-child cohesion at least twice as often for two of the children; of Gia's first three Adversative utterances, two were child-child and Peter's first two utterances were one of each. . . .

Discussion

The first syntactic connective the children learned, *and*, was also the most general: syntactically, *and* was used in both contextual and syntactic structures; semantically, *and* was used to encode conjunction with all of the different conjunction meaning relations, in the order Additive < Temporal < Causal < Adversative. Other syntactic connectives were learned subsequently, with different syntactic structures, and were semantically more specific. These results will be discussed in terms of *form*, and relative linguistic complexity in the adult model, *content*, and the intersection of form with conceptual and semantic factors affecting acquisition, and *use*, in terms of discourse cohesion.

FORM OF COMPLEX SENTENCES

The linguistic complexity of the forms of complex sentences in the adult model provides a partial explanation of the results of this study. There were two factors related to connective forms that appeared to influence the developmental sequence of connectives and syntactic structures observed in this study. First, there seemed to be a conceptual constraint on learning syntactically homonymous forms (see also Bever, 1970). The first connectives the children learned were nonhomonymous (*and, then, because*). The homonymous connectives except for *when* (*what*, *where*, *that*, and *like*), were learned in their nonconnective contexts first. *When*, in contrast, was learned as a connective long before it was learned as a *wh* question form. When homonymous forms were used as connectives, each was used with only one structure: *when* as a conjunction, *what* as a complementizer, and *where* as a relativizer.

The second factor had to do with the pronominalizing function of *wh* forms. Harris (1957) described two functions of *wh* forms in complex sentences: the forms *who*, *what*, *where*, *when*, *which*, as well as *that* can appear as pronominalizing connectives in the structure S_1-Wh-S_2, and either (1) pronominalize an antecedent S_1 noun, as in relativization (e.g., *there's a great hole where the bunny rabbits live*), or (2) pronominalize a subject or object constituent of S_2 as in complementation (e.g., *I don't know what this color is*). However, in the present study, *when* was the first *wh* form to appear and functioned as a conjunction in Temporal relations (as in *I'll get my slippers when I come out*) rather than as a pronominalizing form. *When* functioned in the same way as *and*, *because*, *so*, and *but* functioned in Additive, Causal, and Adversative sentences. The children in the present study learned the S_1-Wh-S_2 connective forms in the order *when* conjunction < *wh* complement < wh relative.

Syntactic Structures

Relativization, which occurred primarily with the main clause and required pronunciation of an antecedent noun, was the last structure that the children learned. Complementation, which also involved pronominalization (of an S_2 constituent) was learned before relativization and after conjunction (which did not involve pronominalization). The children learned complementation *per se* originally in the context of certain matrix verbs that took sentence complements without connectives (for example, *see*, *tell*, *want*, *know*) and that appeared early in their speech along with simple sentences (see also Limber, 1973). For example, *see Mommy busy*, *tell him wake up*, and *I want man stand up* occurred before or at the same time as the first syntactic connective, the use of *and* to code Additive conjunction (see Bloom, Hafitz, Tackeff and Gartner, n.d.).

The complementation that the children learned with pronominalization was constrained by a small set of semantically specific state verbs, including *know*, *think*, *see*, *watch*, and *tell*, which were similar to verbs in the examples of child sentences reported by Limber (1973) and by Rosenbaum (1967) for adult complementation. A semantic distribution of the children's complement-taking verbs is presented in Table 8-2 along with verbs reported by Limber and by Rosenbaum (see also Bloom, 1978). The children's later acquisition of epistemic, notice, and other verb complements appeared to be a formal development, involving pronominalization.

With respect to conjunction, there are two hypotheses in transformational grammar for the derivation of phrasal conjunction, e.g., *I want a green book and a pink book*. In the more traditional analysis, phrasal conjunction is transforma-

Table 8-2. *Complement-Taking Verbs*

	Epistemic	Notice	Communication
Child verbs (Eric, Gia, Kathryn, Peter)	Know Think	See Look Show Watch	Tell Ask Teach Explain
(from Limber 1973)	*all of the above* *Guess* *Remember* *Wonder* *Decide* *Forget*	*all the above*	*all the above* *Say*
Adult verbs (from Rosen baum 1967)	*all of the above* *Understand* *Believe* *Convince* *Surprise* *Doubt* *Worry* *Imagine* *Trust* *Recognize*	*all the above* *Hear* *Observe*	*all the above* *Admit* *Boast* *Promise* *Demonstrate* *Defy* *Persist* *Remind*

tionally derived from an underlying basis that contains two sentential structures, $S \rightarrow S_1$ and S_2 (or NP_1VP_1 and NP_1VP_2) with a general transformation that deletes the second NP_1 (e.g., Chomsky, 1957; Gleitman, 1965; Stockwell, Schacter and Partee, 1973). This first hypothesis suggests the possibility that phrasal conjunction, which is transformationally more complex than sentential conjunction because of the deletion transformation, would be acquired by children after sentential conjunction (i.e., *I want a green book and I want a pink book*). This possibility has been supported by the results of Slobin and Welsh (1973). However, in the present study, phrasal structures appeared at the same time as (for three of the children) or before (for one of the children) sentential conjunction [as reported also by Bates (1976a) for Italian children and by Lust and Mervis (1980) for American children]. These results are consistent with the second hypothesis concerning the derivation of phrasal conjunction: that the phrasal conjunction is, itself, basic in the underlying structure of the sentence (i.e., $S \rightarrow NP_1 \ VP_1$ *and* VP_2) (Stockwell et al., 1973). Such phrases as *green book and pink book* are apparently learned as basic sentence constituents.

CONTENT OF COMPLEX SENTENCES

A fuller explanation of the results of this study appears in the intersection of form with the semantic factors (the meaning relations between clauses and the meaning of connectives) and conceptual factors that affected acquisition. The children

appeared to learn the connective *and* in order to express cooccurrence of events that simply go together to begin with, in both phrasal structures (e.g., *I want to do a boy and a man*) and sentential structures (e.g., *you do one and I do one*).*
The Additive use of *and* was followed developmentally by sentences that combined clauses with different meaning relations between them—that is, Temporal, Causal, and Adversative conjunction.

The general cumulative principle that was used to decide on semantic interpretation proved to characterize the developmental sequence in which the semantic subcategories of conjunction appeared [see Brown and Hanlon (1970) for discussion of syntactic cumulative complexity, and Brainerd (1978) for discussion of cumulative complexity in cognitive development]. In the developmental sequence Additive < Temporal < Causal < Adversative, the Temporal, Causal, and Adversative sentences were all Additive in that two events or states were joined; Causal was both Additive and Temporal; some of the Adversative sentences were Additive, Temporal, and quasi-Causal (e.g., *I was trying to get my crayons but I fell*—meaning, "I couldn't get my crayons because I fell"). Adversative sentences included the new meaning of opposition or contrast (e.g., *I have a puppet/but not a real puppet*).

This cumulative sequence of semantic development has an analogue in children's conceptual development: children learn to form collections of things (e.g., Sinclair, 1970) before they learn to form series of things that are ordered relative to one another (e.g., Inhelder and Piaget, 1964). The children in this study learned to talk about things that go together (Additive conjunction) before they learned to talk about things that go together in ordered relationship (Temporal, Causal, and Adversative conjunction).

COHESION OF COMPLEX SENTENCES

The cohesion analysis in the present study provided evidence that learning increasingly complex structures is not dependent upon or otherwise the result of reciprocity in discourse, as has been claimed, for example, by Greenfield and Smith (1976). The two clauses with complex meaning relations that have been described were expressed most often by the child (child-child cohesion). Adult-child or child-adult-child cohesion occurred most often in expressions of Causality or Adversative relations, was always less frequent than child-child cohesion with the same semantic relations, and increased developmentally. The development of adult-child cohesion appeared to reflect the children's increasing ability to participate in discourse, using newly or already learned linguistic forms, rather than the learning of linguistic forms through discourse. It appears that children have to learn something about the forms of language before learning the situational and interpersonal constraints on using such forms, as has previously been suggested with respect to children's alternating nominal and pronominal forms

*The children also encoded the notion of additive events with the word *too*.

(Bloom et al., 1975) and temporal deixis with the use of verb inflections (Bloom, Lifter and Hafitz, 1980).

The information that a child intends to represent provides certain requirements for the form of the message. The discourse environment provides another source of requirements for the form of the message. In the course of development these two requirements interact with and mutually influence one another. However, in the beginning, the informational requirement appeared to exert the greater influence in determining how and when the children in this study learned to talk about complex meanings. The children appeared to learn complex forms, in order to talk about complex meanings. They began to learn to use such complex forms to meet the requirements of discourse subsequently. . . .

Conclusions

The considerable difficulty involved in learning complex sentences can be inferred from the length of time covered by the results of the study reported here. There is frequent mention in the child language literature of sudden insight in learning, reflected by a precipitous increase in behavior, as children give evidence of what has been referred to as "across the board" learning or awareness. No such learning was evident in the present study. On the contrary, approximately 8-week intervals (for Peter) and 12-week intervals (for Eric, Gia, and Kathryn) separated each of the observations that provided the data for analysis, and the linguistic gains observed were small, although consistent, across the time span for the children. Although there were intervening observations available (since approximately every other observation was used), the data for these observations did not appear (on the basis of cursory scanning) to conflict in any way with the general picture of slow but steady developmental progress toward the acquisition of complex sentences. However, the acquisition that has been reported here can be described only in terms of emergence, as the children presented evidence of learning something about the forms and functions of complex sentences, rather than in terms of achievement. Indeed, even though the procedures used for inferring acquisition were considerably more conservative than those used in other studies (inasmuch as criteria for acquisition included more than use of a single instance of a structure by a single child as had been the case in other studies, e.g., Bates, 1976) it was clear that the children had only just begun to learn about the use of syntactic connectives and meaning relations in conjunction, complementation, and relativization structures.

There was consistency among the children in the sequence in which the different meaning relations emerged and were expressed in complex sentences, but variation among them in the sequence in which they acquired different connectives to encode these meanings. This result—variation in form with similarity in content in the development of individual children—is consistent with reports of other aspects of these children's language acquisition (i.e., Bloom et al., 1975, on nominal/pronominal variation and early sentence relations; Hood and Bloom, 1979, on clause order in expressions of causality; and Bloom et al., 1980, on acquisition of -ed/irregular verb inflections). The variation in age of emergence (of connectives and meaning relations) that was observed is consistent with much of the existing child language literature that has contributed to the consensus that age alone is a poor predictor of acquisition.

To conclude, there were at least three major factors that appeared to influence the acquisition of syntactic connectives and the sequence of development of complex sentences with these connectives: the pronominalization of major constituents, the use of homonymous forms, and cumulative semantic complexity. Additionally, it appears that the children did not learn complex sentences by connecting their own utterance with a prior adult utterance to form the two clauses of a complex sentence. Rather, the informational requirements of the content of the children's messages appeared to be a stronger influence than discourse requirements for determining the form of the children's complex sentences with syntactic connectives.

9

Melissa Bowerman

The Child's Expression of Meaning:
Expanding Relationships among Lexicon, Syntax,
and Morphology

Studies of first-language acquisition typically have shown strong respect for the major components into which linguistic analysis divides language: lexicon, syntax, morphology, and phonology. Thus, researchers explore the acquisition of word meaning (for example), or the characteristics of children's early word combinations, or the acquisition of inflectional morphemes, but only rarely compare the elements of the child's developing linguistic system *across* the major formal categories. The picture of language acquisition built up in this way is fragmented. We may know a great deal about the development of particular subsystems, but we do not yet have a clear understanding of how the different parts fit together, and how they interact and are affected by each other in the course of development.

Interrelationships among the components of the child's developing grammar can be approached in various ways. The most studied problem to date is whether children's initial rules for combining and inflecting words are bound to particular words or groups of semantically similar words rather than extended across all words of the relevant part of speech (e.g., Braine, 1976; Bloom, Lifter and Hafitz, 1980). Limited attention also has been paid to the influence of the infant's phonological system on the "selection" of first words to be learned (Ferguson and Farwell, 1975). The present paper asks still a third question: Given that the child has a certain type of meaning he wants to communicate, what are his lexical, syntactic, and morphological options for encoding that meaning, and

Abridged from "The child's expression of meaning" by M. Bowerman, 1981, in *Native Language and Foreign Language Acquisition* (H. Winitz, Ed.), *Annals of the New York Academy of Sciences*, **379**, 172–189. Copyright 1981 by New York Academy of Sciences. Reprinted by permission of publisher and author.

how do these options change and affect each other over time? This question is elaborated in the first section below. Two issues raised there are considered in more detail in the next two sections. Finally, some possible implications of these issues for second-language acquisition are discussed in the last section.

Alternative Encoding Devices

Useful input to the study of the ontogenetic growth of lexical, syntactic, and morphological options for encoding meaning comes from two relatively independent fields of inquiry: linguistic research on variability in the way the same or closely related meanings are expressed in different languages, and sociolinguistic and pragmatic investigations of alternative ways of accomplishing a given speech act within a language.

CROSS-LINGUISTIC PERSPECTIVES

Languages differ in the devices they employ to express meanings of different kinds. What one language marks syntactically with word order another language encodes morphologically with case endings or phonologically with stress. These cross-linguistic differences mean that the division of labor between lexicon, syntax, and morphology is a matter of discovery for the child. Certain cross-linguistic differences, such as the use of word order versus case endings to mark grammatical relations, already have been discussed extensively by child language scholars (Slobin, 1973). Other, more subtle differences have yet to be investigated systematically, however. One such unexplored difference concerns the question of "what can be a word."

The fluent monolingual speaker may find this a bizarre question: that certain meanings should be dignified with their own words seems self-evident. But cross-linguistic studies have shown fascinating variability in the way complex meanings are packaged, and this variability is, moreover, patterned, with different languages or language families showing internal consistency. For example, categories of meaning that in one language are expressed routinely with single, monomorphemic lexical items may in another language be obligatorily partitioned into two or more components, each of which is assigned to a different word. Still a third alternative, intermediate between these "synthetic" and "analytic" extremes, involves assigning part of the meaning to a lexical root and another part or parts to inflectional or derivational affixes on this root. Languages differ globally from one another with respect to the degree of analyticity they favor (Fillmore, 1978), and they also manifest qualitatively different patterns in what meanings tend to get combined with what other meanings and expressed together as single words (Talmy, 1976b). An intriguing question is whether in the course of acquiring the lexical items to which he is exposed, the child gradually

arrives at an abstract understanding of the characteristic patterns in which semantic material combines to form words in his language.

WITHIN-LANGUAGE OPTIONS

When languages are discussed with an eye toward cross-linguistic comparisons,
they tend to be treated as single, monolithic entities: "language X does things like
this, language Y does them like that." But sociolinguists and pragmaticists re-
mind us that individual languages are anything but monolithic; rather, they are
best seen as complex systems of *linguistic variants,* or alternative ways to encode
roughly the same meanings under different linguistic and nonlinguistic conditions (Hymes, 1972). Becoming a fluent speaker, according to this view, requires
not only mastering a body of linguistic forms but also learning which ones mean
approximately the same thing and which circumstances favor the use of one
variant over another.

The speaker's options can be conceptualized at a variety of levels. At a
relatively global level, for example, a speech act such as requesting something
may be realized by sentences with entirely different semantic contents, cf. *Open
the window* versus *It's hot in here* as alternative methods of getting someone to
open a window. At a more molecular level, what is roughly "the same" semantic
content can be expressed in different ways. Sometimes options involve items
drawn from the same component of the grammar (e.g., two "synonymous"
words). What is particularly important for present purposes, however, is that
roughly synonymous encoding devices may be very dissimilar structurally, often
reflecting the range of variability that is found *across* languages. For example, for
certain meanings, English offers both syntactic and lexical choices: compare, for
instance, how the notion of causation is expressed in *The news of his death made
me sad* versus *The news of his death saddened me,* and in *John opened the door by
kicking it* versus *John kicked the door open;* how repetition is marked in *He read
the book again* versus *He reread the book;* how mode of travel is indicated in *He
drove/flew/bicycled/walked to California* versus *He went to California by car/
plane/bicycle/on foot;* and how location is encoded in *Jack put the wine into
bottles* versus *Jack bottled the wine.*

The within-language availability of alternative devices for expressing given
meanings raises a host of interesting questions. Most extensively discussed has
been what kinds of linguistic and nonlinguistic factors correlate with the use of
one form over another (Hymes, 1972; Talmy, 1976a). Still relatively unexplored,
however, are ongoing psycholinguistic processes at the time of speech: how
speakers keep track of the many contextual factors that are relevant to the form of
their utterances, how they generate linguistic alternatives that meet as many
contextual demands as possible, how they evaluate these alternatives and choose
among them, and how they manage to do all this under considerable time
pressure in ongoing discourse. One particularly interesting question in this connection is how speakers resolve conflicts when alternative incompatible language
forms compete for selection in the same speech context.

Acquiring Lexicalization Patterns

We return now to the question of whether language-learning children acquire an understanding of underlying regularities in the way their language packages semantic material. In principle they need not. They could become fluent speakers simply by memorizing the words they actually have heard and working out their meanings by observing how they are used. In fact, however, children appear to go well beyond this bare minimum: they analyze and compare the words they are learning in such a way as to develop expectations that words with certain semantic properties should exist, regardless of whether they have ever heard them, and they develop a feel for the possible morphological properties of these words. The evidence for this process lies in children's systematic use of words to convey meanings that they do not convey in adult speech.

Three representative categories of these novel usages by English-speaking children are illustrated with a few examples each in Table 9-1 (see Bowerman, 1974, 1977, for more detailed analyses). We shall call these usages "errors," meaning by this term only that they deviate from the conventional adult usage of these words. Most of the data presented in this and subsequent tables come from my two daughters, Christy and Eva, whose language development I followed closely by daily diary notes and periodic tape recording from the time of first words. I have documented each error type with data from a number of other children, however; the processes involved appear to be very general.

Errors 1-11 in Table 9-1 all involve the expression of causal relations, a domain in which particularly rich and interesting cross-linguistic differences in lexicalization patterns have been identified. A succinct summary of these differences has been provided by Fillmore (1978) whose outline we shall follow here.

Given a complex, two-part causal event in which one event, act, or situation is seen as bringing about a second event, act, or situation: let X stand for a verb that names the initial event (act, situation) and let Y stand for a verb or adjective that names the resulting situation. How shall a speaker express the total complex causal event? One possibility is for there to be a verb Z (a "lexical causative" or "causative verb") that represents this event. Such verbs are extremely common in English, e.g., *kill* (do something that causes someone to die) and transitive *break* (do something that causes something to break). Causative verbs are rare in some languages, however, where causal events are encoded more typically by syntactic combinations equivalent to English *make die, make break*, etc.

If a language does have Z verbs, there are several possible ways that these verbs can be related morphologically to X and Y. One is "no relationship," e.g., *kill* means roughly "do something that causes to die" but is morphologically unlike either a possible causing act (*shoot, stab*, etc.) or the resulting event (*die* or *dead*). Another possibility is for Z to be identical to Y, the resulting event, as in, for example, *John* OPENED *the door* (cf. the door OPENED) or *Mother* WARMED *the milk* (the milk became WARM). Still another possibility is for Z to be identical to

Table 9-1. *Errors Showing Grasp of Lexicalization Patterns*[a]

Use of "caused event" predicate as causative verb:

   1. C, 3;1: M: The cow would like to sing but he can't. (As C and M handle broken music box shaped like a cow.)
              C: I'm *singing* him. (Pulling string that used to make cow play.)
   2. C, 4;3: It always *sweats* me. That sweater is a sweaty hot sweater. (Doesn't want to wear sweater.)
   3. C, 4;6: *Spell* this "buy." *Spell* it "buy." (Wants M to rotate blocks on toy spelling device until word "buy" is formed.)
   4. E, 3;2: E: Everybody makes me cry.
              D: I didn't make you cry.
              E: Yes you did, you just *cried* me.
   5. E, 3;7: I'm gonna put the washrag in and *disappear* something under the washrag. (Putting washrag into container while playing in tub. Has been pretending to put on a magic act.)
   6. E, 3;8: I'm gonna *round* it. (Rolling up piece of thread into a ball.)

Use of "causing event" predicate as causative verb:

   7. E, 3;9: A gorilla captured my fingers. I'll *capture* his whole head off. His hands too. (= cause his head to come off by capturing it. As plays with rubber band around fingers.)
   8. E, 3;11: She *jumped* it off for Jennifer and Christy. (= caused it to come off by jumping. After someone jumps up to pull icicle off eaves of house and gives it to C and a friend.)
   9. E, 3;0: The birdies will find the squirrel and *spank* the squirrel from eating their birdseed . . . with their feet. (= cause the squirrel not to eat . . . by spanking him. After squirrel gets into birdfeeder.)
  10. C, 3;6: And the monster would *eat* you in pieces. (= cause you to be in pieces by eating you. Telling M a scary story.)
  11. A, 4;3: When you get to her, you *catch* her off. [= cause her to come off by catching her. A is on park merry-go-round with doll (= her) next to her; wants friend standing nearby to remove doll when doll comes around to her.]*

[a] C, Christy; E, Eva; M, mother; D, daddy; and A, Andrea. Age given in years; months.

*One group of examples omitted. [Eds.]

X, the causing event; in this case the resulting event is expressed separately with a word or phrase: *John* KICKED *the door open* (cf. John KICKED the door, which caused it to open, or John caused the door to become open by KICKING it); *Jim* CHOPPED *the tree down* [Jim CHOPPED (on) the tree, which caused it to fall down]; *Mary* WIPED *the table clean* (Mary WIPED the table, which caused it to become clean). Still other possibilities are for Z to be derived morphologically, e.g., by affixation, from either X (common in German and Hungarian) or Y (common in Turkish) or for Z to be a compound of X and Y (as in Mandarin).

English is unusual among the languages of the world in possessing many Z verbs—lexical causatives—that are identical morphologically to X or Y. But not every X or Y expression can be used as a Z. In some cases there is indeed a Z term, but it is either morphologically unrelated to X or Y (e.g., *kill*) or derivationally related to Y in ways that are no longer productive in contemporary English (e.g., *sharpen, flatten, legalize, enrich*). In other cases, there simply *is* no Z, no single-word lexical causative.

It is well known that when children discover a patterned way of doing things in language, they regularize forms that are exceptions to this pattern. Apparently the use of X or Y forms as Z—lexical causatives—is prevalent enough in English that the child extracts a pattern from the particular lexical causatives she has encountered and comes to *expect* that X or Y terms can be used, without morphological modification, as lexical causatives regardless of whether she has ever heard them so used. In 1-6 in Table 9-1, the child uses Y (a predicate for the caused event) as a lexical causative where English simply *has* no verb with the meaning of the converted Y (in many equivalent errors, the child's novel Z form replaces in existing Z form, e.g., transitive *die* for *kill*, cf. 7 in Table 9-2). In 7–11 it is X, a predicate specifying the causing act, that is used as a novel lexical causative. Errors of these types are quite analogous to more familiar overregularizations involving inflectional morphology, such as *foots* and *breaked*. . . .

It should be noted, but cannot be elaborated here (see Bowerman, 1974,

Table 9-2. *Interchangeable Use of Lexical and Periphrastic Causatives*[a]

Periphrastic causative used where lexical causative is required:

1.	C, 2;11:	I *maked* him *dead* on my tricycle. (= *killed* him. Re: imaginary monster she had run over.)
2.	C, 3;1:	I don't want you to *make* him *go off.* (= *brush* off, *knock* off. After M tries to brush a moth off C's car seat with her hand.)
3.	E, 2;3:	Then I'm going to sit on him and *made* [sic] him *broken.* [= *break* (squash). Looking at ant on seat of her toy tractor.]

Lexical causative where periphrastic causative is required:

4.	C, 5;10:	Water *bloomed* these flowers. (= *made* these flowers *bloom.*)
5.	C, 4;0:	The machine might *put* him away. (= *make* him *disappear/go* away. C watching "Captain Kangaroo" story about a magic machine that caused Captain Kangaroo to disappear for a while: she's now suggesting same thing may happen to Mr. Greenjeans.)
6.	C, 5;8	It's not worse. But the airplane's *keeping* it. [Re: stomachache C had before boarding plane. Now, as we fly, the plane (ride) is *making* stomachache *continue, go on.*]

Successive use of periphrastic and lexical causatives in same speech context:

7.	C, 5;0:	OK. If you want it to *die.* Eva's gonna *die* it. She's gonna *make* it *die.* (Upset because E is about to touch a moth.)
8.	E, 2;8:	*Put* it on her. *Make* it *be* on her. (Wants M to put a dress on her doll.)
9.	E, 3;9:	Can you *make* this *flattened* and *round?* You *round* it and then I'll *flatten* it. (To M, as E plays with a piece of play dough.)
10.	EM, 2;11:	You *make* me *swing* around. You *swing* me around. (To Melissa, who is rotating chair Emily is sitting in.)

[a] Names and ages as in Table 9-1. Em, Emily.

1977), that errors like those in Table 9-1 are *not observed* in the early stages of the child's use of the verbs in question. To the contrary, errors of each type are preceded by months or in some cases even years during which usage is syntactically impeccable. This rules out an interpretation according to which the child simply is confused, e.g., does not know yet whether a verb is transitive or intransitive, or whether it can take a locative complement. The period of correct usage before the onset of the errors strengthens the inference that, far from reflecting basic ignorance of the linguistic system, these errors are signs of a rather sophisticated grasp of underlying regularities in the English lexicon.

Conflict and Harmony among Components of Grammar

The choices that speakers make as they piece together sentences from the lexical, syntactic, and morphological resources of their language are not carried out independently of one other. Rather, choices in one domain can severely restrict or eliminate choices in another domain. Learning how to coordinate the components of grammar is an important aspect of first-language development that may have interesting implications for second-language learning.

CHOOSING THE RIGHT ALTERNATIVE

There is evidence that early in development, children seek a relatively direct mapping between underlying meanings and overt linguistic forms. That is, a particular meaning will be associated with a unique form (or allomorphs of a form) and, conversely, this form can be seen as the procedure invoked to express this meaning and no other (Slobin, 1973). It is not long, however, before roughly equivalent forms begin to multiply. The child with several forms at his disposal must learn how to make principled choices among them. The learning process can be extended, and marked by many errors.

Consider the child who, like Christy and Eva at 24 months, can express causal events either with single-word causative verbs (e.g., *kill, break,* or novel forms like transitive *die*) or with syntactic ("periphrastic") causatives (*make die, make break*). How does he choose between them? In adult English, the choice hangs on a complex set of distinctions involving, most critically, how directly the "causer" brings about a change of state in the "causee" (Shibatani, 1976). Children at first may fail to appreciate these distinctions, however. The evidence is that they initially make many errors in which the lexical form is used where the periphrastic is called for, or the other way around, or *both* forms are used within the same context as if they were regarded as interchangeable. Some examples are shown in Table 9-2 . . . Further development consists of working out the conditions under which each form is preferred.

A different kind of conflict between roughly equivalent forms is shown in

Table 9-3. The semantic domain involved here can be termed "acts of separation." English encodes acts of separation in several ways. In some cases, separation is entailed by the reversal of an action of coming together or fastening, and is expressed with the reversative prefix *un-*: *untie, unbuckle, uncoil, unbutton*, etc. In other cases, separation is encoded by a locative particle following the verb, e.g., *take off/out/apart/away*. In still other cases, separation is more implicit, incorporated directly into the meaning of a monomorphemic lexical item such as *open, break, peel*, or *split*.

Children initially seem to learn the correct method for each lexical item independently, and make no errors. Later, however—starting around age 4 for Christy and Eva—they begin to make occasional errors. For example, in 1 and 2 of Table 9-3 the child has prefixed *un-* to verbs that require *off* or *out*. Examples 3 and 4 show the reverse type of error, adding *out* to a verb that requires *un-*. In examples 5 and 6 the child has simultaneously selected both *un-* and a postverb particle. Finally, in 7–9 the child has redundantly and incorrectly prefixed *un-* to a verb that already expresses separation simply by virtue of its lexical meaning.

Errors like these indicate that beyond a certain point in development, the

Table 9-3. *Errors in Encoding Acts of Separation*[a]

un- prefixed to verb that requires *off/out*, etc.:

1. E, 4;2:   D: Pull your pants up, Eva. (E has pants sagging down.)
              E: Somebody *unpulled* 'em. (= pulled them down/off.)
2. C, 5;6:   . . . So I had to *untake* the sewing. (= take the sewing/stiches out. Telling about sewing project at school.)

out following verb that requires *un-*:

3. C, 4;5:   (Wants to move electric humidifier): I'll get it after it's *plugged out*. (Shortly after): Mommy, can I *unplug* it?
4. E, 4;5:   M: The end is tucked in. (Discussing state of E's blanket as puts E to bed.)
              E: Will you *tuck* it *out*?

un- and *out/off* both selected:

5. E, 3;5:   How do I *untake* this *off*? (= take this off. Trying to get out of swimsuit.)
6. E, 4;11:   . . . and then *unpress* it *out*. (Showing how she gets play dough out of a mold by pressing it through.)
              M: How do you unpress it out?
              E: You just take it out.

un- prefixed to lexical item that already incorporates notion of separation:

7. C, 4;11:   Will you *unopen* this? (Wants D to take lid off Styrofoam cooler.)
8. E, 4;7:   E: (Holding up chain of glued paper strips): I know how you take these apart. *Unsplit* them and put 'em on.
              M: How do you unsplit them?
              E: Like this. (Pulling a link apart.)
9. S, 5;2:   How do you *unbreak* this? (Trying to pull sheet of stamps apart.)

[a]Names and ages as in Table 9-1. S, Scott.

intention to encode a given act of separation does not present itself to the mind as a unit, neatly tagged with a suitable lexical item. Rather, the notion of separation apparently is "pulled out" from the surrounding semantic specifics and mentally represented in a form that is neutral enough to simultaneously activate encoding devices from different components of the grammar. Errors result when the child fails to choose successfully among them.

COORDINATING VERB CHOICE AND SYNTACTIC ARRANGEMENT

When a speaker chooses a certain verb for a simple, active, declarative sentence, she is not free to assign the noun arguments of that verb to any syntactic role she likes. Rather, the verb imposes a certain syntactic arrangement on these arguments. If the verb is *sell*, for example, the noun phrase naming the one who hands over the goods must function as the subject while a name for the recipient of the goods, if present, is the oblique object. *Buy*, in contrast, requires the opposite arrangement:

    1. Harry *sold* a car to John/*John *sold* a car from Harry.
    2. John *bought* a car from Harry/*Harry *bought* a car to John.

Similarly, but with respect to the direct object, we have a contrast between verbs such as *pour* and *fill*. *Pour* requires the name for the moving liquid to be the direct object while the name for the container, if mentioned, is the oblique object; it is precisely the other way around for *fill*:

    3. John *poured* water into the cup/*John *poured* the cup with water.
    4. John *filled* the cup with water/*John *filled* water into the cup.

On the whole, children do a remarkably good job of learning the syntactic roles associated with the noun arguments of the verbs in their vocabularies. But mistakes do occur, and these give interesting clues to the processes involved in coordinating verb choice and syntax.

In the examples given in Table 9-4, verb choice and syntax do not harmonize. The child has selected the wrong syntactic arrangement for the verb or, to look at it the other way around, the wrong verb for the syntactic arrangement. The precise cause of such errors is not easy to establish. Different errors—even different tokens of the same type of error with a given verb—may have somewhat different causes. Some errors, particularly errors made under the age of about 4 or 5 with familiar, high-frequency verbs such as *spill* and *fill*, appear to reflect generalizations about the proper or possible syntactic treatment of the noun arguments of "verbs of this semantic type" (Bowerman, 1982). Others, especially with later-learned verbs of lower frequency that are members of a set of semantically closely related verbs (e.g., *cost/spend/pay/charge; mind/matter/care; rob/ steal; enjoy/appeal to*), may stem from "contamination" among members of the

Table 9-4. *Errors in Coordinating Verb Choice with Assignment*
of Syntactic Roles to Noun Arguments[a]

1.	E, 7;7:	She doesn't *picture* to me like a "Henrietta." Does she to you? (= I don't *picture* her as—/she doesn't *look like*/*strike* me as—. After telling that a friend's middle name is "Henrietta.")
2.	E, 7;2:	Does it not *care* if I see the eggs? (= does no one *care* if—/does it not *matter* if—. After M suggest that E and D buy chocolate Easter eggs together; E wondering whether she should see them ahead of time.)
3.	C, 6;10:	*Feel* your hand to that. (= *feel* that with your hand/*put* your hand on that. Wants M to put her hand on one end of a hose; then she blows into the other end.)
4.	E, 7;2:	(Dipping water out of tub and letting it run down he stomach; has discovered with delight that her navel holds water): My belly holds water! (= belly button).
		Look, Mom, I'm gonna *pour* it with water, my belly. (= *pour* water into my belly button/*fill* my belly button with water.)
5.	E, 4;11:	(M sees uneaten toast at end of breakfast, has asked if E plans to eat it): I don't want it because I *spilled* it of orange juice. [= *spilled* orange juice on it/ *got it wet*; (poor choices): *wetted* it, *moistened* it with orange juice.]*

[a]Names and ages as in Table 9-1.

*Some examples omitted. [Eds.]

set. That is, the differing syntactic requirements of verbs that are semantically very similar may confuse the child. Beyond the age of 5 or 6 there is increasing reason to suspect a third cause for error: the child's growing awareness of syntactic structure as a device for conveying perspective and her attempts to actively manipulate it in service of this goal.

"Perspective" is a complex psychological construct having to do with where the speaker mentally places himself with respect to the event described by his sentence (Fillmore, 1977). One important device through which perspective is conveyed in English is the way in which the noun phrases of a sentence are arranged syntactically with respect to the verb. Those entities referred to by the noun phrases functioning as subject and direct object of the verb are perceived as "in perspective," whereas entities mentioned only as oblique object or omitted entirely are, relatively speaking, perceived as "out of perspective." Thus, a speaker would utter sentence 2 above if he took the perspective of John, the receiver of the car, whereas he would choose 1 if he took the perspective of Harry, who gives over the car. Which entities are chosen for placement "in perspective" is influenced by a variety of factors, such as whether they have been the subject of prior discourse, whether they are animate or inanimate, stationary or moving, definite or indefinite, etc.

Some semantic domains in English are characterized by great flexibility with respect to the taking of perspective. In some cases this flexibility is due to the availability of a variety of verbs that encode the same meaning from different perspectives (e.g., *buy/sell; give/take; lend/borrow; rob/steal*). Alternatively, it may stem from the presence of syntactically versatile verbs that permit more than one perspective (e.g., *her face radiated joy/joy radiated from her face; the farmer loaded hay into the wagon/the farmer loaded the wagon with hay*). In other semantic domains, however, there is less flexibility and the verb that semantically is ideally suited to the meaning to be conveyed may require a syntactic arrangement that is counter to the desired perspective.

The resources of language are riddled with such gaps; speakers must learn to work around them, to find compromises. Adults have impressive skill at unconsciously and effortlessly striking balances in which one communicative goal is met less satisfactorily than it otherwise could be in the interests of maximizing another goal deemed more important (Talmy, 1976a). Children, in contrast, make many errors in which they apparently try to "eat their cake and have it too." That is, they attempt to establish a desired perspective through the manipulation of syntactic roles, they select a verb that on semantic or other grounds is "just right," and they proceed to weave these two choices together without attending to whether the choices can be realized harmoniously in the same sentence. *

Example 4 from Table 9-4 illustrates the genre (as does 5). Here, the child is concentrating on her navel. In the first utterance, she places it maximally in perspective by making it the sentence subject (*belly* apparently is a shorthand for *belly button* in this monologue). In the second utterance, the agent (*I*) takes over the subject slot, but the navel clearly is still more in perspective than the water; its placement as direct object rather than oblique object thus is well motivated pragmatically. But *pour* does not allow this arrangement: *belly* must be the oblique object. If Eva wants *belly* as direct object, she should switch to another verb that allows this. But *fill* is the only plausible candidate, and *fill* is semantically odd here: can one speak of "filling" a "container" as shallow as a navel, which is, moreover, oriented sideways? Under the circumstances, sentence 4 can be seen as well tailored to both the perspectival and semantic requirements of the situation—unfortunately, however, English does not permit this nice combination of goals.

As this example suggests, new problems for the child to resolve are created by her own growing ability to take perspective into account and to manipulate it through syntactic role assignment. A first step in the resolution of such problems is for the child to recognize that conflict exists—that some constraints are binding

*An experimental study by A. Karmiloff-Smith indicates that prior discourse does not begin to influence the child's selection of sentence subject until about age 6 (Karmiloff-Smith, 1981), which is approximately the time at which Christy and Eva began to make errors attributable to manipulation of perspective.

and that she may not be able to meet all goals satisfactorily with her "first choices" of lexical items and syntactic structures. Beyond this, she must learn how to search for suitable "near synonym" verbs, how to exploit alternative devices for handling perspective such as passivization or clefting, and, when all else fails, how to give up a less important goal in the interests of preserving grammaticality.*

*Section dealing with implications for second language acquisition is omitted. [Eds.]

10

Eve V. Clark

Lexical Innovations: How Children Learn to Create New Words

As speakers, we often find ourselves in situations in which there appears to be no word that is quite appropriate for the entity or event we wish to convey to a listener. At such times we have recourse to coinage and create new lexical items from the lexical resources available in our language. And we create these new lexical items in just such a way that our listeners will be able to compute the intended meanings, readily and uniquely, on each occasion of use. Although it often goes unnoticed, the process of coining new words—new meanings expressed with forms that fit the word-formation paradigms of the language—is widespread in adult speech (e.g., Clark and Clark, 1979; Downing, 1977; Gleitman and Gleitman, 1970). It is no less widespread in children's speech and, I will argue, serves the same function—that of filling lexical gaps. Moreover, in children's speech coinages provide a window on the developmental process whereby children acquire both the adult conventions governing the creation of new meanings and the conventions on uses of the word forms that carry those meanings. In the present chapter, I shall consider both the kinds of *meanings* young children create and the *forms* they employ for their expression.

To keep the two sides of the coin distinct, the chapter is divided into two parts. In the first, I take up the *why* of children's lexical creativity—why they create new meanings and the circumstances under which they do this. Under this heading I will consider the evidence that children's lexical innovations play the same role, communicatively, as the adults', and I will draw on illustrations from a variety of sources: diaries, vocabulary studies, and my own observational and experimental data, mainly from children aged between 2 and 6. . . .

Abridged from "Lexical innovations: How children learn to create new words" by E. Clark, 1981, in *The Child's Construction of Language* (W. Deutsch, Ed.), pp. 299–328. New York: Academic Press.

Lexical Innovations*

LEXICAL GAPS

The lexical inventories of languages differ and no language has words for every possible concept its speakers might want to talk about. The result is that the stock of vocabulary is constantly renewed through the acceptance of those newly coined meanings that are useful enough for large groups of speakers to take up and add to the idiomatic or well-established meanings already in the lexicon. Many innovations, of course, remain nonce uses—coinages that were quite interpretable on the occasion of their use but failed to retain a permanent place in the lexicon. But even the nonce uses of lexical innovations *fill lexical gaps*. They supply a meaning not otherwise expressed by any lexical items available to the speaker in question (cf. Lehrer, 1970; Lyons, 1977).

Lexical gaps may be *momentary*—as when someone has difficulty retrieving that right word form from memory—or *chronic*—where there is no word form that is conventionally used to express that particular meaning. In order to fill *chronic gaps*, there are three general conditions that must pertain. First, the exact meaning to be expressed must not be expressed by any other lexeme already in the lexicon. (This condition is violated in the case of momentary gaps, where the gap results from loss of memory or some retrieval difficulty that prevents the speaker from coming up with the form conventionally used for a particular meaning. Fromkin (1973) cites a number of speech errors where speakers constructed new word forms in lieu of those conventionally used. Second, the new meaning has to be carried by an appropriate form, one that fits the word-formation rules of the language in question. And third, the speaker and listener must jointly observe whatever conventions govern the use of such innovative meanings in such a way that the innovation will be readily understood as the speaker intends it on the occasion of its use.

These three general conditions on chronic gaps are so frequently met on an everyday basis that most of us do not even notice how often we process lexical innovations in the course of understanding utterances. As long as the utterance containing an innovation is interpretable in context, we tend to take it for granted. Only when we pause to reflect might we notice that we have just heard a new verb formed from a noun ("I've got to *launderette* those sheets," meaning "take those sheets to be washed at the launderette"), a new noun compound ("Why don't you sit in the *apple-juice chair?*," meaning "the chair nearest the glass of apple juice on the table"), or a new derived agentive noun ("Dare to be a *juicer!*," meaning "a drinker of juice," from an advertisement on a bottle of apple juice). These meanings are all novel in that they are not expressed by any well-established expressions already in the English lexicon. Despite their innovative status, each of them is easily interpreted in context.

---

*All endnotes omitted. [Eds.]

Both adults and children, I claim, fill lexical gaps, but the process of filling gaps is in one case the same and in the other different for the two populations. Like adults, children may experience momentary gaps: when they have difficulty retrieving a known word form, they may construct a new one on the spot. Two examples from my data are the construction of *sleeper* (in lieu of *bed*) by a 3 year old, and the construction of *pourer* (in lieu of *cup*) by a 4 year old. These children knew the correct terms, but because of a passing difficulty in retrieving the "right" words, constructed alternatives. (These momentary forms are often corrected seconds later when the right word comes through.)

The process is different, however, for chronic gaps. Adults fill what are gaps in the adult lexicon: ideally, they work from what is already *in* the well-established vocabulary and coin new words only where there are discernible gaps that require filling on particular occasions, e.g., the verb *to charcoal* (meaning, make into charcoal, said of potatoes that boiled dry). Children, though, have not yet mastered the adult lexicon. What they know about it is not only fragmentary; it can change from day to day as they acquire additional well-established lexical items. As a result, they may fill many chronic gaps that are *not* gaps for adult speakers (e.g., *to needle* in lieu of *mend*, *to nipple* in lieu of *nurse*, a *fixer* in lieu of *tool*, a *plant-man* in lieu of *gardener*) in addition to those that are gaps for adults. One way to differentiate these two situations is to characterize the innovations adults produce as *legitimate innovations*: these fill true gaps in the (adult) lexicon where there are meanings to be expressed that lack any conventional (well-established) means for doing so. Children, in contrast, produce both *legitimate* and *illegitimate* innovations. Their legitimate innovations fill true chronic gaps and could as well have been produced by adults, while their illegitimate ones fill what are currently gaps in the child's but not in the adult's lexicon.

Illegitimate innovations are illegitimate precisely because they are pre-empted for adult speakers by the existence of well-established lexical items with the requisite meanings. Illegitimate innovations, such as the verbs *to needle* and *to broom*, should therefore give way to the appropriate well-established terms, here *to mend* and *to sweep*, as soon as children acquire them. The criterion for legitimacy for children's innovations is simply the existence of a gap in the adult lexicon. For a child innovation to be illegitimate, then, it must coincide in meaning with some well-established lexical item that takes precedence or pre-empts that innovation.

Lexical innovations in adult speech are relatively easy to detect, although what is an innovation for one speaker may not be for another (Clark and Clark, 1979). In children's speech, detection should be rather more of a problem. First, their legitimate innovations may be underestimated by the observer just because they conform or appear to conform to the adult conventions on innovation and will thus be less noticeable than illegitimate innovations. The latter, by their very nature, will be more noticeable and more likely to be noted in diary and vocabulary studies. Second, children's lexical creativity may be further underestimated wherever their innovations happen to coincide with actual well-established forms. For example, a child might coin the agentive noun *gardener* from *garden*, meaning "the person who usually works in the garden." Such innovations will generally be indistinguishable from all the other well-established terms that children have picked up wholesale from the adult speakers around them. Re-creations, like *gardener*, coincident with well-established or conventional adult forms, will be virtually undetectable as innovations.

The hypothesis I am putting forward is that filling chronic lexical gaps provides the major motivation for both adult and child innovations in the lexicon. Adults have little reason to duplicate exactly meanings that are already expressed by well-established lexical items and indeed avoid doing so (e.g., Bolinger, 1977). But filling a lexical gap, for adults, has an obvious communicative function: it allows a speaker to be more precise in conveying his intended meaning on a particular occasion where no well-established term is entirely adequate to the task.

What would constitute evidence for or against this hypothesis in the case of children's innovations? Evidence for such an hypothesis would be children's making up new words—new meanings—where they lacked other words to express their meanings, e.g., the agentive noun *fix-man* in the absence of *mechanic*. Such innovations should be more likely to occur in domains where children's vocabulary of available terms is relatively small, and the innovations they produce should contrast in meaning with the vocabulary items they have already acquired. On the other hand, it would be evidence against the hypothesis if children coined synonyms for meanings they had already acquired, and simply used innovations and well-established terms interchangeably with no contrast in meaning.

In fact, there is considerable evidence *for* the hypothesis. First, even very young children treat words as if they contrast in meaning. Upon learning a new animal term like *horse*, for example, they will narrow the domain of a previously overextended term, *dog*, in order to contrast it with the new term just acquired (e.g., Clark, 1978). Moreover, there is evidence from the language acquisition of bilingual children that at one stage they will reject having two separate labels (from different languages) for the same entity and, for instance, will accept only one of *dog* and *perro* or of *water* and *agua* (e.g., Fantini, 1976). Children also seem to assume that any new words introduced to them by adults contrast with the known set they cooccur with. Thus, children introduced to the term *chromium* in the context of other color terms, took it to be a color term that contrasted with the ones they already knew (Carey, 1978a), and, introduced to a novel (nonsense) word in the physical context of objects differing in either color or shape, children took it to encode a color in the one case, a shape in the other (Dockrell, 1979).

Second, more direct evidence for the hypothesis comes from children's lexical innovations. I will present illustrations from three domains: (1) children's coining of innovative denominal verbs, (2) their coining of names for subcategories, and (3) their coining of new agent and instrument nouns. In all three domains, as in most adult innovations, precision of communication appears to be what is at stake (e.g., Downing, 1977; Clark and Clark, 1979). To take the first domain of examples, why do children coin new verbs? Children are much slower in mastering well-established verb meanings than they are in mastering noun meanings (e.g., Clark, 1978; Gentner, 1978). As a result, they have few verbs available early on for talking about a large range of actions. To communicate about particular actions, many children take up the option of coining new verbs from nouns where the noun in question designates one of the objects involved in the particular action being talked about. Some typical examples of such denominal verbs from English-speaking children are listed in Table 10-1. Such verbs are also coined by young children acquiring other languages (see Clark, 1982). The importance of such innovative verbs is that they allow small children—as young as 2—to be very precise, in context, about the actions they are talking about.

Second, in labeling things, even very young children set up contrasts and will divide up known categories into subcategories. But since they lack well-established terms for each subcategory (and these may be lacking altogether in the language), they may opt to coin new compound nouns—combining two (or more) nouns with the appropriate stress pattern and modifier-head word order. One child, for example, at 1;11 contrasted *baby-bottle* (a bottle used when she was a baby) with *bottle* alone (Leopold, 1949). Another, aged 2;0, distinguished fried from boiled eggs (her breakfast fare) with the expressions *plate-egg* and *cup-egg*. The same child distinguished dogs in general, *dog*, from a particular yellow dog found at the site of a local fire and subsequently given to a neighboring child, by use of the compound *fire-dog*, which she used frequently in requests for a similar pet (Pelsma, 1910). Other 2 year olds I have observed consistently con-

Table 10-1. *Some Typical Examples of Innovative Denominal Verbs*[a]

1.	S	(2;4, wanting to have some cheese weighed): *You have to scale it.*
2.	EB	(2;8, after roaring with "claws" outstretched at a towel): *I monstered that towel.*
3.	S	(3;0, watching a truck pass): *It's trucking.*
4.	S	(3;2, putting on a cowboy hat, fastened with a bead-and-string): *String me up, mommy.*
5.	CB	(3;11, putting crackers in her soup): *I'm crackering my soup.*
6.	JA	(4;0, playing the role of a doctor dealing with a broken arm): *We're gonna cast it.*
7.	ME	(4;11, talking about Chistmas trees): *We already decorationed our tree.*
8.	JW	(5;7, hitting a ball with a stick): *I'm sticking it and that makes it go really fast.*

[a]Based on Clark (1982).

trasted subcategories by means of such compounds: one distinguished kinds of smoke such as *house-smoke* (from a chimney) versus *car-smoke* (exhaust), and another kept his T-shirts apart with the same device, with *butterfly-shirt*, for instance, for the one with a butterfly design on it. While I have listed only a few examples here, they are widespread both in the vocabulary and diary literature and in my own longitudinal records.

The third domain of innovations illustrated here is that of agent and instrument nouns. Young children will construct new compound nouns for these categories, e.g., the spontaneous *fix-man* (for a car mechanic), *garden-man* (for a gardener), or *rat-man* (for a man who worked with rats in a psychology laboratory, a colleague of the child's father)—all from 2 year olds. Moreover, children as young as $2\frac{1}{2}$ or 3 will coin such terms on demand. In an elicitation study, Barbara Hecht and I specified meanings—describing what the agent or instrument did—and asked young children for a way of conveying those meanings. Examples typical of the agentive forms we elicited are shown in the top half of Table 10-2. The commonest type of compound noun children produced combined a noun or verb base as the first element with the noun *-man* in second place, as in *fire-man* and *sweep-man*. This type fits a common adult pattern for constructing agent nominals. These children sometimes marked the agent redundantly, adding an *-er* to the verb base in addition to combining it with the noun *-man*, as in *hitter-man*. This pattern is comparatively rare in adult English, and the occasional well-established form like *fisherman* seems an unlikely model for children this age to work from. Since the derivational ending *-er* marks instruments as well as agents in English, it could be that the children add *-man* to a *verb + er* form just to make quite clear they are designating an agent and not an instrument. (The older children tended to opt simply for the forms composed of a *base + er* to mark agents.) Some typical instrument nouns coined by the same children are shown in the bottom half of Table 10-2. The head nouns (in second place) were usually *-thing* or *-machine*, and they followed a verb base, a verb + *ing*, a verb + *er*, or a noun base. Again, older children tended to opt for forms combining a noun or verb base with the derivational *-er* ending, just as for the agent nouns.

What is important, for all three domains illustrated here, is that these children lacked other words to express these innovative meanings. This is particularly clear in the case of diary and vocabulary records, but it was also the case for our experimentally elicited innovations. The children did not have other terms to express the meanings we offered since we deliberately chose meanings for which there was not any obvious English word. These data, then, offer strong preliminary support to the hypothesis that children, like adults, innovate in order to fill lexical gaps.

CONTEXTUAL INNOVATIONS

Do children's innovations have any particular properties, apart from the variety of forms they draw on in their coinages? As the glosses in Table 10-2 suggest, the

Table 10-2. *Typical Agent and Instrument Nominals Elicited from Young Children*[a]

Agent nominals: some compound forms produced by 3 year olds
1. *Fire-man:* someone who burns things[b]
2. *sweep-man:* someone who sweeps things
3. *Smile-person:* someone who smiles at people
4. *Hitter-man:* someone who hits things
5. *Kicker-man:* someone who kicks things
6. *Reader-man:* someone who reads things
7. *Hider-man:* someone who hides things

Instrument nominals: some compound forms produced by 3 to 5 year olds
1. *Jumping-thing:* thing for jumping with[b]
2. *Hugging-machine:* thing for hugging people
3. *Eating-thing:* thing for eating with
4. *Knock-thing:* thing for knocking with
5. *Blow-machine:* machine for blowing with
6. *Package-machine:* machine for pushing things
7. *Rock-machine:* machine for throwing things
8. *Kicker-machine:* machine for kicking things

---

[a]Based on Clark and Hecht (1982).

[b]The glosses represent the meanings given to the child for which the pertinent form was elicited.

context is often, and maybe always, critical to the meaning being expressed. Without the gloss—here the meaning offered to the child for expression—there is no way to tell that the combination of *fire* and *man* in the compound *fire-man* on this occasion designated not someone who puts out fires (the well-established adult meaning of this form) but someone who sets fire to things. Equally, the meaning of *rock-machine* is not a transparent composition of the two constituent nouns, *rock* and *machine*. One has to know that on this occasion, the machine so designated was one that could throw rocks rather than grind them up, arrange them in lines, polish them, or the myriad other activities that could link rocks and machines. Without the context, utterances containing innovations like these are often uninterpretable. Although we supplied the meanings in these instances, this dependence on context is just as typical of children's spontaneous coinages as of those we elicited.

Elsewhere, I have characterized innovations like these—dependent on context on the occasion of their use for proper interpretation—as *contextuals* (Clark and Clark, 1979). They contrast with innovations whose interpretation can be computed from the composition of the constituent elements of the innovative expression alone. For instance, adjectives plus the ending *-ness* all have the meaning "quality of being X," as in *smoothness, quickness, flashiness,* etc., while most verb stems plus *-able* have the interpretation "possible to be X-ed," as in *houseable, rideable,* etc. (see Aronoff, 1976). The combination of ending plus base in such cases makes for a predictable meaning, a composition of the parts.

Contextuals, as a type of innovation, have the following properties:

1. They have an indefinitely large number of potential senses. An innovative denominal verb (like *launderette*), a compound noun (like *apple-juice chair*), or a derived noun (like *juicer*) could be used with one sense on occasion, another on another, and so on. This, I would argue, also appears typical of many child innovations. For example, one 2 year old I have been recording used the noun *broom* as a verb on one occasion to mean "hit with a broom" and on another to mean "sweep with a broom" (an illegitimate coinage given the existence of adult *sweep*).

2. Contextuals depend for their interpretation on the context in which they are produced. As a result, they bear a strong resemblance in many ways to indexicals or deictic terms such as *he* or *there*. This dependence on context is especially obvious when it comes to interpreting children's innovations: without contextual information, they are usually just as opaque as children's uses of deictics like *that* or general purpose verbs like *do*.

3. Contextuals demand cooperation between the speaker and the listener in the following way: the speaker has to assess what the listener knows or could infer from the context, and the listener has to use clues from the context plus any other facts he could assume the speaker would expect him to use in arriving at the speaker's intended interpretation of the innovation. With children, such deliberate cooperation is usually lacking, but the fact that young children restrict much of their conversation to the here-and-now allows it by default. The adult listener can nearly always rely on the context to provide clues to the child-speaker's meaning for an innovative term.

Among adults, speakers and listeners rely on conventions governing such innovations in order to arrive at the intended interpretations. These conventions spell out the conditions under which the speaker can expect the listener to arrive at a readily computable, unique interpretation on each particular occasion of use. This is done essentially by considering both the expression itself—in the examples given above: a denominal verb, a compound noun, or a derived noun—and the speaker's and listener's mutual knowledge in a particular context of use.

The adult convention on innovative denominal verbs takes the following form, where the first five conditions seem to be conditions that would apply to any contextual:

The Innovative Denominal Verb Convention. In using an innovative denominal verb, the speaker means to denote:

1. the kind of situation
2. he has good reason to believe
3. that on this occasion the listener can readily compute

4. uniquely
5. on the basis of their mutual knowledge
6. such that the parent noun denotes one role in the situation and the remaining surface arguments of the denominal verb denote other roles in the situation (Clark and Clark, 1979, p. 787).

The sixth condition applies specifically to innovative denominal verbs, and the form of this condition would clearly change for each type of contextual—denominal adjectives, compound nouns, derived agent, and instrument nouns, and so on, to name just a few such categories in English. However, the first five conditions specify the general circumstances required for the appropriate interpretation of contextuals, specifying their dependence on mutual knowledge and context for ready computation of a unique meaning by the listener.

A convention of this type places constraints on what can be used as an innovation—in this instance, which nouns can be used as innovative denominal verbs. However, children do not yet observe these constraints and therefore produce a number of illegitimate innovations alongside their legitimate ones. A major constraint imposed by the denominal verb convention can be called the principle of preemption by synonymy. Innovations are preempted or accounted illegitimate if there is a common term already in the language with just the meaning the innovation was intended to have. For denominal verbs there are several subtypes of such preemption.

First, there is preemption by suppletion, where there already exists some other verb [morphologically unrelated to the parent noun of the (potential) innovation] with just the meaning the innovation would have supplied. For example, among vehicle terms in English, noun/verb pairs form a highly productive paradigm (*taxi*/to *taxi*, *canoe*/to *canoe*, *helicopter*/to *helicopter*, etc.); but there are some striking exceptions. Neither *car* nor *airplane* fits the verb paradigm since, for adult speakers, the verbs *drive* and *fly* fill the respective meaning slots for these two vehicles. The verb *drive* is in a suppletive relation to the noun *car* since it preempts use of *to car* for the meaning "go by vehicle."

Suppletion accounts for the illegitimacy of one child example mentioned earlier, the verb *broom*. For adults, the noun *broom* is not a number of the noun/verb paradigm of instruments that can be exemplified by pairs like *saw*/to *saw*, *hammer*/to *hammer*, and so on. *Broom* is paired with *to sweep*, which preempts the use of *broom* as a verb with the meaning, "clean with a broom." Other examples of where children fail to use the adult suppletive forms are *scale* for *weigh*, *nipple* for *nurse*, *gun* for *shoot*, and *axe* for *chop*. Failure to use suppletion is a common source of illegitimate child innovations among denominal verbs (Clark, 1982).

A second type of preemption by synonymy is preemption by entrenchment. Although one can form the verb *to jail* from the noun *jail*, one cannot use *to prison*, from *prison*, meaning "to put into prison," because of the existence in the language of the verb *imprison* with just that meaning. And one can *house* someone (from the parent noun *house*) but not *hospital* someone ("put into a hospital") because of the prior existence of *hospitalize*. In all cases of entrenchment there is already in use a verb derived ultimately from the same parent noun, with just the meaning that would be carried by the proposed innovation. The verbs already entrenched in language, like *imprison, enthrone,* or *hospitalize,* take precedence over the innovations. Because children often lack the necessary adult knowledge of the lexicon, they produce illegitimate innovations of this type.

A third type of preemption by synonymy is preemption by ancestry. If the potential parent noun the speaker uses is itself derived from another noun or verb base, then that noun cannot normally become the parent of an innovative denominal verb. Consider the noun *baker.* This noun cannot give rise to a verb *baker* with the meaning "do what a baker would do professionally" in the way *butcher* can give rise to *to butcher,* because the noun *baker* itself was originally derived from the verb *to bake,* which has just the meaning in question. Equally, the noun *farmer* does not provide for *to farmer* because the meaning ("to do what a farmer would do professionally") is itself carried by the (denominal) verb *to farm* from which the noun *farmer* derives. The morphological relations in cases of ancestry are usually transparent, so it is normally clear that a particular noun is related by both meaning and form to a particular source. Children also produce illegitimate innovations of this type; for instance, they use a noun like *decoration* as the parent noun of a verb, *to decoration*—presumably because they do not know *to decorate* or fail to recognize the synonymy of *to decorate* and *to decoration.*

A second principle that seems to place constraints on innovations, although it does not seem to have such force as the avoidance of synonymy, is the principle of preemption by homonymy. This constraint covers coincidence of forms with difference of meanings. If a potential innovation coincides in form with a common verb, say, that has a quite different meaning, the innovation tends to be avoided. For example, although one can use all sorts of car names as verbs where that level of specificity is required ("He didn't VW to New York, he Chevied"), one would avoid saying *he Forded to New York* (meaning "go by Ford car") because of the presence of the common verb *to ford,* meaning "to cross by a ford." Equally, *to Dodge,* meaning "go by Dodge car," is avoided because of *to dodge,* "to evade pursuit." And while season names like *winter* and *summer* occur as verbs, the potential verbs *spring* and *fall* are preempted by the common verbs *fall* ("let drop") and *to spring* ("to jump"). There seem to be relatively few instances of children's using illegitimate innovations of this type. However, one could perhaps consider here such uses as *button* ("turn on by pressing a button") preempted by adult *button,* "fasten by means of a button"; *key* ("open with a key"), preempted by adult "make a key for"; *needle* ("mend with a needle"), preempted by adult "irritate"; and *cement* ("make cement"), preempted by adult "put cement on."

Since children produce numerous illegitimate innovations, both among their denominal verbs and in other categories of innovations, it is clear that, for them as for adult speakers, filling gaps is relative to what vocabulary one knows.

The difference is that adults normally know a great deal more vocabulary—and hence the meanings conventionally available—in their language. This knowledge, in combination with the conventions on innovations, is what constrains the process of innovation. Young children, however, at first have only a limited vocabulary, and while they add to it steadily, both through the acquisition of well-established lexical items and through coinages, it takes them a long time to acquire the vocabulary that limits innovations. As a result, they produce both illegitimate and legitimate innovations, with the former only lessening in number as they acquire more vocabulary. This finding, observed first for children's denominal verbs (Clark, 1982), also seems to hold for innovative nominals, both in the diary and vocabulary study data and in our experiments (Clark and Hecht, 1982). Children produce a number of illegitimate innovations in lieu of the terms adult speakers would normally use. They also, of course, produce many quite legitimate innovative nominals—innovations that fill true gaps in the adult lexicon.

In summary, innovations drawn from three areas of the lexicon—denominal verbs, object nominals, and agent and instrument nominals—strongly suggest that children, like adults, coin new words in order to communicate more precisely what they mean. They are engaged in filling chronic lexical gaps. But innovations are constrained by the well-established lexicon, so the elimination of illegitimate innovations depends on children's acquisition of the pertinent well-established vocabulary, an acquisition that takes considerable time. *

Conclusion

In this brief chapter, I have sketched some hypotheses and issues that arise in the study of children's knowledge of word formation. I have distinguished the meanings of their lexical innovations from the forms they rely on to convey these meanings, even though, in fact, the two—meaning and form—are tightly linked. Children's innovative meanings are often contextual. They require knowledge of the context, and what mutual knowledge that would entail, for the addressee to arrive at the child-speaker's intended meaning. This is often achieved by default, since children tend to limit their early conversations to the here-and-now, thus making it possible for the addressee to use the context even when the speaker is not taking it explicitly into account. Learning to assess what the addressee does and does not know is only one of the factors children must eventually attend to as they acquire the conventions on innovation.

Lexical innovations require word forms for their expression. These seem to be acquired in a predictable order, with forms that are productive in the language—and hence more readily available—being mastered earlier. In addition to

---

*Section on constructing lexical forms is omitted. [Eds.]

the principle of productivity, children also attend to the semantic transparency of the new forms they are constructing, and they regularize the lexical paradigms that result, for instance, choosing a single form for all agent nouns. But the three principles outlined here—productivity, semantic transparency, and regularization—are only some of those that operate in the acquisition of the word formation rules for a language.

To study word formation, and children's acquisition of word formation rules, one has to take into account both the meanings of lexical innovations and the forms used to convey them. The present chapter represents a preliminary step toward that goal.

11

Stan A. Kuczaj II
Factors Influencing Children's Hypothetical Reference

In an earlier study of the development of hypothetical reference skills in the speech of young children, Kuczaj and Daly (1979) found that reference to future hypothetical events (hereafter referred to as *future hypothetical reference*) emerged earlier than reference to past hypothetical events (hereafter referred to as *past hypothetical reference*). Kuczaj and Daly suggested that this developmental pattern is due to the greater cognitive complexity of past hypotheticals than future hypotheticals. In their view, past hypotheticals are more cognitively complex than future hypotheticals in that past hypothetical reference involves the comparison of an actual past event (i.e., one that has occurred) with an unactual hypothetical event, whereas future hypothetical reference involves the comparison of an unactual but expected future event with an unactual hypothetical (unexpected) event. Thus, past hypothetical reference involves across-category comparisons (actual/unactual) and future hypothetical reference involves within-category comparisons (unactual/unactual). Kuczaj and Daly hypothesized that young children find it more difficult to make actual/unactual comparisons than unactual/unactual comparisons, on the assumption that young children find it more difficult to engage in across-category comparisons than within-category comparisons.

The present investigation tested this hypothesis by contrasting children's responses to hypothetical questions varying along two dimensions: (1) past/future and (2) parents/fantasy characters. As noted earlier, past hypotheticals involve unactual/actual comparisons, and such is also the case for hypothetical reference involving parental behavior (at least in the context of the present investigation, as will be demonstrated below). Future hypotheticals and hypothetical reference involving fantasy characters involve unactual/unactual comparisons. Based on the hypothesis that unactual/unactual comparisons are easier for the child than actual/unactual comparisons, the following predictions are derived.

1. Hypothetical reference involving fantasy characters should be easier for children than hypothetical reference involving their parents, since all events involving fantasy characters are unactual while at least some events involving parents are actual, thus leading to actual/unactual contrasts in hypothetical contexts involving parents.

2. Past hypothetical reference involving fantasy characters should be easier for children than past hypothetical reference involving parents in that all behavior of fantasy characters is unactual. Thus, although past hypothetical reference usually involves actual/unactual comparisons, past hypothetical reference involving fantasy characters involves unactual behavior. The hypothetical contrast in such cases may be unactual/unactual or imagined actual/unactual (in the latter case, past hypothetical reference involving fantasy characters involves a contrast similar to that involved in future hypothetical reference).

3. Future hypothetical reference involving fantasy characters should be easier than that involving parents since children might have certain expectations about their parents' behavior and so have to contrast this expectation with the hypothetical event even in future hypothetical reference, such a conflict between the child's expectations and the proposed hypothetical event not existing to impede future hypothetical reference about fantasy characters.

4. Past hypothetical reference should be more difficult for children than future hypothetical reference.

To sum up, then, children should find it easiest to engage in future hypothetical reference about fantasy characters, future hypothetical reference about parents being slightly more difficult, past hypothetical reference about fantasy characters being even more difficult, and past hypothetical reference involving parents being the most difficult.

Method

SUBJECTS

Sixty (26 female, 34 male) children participated in the present study. This sample was divided into four groups of 15 children each, based on chronological age.

Group I consisted of 15 3 year olds between 3;2 and 3;11 ($\overline{X}$ age = 3;7).
Group II consisted of 15 4 year olds between 4;0 and 4;10
   ($\overline{X}$ age = 4;7).
Group III consisted of 15 5 year olds between 5;2 and 5;11
   ($\overline{X}$ age = 5;9).
Group IV consisted of 15 6 year olds between 6;3 and 6;11
   ($\overline{X}$ age = 6;8).

PROCEDURE

Each child was tested individually at his or her preschool. Initially, the child was introduced to two fantasy characters—Bingo and Todo. Bingo was a blue unicorn with red spots. Todo was a friendly yellow dragon. Immediately following this exposure to the fantasy characters, the fantasy characters were taken away, and the child was told that the experimenter needed the child's help in answering some questions and was then asked 16 question–counterquestion pairs. Four of these pairs dealt with past hypothetical events involving fantasy characters. Four other pairs dealt with past hypothetical events involving the child's parents. The remaining eight question pairs dealt with future hypothetical events, four pairs involving fantasy characters and four pairs involving the child's parents.

The 16 questions asked each child were as follows: (1) "Do you think Bingo ate ice cream last night?" (past fantasy). (2) "Do you think Bingo went swimming yesterday?" (past fantasy). (3) "Do you think Todo took a nap yesterday?" (past fantasy). (4) "Do you think Todo saw Santa Claus last night?" (past fantasy). (5) "Do you think your mommy played football yesterday?" (past parent). (6) "Do you think your mommy drank some coffee last night?" (past parent). (7) "Do you think your daddy mowed the yard yesterday?" (past parent). (8) "Do you think your daddy ate a sandwich last night?" (past parent). (9) "Do you think Bingo will kiss a girl tomorrow?" (future fantasy). (10) "Do you think Bingo will break his horn tomorrow?" (future fantasy). (12) "Do you think Todo will eat breakfast tomorrow?" (future fantasy). (13) "Do you think your mommy will fall out of bed tomorrow?" (future parent). (14) "Do you think your mommy will go to work tomorrow?" (future parent). (15) "Do you think your daddy will cook dinner tomorrow?" (future parent). (16) "Do you think your daddy will ride a bicycle tomorrow?" (future parent). (Prior to testing, it was ascertained whether each child had an absent mother or father. If so, each of the parent questions was concerned with the present parent.)

Following the child's response to a question, the child was asked a hypothetical question that supposed a condition counter to that which the child had stated. For example, if the child responded "no" to question (1), she or he was then asked "what would have happened if Bingo had eaten ice cream last night?" If the child responded "yes" to question (14), she or he was then asked "what would happen if she did not go to work tomorrow?"

The order of presentation of the question–counterquestion pairs was randomized for each child. The entire procedure was recorded on a portable tape recorder.

SCORING

Only the responses to the hypothetical questions were considered. Such responses were scored as correct or one of three incorrect categories. Correct responses were those in which the child used obligatory hypothetical forms such as *would* or *would have*. Incorrect responses were those in which the child responded with (1) an "I don't know" statement (or its equivalent), (2) a completely irrelevant response, or (3) a relevant but inappropriate response. An example of a completely irrelevant response was that of a 4-year-old child who responded to the question "what would happen if your mommy went to work tomorrow?" with "my dog ate a birdie yesterday." The relevant but inappropriate incorrect response category reflects two types of errors in which the conversational topic was maintained but not in the appropriate hypothetical context. For example, a 4-year-old child responded to "what would happen if your daddy cooked dinner tomorrow?" with "he cooked hamburgers one time." In errors such as these, the child's response is clearly not hypothetical. The other type of error for this category was that in which the child responded with a future hypothetical to a past hypothetical question. For example, a 5-year-old child responded to "what would have happened if your mommy had played football yesterday?" with "she would make a touchdown."

Results

Initially, responses to affirmative questions (e.g., "what would have happened if Bingo had gone swimming yesterday?") were compared with responses to negative questions (e.g., "what would have happened if Bingo had not gone swimming yesterday?"). No significant difference was found in these comparisons, and subsequent analyses were based on responses to both affirmative and negative questions.

As expected, correct responses increased with age, $F(3, 66) = 12.5$, $p < 0.01$. Correct responses were also more common in response to future hypothetical questions than in response to past hypothetical questions, $F(1, 56) = 7.57$, $p < 0.01$. "Fantasy" hypothetical questions elicited more correct responses than did "parent" hypothetical questions, $F(1, 56) = 4.33$, $p < 0.05$.

"I don't know" incorrect responses decreased with age, $F(3, 66) = 9.11$, $p < 0.01$, as did irrelevant responses, $F(3, 66) = 5.86$, $p < 0.01$, whereas relevant but inappropriate responses increased from age 3 to age 4 and then steadily declined, $F(3, 66) = 3.71$, $p < 0.05$. Irrelevant responses occurred more often in response to past hypothetical questions than in response to future hypothetical questions, $F(1, 56) = 4.48$, $p < 0.05$, as did relevant but inappropriate responses, $F(1, 56) = 16.45$, $p < 0.01$. Relevant but inappropriate responses also occurred more often in response to hypothetical questions involving parents than in response to those involving fantasy characters, $F(1, 56) = 5.63$, $p < 0.05$. These data are summarized in Tables 11-1 and 11-2.

The predicted order of difficulty of each of the four hypothetical question categories was also supported by the data. Children responded correctly more often to past fantasy hypothetical questions than to past parent hypothetical questions $t(59) = 2.38$, $p < 0.05$. Future parent questions were correctly re-

Table 11-1. *Mean Number of Correct Responses by Each Age Group for Each Type of Hypothetical Question*

Group	Past parent	Past fantasy	Future parent	Future fantasy
I	0.53	0.73	1.6	2.2
II	0.87	1.47	1.93	2.73
III	1.87	2.07	2.67	3.13
IV	2.07	2.07	2.73	3.13

Table 11-2. *Mean Number of Each Type of Incorrect Response by Each Age Group for Each Type of Hypothetical Question*

	Past parent			Past fantasy		
Group	a	b	c	a	b	c
I	1.8	1.0	0.67	1.54	1.53	0.2
II	0.27	0.87	2.0	0.13	0.67	1.73
III	0.27	0.47	1.4	0.2	0.53	1.2
IV	0.27	0.4	1.27	0.4	0.47	1.07
I	1.34	0.53	0.53	0.67	0.93	0.2
II	0.27	0.73	1.07	0	0.6	0.67
III	0.13	0.2	1.0	0.13	0.33	0.4
IV	0	0.53	0.73	0.33	0.2	0.33

[a]"I don't know" response.

[b]Irrelevant response.

[c]Relevant but inappropriate response.

sponded to more often than were past fantasy questions, $t(59) = 5.0$, $p < 0.001$, while future fantasy questions were correctly responded to more often than were future parent questions, $t(59) = 4.07, p < 0.001$.

Discussion

The results support the hypothesis advanced by Kuczaj and Daly that young children find it more difficult to contrast an actual event with an unactual event than to contrast two unactual events. Thus, young children find it easier to compare an expected future event with a hypothetical future event then to compare an actual past event with a hypothetical past event. They also find it easier to deal with hypothetical questions about fantasy creatures than hypothetical questions about their parents, parental behavior having more of a "reality orientation" than does the behavior of fantasy characters, the result being that hypothetical questions about parents frequently result in actual–unactual comparisons, whereas hypothetical questions about fantasy objects are more likely to result in unactual–unactual comparisons.

However, the simple distinction between actual–unactual comparisons and unactual–unactual comparisons is not sufficient to account for all of the data, namely the interaction of the past future and fantasy parent dimensions. If in fact unactual–unactual comparisons are always easier than actual–unactual comparisons, young children should find it easier to deal with hypothetical questions about fantasy characters than hypothetical questions about their parents, regardless of whether the question refers to past or future events. This is not the case. Past hypothetical questions in general yielded fewer correct responses than future hypothetical questions in general, with questions about fantasy characters resulting in more correct responses than questions about parents for both past and future hypothetical questions. Importantly, children more often responded correctly to future fantasy questions than to past fantasy questions. Thus, past hypotheticals are more difficult than future hypotheticals for children even when the past hypotheticals involve unactual–unactual comparisons (as in the past fantasy condition). However, even past fantasy hypotheticals may involve actual–unactual comparisons in that such hypotheticals may require the establishment of a *supposed* actual past event with which to contrast the hypothetical event. The finding that past parent hypotheticals were more difficult than past fantasy hypotheticals suggests that actual–unactual comparisons are more difficult than "supposed actual"–unactual comparisons. Similarly, the finding that future parent hypotheticals were more difficult than future fantasy hypotheticals suggests that unactual–unactual comparisons that involve the expected behavior of familiar others are more difficult than unactual–unactual comparisons that involve the unique behavior of fantasy characters.

These data, in conjunction with those from previous investigations, suggest that the development of hypothetical reference is influenced by a number of factors. One of these factors is the relative ease of making across-category comparisons as opposed to within-category comparisons, the latter type apparently being easier than the former. However, this factor interacts with syntactic complexity, temporal reference skills, and familiarity with the content material to yield the observed developmental patterns. Although syntactic complexity alone is insufficient to account for the relative difficulty of past hypothetical reference in comparison to future hypothetical reference (Slobin, 1973; Cromer, 1974; Bates 1976a; Kuczaj and Daly, 1979), the greater complexity of past hypothetical reference forms undoubtedly contributes to the developmental disparity between past hypothetical reference and future hypothetical reference. For example, in the present study, past/fantasy and past/present hypothetical reference were more difficult than future/fantasy and future/parent hypothetical reference, although fantasy hypothetical reference was in general easier than that involving parents. Thus, syntactic complexity interacts within comparison type (across versus within) to influence ease of hypothetical reference.

Temporal reference skills contribute to hypothetical reference in several ways. First, the child must be able to distinguish past events, present events, and future events. Thus, the child must distinguish memories, perceptions, and anticipations. These abilities, of course, are necessary but not sufficient for hypothetical reference. To engage in hypothetical reference, the child must also be able to distinguish actual and unactual events and compare them when necessary. Moreover, the child must be able to distinguish unactual past events (hypothetical) from unactual future events (anticipated or hypothetical).

Familiarity with the content material may also influence the child's hypothetical reference. In the present study, we have seen how the young child's hypothetical reference skills vary, depending on whether the child was questioned about his parents or the fantasy characters. Familiarity with the content material apparently affects the ease with which the child perceives and then makes actual/unactual and unactual/unactual contrasts. In this way, familiarity with the content material affects the child's hypothetical reference.

To sum up, children's hypothetical reference appears to be determined by a number of factors. These factors include syntactic complexity, temporal referencing skills, familiarity with content material, and relative ease of making unactual/unactual comparisons and actual/unactual comparisons. Future research should be directed at investigating the interaction of the various factors that affect the development of hypothetical reference skills in young children.

12

Ellen M. Markman and Jean E. Hutchinson

Children's Sensitivity to Constraints on Word Meaning: Taxonomic versus Thematic Relations

One of the major problems confronting someone learning a language is to figure out the meaning of a word given the enormous number of possible meanings for any particular word. Children commonly learn their first words (category terms) through ostensive definition: a parent or other teacher points to an object and labels it. Especially in the early phases of language acquisition, when children cannot understand a description of a category, children's learning of new category terms must depend heavily on ostensive definition. Once an adult points to an object and labels it, how does the child settle on an interpretation? At first sight this would seem to be a simple problem, and in fact children make hundreds of such inferences correctly when acquiring new vocabulary. This apparent simplicity, however, belies a complex inferential problem that was formulated by Quine (1960) in his well-known argument about translation. Imagine that someone points to a dog and says "chien," and our job is to figure out what "chien" means. An obvious hypothesis is that it means "dog." But this is not necessary. It could mean "furry object," or "brown object," or "medium-sized object," and so on. To decide if the new term refers to dogs, one might set up test situations by pointing to various objects and asking whether or not "chien" applies. Quine's argument is that no matter how many test situations one constructs, there will always be more than one hypothesis for the meaning of a new term that is consistent with the existing evidence.

Young children beginning to acquire their native language continually face this problem of narrowing down the meaning of a term from an indefinite

Abridged from "Children's sensitivity to constraints on word meaning: Taxonomic vs. thematic relations" by Ellen M. Markman and Jean E. Hutchinson, 1984, *Cognitive Psychology*, 16, 1–27. Copyright 1984 by Academic Press. Reprinted by permission of publisher and authors.

number of possibilities. Someone points in some direction and then utters a word. On what grounds is the child to conclude that a new unfamiliar word, e.g., "dog," refers to dogs? What is to prevent a child from concluding that "dog" is a proper name for that particular dog? What prevents the child from concluding that "dog" means "four-legged object" or "black object" or any number of other characteristics that dogs share? And finally, what prevents the child from concluding that "dog," in addition to referring to that particular dog, also refers to the bone the dog is chewing on or to the tree the dog is lying under? These last examples of thematic relations pose a particular problem because children are very interested in such relations and may find them more salient than categorical relations. Before continuing to discuss how children narrow down the possible meanings of terms, we briefly review the work on classification showing children's fascination with thematic relations.

One widely used procedure for studying how children form categories of objects is to ask them to sort objects into groups. Typically children are presented with objects from several different categories, for example, vehicles, animals, clothing, and people. They are instructed to put together the objects that are alike or that go together or are given freedom to manipulate and group the objects as they like. Another variant of the sorting procedure is a match to sample task. In this case, children are shown a target object and two choices, one in the same category as the target and one in a different category. Children must choose which is most like the target. This task in particular is similar to the one that children face in ostensive definition, in that someone points to an object and the child must determine which other objects are like it.

Here is a somewhat oversimplified summary of what is often found in these studies. Children older than about 7 sort objects on the basis of the object's taxonomic category. For example, they place all and only the vehicles together, all and only the clothing together, and so on. They perceive the perceptual or functional properties that the objects share [perhaps in a family resemblance structure (Rosch and Mervis, 1975)] and so find the common taxonomic category to be a natural way of organizing objects. Younger children sort on some other basis. Sometimes, especially when geometric figures are used, young children create spatial configurations with the objects, arranging them into designs or patterns. When more meaningful objects are used, children represent causal and temporal relations among the objects as well as spatial relations. These thematic relations emphasize events rather than taxonomic similarity. For example, children might sort a man and a car together because the man is driving the car. Or they might place a boy, a coat, and a dog together because the boy will wear his coat when he takes the dog for a walk.

This attention to thematic relations between objects rather than to how objects are alike is a common finding replicated in many studies. In addition to sorting experiments, this thematic bias shows up in studies of memory clustering and word association (Inhelder and Piaget, 1964; Denney, 1974; Denney and

Ziobrowski, 1972; Nelson, 1977b). These findings indicate that children are more interested in the thematic relations among objects or that thematic relations are simpler or more readily constructed than categorical relations.

It is not surprising that children notice these thematic relations. They are obviously very important for making sense of the world for adults and children alike. As we move about in our daily life, we observe people interacting or using tools or other artifacts to accomplish goals. We view natural occurrences such as storms, and we admire scenery. Much of our perception is interpretive, trying to figure out what is happening and how. Even infants tend to place causal interpretations on events they perceive (cf. Gibson and Spelke, 1983). Thus, these event-like structures are a fundamentally important and natural way of organizing information. Moreover, there seem to be fewer developmental and cross-cultural differences in understanding this type of organization (Mandler, Scribner, Cole, & DeForest, 1980). This is in marked contrast to the cross-cultural and developmental differences found in studies of taxonomic classification. In sum, interest in thematic relations is not limited to young children. Nor should attention to thematic relations be viewed as a useless or nonproductive bias. Noticing causal, spatial, and temporal relations between objects is essential for understanding the world. It is children's attention to categorical relations and not their attention to thematic relations that changes most with development.

When the procedures used in sorting tasks specifically guide children's attention toward categories and away from thematic relations, children do show some understanding of categorical organization (see Carey, 1985; Gelman and Baillargeon, 1983; Markman and Callanan, 1983). To take one example, Smiley and Brown (1979) tested whether 5- and 6-year-old children could understand taxonomic relations even though they prefer thematic ones. They presented children with a target picture and two choice pictures. One of the choices was thematically related to the target, and one of the choices was taxonomically related to the target. For example, children were shown a spider (target), a spider web (thematic choice), and a grasshopper (taxonomic choice). The experimenter pointed to the spider and asked for "the one that goes best with this one." As usual, these young children tended to pick the spider web, rather than the grasshopper, thereby indicating a thematic relation. Nevertheless, when they were asked about the grasshopper, all of the children could explain the taxonomic relation. Thus, children have a rudimentary ability to organize objects taxonomically, but it is often obscured by their attention to thematic relations.

Although children are biased toward organizing objects thematically, single words, in particular count nouns, do not often encode thematic relations.* English does not have a single noun for thematically related objects such as a boy and his bike, a spider and its web, or a baby and its bottle. Thus, to return to

*Footnote omitted.[Eds.]

Quine's problem of induction, we are faced with a kind of paradox. Children seem to readily learn concrete nouns like "ball" or "dog" that refer to object categories. Yet they tend to notice and remember thematic relations between objects more readily than categorical relations. How is it that children readily learn labels for categories of objects if they are attending to these thematic relations between objects instead? To take a concrete example, imagine a mother pointing to a baby and saying "baby." Based on the sorting studies, we should assume that the child will be attending to the baby shaking a rattle or to the baby being diapered. Why, then, doesn't the child infer that "baby" also refers to the rattle or to the diaper, in addition to the particular baby?

As a possible solution to this problem, we propose that children have implicit hypotheses about the possible meaning of words that help them acquire words for categories. Children may well prefer to construe the environment in a way that conflicts with the way that language is organized. But even very young children may be aware of the constraint on word meaning so that when they believe that they are learning a new *word*, they shift their attention from thematic to categorical organization.

This proposal has a strong and a weak form. The strong form is that sensitivity to the constraint on word meaning can help children discover and learn new categories. That is, on hearing an unfamiliar word, children will search for categorical relations. If no familiar, previously unlabeled category is available, children will analyze the environment to form a new categorical relation to label. In this way, the constraint on possible word meanings could help children acquire new categories. The weak form of the proposal is that children use the constraint to help them link a new word to a concept they already know. If a familiar categorical relation is not available, however, children will not attempt to search for a new one.

The four studies that follow test mainly the weak form of the hypothesis. Experiment 1 focuses on 2- and 3-year-old children's knowledge of the constraint on word meaning for basic level categorization. Experiments 2 and 3 focus on 4- and 5-year-olds sensitivity to the constraint for superordinate level categories. And Experiment 4 tests the hypothesis for 4- and 5-year-olds who were taught new taxonomic and new thematic relations for unfamiliar objects.

All of the experiments use a match to sample procedure with a target picture, taxonomic choice, and thematic choice. In the No Word condition, children are shown the target and asked to simply "find another one." In the Novel Word condition, children hear a new label for the target (e.g., "biv") and are asked to "find another biv." The Novel Word task is quite like ostensive definition: someone points to an object and labels it, and the child must figure out what else the label refers to. We predicted that the majority of choices in the Novel Word condition would be taxonomic. The No Word task also has much in common with ostensive definition, except that no label is given. We expected children in this condition to give many more thematic responses than children in the Novel Word condition.

Experiment 1

This first study investigates whether hearing a novel word will cause 2- to 3-year-old children to shift their attention from thematic to categorical relations. Basic level categories (such as "dog" or "chair") were used with these young children rather than general superordinate level categories (such as "animal" or "furniture"). The basic level, according to Rosch and her colleagues, is the level of categorization at which category members have the most features in common without being confusable with members of contrasting categories (Rosch, 1978; Rosch, Mervis, Gray, Johnson, and Boyes-Braem, 1976; Mervis and Rosch, 1981).*

METHODS

Subjects

Forty-one children from nursery schools in Palo Alto, California, participated in the study. They ranged in age from 2 years 5 months to 3 years 11 months, with a mean age of 3 years 4 months. An additional two children failed to pass a pretest described below and were not included in the study. Children were randomly assigned to one of two conditions with the constraint that the conditions be roughly equated for age and sex.

Procedure

PRETEST. A simple pretest was given to ensure that the children understood instructions to find an object that is the same as another. A target picture was propped up against a frame and the child's attention was drawn to the picture. Then another identical picture and a distractor were placed on the table in front of the child, and the child was asked to "find one that is the same as this one" (the target picture). Three sets of pictures were used: two identical circles with a

---

*Rosch et al., (1976) showed that 3-year-old children are capable of using category membership to sort objects at the basic level of categorization, even though they fail to sort objects taxonomically at the superordinate level. In the Rosch et al. (1976) study children were presented with two objects related at the basic level, along with an unrelated distractor, and were asked to find the two that are alike. Three-year-olds almost always selected the two category members over the unrelated distractor. Because this study failed to include any competing thematic relations, however, it did not establish the relative salience of thematic and categorical relations. In a preliminary study, we demonstrated that when a competing thematic relation is present (e.g., a baby and a bottle), 2- and 3-year-olds often select it over the basic level category (e.g., two babies). When an unrelated distractor was used, children selected the categorical associate 94% of the time, as in the Rosch et al. (1976) study. When a thematically related distractor was used, however, children selected the categorical associate only 56% of the time. This finding allows us to address the main question about the role of a word in inducing categorical organization.

squiggle as the distractor, two rectangles with a *z* as the distractor, and two arrows with a U-shaped figure as the distractor. Children were scored as passing the pretest only if they answered all three items correctly.

NO WORD CONDITION. The procedure used in this condition was very similar to the pretest procedure. Children were first introduced to a hand puppet and were told to put the picture they chose in the puppet's mouth. On each trial, the experimenter propped the target picture against the frame and told the child, "Look carefully now. See this?" as she pointed to the picture. Then the experimenter placed the two choice pictures on the table and told the child to "find another one that is the same as this," as she continued to point to the target picture. The instructions were designed to make it as clear as possible to these young children that we were looking for a taxonomic match.

One of the choice pictures was a member of the same basic level category as the target: for example, the target might be a poodle and the choice a German shepherd (both dogs). We attempted to make the two category exemplars fairly dissimilar yet still readily identifiable to these young children. The other choice picture was a strong thematic associate to the target—in this case, dog food. There were 10 such triads in all. They are listed in Table 12-1. The left–right placement of the thematic and category choices was randomly determined for each subject with the constraints that half of the thematic choices be on the left and half be on the right. The presentation order of the 10 items was also randomly determined for each subject.

NOVEL WORD CONDITION. The materials and procedure for this condition were identical to those of the No Word condition, with one change. Children in this condition were told that the puppet could talk in puppet talk. They were instructed to listen carefully to find the right picture. The puppet gave the target picture an unfamiliar name and used the same name in the instructions for picking a choice picture. For example, the puppet might say, "See this? It is a sud. Find another sud that is the same as this sud." Ten meaningless one-syllable words were used and a different random assignment of words to pictures was made for each child.

RESULTS

When children in the No Word condition had to select between another category member and a thematically related object, they chose the thematic relation almost half of the time. They selected other category members a mean of 5.95 times out of 10 (59%), $sd = 2.28$. This was not significantly different from chance. When the target picture was labeled with an unfamiliar word children were much more likely to select categorically. They now chose the other category member a mean of 8.29 times out of 10 (83%), $sd = 1.82$. This was significantly different from chance, $t(20) = 8.08$, $p < 0.01$, and was significantly different

Table 12-1. *Stimulus Materials for Experiment 1*

Standard object	Taxonomic choice	Thematic choice
Police car	Car	Policeman
Tennis shoe	High-heeled shoe	Foot
Dog	Dog	Dog food
Straight backed chair	Easy chair	Man in sitting position
Crib	Crib	Baby
Birthday cake	Chocolate cake	Birthday present
Blue jay	Duck	Nest
Outside door	Swinging door	Key
Male football player	Man	Football
Male child in swimsuit	Female child in overalls	Swimming pool

from the No Word condition, $t(39) = 3.63, p < 0.001$. The effect held up over every item and was significant when items rather than subjects were treated as a random factor, paired $t(9) = 8.40, p < 0.001$. As predicted, when children think they are learning a new word they look for categorical relationships between objects and pay less attention to thematic relations. These results support the hypothesis at least for very young children and basic level categories. The next three studies examine whether the effect holds up for familiar superordinate level categories and for newly learned object categories.

Experiment 2

This study tests the hypothesis that hearing a new word will induce older pre-schoolers to look for superordinate level taxonomic relations rather than thematic relations. The superordinate level of categorization, according to Rosch and her colleagues, is more abstract than the basic level. Members of superordinate level categories share fewer attributes, especially perceptual attributes, than members of basic level categories (Rosch, 1978; Rosch et al., 1976; Mervis and Rosch, 1981).

METHODS

Subjects

Sixty children attending nursery schools in Palo Alto, California and surrounding towns participated in the study. They ranged in age from 4 years 4 months to 5 years 3 months, with a mean age of 4 years 10 months. An additional two children were dropped from the study, one who did not cooperate with the experimenter and one who did not understand the task. The children were randomly assigned to four conditions, 15 per condition, with the constraint that the conditions be roughly equated for age and sex.

Procedure

NO WORD CONDITION. The procedure used in this condition was very similar to that used in the No Word condition of Experiment 1, except that superordinate level categories were used instead of basic level categories. The experimenter saw each child individually for one 15- to 20-minute session. Subjects were shown 30 colorful pictures of common objects. Ten of the pictures served as targets. Associated with each of the target pictures were two choice pictures. One of the choice pictures was related in a thematic way to the target (e.g., milk/cow). The other choice picture was a member of the same superordinate category as the target (e.g., pig/cow). An attempt was made to use a variety of thematic relations rather than just one, so as not to limit the generality of the results. A complete list of the stimulus materials appears in Table 12-2. As in Experiment 1, the instructions in the No Word condition were designed to make it as clear as possible that we were looking for a taxonomic match.

On each trial in the No Word condition, the experimenter, using a hand puppet, said, "I'm going to show you a (new) picture. Then you'll have to find another one that is the same kind of thing." The experimenter then placed the target picture face up on the table directly in front of the child, and said, "See

Table 12-2. *Stimulus Materials for Experiments 2 and 3*

Standard object	Taxonomic choice	Thematic choice
Cow	Pig	Milk
Ring	Necklace	Hand
Door	Window	Key
Crib	Adult bed	Baby
Bee	Ant	Flower
Hanger	Hook	Dress
Cup	Glass	Kettle
Car	Bicycle	Car tire
Sprinkler[a]	Watering can	Grass
Paintbrush[a]	Crayons	Easel
Train[b]	Bus	Tracks
Dog[b]	Cat	Bone

[a]This set was used only in Experiment 2.

[b]This set was used only in Experiment 3.

this?" She placed the two choice pictures to the left and right of the target, then said, "Can you find another one that is the same kind of thing as this one? Find another one that is the same kind of thing as this one." The left–right position of the choice pictures was randomized for each child in such a way that thematic and taxonomic choices each appeared half the time on the left and half the time on the right, across the 10 stimulus triads. The order of presentation of triads was also randomized for each subject. After children made a choice, they were asked to justify their response: "How do you know these two are the same kind of thing?"

NOVEL WORD CONDITION. The materials and procedure for this condition were identical to those of the No Word condition, except that the target picture was now labeled with a novel word. Children were told that the puppet could talk in puppet talk, and that they were to listen carefully to what he said. The instructions now included an unfamiliar label for the target: "I'm going to show you a kind of dax. Then you'll have to find another kind of dax. See this? It's a kind of dax. Can you find another kind of dax?" A different meaningless one-syllable word was used for each target picture. Children again were asked to justify their choices. Because they were given a label, we expected children in the Novel Word condition to choose the taxonomically related picture more often than children in the No Word condition.

Two additional control conditions were included to attempt to rule out one alternative explanation for increased taxonomic responding in the Novel Word condition. We are arguing that when children hear a word, they focus on categorical relationships because of general knowledge of what nouns encode, and not because of specific knowledge about the word's meaning. But children already knew real word names for the target pictures and they conceivably could have translated the unfamiliar labels. Translation of the unfamiliar words into known words might help children choose taxonomically. We could not control for the possibility that children were translating, but we did run one condition to determine what word children might translate into if they were translating, and another condition to determine what effect such translation would have.

TRANSLATION CONDITION. Children might translate the unfamiliar word either into a basic level word or into a superordinate level word. For instance, given a cow as a target picture and told that it was a "dax," they might translate "dax" into "cow" (basic level) or they might translate "dax" into "animal" (superordinate level). In the Translation condition, we looked at the kinds of translations children make when they are explicitly asked to translate the unfamiliar word. The procedure was identical to that of the Novel Word condition except children were also asked "What do you think dax means?"—once right after the target picture was introduced (but before children saw the choice pictures), and again after they made a choice.

When we analyzed the children's translations of these novel words, we found that on the first translation, before seeing the choice pictures, children almost never translated the unfamiliar labels into superordinate terms (only 6.7% of the time). Forty-seven percent of the first translations were basic level words. The rest of the translations were descriptive phrases. Even after making a choice, subjects still produced superordinates only 7.3% of the time, while the mean percentage of basic level translations decreased to 19%. Thus if children in the Novel Word condition spontaneously translated the unfamiliar word, they would be very unlikely to translate it into a superordinate level word.

BASIC WORD CONDITION. If children are going to translate into a single known word, it will be into a basic level category term. The Basic Word condition tested whether translation into a basic level word would facilitate taxonomic responding.

The materials and procedure for this condition were identical to those in the Novel Word condition. The instructions simply substituted the basic level word for the target, in place of the unfamiliar label. For the example with the cow target, the experimenter said: "I'm going to show you a picture of a cow. Then you'll have to find another picture that is the same kind of thing. See this? It's a cow. Can you find another one that is the same kind of thing as this one?" As in the other three conditions, children were asked to justify their choices.

RESULTS

As is typical for children this age, when no word was present they made a number of thematic choices. When children in the No Word condition had to select between another member of the same superordinate category and a thematically related object, they chose the categorical relation only 4.93 times out of 10 (49%), $sd = 2.88$. This was not different from chance. As predicted, the presence of a new word caused children to focus more attention on taxonomic relations. When the target picture was labeled with an unnfamiliar word, children now chose the other category member a mean of 6.87 times out of 10 (69%), $sd = 2.55$. This was more often than would be expected by chance, $t(14) = 2.75$, $p < 0.05$. The difference between the conditions was significant by a one-tailed t test, $t(28) = 1.88$, $p < 0.05$.

Children who heard the target described with a basic level word chose the categorically related object 57% of the time. This was not significantly different from either the Novel Word or the No Word condition. It was also not significantly different from chance.

The results were more clear-cut when items were treated as a random factor and conditions as a within groups factor. Pictures labeled with unfamiliar words elicited significantly more taxonomic responses than the same pictures not labeled, paired $t(9) = 4.95$, $p < 0.002$. This effect held up for 9 out of the 10 stimulus triads. Pictures labeled with a basic object word elicited an intermediate number of taxonomic responses: significantly more than in the No Word condition, paired $t(9) = 4.14$, $p < 0.01$, but significantly fewer than in the Novel Word condition, paired $t(9) = 2.49$, $p < 0.05$.

Converging evidence for the hypothesis came from the justifications that children gave for their choices. Two raters coded the justifications as thematic, categorical, or irrelevant, and agreed on 90% of the classifications. Thematic justifications expressed an interactive relationship between the target and the object chosen. An example is "The *cow* makes *milk*." Children justified more of their choices thematically when they heard no word (51%) than when they heard an unfamiliar word (19%), $t(28) = 3.17$, $p < 0.005$. Likewise, they justified more of their choices thematically when they heard a familiar basic level word (38%) than when they heard an unfamiliar word, $t(28) = 1.92$, $p = 0.062$. There was no difference in the numbers of thematic justifications given in the No Word and Basic Word conditions.

Justifications and choices were not perfectly correlated, as the kind of justification children gave did not always match the kind of choice they made. Children seemed to explain their choices in terms of the task as they saw it. For example, when children chose thematically in the Novel Word condition, they seemed reluctant to justify the thematic choice with a thematic explanation. When they heard a novel word, they justified thematic choices with a thematic explanation an average of only 44% of the time. The children seemed to be in conflict between having chosen thematically but believing that the word implies a taxonomic relation. After choosing a cow and milk as being the same kind of thing, for example, many children did not justify their selection in the most natural way (stating that milk comes from a cow). They had to manufacture some justification to satisfy the experimenter, and so ended up giving a relatively high proportion of irrelevant justifications for their thematic choices such as "I don't know" (mean = 39%), compared to children in the No Word condition (mean = 6%), $t(24) = 2.52$, $p < 0.02$. When children in the No Word condition made a thematic choice they did not have the same conflict and were quite willing to give thematic justifications. These children, who did not hear a word, justified their thematic choices thematically the majority (a mean of 84%) of the time. The difference between the Novel and No Word conditions in propensity to justify thematic choices thematically was significant, $t(24) = 2.71$, $p < 0.02$. Children in the Basic Word condition justified thematic choices thematically an average of 67% of the time. This was not significantly different from either the Novel Word or No Word condition.

In sum, when an object was labeled with an unfamiliar word, children were more likely to look for another object from the same superordinate level category than when the object was not labeled. Children almost certainly were not translating the novel word into a superordinate level term, so that cannot account for the effect. If children were translating the term into a basic level word for the object, that would have helped them to choose a categorically related object. However, the justifications from children hearing a novel word differed from those of children hearing a basic level word, suggesting that translation into known terms was not accounting for the results.

Experiment 3

Experiment 3 is a modified replication of Experiment 2. In Experiment 2 the No Word instructions ("Find another one that is the same kind of thing") were designed to promote as much taxonomic responding as possible. The No Word condition was the baseline measure of taxonomic responding, and we hypothesized that the presence of a new word would elevate taxonomic responses above even this baseline. Thus, this was a conservative test of the hypothesis.

In Experiment 3 we attempted to make the No Word instructions more neutral. A neutral instruction is more like the natural language learning context since, in both cases, children view objects and hear them labeled without instructions about what relations to attend to. In this study, children were asked to "Find another one." This is less explicit than the earlier instructions, but for adults still clearly implies that taxonomic similarity is called for. In this way we could compare what children naturally found salient to their choices when they heard a novel word. In Experiment 3 we also used slightly younger children, who would be expected to show a greater baseline preference for thematic relations. *

In sum, the results for Experiment 3 replicated the findings of Experiment 2, providing even stronger support for the hypothesis. Hearing a new word diminishes children's tendency to look for thematic relationships, and causes them to look for categorical relationships instead. There is at least some evidence that children focus on categorical relationships because of the sheer presence of the word, and not because of any particular knowledge about the meaning of the word.

Experiment 4

Experiment 4 is designed to provide additional evidence that children use abstract knowledge about words rather than specific known meanings to facilitate taxonomic responding. In this study, pictures of artificial objects were used instead of real objects. Children are not likely to translate unfamiliar names for these pictures into known words, because they do not know real word names for them. If the presence of an unfamiliar word still causes children to shift from thematic to taxonomic responding when the materials are also unfamiliar, then this would rule out translation as an explanation for the effect.

---

*Methods, results, and discussion of Experiment 3 omitted. [Eds.]

METHODS

Subjects

Thirty-two children attending nursery schools in Palo Alto, California, and surrounding towns participated in the study. The children ranged in age from 4 years 6 months to 5 years 11 months, with a mean age of 5 years 2 months. An additional three children were dropped from the study because of response bias. The children were randomly assigned to two conditions, 16 per condition, with the constraint that the conditions be roughly equated for age and sex.

Procedure

The design and procedure for this study are essentially the same as that of Experiment 3. The main difference is that the experimenter first described the taxonomic and thematic relations for the artificial objects before asking children to select the picture that was like the target.

NO WORD CONDITION. Each child was seen individually for one 20-minute session. Subjects were shown eight sets of pictures in random order. Each set included a target picture, and two choice pictures, one thematically related and one taxonomically related to the target. Before children saw the target picture and the two choices, they were shown two training pictures that illustrated how the target picture related to each of the choice pictures. One picture showed the target object and the taxonomic choice, side by side. For these pairs, children were told a common function that the two objects shared. An example taxonomic training picture is shown in Fig. 12-1. For this example, the experimenter said, "This swims in the water" (pointing to the left-hand object). "This swims in the water" (pointing to the right-hand object).

A second training picture showed the target and the thematic choice in an interactive relationship. The experimenter told the children how the two objects interacted. The thematic training picture for the set just given is shown in Fig. 12-2. For this example, the experimenter said, "This catches this" (pointing to the objects she was referring to as she said the sentence). Children were asked to repeat the spoken information to make sure that they were paying attention. The first training picture was left on the table as the second training picture was

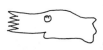

Fig. 12-1. *Sample taxonomic training picture in Experiment 4.*

Fig. 12-2. *Sample thematic training picture in Experiment 4.*

introduced, so that children could see the connection between the target in the first picture and the target in the second picture. The order of presentation of training pictures was randomized so that taxonomic and thematic training pictures were each presented first half of the time.

A second example taxonomic training picture is shown in Fig. 12-3. For this example the experimenter said, "This pokes holes in things" (pointing to the left hand object). "This pokes holes in things" (pointing to the right hand object). The thematic training picture for the same set is shown in Fig. 12-4. For this picture, the spoken information was "You keep this in here."

After children saw the two training pictures in a set, the pictures were removed from the table. The rest of the trial was a match to sample task following the same procedure as the No Word condition of Experiment 3. The experimenter said, "I'm going to show you something. Then I want you to think carefully, and find another one." The experimenter then placed the target picture face up on the table directly in front of the child and said, "See this?" She placed the two choice pictures to the left and right of the target and said, "Can you find another one?" Note that the choices were pictures of the individual objects as in the previous studies, rather than pictures of two objects together. After children made a choice, the experimenter asked them to justify their response: "How did you know it was this one?" The left–right order of choices was randomized so that taxonomic choices each appeared half the time on the left and half the time on the right.

NOVEL WORD CONDITION. The materials and procedure for this condition were identical to those of the No Word condition, except that a novel word was used to label the target picture during the match to sample task. After children saw the training pictures, the experimenter said, "I'm going to show you a dax. Then I want you to think carefully, and find another dax. See this dax? Can you say dax? Can you find another dax?" A different unfamiliar word was used for each set. Children again were asked to justify their choices. Because of the unfamiliarity

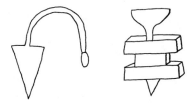

Fig. 12-3. *Sample taxonomic training picture in Experiment 4.*

Fig. 12-4. *Sample thematic training picture in Experiment 4.*

of the materials, children in both conditions found it difficult to justify their responses, so the justifications will not be discussed.

RESULTS

The results for the choices were parallel to those found for Experiments 2 and 3. As usual, when children in the No Word condition had to select between another member of the same category and a thematically related object, they often chose the thematic relation. They selected the other category member a mean of only 3.00 times out of 8 (37%), $sd = 1.79$. This was significantly less than chance, $t(15) = 2.24$, $p < 0.05$. When the target picture was labeled with an unfamiliar word, children were more likely to select categorically. They now chose the other category member a mean of 5.06 times out of 8 (63%), $sd = 2.38$. This was more than chance by a one-tailed t test, $t(15) = 1.78$, $p < 0.05$. Children hearing a novel word were significantly more likely to select an object from the same category than children not hearing a label, $t(30) = 2.77$, $p < 0.01$.

When the results were analyzed with items as a random factor and conditions as a within-groups factor, we again found the predicted difference. Pictures labeled with unfamiliar words elicited significantly more taxonomic responses than the same pictures not labeled, paired $t(7) = 4.07$, $p < 0.005$, and the difference held up for every item.

Discussion

The hypothesis tested by these studies is that children place an abstract constraint on what single nouns might mean. Children limit words to refer mainly to objects that share some property or function rather than allowing words to refer to objects that are united by thematic relations. This would help explain how children acquire words that refer to categories even though, in many other situations, they seem to find the thematic associations between objects to be more salient. The simple presence of a noun, even an unfamiliar one such as "dax," should cause children to search for objects that share perceptual or functional properties. Thus, labeling a picture as "a dax" and asking children to find "another dax" should help override their preference for choosing thematically.

OVERVIEW OF RESULTS

The results from four studies supported the hypothesis. The main results from all of the studies are summarized in Table 12-3.

As can be seen from the results of Experiment 1, even children as young as 2 and 3 years place constraints on what an unfamiliar word might mean. When presented with two basic level objects—for example, two different kinds of dogs—and a third object that was thematically related, such as dog food, very young children often selected a dog and dog food as being the same kind of thing. If,

Table 12-3. *Main Results for Experiments 1 to 4*

	Percentage of taxonomic choices (%)	Percentage of all choices justified thematically (%)	Percentage of thematic choices justified thematically (%)
Experiment 1: Basic level categories in 2 to 3 year olds (taxonomically biased instructions)			
No Word	59	—	—
Novel Word	83	—	—
Experiment 2: Superordinate level categories in 4 to 5 year olds (taxonomically biased instructions)			
No Word	49	51	84
Novel Word	69	19	44
Basic Word	57	38	67
Experiment 3: Superordinate level categories in 4 year olds (neutral instructions)			
No Word	25	67	79
Novel Word	65	25	44
Basic Word	62	38	70
Experiment 4: Unfamiliar categories in 4 to 5 year olds (neutral instructions)			
No Word	37	—	—
Novel Word	63	—	—

however, one of the dogs was called by an unfamiliar label, e.g., "dax," and children were told to find another dax, they were now much more likely to select the two dogs.

By 4 or 5 years of age, children have set further constraints on what a word might mean, as Experiments 2 and 3 demonstrate. A word induces them to search for categorical relations even among objects that can only be related at the superordinate level of categorization. For example, with no word present, children often selected a dog and dog bone as being the same kind of thing because of the strong thematic association between dog and bone. When one of the dogs was called a "dax," however, and children were asked to find another dax, they more often selected a dog and a cat as being the same, because they are both in the same superordinate category, animals.

At the superordinate level of categorization, the same pattern of choices was obtained for two different sets of instructions. Even when the No Word instructions emphasized taxonomic relations, as in Experiment 2 ("Find another one that is the same kind of thing as this one."), we found an increase in taxonomic responding in the Novel Word condition. In Experiment 3 when the No Word instructions were more neutral ("Find another one."), there was an even bigger shift toward more taxonomic responding in the presence of a new word.

The justification data corroborated the choices. Children who heard a novel word tended to give more justifications that referred to the categorical relations between the objects, whereas children who did not hear a label for the objects referred more to thematic relations (see column 2 of Table 12-3). Even when children chose thematically in the Novel Word condition, they seemed reluctant to justify the thematic choice with a thematic explanation (see column 3 of Table 12-3). For example, when children select a dog and a dog bone as being the same, they ordinarily justify this by saying that the dog eats the bone. However, those children who had heard the dog labeled with an unfamiliar term, yet nevertheless selected the dog bone, now justified their choice by saying that the dog and the bone were both white, for example, or refused to explain their selection. There was no such reluctance to justify thematic choices thematically when no label was given.

The hypothesis is that the presence of an unfamiliar word shifts children's attention to taxonomic relations because of an abstract constraint children place on possible word meanings, and not because they know the meaning of the word. Thus, we would like to rule out translation into a known word as accounting for the effect. Based on our results and on other research on language acquisition (e.g., Anglin, 1977; Clark, 1973b; Mervis and Rosch, 1981), it is extremely unlikely that children would translate the unfamiliar terms into superordinate level terms. Children seeing a dog and hearing the word "dax," for example, would be very unlikely to translate "dax" into "animal" or "mammal" or even "pet." If they were translating at all, they would think that "dax" meant "dog." Even when children were specifically asked to translate the novel word in the Translation condition of Experiment 2, they rarely translated it into a superordinate level term. Thus translation into a superordinate level word cannot account for the increase in taxonomic responding for children who heard the picture labeled with an unfamiliar word.

Had children been translating into a basic level term, it would have helped them to select taxonomically. When the target picture was labeled with a basic object word, children selected more taxonomically related pictures than children who heard no label (see column 1, Experiments 2 and 3 in Table 12-3). How-ever, the increase in taxonomic responding when children heard a novel word cannot be fully accounted for by translation of the novel word into a basic level word. Children's justifications provide one source of evidence that they were not simply translating the word into a basic level term. When children heard the novel words they seemed reluctant to justify their choices thematically, even in those cases where they had selected a thematically related picture. In contrast, when children heard familiar basic level words, they were happy to justify their choices in terms of thematic relationships (see columns 2 and 3 of Table 12-3). In the Basic Word condition, children heard, for example, the dog called "dog" and were told to "find another dog." When these children selected the dog and dog bone, they showed no reluctance to justify their choice by saying that the dog eats the bone. Perhaps when children heard the basic level term they tried to generalize it to other items. When they failed, the fact that the familiar term was a count noun may not have been salient enough to prevent them from claiming that it referred to a thematic relationship. In contrast, children who heard the novel word tried to figure out what it might mean. This may have heightened their awareness that a word was involved. As a consequence, children in the Novel Word condition may have felt more reluctant than children in the Basic Word condition to describe the word as referring to a thematic relation.

The most compelling evidence that translation into known terms cannot account for the results comes from the fourth study, where unfamiliar objects were used as well as unfamiliar words. Here children were shown three novel objects. They were taught a taxonomic relation for two of the objects and a thematic relation for two. When no label was used children often selected the two objects that were related thematically as being the same. When an unfamil-iar word was used to label the target picture, children now selected the two objects that were related taxonomically. Children could not have been translat-ing in this study because they did not know what these unfamiliar objects were and had no familiar labels for them. Nevertheless, the results from this study replicated the results from the studies that used familiar objects. Again, the presence of an unfamiliar meaningless word caused children to shift from select-ing objects that are thematically related to selecting objects that are taxonomi-cally related. This suggests that children have placed an abstract constraint on what words can mean that is not mediated by the meaning of known terms.

By constraining the meaning of a term to categorical relations, children are able to rule out a huge number of other potential meanings for any given term. For example, suppose an adult points to a cup and says "cup." With no constraints on possible meanings, a child would have to consider that the table might also be a "cup" because the cup was on the table, or that coffee is also called "cup" because the cup was filled with coffee, or that mother might be a "cup" because mother was lifting the cup. All of these relational meanings would be eliminated from consideration by the constraint that nouns refer to object categories. By limiting the number and kind of hypotheses that children need to consider, this constraint tremendously simplifies the problem of language learning.

ORIGINS OF SENSITIVITY TO CONSTRAINTS ON WORD MEANING

These findings raise the question of how children come to constrain their hypotheses about what a word can mean. What leads children to assume that a word is likely to refer to objects that are similar in some way rather than to objects that participate in the same event or context? There are at least two possibilities. One is that sensitivity to the constraint is innate—from the start, children assume words will refer to categories of similar objects. Having such implicit knowledge would provide children with an entry into the formidable problem of learning language. Children would at least be able to readily acquire count nouns, and once they had a reasonable vocabulary of category terms, they could then begin to comprehend other linguistic forms. In fact, the huge majority of children's first words are count nouns (Clark, 1983; Nelson, 1973; Huttenlocher, 1974).

Another possibility is that the constraint is induced from early language experience. Having learned many count nouns, almost all of which refer to objects that are taxonomically related, children may come to expect this to be true of subsequent terms they learn. If so, then this induction must take place fairly rapidly at an early point in language acquisition, since we found that even 2-year-olds believe that count nouns are more likely to refer to objects that belong to the same category than to objects that are thematically related.

It is not clear whether or not very young language learners limit the constraint to count nouns. Particularly if children have some innate knowledge of the constraint, they may at first overextend it, indiscriminately believing that any word they hear must refer to a taxonomic category. Only somewhat later might they become sensitive to form class and expect count nouns to be more likely than other classes of words to refer to categorical relations.

THE ROLE OF LANGUAGE IN AIDING CONCEPT ACQUISITION

Children's sensitivity to this constraint raises the possibility that language may help children acquire new categories. In contrast, it is often argued that words must map onto concepts that have already been worked out nonlinguistically (Clark, 1973b; Huttenlocher, 1974; Macnamara, 1972; Nelson, 1974; Wittgenstein, 1953, 1958). In this view, language plays little role in concept learning. But this view may underestimate the importance of language. Young children may create concepts to fit new words, guided by abstract constraints on word meaning. This alternative view is a mild form of linguistic determinism (Whorf, 1956), in that language is believed to shape thought. It is quite different, however, from Whorf's conception that each language imposes a particular world view on its speakers and that cognition is determined and limited by the specific language one speaks. First, all languages are likely to share similar constraints on possible meanings for count nouns. Thus, the hypothesis is that, regardless of native language, children look for categories of similar objects when they hear new nouns. Second, although nouns help focus children's attention on categorical relations, we are not arguing that children would be incapable of forming categories without exposure to language.

The small amount of research that bears on this milder form of linguistic determinism suggests that children can use abstract knowledge of the semantic correlates of form class to help them discover the concept to which a word refers. Brown (1957) found that 3- to 5-year-old children interpreted an unfamiliar count noun ("a dax") as referring to a new concrete object, whereas they interpreted an unfamiliar mass noun ("some dax") as referring to a novel undifferentiated mass. In a study by Katz, Baker, and Macnamara (1974), children as young as $1\frac{1}{2}$ years old interpreted an unfamiliar proper noun ("Dax") as referring to an individual. At the same time, these young children understood an unfamiliar count noun ("a dax") as referring to a category of similar objects.

To return to our findings, hearing a noun caused children to shift their attention from thematic to taxonomic organization. These results lead us to speculate that linguistic input may serve more generally to shape the conceptual structure of the child in the direction of greater taxonomic organization. A word may draw members of a category together for a child, highlighting their common category membership. Language may thus play a direct role in making categorical relations a salient and highly structured mode of organization.

POSSIBLE REASONS FOR TAXONOMIC ORGANIZATION OF LANGUAGE

The question arises as to why language is organized this way. Why don't words refer typically to objects that are thematically related? As we earlier pointed out, thematic relations between objects certainly are important for adults as well as for children. In naturally occurring situations, objects are not found organized by category, but rather are embedded in spatial, temporal, and causal contexts. Such relational structures as events and themes are a common way of organizing information to make sense of what we encounter (cf. Mandler, 1979; Markman, 1981).

Given that these thematic event-like organizations are a natural way of construing the world, why should languages force a taxonomic or categorical structure rather than capturing this thematic bias? Why don't we have single words for a boy and his bike, a baby and its bottle, a spider and its web? One reason may be that if nouns referred exclusively to relations such as a baby and its bottle or a boy and his bike, there would be no easy way to express hierarchical taxonomic relations. Because a taxonomy groups objects into categories nested within broader categories, it allows deductive inferences to be made that go beyond the first-hand knowledge one has about a specific object. If one knows, for example, that a particular object is an animal, one can be fairly sure that it takes in food, moves about, reproduces, and has internal organs. In contrast, knowing that something is a "dax," where "dax" could be a boy or his bike, tells one very little else about it. One reason why nouns tend not to refer to thematically related objects, then, may be because of the advantages of hierarchical organization.

Another more important reason may be that if a language had single nouns refer exclusively to pairs of thematically related objects, it would be at great cost. The enormous expressive power of language would be lost. The expressive power of language derives from its ability to convey new relations through combinations of words. There are a potentially infinite number of thematic relations that one might want to express. The many thematic relations can easily be described through combinations of words—e.g., sentences and phrases. If single words referred only to thematic relations, however, there would be an extraordinary proliferation of words, probably more than humans could learn. One would need separate words for a baby and its bottle, a baby and its crib, a baby and its mother, a baby and its diaper, etc. Thus, the combinatorial power of language would be wasted. This, then, may be the major reason why nouns refer primarily to taxonomic categories rather than to thematically related objects.

13

Lila R. Gleitman
Biological Dispositions to Learn Language

Language learning clearly is an outcome of specific exposure conditions, but just as clearly requires specific biological adaptations. There is no controversy about this claim as stated, for it is obvious to the point of banality. To believe that special biological adaptations are a requirement, it is enough to notice that all the children but none of the dogs and cats in the house acquire language. To believe that language is nevertheless learned, it is sufficient to note the massive correlation between living in France and learning French, and living in Germany and learning German. Controversy does arise, however, on the issue of whether language knowledge is based on a specific and segregated mental faculty, or instead utilizes the same machinery in the head that is implicated in the acquisition of all complex cognitive functions. Many linguistic theories postulate not only a distinct mental representation or faculty of language (a "language organ," in Chomsky's wording, functioning as autonomously as, say, the liver), but a highly modularized system internal to language itself (Chomsky, 1981). Proponents of such positions expect that language learning will be largely maturationally determined, that the maturation functions may be quite separate from those in other cognitive domains, and that different modules within the language system may mature quasi-independently. In clear contrast, most developmental psycholinguists hold that language acquisition is best described by a global learning procedure that is responsible for the acquisition of, say, knitting, arithmetic, and ancient history as well as, English (e.g., Slobin, 1973; Bever, 1982). They expect that the unfolding of language will be jointly dependent on specific opportunities to receive relevant data and on cognitive development.

Rudimentary current evidence about learning is insufficient to adjudicate these distinct claims about how biology and experience interact to produce language knowledge. Exacerbating these difficulties, there are at present many contending descriptions of grammar—of what is finally learned. Given disagreements on *what* is learned, it is hard to devise an adequate description of *how* it is learned (see Wexler and Culicover, 1980, and Pinker, 1982, for quite disparate formal models of a learning procedure based on correspondingly disparate conjectures about the grammar that is attained). But in my view, the presently available evidence tips the balance of plausibility toward a biologically preprogrammed learning procedure specific to language.

In the present discussion, I first present a schematic description of the language-learning task, followed by a sketch of the kinds of argument often put forward in favor of significant and relatively autonomous biological preprogramming suppporting that learning. Thereafter, I summarize the kinds of investigation that are being carried out by our own group of investigators.

Analysis of the Language Learning Problem

Chomsky (1965) and other investigators (Pinker, 1979; Wexler and Culicover, 1980) have provided a schematic analysis of language learning; roughly, it looks like this:

1. The learner receives some sample utterances from the language.
2. The learner simultaneously observes situations: objects, scenes, and events in the world.
3. These utterance/situation pairs constitute the input to language learning.
4. The learner's job is to project from these sample utterance/situation pairs a system, or grammar, that encompasses all sentence/meaning pairs in the language. This job includes, of course, learning the meanings and forms of words, for these affect the meanings of sentences. But it also includes learning the syntactic structures, for these affect the meaning of sentences even when the component words are held constant (i.e., *Caesar killed Brutus* and *Brutus killed Caesar* mean different things).
5. For learning to proceed, the learner must have some means for representing the utterances and the situations to himself in a linguistically relevant way. For example, though the learner receives utterances in the form of continuously varying sound waves, he must be disposed to represent these as sequences of discrete formatives such as phone, syllable, word, phrase, and sentence. And though he receives impressions of some single object, he must be disposed to represent it in various ways, such as "Fido," "dog," "mammal," "physical object," and not in other ways, such as "undetached dog-parts."

6. The learner must also have some strategies for manipulating these data in the interest of extracting the regularities that bind them.

7. The learner must have some perspective on the kinds of descriptive devices, or rule systems, that he is willing to countenance as statements of the regularities. To put this another way, different language-learning "machines" (particular representational systems, with particular computational procedures) will construct different grammars, based on the same data.

8. Finally, the learner must have some criterion that will lead him to stabilize on a particular conjecture about the grammar, to decide once and for all that his learning job is completed.

As presented, this analysis is neutral about many issues. For example, it is possible that tutors are required for some of these steps to be taken successfully. Perhaps the learner requires the caretakers to say only very simple sentences, or sentences of restricted kinds, early in the learning period; and perhaps the learner requires reinforcement for correct performances and correction of errors he makes along the way. Depending on whether these additional conditions are met, quite different kinds of machines will be able to learn a human language. Therefore it is of some interest to examine the real input circumstances of children and the early generalizations they draw from these inputs. This may help to disentangle the kinds of internal and external resources learners recruit to crack the language code.

A Significant Innate Basis for Language Learning

Three main kinds of argument favor the supposition that language and its learning are biologically preprogrammed. The first two derive from empirical study of learning: (1) language learning proceeds in uniform ways within and across linguistic communities, in spite of extensive variability of the input provided to individuals, and (2) the character of what is learned is not simply related to the input sample. A third argument is logical: (3) the child acquires many linguistic generalizations that experience could not have made available.

UNIFORM LEARNING

Inquiry into language learning is constrained by one main principle. The right theory has to cope with the fact that everybody does it, by specifying a learning device guaranteed to converge on the grammar of any language to which it is exposed, in finite time, and in fair indifference to particulars of the sample data received (Wexler, 1982). This principle is based on the real facts of the matter. Under widely varying environmental circumstances, learning different languages under different conditions of culture and child rearing, and with different motivations and talents, all nonpathological children acquire their native tongue at a high level of proficiency within a narrow developmental time frame. (This does not mean there are no differences in final attainment, but these differences pale into insignificance when compared with the samenesses.)

Moreover, there are very interesting similarities in the course this learning takes. Isolated words appear at about age 1, followed by two-word utterances at about age 2. Thereafter, sometime during the third year of life, there is a sudden spurt of vocabulary growth accompanied, coincidentally or not, by elaboration of the sentence structures. By about 4 years of age the speaker sounds essentially adult, though his sentences tend to be quite short because the use of embeddings is limited, and though some item-specific information continues to come in about through age 8 or 9. (By item-specific information I have reference particularly to some features of derivational morphology, and significant growth of vocabulary.)

Summarizing, similarities in the pattern of learning are observed across individuals and across linguistic communities. Lenneberg (1967) was perhaps the first to argue that these uniformities in course of learning, in spite of differences in experience, are a beginning indicant that language learning has a significant biological basis. He provided some normative evidence that the achievement of basic milestones in language learning is predictable from the child's age and seems to be intercalated quite closely to developments that are known on other grounds to be maturationally dependent (e.g., sitting, standing, walking, and jumping). Other findings were used by Lenneberg to argue that there is a sensitive (or critical) period for language learning. For example, foreign accents are typical in adult learners but not child learners of second languages, even when time of exposure and use are equated. Downs Syndrome individuals that he studied seemed to acquire language in the same way as normals, only slower; and their learning seemed to stop at about puberty whatever their current competence with the language. Finally, Lenneberg maintained that recovery from brain injury that implicates language is likely in children but rare in adults. On such evidence, he conjectured that the capacity for language learning tends to whither away as the brain matures.

Not all of Lenneberg's findings have withstood subsequent review too well, however. For example, in later discussion I will present a rather different picture of learning in Downs Syndrome individuals. Moreover, the results about the course of learning (from Lenneberg and others) are so fragmentary as to be consistent with quite distinct conjectures about the processes that underlie this learning: although there are gross similarities among children whose age is the same, there may be detailed distinctions among them consequent on distinctions in their exposure conditions. Certainly that is true for specific vocabulary learning, and who is to say, and on what grounds, that this detail is "unimportant"? Symmetrically, the differences in environment may have been overestimated.

Indeed, no two mothers will say exactly the same sentences to their offspring. But still the set of input utterances may be constrained in various ways (they may be especially "simple" sentences) and they may be presented under special conditions (e.g., accompanied by corrections or relevant didactic comments, said only in the presence of "easily interpretable events," etc.). Under these improved conditions, perhaps any open-minded all-purpose inductive device would generate the same uniformities in the course of learning as are observed for young children acquiring their native tongue. However, as I will now try to show, closer inspection of patterns of development gives more weight to the view that special dispositions in the learner are guiding language acquisition.

CHARACTER OF LEARNING; DISPARITIES BETWEEEN INPUT AND OUTPUT

The character of language knowledge at various developmental moments is hard to reconcile with the superficial properties of the input data. To be sure, the child learns from what he hears. But he does not directly copy these heard sentences, but makes systematic errors. These errors can be understood, but only by claiming the learner filters the input data through an emerging system of rules of grammar, to which he is never directly exposed.

Noncanonical Sentences In; Canonical Sentences Out

Some convincing examples were developed by Bellugi (1967). One of her cases concerned interrogative structures. In simple sentences of English, auxiliary verbs appear after the subject noun phrase but before the verb (e.g., *I can eat pizza*). But in yes–no questions, the auxiliary precedes the subject (e.g., *Can I eat pizza?*). And in so-called *wh* questions, this subject/auxiliary inversion appears again (e.g., *What can I eat?*), this time without the object noun phrase (*pizza*) and with an initial "*wh* word" (e.g., *what* or *when* or *who*) instead. The learner of English is exposed by his caretakers to many such *wh* questions (about 10% of all the utterances he hears, according to the estimate of Newport, 1977). Nevertheless, young learners generally do not reproduce these forms that they hear so often. Instead they produce a form that is virtually never spoken by adults, namely, *What I can eat?* or sometimes even *What can I can eat?* A related finding, also from Bellugi (1967), is that, while over 90% of maternal auxiliaries in declaratives are contracted (e.g., *We'll go out now*), the child uses only the uncontracted forms early in the learning period (*We will go out now*). In light of such findings, the sense in which the child is learning the language from the presented environment of utterances is evidently quite abstract.

    There is a generalization that predicts these errors, as Bellugi pointed out: The child is biased toward "canonical" surface structure formats for his utterances (see also Gleitman and Wanner, 1982; Slobin and Bever, 1982). In the canonical declarative sentence of English, the subject does precede the whole verb phrase, including its auxiliary. An abstract movement transformation reorders these elements in questions.* If it is supposed that the child acquires formation rules that underlie the declarative first and countenances movement rules only later, this particular error is predictable. Similarly, it is possible to suppose that only the full canonical forms (*will*) of words like *'ll* are entered into the learner's mental lexicon. Contraction is achieved by a rule that operates on these abstract lexical representations under restricted circumstances. (For further discussion, see the section on "Language Knowledge" below.) In sum, it is certainly possible to explain why the young child does not behave exactly like his models, who contract and invert. To explain this, one can invoke a bias toward canonical forms in the language being learned. But this, in turn, implies that the young learner has an ability to reconstruct the canonical forms for questions and for words such as *'ll*. These canonical forms are related to the utterances he actually hears, but only by covert rules. Considering the tender age of the language-learning humans who apparently can perform the complex data manipulations required to recover these rules—quite effortlessly and unconsciously—it is likely that significant biological dispositions are guiding their analyses.

Open Class/Closed Class

An even more general disparity between input and output, as Brown (1973), Gleitman and Wanner (1982), and many others have discussed, has to do with the differential pattern of acquisition of the so-called open class and closed class stock of morphological items (usually called *content* and *functor* words by psychologists) . . . It has been known for some time that there are lexical categories that admit new members freely: new verbs, nouns, and adjectives are being created by language users every day (hence "open class"). Other lexical categories change their membership only very slowly over historical time (hence "closed class"). The closed class includes the "little" words and affixes, the conjunctions, prepositions, inflectional and derivational suffixes, relativizers, and verbal auxiliaries. These examples given, it is obvious that the closed class and open class morphemes are different in many ways. The closed class items are restricted in semantic content (nobody's name is a preposition) and in syntactic function (as follows from the fact, stated above, that they belong to only certain lexical classes). They differ phonologically as well: closed class morphemes are in most usages unstressed, some are subsyllabic, and many more become subsyllabic by contraction (e.g., *will* contracts to *'ll*).

Perhaps the most striking fact about early speech and the context in which it is learned is that open class and closed class materials are made available to the learner simultaneously, but these subcomponents of the morphological stock are incorporated into the child's speech at different developmental moments. The mother's speech consists of simple sentences like "The book is on the table,"

---

*Footnote omitted. [Eds.]

including the closed class items *the*, *is*, and *on*. But there is a well-known stage of language learning, the so-called two-word or telegraphic stage, at which the output is "Book table," with all the closed class items omitted. Thus, the most primitive learners seem to have certain devices that allow them to filter out the closed class.

It is not obvious how to explain these developing speech patterns without begging the questions of language learning. For example, even if it were possible to say that the omitted items were the meaningless ones, which it emphatically is not, one would not want to claim that the child examines the semantics of closed class words and, on the basis of this, decides to omit them all. This would beg the question at issue: how the semantics of such items are arrived at in the first place. The same for a claim based on the syntactic functioning of closed class items. Gleitman and Wanner (1982, 1984) conjectured that it is the special phonology of the closed class items that renders them opaque to youngest learners—they are subsyllabic items or unstressed syllables. Differential attention to the unit *stressed syllable* in the incoming speech wave represents, we believe, one of the significant biases of young learners.* Because of the child's selective attention to stressed syllables, the pattern of acquisition does not mirror the environment directly, but mirrors the environment only as it is mediated by these preexisting biases as to how to represent the sound wave. (See Fernald, 1984, for a full discussion of acoustic-perceptual dispositions in infants, and the position that the filtering effect of these predispositions plays a role in language learning) . . .

Lexical Selections and Argument Roles

So far I have noted learning biases of the child in the syntactic and morphophonological domains that act to predict a difference between what goes into the child's ear and what first comes out of his mouth. The case for lexical category acquisition is just as clear. Evidently, a learner hears verbs and adjectives as well as nouns early in life. But the child's earliest words are overwhelmingly nouns that encode simple concrete objects; verbs that encode activities tend to appear later, and verbs that encode mental states later still; finally, adjectives that encode properties of things are later than all these others (e.g., Nelson, 1973; Gentner, 1982; Feldman, Goldin–Meadow, and Gleitman, 1978). Similarly, certain syntactically rather than lexically encoded semantic-relational categories (e.g., "agent of the action," for example, *John* in *John eats peas*) uniformly appear early and others (e.g., "instrument of the action," for example, *knife* in *John eats peas with a knife*) are uniformly found later, again although instances of all of them appear in the child's database—his mother's speech—from the beginning (Bloom, Lightbown and Hood, 1975).

In sum, the child is clearly learning from what he hears (English from English, French from French), but the detailed properties of the development

---

*Footnote omitted. [Eds.]

are hard to describe as arising very simply or directly from the environment of heard utterances. Likely, global aspects of cognitive development will account for many of these learning patterns: the fact that there is attention to concrete objects and physical activities before mental states and properties is unlikely to have specifically linguistic sources. But the morphophonemic and syntactic choices of novice language learners are less likely to be explained as deriving from general properties of cognitive development.

LANGUAGE KNOWLEDGE THAT EXPERIENCE
COULD NOT PROVIDE

Another kind of argument for innate language-learning capacities comes from logical analyses by Chomsky (1975). This has to do with the learning of certain language properties that experience could hardly have made available. Taking one of his examples, a distinction between higher and lower clause in a phrase structure configuration determines certain properties of movement transformations and of the reference of pronouns. (The characterization of the linguistic facts are perforce rough in this discussion, but will have to do for a sketch.) Specifically, consider again the movement of certain materials in English yes–no questions. In the sentence *Is the man a fool?*, the *is* has moved to the left from its canonical position in declarative sentences, *The man is a fool.* But can any *is* in a declarative sentence be moved to form a yes–no question? It is impossible to judge from one-clause sentences alone. The issue is resolved by looking at more complex sentences that contain more than one clause: It is the *is* in the higher clause, never the *is* in the lower clause, that moves to form yes–no questions from structures underlying, e.g., *The man who is a fool is amusing* and *The man is a fool who is amusing.* This generalization explains the acceptability of yes–no questions such as *Is the man who is a fool amusing?* and *Is the man a fool who is amusing?* but the absence of *Is the man who a fool is amusing?* and *Is the man is a fool who amusing?* Whether *is* moves depends on its structural position in the sentence.

Notice that an alternative analysis, namely serial position of the two *is*'s in the string of words, as opposed to structural position of the two *is*'s in a clause hierarchy, could not explain the facts about English structure: in the examples just given, the moving *is* was once the first *is* in the sentence, but once the second. Learners apparently know that movement rules are structure dependent, not simply serial-order dependent. To my knowledge, no child ever makes the mistake of saying "Is the man is a fool who amusing?" The important point here is that it is hard to conceive how the environment literally gives the required information to the learner. Surely only the correct sentences, not the incorrect ones, appear in the input data. But the generalization required for producing new correct sentences is not directly presented, for no hierarchy of clauses appears in real utterances—only a string of words is directly observable to the listener. And certainly there is no instruction about clauses. Even if mothers knew something explicit about these matters, which they do not, it would not do much good for them to tell the aspiring learners that "It's the *is* in the higher clause that moves."

Many generalizations about sentence form turn on the same or related configural distinctions (though again the characterization being used here is rough and underestimates the complexity of the descriptive facts). To give one more example, coreference is possible when the pronoun precedes its antecedent but only if the pronoun is in a lower clause than the antecedent. For example, the man mentioned in the second clause could be the one who arrived in the sentence *When he arrived, the man danced* but not in the sentence *He arrived when the man danced*. Even in these hard cases where the pronoun precedes its potential antecedent, learners come to interpret coreference correctly, without special tutoring, and without an opportunity directly to experience the hierarchical structures. *

Summarizing, it is hard to imagine how the environment instructs the learner that not serial order simply, but the hierarchical arrangement of clauses, determines properties of sentences and their interpretations. Yet errors on these properties are so rare that no one, to my knowledge, has so far succeeded in observing one made by a child. In short, errorless learning of structural properties of the language not transparently offered to experience—the poverty of the stimulus information—forms still another sort of argument that learning biases, this time biases in the formation and interpretation of configural structures underlying sentences, are required as explanations of how language organization is achieved by the child.

The Deprivation Paradigm

During the last several years, my associates and I have looked at some natural cases in which some of the components of the language-learning situation are varied. We have operated by taking to heart the view that utterance/situation pairs are required input to language learning, as described in the schema for learning with which I began. Therefore we have looked at situations in which this information is changed. Certain populations of learners allow us to see what happens if there is less or different information about the utterances; other populations allow us to see what happens if there is less or different information about the world. Symmetrically, certain populations are exposed to normal input data but differ from the normal in their current or final mental state. In these latter cases, we are asking what happens when different learning devices are exposed to the same data.

*Section on null elements omitted. [Eds.]

VARYING THE LANGUAGE SAMPLES

There seems to be quite general agreement that a learner exposed to random samples of the sentences of a language would be unable to converge on the grammar. The main difficulty is the richness of the incoming data, which would seem to support so bewildering a variety of generalizations, including wrong and irrelevant ones, that we would expect learners to vary extremely in the time at which they hit on the grammar of their language. It is usually assumed, following findings from Brown and Hanlon (1970), that negative feedback, or correction, from the environment cannot be relied on to solve this problem. This is not so much that feedback for ungrammaticalness is never given, although Brown and Hanlon have shown it is rare. The main problem is that for a variety of structures and contents—such as those described in the preceding section—the child never errs in the first place so no opportunity to correct him, or to describe his learning as a consequence of such correction, arises. Another problem, as Brown and Hanlon showed, is that correction is given very often for matters other than grammaticalness of the child's utterances, for example, their truth or moral propriety. Should the child construe all corrections, then, as grammatical corrections, he might falsely conclude that *ink-on-the-wall* is an outlawed phrase, rather than an outlawed act. In light of these difficulties, most investigators assume that language learning is on positive examples only. Formally speaking, it is a lot easier to develop a mechanical procedure for learning from presented sample utterances if it is assumed that that procedure receives negative feedback when it makes a false generalization, i.e., if it is told that some new sentence it tries out is not a correct sentence of the language being learned (for that demonstration, see Gold, 1967). Hence some proposals have considered whether restrictions or simplifications of sentences presented to novices can substitute for overt corrections.

Effects of Maternal Simplification: The Motherese Hypothesis

The paradox so far is that language learning is hard to describe given positive data only (a sample of the correct sentences) and yet all the real learners seem to do very well even though they receive only, or almost only, such positive data. A very popular response to this problem among developmental psycholinguists has been to suppose the environment provides detailed support for learning by ordering the input utterances (see the collection of articles edited by Snow and Ferguson, 1977, for many papers adopting this position). We have called this "the Motherese Hypothesis." It holds that caretakers present linguistic information in a set sequence, essentially smallest sentences to littlest ears. And in fact there is no doubt that adults speak quite differently to children than to adults, so the utterances heard by the children are not random selections from the adult language. The utterances to youngest learners are very short, slow in rate, and the like. Some investigators propose that this natural simplification from caretakers (whatever its source of motivation) plays a causal role in learning. Evidence favoring this hypothesis comes from Fernald (1984), who has shown that infants prefer to listen to the prosodically exaggerated forms of Motherese, which is used in every known culture: apparently, as Fernald states, Motherese is "sweet music to the species." Gleitman and Wanner have proposed that these exaggerated prosodic cues can help an appropriately preprogrammed learner to reconstruct a global parse of the input sentences, a reconstruction that materially simplifies subsequent steps in the language-learning task.

But evidently there are limits on the work that Motherese can do for the learner. Particularly it is hard to maintain the view that the preselection of syntactic types by caretakers can bear materially on the acquisition of grammar. Though restricting the sentence types may exclude certain hypotheses from being considered early, it may also make available hypotheses that would be insupportable given the full range of the language structures. As I described in the preceding section, the child would be unable to distinguish the "string movement" hypothesis from the "structure movement" hypothesis if all the input sentences were uniclausal (for discussion see Chomsky, 1975, and Wexler and Culicover, 1980); if more complex sentences are offered, the string movement hypothesis fails on data. However, there is at least some surface plausibility to the idea that the mother first teaches the child some easy structures. After he learns these, she moves on to the next lesson. To help this idea go through, we would have to grant the caretaker some implicit metric of syntactic/semantic complexity so that in principle she could choose judiciously the sentences that might be good to say to learners. Here too there are some initial supportive findings: caretakers' speech changes to some degree, in correspondence with the learner's age (Newport, 1977).

In our studies of the Motherese hypothesis (Newport, Gleitman, and Gleitman, 1977), we first collected extensive samples of maternal speech to young learners (age range 15 to 27 months). Rather to our surprise, the properties of this speech did not seem promising as aids to learning syntactic forms. The mothers' speech forms were only rarely (less than 10% of the time) canonical sentences, and they were neither uniform syntactically, nor more explicit in how they mapped onto the meanings, than the sentences used among adults. They *were* short and clear, but this hardly suggests anything very specific about how they reveal the syntax of the language. But it is still possible that some less obvious properties of maternal speech are especially useful to learners. To study this, we revisited the original mother–child pairs 6 months after the first measurement. Analyzing the child's speech at these two times, we were in a position to compute growth scores for each child on many linguistic dimensions. The question was which properties of the mother's speech at time one had predicted the child's rate of growth on each measure, explaining his status at time two. (The correlational analysis used a partialling procedure that removed baseline differences among the learners.)

One interesting outcome of these studies was that a number of dimensions of learning rate were utterly indifferent to large differences in the speech pattern of the mothers. For example, the child's increasing tendency to express predicates (as verbs) and their obligatory arguments (as nouns) was not predictable from the particular speech forms presented. In contrast, in the age range studied, the child's progress with the closed class morphology was a rather strict function of maternal speech style. For example, almost all the variance in rate of learning the English auxiliary verbs is predicted by the preponderance of yes–no questions in maternal speech (for a replication of this finding, see Furrow et al., 1979). The effect of these is to place the closed class items in first serial position, with stress and without contraction (e.g., *Will you pass the salt?* rather than *You will pass the salt, You'll pass the salt,* or *'Ll you pass the salt?*). Thus either, or both, positional biases or biases toward stressed syllables (as conjectured by Gleitman and Wanner) can be postulated for the child; and mothers whose usage gets through these child filters have children who learn the closed class materials the faster.

Recall from the earlier discussion, however, that these environmental factors do not say much about *what* is learned. For one thing, as just stated, no known special properties of Motherese explain the learning patterns for open class materials or their organization in the child's sentences. Further, the evidence is clear that children first learn to say declaratives with auxiliaries in *medial unstressed* position even though the environment favoring learning how to do so is hearing those auxiliaries in *initial stressed* position.

In sum, certain universal properties of natural languages (e.g., expressing the predicates and arguments of propositions) seem to emerge in the child at maturationally fixed moments, and are insensitive to the naturally occurring variation among mothers. But elements and functions of the closed class, for children in this age range, seem to be closely affected by specifiable facts about the input. Even here, however, the environment exerts its influence only as the information it provides is filtered through the child's learning biases. For example the serial position, but not the frequency, of maternal auxiliary use affected the learning rate (for a general discussion of the Motherese hypothesis and its limitations, see Gleitman, Newport, and Gleitman, 1984).

Unfortunately, while these studies preclude certain strong forms of the Motherese hypothesis, they leave almost everything unresolved. First, the limited effects of environment on language learning that we found may be attributable to threshold effects of various sorts, to the attenuated sample, or to the measures or analyses used. These complaints are fair even though they lose some force given the positive findings for the closed class component. Nonetheless, there was clear impetus for looking at cases in which the child's environment was more radically altered.

The Creation of Language: Isolated Deaf Children

We therefore next studied a population grossly deprived of formal linguistic stimulation (Feldman et al., 1978). These were six deaf children of hearing parents who had decided to educate their children orally, by having them taught to vocalize and lip read. Accordingly, in advance of the planned training period, the parents made no attempt to teach a manual language. More important, these parents did not *know* a manual language, so they were not in a position to present the easiest sentences first, the harder ones later. It has been observed that children in these circumstances develop an informal system of communicative gestures, called "home sign." It was the genesis of this system that we wished to study. Though many questions arise about how precisely we could analyze this exotic communication system, it is fair to say that the interpretive puzzles we faced are not materially different from those confounding the study of 2- and 3-year-old English speakers by adult English-speaking psycholinguists. In each case, one has to try to interpret the child's messages relying heavily on their real-world context of use (cf., Bloom, 1970). In doing so, one encounters the same perils and pitfalls as the language learner himself. We settled for using the methods traditionally employed in studying normal language learning. And we achieved about the same results, for early stages.

These linguistic isolates began to make single gestures (invented by themselves) at the same developmental moment that hearing learners of English speak one word at a time. Two- and three-sign sequences, encoding the same semantic relational roles, appeared at the same age as hearing learners speak in two- and three-word sentences. To the (rough) extent that the words in these primitive sentences are serially ordered by young hearing learners according to these semantic roles, similar serial ordering of the same categories described the self-generated gesture system. It seems then that even if the environment provides no sample sentences, the child has the internal wherewithal to invent forms himself, to render the same meanings.

These results become more interesting when compared to the findings mentioned earlier, concerning the hearing learners. To the degree that the propositional forms and meanings appeared in indifference to variations in maternal input, these same properties appeared at the same time in the deaf learners, exposed to no formal language input. The closed class subcomponent, responsive at this stage to variations in maternal input, did not appear at all in the signing of the isolated youngsters. The first suggestion here is that the closed class is laid down later, and in a different developmental pattern than other properties of the language system, an argument I made earlier based on quite different observational evidence (see the section on "Significant Innate Basis for Language Learning" above). The second suggestion is that the one subcomponent of the language system is more environmentally dependent than the other, and may not appear in some exposure conditions. *

VARYING THE INTERPRETIVE INFORMATION

There is more to the child's input than a sample of utterances—presumably it would be impossible to learn language just from listening to the radio. Specifically, in the logic sketched earlier, it was asserted—in agreement with most

---

*Section on creolization omitted. [Eds.]

investigators, whatever their theoretical persuasions—that the child requires a real world context that accompanies the speech events: some situation that he can interpret. In fact, many investigators assert that there is little mystery left in the language-learning feat once it has been acknowledged that the child can interpret the extralinguistic world meaningfully (e.g., Bates and MacWhinney, 1982). However, it is not so easy to state just how "relying on meaning" *succeeds* in helping a child learn language.

One difficulty is that every object in the world can be described by many different kinds of words, a fact I alluded to earlier: the same object out there can be called *Felix*, a *cat*, a *mammal*, etc. On seeing the object then, the child still has a problem in determining the intended meaning of a word used to refer to it (the analysis of "basic level categories," e.g., Rosch et al., 1976, is sure to be of use in approaching such problems but the fact is that children finally acquire superordinate and subordinate terms as well as basic terms). Similarly, any given scene or event in the world can be described by many different sentences. For instance, scenes suitable to *The cat is on the mat* are just as suitable to *The mat is under the cat* and *Get that damn cat off the new mat*. Thus there is a considerable distance between meaningfully interpreting a scene and catching just how a heard sentence relates to it. To maintain the position that the scene helps the child learn, it will be necessary to provide the natural (perceptual and/or cognitive) analysis of the world that biases the learner to see cats-on-mats, not mats-under-cats, plus a conspiratorial agreement between mother and child such that the mother refer to scenes only in ways that match these biases, whatever they will turn out to be (for very useful discussions of the relations between language and perception, see Miller and Johnson-Laird, 1976, and Jackendoff, 1984). In addition, there will have to be a further conspiracy for marking specially any other intents for, after all, the grammar that is ultimately learned has to allow for the saying and comprehension of *mat-under-cat*.

A related problem has to do with how the utterance is to be analyzed, even assuming that the coconspirators have figured out how to be united on the interpretation. For example, suppose the mother says "Rabbit jumps" when the learner can see a rabbit jumping. And suppose, with Pinker (1982), that the child believes things are to be the nouns and actions are to be the verbs. Even in these very favorable circumstances there seem to be at least two choices the learner can make. He can suppose English is a noun or subject-first language, in which case *rabbit* is the required noun; or he can suppose English is a verb or predicate-first language, in which case *rabbit* is the required verb. Given all this, it's hard to know how the child gets started.

Summarizing once again, all parties agree that language is learned in partial dependence on the real scenes that are there to be interpreted in the world. However, to my knowledge, nobody has succeeded in providing the required cognitive-perceptual analysis of how scenes are to be interpreted against heard utterances.

Our approach (Landau, 1982; Landau and Gleitman, 1985) to these problems has been to look once more at differing environments in which language is learned. In the studies I have mentioned, the learner was in some ways deprived of information about language forms. What happens if the child is deprived of some opportunities to interpret heard utterances against the world of objects and events? Surely, a blind learner suffers some such deprivations. Though he can hear, and touch objects, so can a sighted learner. A claim in the literature (Bruner, 1975a) is that a child learns which words refer to what—and hence their meanings—because, as he listens, he follows his mother's gaze and pointing gestures. Even supposing (falsely) that the mother of a blind child names objects only when the child is holding them, in what sense could this be equivalent to gazing and pointing, in directing reference making?

In the light of these limitations on the blind learners' opportunities to discern the referents of many heard words and sentences, we have been surprised to discover that blindness hardly delays language onset; moreover, after the first few words are said, the pattern of linguistic development is virtually identical for sighted children and for neurologically intact blind children. This includes both the development of a lexicon, used appropriately to map onto the world, and the development of syntactic structure and the semantic/relational categories this describes. Apparently, receiving different, and less, interpretive information has no dramatic effect on overall acquisition rate or the character of that learning.

Some details of the blind child's learning are quite interesting. We expected to find the largest differences between blind and sighted children in acquiring the visual vocabulary, words like *look* and *see*, for here the information base is maximally different from the normal. However, blind children seem to use these words as early as do sighted children. In the education literature, such uses are called *verbalism*, often said to be detrimental to the child, who should be discouraged from use of the sighted vocabulary lest he fall victim to "loose thinking." But, on the contrary, the meanings a blind child comes up with seem quite appropriate, though of course they map onto a different sensory world . . .

Our conclusion in the investigations of the blind is that these children recruit several sources of information that jointly can be informative about which verb has which meaning. A contribution is made by the situational factors (e.g., *look* but not *get* or *come* is usually used when a target object is near by). But a separate contribution is made by examining the constraints on the syntactic forms in which the different verbs participate. Space forbids reproducing a full description here. But as an example, notice that *give* is a verb that takes three noun phrases, the first of which expresses the agent of the action (e.g., *John gives Mary the ball*). But *look*, an inalienable perceptual activity, can express no agent (i.e., it is semantically incoherent and syntactically anomalous to say *John looks Mary the ball*). We take the position that a child disposed by nature to analyze these syntactic formats can extract and differentiate the verb meanings, whereas a learner dependent on observation of linguistic circumstances alone has an insufficient basis for making these inductions. Considering the intricacy of the syntactic analyses required even of blind toddlers, we take their success as another argument for significant biological support of language learning.

VARYING THE ENDOWMENT OF THE LEARNER

The literature just sketched is consistent with a maturationally driven acquisition process, heavily dependent on specific linguistic and perceptual representations, with progress relatively independent of exposure time or type. If this position is correct, then organisms differently endowed should not be able to learn under anything like the same exposure conditions. For cats and dogs, however, there are many arguments much weaker than their lack of a "language faculty" that will serve to explain why they do not learn English. The case has been made more interestingly for primates by Premack and Premack (1983), for they have shown that chimpanzees have certain general conceptual wherewithal in common with humans: but that still does not allow them to function with syntactic categories like those of a human language. My colleagues and I have begun to look at special human populations to pursue this kind of issue.

Language Learning in Downs Syndrome (DS) Retardates

Fowler (1981) first examined the linguistic functioning of a small group of Downs Syndrome adolescents who for 3 years had shown no further linguistic development (had arrived at some steady final state). They were selected for homogeneity on several measures of cognitive function (e.g., mental age, about 6 years) and an anchor measure of language function (mean length of utterance, MLU, 3.0 to 3.5). This is the level usually achieved by normals between ages 2 and 3. It is important to note that these individuals differ extensively from one another in other aspects of cognitive functioning, for example, some of them were vastly better than others at primitive arithmetic, but this did not predict differences among them in language skill. Not only their gross language level as assessed by MLU, but also the internal properties of their language knowledge, as assessed by a variety of standard instruments used by developmental psycholinguists, were found to be the same as that of $2\frac{1}{2}$ year old normal controls. The similarity in the course and character of early language learning between normal and DS children has also been found by many others (e.g., Lenneberg, 1967; Lackner, 1976). Hence it looks as if DS individuals may be a diminished case of the normal endowment. (In contrast, non-DS retardates we have studied differ both from the DS individuals and from each other in linguistic developmental patterning, making them a less likely group to study for the present questions.)

The important issue to Fowler, Gelman, and Gleitman had to do with the course of language development in the DS population, and so we instituted a longitudinal study of individuals whose IQ was about the same as the original adolescent group. This study is still underway, and the number of subjects is very small, but a few generalizations are already apparent, particularly from the detailed case history of an individual, "Jenny," whose learning has so far been studied for about 3 years. These individuals began to speak very late, at about 5 years of age. But once language was manifest at all in Jenny, her rate of growth was normal for some succeeding time. Correcting for the onset-time difference, she traversed Roger Brown's (1973) first four stages of language learning in the same absolute period of time required by normals. The internal structure of the knowledge at each interim measurement was virtually identical to that of much younger normals traversing the same stages. However, at this point (MLU about 3.5) Jenny's learning came to a halt. Perhaps the halt is permanent: it has extended 14 months so far, but we have to wait to see if learning starts up once more. The same halt in progress, extending for more than a year subsequent to observed growth—and at chronological ages as young as 7 or 8 years—has been observed for other subjects being studied, but it remains to be shown whether these apparent halt points will turn out to be coherent—as they seem to be for Jenny—with specifiable stages in the normal growth of language. The adolescent population mentioned above suggests, however, that at least some DS individuals at this IQ level reach just the ceiling of attainment that characterizes Jenny's steady state (equivalent to that of 2-year-old normals) and then learn no more.

Summarizing, the interest of the longitudinal findings has to do with two main points: (1) learning is not slow, but at normal pace, until some ceiling is achieved, often at a point very early in life, and (2) the character of knowledge is the same as for normals at the same stage of language development. The progress of the DS individuals, limited as it is, suggests to us that a very low-level, automatic process is at work to determine the rockbottom aspects of linguistic function.*

Conclusions

I have tried to describe some of the complex facts about language learning that I suppose are at least within calling distance of an explanation just in case there are task-specific, biologically given predispositions in humans to support them. I know of no extant learning theory specific enough in its claims about the human representational system and learning strategies to explain these same facts, and to subsume as well learning and knowledge of other human cognitive systems. Possibly, such a global learning theory can be developed and can be successful. Until or unless such a theory is developed, such language-specific learning devices as proposed, for example, by Wexler and Culicover (1980), are the closest thing we have to an account of how language is acquired. I myself therefore do not take Chomsky's postulation of an autonomous "language faculty" with principles of learning all its own as an approach that makes extravagant claims on fragmentary evidence. On the contrary, I take that claim as repesenting appropri-

*Section on "Other Populations" omitted. [Eds.]

ate scientific modesty given the state of the art in describing *either* language or its learning. At their best, schematic models offered by linguists and learnability theorists go some small way toward describing the awesomely complex facts about the learning of human language. They go no distance whatsoever in describing "all learning" or "all human knowledge." Therefore, at present, they are best interpreted as interim descriptions of language, and nothing else. It will be a victory for psychology, but one I scarcely anticipate in the near future (say, within a millenium), if that task-specific view turns out to be too modest after all.

III

SOCIAL AND PRIVATE
SPEECH

In *The Language and Thought of the Child*, Piaget (1926) opened contemporary debate on the relation between sociality and the forms of speech in young children. He classified samples of children's talk in terms of communicative function and found it to be predominantly asocial or "egocentric," in that children do not adopt the perspective of the addressee in their talk. After the age of 7, children are increasingly oriented toward communication with others, and their speech becomes "socialized" as they aim to make themselves understood and to ask and answer genuine questions. Children's concern with effective communication parallels and facilitates the development of forms of speech that make successful communication possible. The shift from relatively egocentric to more socialized uses of speech occurs, according to Piaget, through interchange with peers in the form of disagreement and collaborative work.

Piaget believed that the child begins life within a private universe, where speech merely acccompanies affect and action, serving neither a cognitive nor a social function. Vygotsky took the contrary position that the child is born a social being, one who is turned toward others from the start. While Vygotsky retained Piaget's term "egocentric speech," he provided evidence that much of the child's early speech is not merely an accompaniment to action but serves to sustain and direct thinking in the present and to anticipate and plan future activities.

In the selection by **Vygotsky** included in this volume, Vygotsky elaborates on the major differences between his view and Piaget's, particularly with regard to the fate of egocentric speech. According to Piaget, as the proportion of egocentric to socialized speech decreases, egocentric speech is superseded by socialized speech. By contrast, as Vygotsky proposes in this selection, egocentric speech is internalized as inner speech, and merely its vocal aspect disappears. The debate between these pioneers, which initially centered on the nature of egocentric speech and its relation to thought, also involves the relation between the forms of speech and the intended addressee. As Vygotsky saw it, when the addressee is psychologically close to the speaker—in the extreme case being the speaker himself—speech (and thought) takes an abbreviated and implicit form. Whenever the speaker believes that he is understood, whether or not this is the case, the message approaches "egocentric speech," and thus the proportion of egocentric speech reflects not only the ability to take the other's perspective into account, but also the speaker's conception of the psychological distance and communication needs of the addressee.

In addition to stressing the relation between form of speech and intended addressee, Vygotsky laid the groundwork for considering the cognitive functions of the young child's speech. Whereas Piaget had argued that language and action are independent in young children, Vygotsky states in the selection included in this volume that some of the young child's speech "serves mental orientation" and "helps in overcoming difficulties." In Vygotsky's view, the phenomenon of private speech is not totally explained as cognitive or social immaturity. The self-directing or self-guiding functions of speech can be seen as positive functions that integrate speech, action, and thinking.

Although **Halliday** does not trace his viewpoint to Vygotsky, he also emphasizes the functional diversity of language, which he claims has been ignored or misunderstood by theorists working with too limited a "model" of language. Halliday argues that most psychologists have been aware only of the representational use of language for labeling content, and have tended to overlook and minimize other uses of language, such as expressing individuality, controlling others, and sustaining solidarity.

Current developments in the area of private and social speech have taken several forms. One stream of research—parallelled in other studies of cognitive development—stresses the early emergence of a social orientation in the speech of young children. **Garvey and Hogan,** in the selection included in this section, show that children as young as $3\frac{1}{2}$ years of age clearly talk to their peers, indicating a remarkable capacity to adapt messages to one another. Measures of socially coordinated ("in-focus") communications include waiting for an answer, giving an appropriate reply, and making a relevant comment on the action of another. Following Vygotsky, Garvey and Hogan claim that a social orientation appears early, but that it takes time for children to develop linguistic proficiency in organizing their play interactions and social life in general.

A second avenue of research bears directly on Vygotsky's assumptions regarding the social origins of speech and differences in the functions of social and private speech. In his study of naturally occurring speech in 2 year olds, **Furrow** examines the differences between the functions of speech when it is directed toward others and when it is not (social versus private "contexts"). The evidence of both social and private speech in this age group lends support to Vygotsky's assumption that young children's talk is not inherently asocial. Furthermore, in private contexts, children use speech for the positive functions of describing and directing their own activity, suggesting the inadequacy of an explanation of private speech solely in terms of an *absence* of social-communicative ability. Furrow's article supplements Halliday's categorization of the functions of speech in that it suggests social situational determinants of the various uses, and also considers private as well as social occasions of use.

The third avenue of research deals with ways in which children modify their speech as a function of the particular addressee. Beginning with the assumption that speech for self and speech for others differs structurally, this line of investigation asks whether children adopt different speech registers in talking to dolls, peers, and adults. **Sachs and Devin** demonstrate that children as young as 3;9 begin to talk to real babies and baby dolls in a manner resembling caretakers' talk to babies, not only in content, but in syntax and intonation as well. In addition to casting further doubt on the extent of "egocentricity" in young children, the findings of Sachs and Devin of a developmental trend between 3;9 and 5;5 point to this age span as a crucial period for the use of language in differentiating social relations.

The final selection in Part III differs from the others in that it deals not with language production, but with factors that might underlie the capacity for successful social speech. **Beal and Flavell** examine young children's ability to gauge the listener's ability to understand a message, using metalinguistic tasks developed by Markman. Children seem able to monitor and modify communications to one another quite adequately without the ability to explicitly evaluate and comment upon the listener's state of comprehension. As Beal and Flavell report, preschoolers and kindergartners rely on the listener's feedback to evaluate message adequacy, and only gradually begin to estimate the hearer's state of comprehension on the basis of the consistency and clarity of the message. Thus, successful communication must rest upon the capacity to monitor and regulate the adequacy of one's own messages, not merely on taking the perspective of the other. Children's growing ability to jointly construct talk with others is one of the foundations for the development of conversation and story telling.

14

Lev Semenovich Vygotsky

On Inner Speech

We must probe still deeper and explore the plane of inner speech lying beyond the semantic plane. We shall discuss here some of the data of the special investigation we have made of it. The relationship of thought and word cannot be understood in all its complexity without a clear understanding of the psychological nature of inner speech. Yet, of all the problems connected with thought and language, this is perhaps the most complicated, beset as it is with terminological and other misunderstandings.

The term *inner speech*, or *endophasy*, has been applied to various phenomena, and authors argue about different things that they call by the same name. Originally, inner speech seems to have been understood as verbal memory. An example would be the silent recital of a poem known by heart. In that case, inner speech differs from vocal speech only as the idea or image of an object differs from the real object. It was in this sense that inner speech was understood by the French authors who tried to find out how words were reproduced in memory—whether as auditory, visual, motor, or synthetic images. We shall see that word memory is indeed one of the constituent elements of inner speech but not all of it.

In a second interpretation, inner speech is seen as truncated external speech—as "speech minus sound" (Mueller) or "subvocal speech" (Watson). Bekhterev defined it as a speech reflex inhibited in its motor part. Such an explanation is by no means sufficient. Silent "pronouncing" of words is not equivalent to the total process of inner speech.

The third definition is, on the contrary, too broad. To Goldstein (1927,

From *Thought and Language* (pp. 130–138) by L.S. Vygotsky (translated and edited by E. Hanfman and G. Vakar), 1962, Cambridge, MA: M.I.T. Press. Copyright 1962 by Massachusetts Institute of Technology. Reprinted by permission of publisher.

1932) the term covers everthing that precedes the motor act of speaking, includ-ing Wundt's "motives of speech" and the indefinable, nonsensory, and nonmotor specific speech experience—i.e., the whole interior aspect of any speech activity. It is hard to accept the equation of inner speech with an inarticulate inner experience in which the separate identifiable structural planes are dissolved with-out trace. This central experience is common to all linguistic activity, and for this reason alone Goldstein's interpretation does not fit that specific, unique function that alone deserves the name of inner speech. Logically developed, Goldstein's view must lead to the thesis that inner speech is not speech at all but rather an intellectual and affective-volitional activity, since it includes the motives of speech and the thought that is expressed in words.

To get a true picture of inner speech, one must start from the assumption that it is a specific formation, with its own laws and complex relations to the other forms of speech activity. Before we can study its relation to thought, on the one hand, and to speech, on the other, we must determine its special characteristics and function.

Inner speech is speech for oneself; external speech is for others. It would indeed be surprising if such a basic difference in function did not affect the structure of the two kinds of speech. Absence of vocalization per se is only a consequence of the specific nature of inner speech, which is neither an antecedent of external speech nor its reproduction in memory but is, in a sense, the opposite of external speech. The latter is the turning of thought into words, its materialization and objectification. With inner speech, the process is reversed: Speech turns into inward thought. Consequently, their structures must differ.

The area of inner speech is one of the most difficult to investigate. It remained almost inaccessible to experiments until ways were found to apply the genetic method of experimentation. Piaget (1926) was the first to pay attention to the child's egocentric speech and to see its theoretical significance, but he re-mained blind to the most important trait of egocentric speech—its genetic con-nection with inner speech—and this warped his interpretation of its function and structure. We made that relationship the central problem of our study and thus were able to investigate the nature of inner speech with unusual completeness. A number of considerations and observations led us to conclude that egocentric speech is a stage of development preceding inner speech: Both fulfill intellectual functions, their structures are similar; egocentric speech disappears at school age, when inner speech begins to develop. From all this we infer that one changes into the other.

If this transformation does take place, then egocentric speech provides the key to the study of inner speech. One advantage of approaching inner speech through egocentric speech is its accessibility to experimentation and observation. It is still vocalized, audible speech, i.e., external in its mode of expression, but at the same time inner speech in function and structure. To study an internal process it is necessary to externalize it experimentally, by connecting it with some outer activity; only then is objective functional analysis possible. Egocentric speech is, in fact, a natural experiment of this type.

This method has another great advantage: Since egocentric speech can be studied at the time when some of its characteristics are waning and new ones forming, we are able to judge which traits are essential to inner speech and which are only temporary, and thus to determine the goal of this movement from egocentric to inner speech—i.e., the nature of inner speech.

Before we go on to the results obtained by this method, we shall briefly discuss the nature of egocentric speech, stressing the differences between our theory and Piaget's. Piaget contends that the child's egocentric speech is a direct expression of the egocentrism of his thought, which in turn is a compromise between the primary autism of his thinking and its gradual socialization. As the child grows older, autism recedes and socialization progresses, leading to the waning of egocentrism in his thinking and speech.

In Piaget's conception, the child in his egocentric speech does not adapt himself to the thinking of adults. His thought remains entirely egocentric; this makes his talk incomprehensible to others. Egocentric speech has no function in the child's realistic thinking or activity—it merely accompanies them. And since it is an expression of egocentric thought, it disappears together with the child's egocentrism. From its climax at the beginning of the child's development, egocentric speech drops to zero on the threshold of school age. Its history is one of involution rather than evolution. It has no future.

In our conception, egocentric speech is a phenomenon of the transition from interpsychic to intrapyschic functioning, i.e., from the social, collective activity of the child to his more individualized activity—a pattern of development common to all the higher psychological functions. Speech for oneself originates through differentiation from speech for others. Since the main course of the child's development is one of gradual individualization, this tendency is reflected in the function and structure of his speech.

Our experimental results indicate that the function of egocentric speech is similar to that of inner speech: It does not merely accompany the child's activity, it serves mental orientation, conscious understanding, it helps in overcoming difficulties; it is speech for oneself, intimately and usefully connected with the child's thinking. Its fate is very different from that described by Piaget. Egocentric speech develops along a rising, not a declining, curve; it goes through an evolution, not an involution. In the end, it becomes inner speech.

Our hypothesis has several advantages over Piaget's: It explains the function and development of egocentric speech and, in particular, its sudden increase when the child faces difficulties which demand consciousness and reflection—a fact uncovered by our experiments and which Piaget's theory cannot explain. But the greatest advantage of our theory is that it supplies a satisfying answer to a paradoxical situation described by Piaget himself. To Piaget, the quantitative drop in egocentric speech as the child grows older means the withering of that form of speech. If that were so, its structural peculiarities might also be expected to decline; it is hard to believe that the process would affect only its quantity, and not its inner structure. The child's thought becomes infinitely less egocentric between the ages of 3 and 7. If the characteristics of egocentric speech that make it incomprehensible to others are indeed rooted in egocentrism, they should become less apparent as that form of speech becomes less frequent; egocentric speech should approach social speech and become more and more intelligible. Yet what are the facts? Is the talk of a 3 year old harder to follow than that of a 7 year old? Our investigation established that the traits of egocentric speech which make for inscrutability are at their lowest point at 3 and at their peak at 7. They develop in a reverse direction to the frequency of egocentric speech. While the latter keeps falling and reaches zero at school age, the structural characteristics become more and more pronounced.

This throws a new light on the quantitative decrease in egocentric speech, which is the cornerstone of Piaget's thesis.

What does this decrease mean? The structural peculiarities of speech for oneself and its differentiation from external speech increase with age. What is it then that diminishes? Only one of its aspects: vocalization. Does this mean that egocentric speech as a whole is dying out? We believe that it does not, for how then could we explain the growth of the functional and structural traits of egocentric speech? On the other hand, their growth is perfectly compatible with the decrease of vocalization—indeed, clarifies its meaning. Its rapid dwindling and the equally rapid growth of the other characteristics are contradictory in appearance only.

To explain this, let us start from an undeniable, experimentally established fact. The structural and functional qualities of egocentric speech become more marked as the child develops. At 3, the difference between egocentric and social speech equals zero; at 7, we have speech that in structure and function is totally unlike social speech. A differentiation of the two speech functions has taken place. This is a fact—and facts are notoriously hard to refute.

Once we accept this, everything else falls into place. If the developing structural and functional peculiarities of egocentric speech progressively isolate it from external speech, then its vocal aspect must fade away; and this is exactly what happens between 3 and 7 years. With the progressive isolation of speech for oneself, its vocalization becomes unnecessary and meaningless and, because of its growing structural peculiarities, also impossible. Speech for oneself cannot find expression in external speech. The more independent and autonomous egocentric speech becomes, the poorer it grows in its external manifestations. In the end it separates itself entirely from speech for others, ceases to be vocalized, and thus appears to die out.

But this is only an illusion. To interpret the sinking coefficient of egocentric speech as a sign that this kind of speech is dying out is like saying that the child stops counting when he ceases to use his fingers and starts adding in his head. In reality behind the symptoms of dissolution lies a progressive development, the birth of a new speech form.

The decreasing vocalization of egocentric speech denotes a developing abstraction from sound, the child's new faculty to "think words" instead of pronouncing them. This is the positive meaning of the sinking coefficient of egocentric speech. The downward curve indicates development toward inner speech.

We can see that all the known facts about the functional, structural, and genetic characteristics of egocentric speech point to one thing: It develops in the direction of inner speech. Its developmental history can be understood only as a gradual unfolding of the traits of inner speech.

We believe that this corroborates our hypothesis about the origin and nature of egocentric speech. To turn our hypothesis into a certainty, we must devise an experiment capable of showing which of the two interpretations is correct. What are the data for this critical experiment?

Let us restate the theories between which we must decide. Piaget believes that egocentric speech stems from the insufficient socialization of speech and that its only development is decrease and eventual death. Its culmination lies in the past. Inner speech is something new brought in from the outside along with socialization. We believe that egocentric speech stems from the insufficient individualization of primary social speech. Its culmination lies in the future. It develops into inner speech.

To obtain evidence for one or the other view, we must place the child alternately in experimental situations encouraging social speech and in situations discouraging it, and see how these changes affect egocentric speech. We consider this an *experimentum crucis* for the following reasons.

If the child's egocentric talk results from the egocentrism of his thinking and its insufficient socialization, then any weakening of the social elements in the experimental setup, any factor contributing to the child's isolation from the group, must lead to a sudden increase in egocentric speech. But if the latter results from an insufficient differentiation of speech for oneself from speech for others, then the same changes must cause it to decrease.

We took as the starting point of our experiment three of Piaget's own observations. (1) Egocentric speech occurs only in the presence of other children engaged in the same activity, and not when the child is alone, i.e., it is a collective monologue. (2) The child is under the illusion that his egocentric talk, directed to nobody, is understood by those who surround him. (3) Egocentric speech has the character of external speech: It is not inaudible or whispered. These are certainly not chance peculiarities. From the child's own point of view, egocentric speech is not yet separated from social speech. It occurs under the subjective and objective conditions of social speech and may be considered a correlate of the insufficient isolation of the child's individual consciousness from the social whole.

In our first series of experiments (Vygotsky, Luria, Leontiev and Levina, unpublished; Vygotsky and Luria, 1930), we tried to destroy the illusion of being understood. After measuring the child's coefficient of egocentric speech in a situation similar to that of Piaget's experiments, we put him into a new situation:

either with deaf-mute children or with children speaking a foreign language. In all other respects the setup remained the same. The coefficient of egocentric speech dropped to zero in the majority of cases, and in the rest to one-eighth of the previous figure, on the average. This proves that the illusion of being understood is not a mere epiphenomenon of egocentric speech but is functionally connected with it. Our results must seem paradoxical from the point of view of Piaget's theory: The weaker the child's contact is with the group—the less the social situation forces him to adjust his thoughts to others and to use social speech—the more freely should the egocentrism of his thinking and speech manifest itself. But from the point of view of our hypothesis, the meaning of these findings is clear: Egocentric speech, springing from the lack of differentiation of speech for oneself from speech for others, disappears when the feeling of being understood, essential for social speech, is absent.

In the second series of experiments, the variable factor was the possibility of collective monologue. Having measured the child's coefficient of egocentric speech in a situation permitting collective monologue, we put him into a situation excluding it—in a group of children who were strangers to him, or by himself at a separate table in a corner of the room; or he worked quite alone, even the experimenter leaving the room. The results of this series agreed with the first results. The exclusion of the group monologue caused a drop in the coefficient of egocentric speech, though not such a striking one as in the first case—seldom to zero and, on the average, to one-sixth of the original figure. The different methods of precluding collective monologue were not equally effective in reducing the coefficient of egocentric speech. The trend, however, was obvious in all the variations of the experiment. The exclusion of the collective factor, instead of giving full freedom to egocentric speech, depressed it. Our hypothesis was once more confirmed.

In the third series of experiments, the variable factor was the vocal quality of egocentric speech. Just outside the laboratory where the experiment was in progress, an orchestra played so loudly, or so much noise was made, that it drowned out not only the voices of others but the child's own; in a variant of the experiment, the child was expressly forbidden to talk loudly and allowed to talk only in whispers. Once again the coefficient of egocentric speech went down, the relation to the original figure being 5:1. Again the different methods were not equally effective, but the basic trend was invariably present.

The purpose of all three series of experiments was to eliminate those characteristics of egocentric speech that bring it close to social speech. We found that this always led to the dwindling of egocentric speech. It is logical, then, to assume that egocentric speech is a form developing out of social speech and not yet separated from it in its manifestation, although already distinct in function and structure.

The disagreement between us and Piaget on this point will be made quite clear by the following example: I am sitting at my desk talking to a person who is behind me and whom I cannot see; he leaves the room without my noticing it, and I continue to talk, under the illusion that he listens and understands. Outwardly, I am talking with myself and for myself, but psychologically my speech is social. From the point of view of Piaget's theory, the opposite happens in the case of the child: His egocentic talk is for and with himself; it only has the appearance of social speech, just as my speech gave the false impression of being egocentric. From our point of view, the whole situation is much more complicated than that: Subjectively, the child's egocentric speech already has its own peculiar function—to that extent, it is independent from social speech; yet its independence is not complete because it is not felt as inner speech and is not distinguished by the child from speech for others. Objectively, also, it is different from social speech but again not entirely, because it functions only within social situations. Both subjectively and objectively, egocentric speech represents a transition from speech for others to speech for oneself. It already has the function of inner speech but remains similar to social speech in its expression.

The investigation of egocentric speech has paved the way to the understanding of inner speech, which we shall examine next.

15

M. A. K. Halliday
Relevant Models of Language

The teacher of English who, when seeking an adequate definition of language to guide him in his work, meets with a cautious "well, it depends on how you look at it," is likely to share the natural impatience felt by anyone who finds himself unable to elicit "a straight answer to a straight question." But the very frequency of this complaint may suggest that, perhaps, questions are seldom as straight as they seem. The question "what is language?," in whatever guise it appears, is as diffuse and, at times, disingenuous as other formulations of its kind, for example "what is literature?" Such questions, which are wisely excluded from examinations, demand the privilege of a qualified and perhaps circuitous answer.

In a sense the only satisfactory response is "why do you want to know?," since unless we know what lies beneath the question we cannot hope to answer it in a way which will suit the questioner. Is he interested in language planning in multilingual communities? Or in aphasia and language disorders? Or in words and their histories? Or in dialects and those who speak them? Or in how one language differs from another? Or in the formal properties of language as a system? Or in the functions of language and the demands that we make on it? Or in language as an art medium? Or in the information and redundancy of writing systems? Each one of these and other such questions is a possible context for a definition of language. In each case language "is" something different.

The criterion is one of relevance; we want to understand, and to highlight, those facets of language which bear on the investigation or the task in hand. . . .

It is not necessary to sacrifice a generation of children, or even one classroomful, in order to demonstrate that particular preconceptions of language are inadequate or irrelevant. In place of a negative and somewhat hit-and-miss

approach, a more fruitful procedure is to seek to establish certain general, positive criteria of relevance. These will relate, ultimately, to the demands that we
make of language in the course of our lives. We need therefore to have some idea
of the nature of these demands, and we shall try to consider them here from the
point of view of the child. We shall ask, in effect, about the child's image of
language: what is the "model" of language that he internalizes as a result of his
own experience? This will help us to decide what is relevant to the teacher, since
the teacher's own view of language must at the very least encompass all that the
child knows language to be.

The child knows what language is because he knows what language does.
The determining elements in the young child's experience are the successful
demands on language that he himself has made, the particular needs that have
been satisfied by language for him. He has used language in many ways—for the
satisfaction of material and intellectual needs, for the mediation of personal
relationships, the expression of feelings, and so on. Language in all these uses has
come within his own direct experience, and because of this he is subconsciously
aware that language has many functions that affect him personally. Language is,
for the child, a rich and adaptable instrument for the realization of his intentions;
there is hardly any limit to what he can do with it.

As a result, the child's internal "model" of language is a highly complex
one, and most adult notions of language fail to match up to it. The adult's ideas
about language may be externalized and consciously formulated, but they are
nearly always much too simple. In fact it may be more helpful, in this connection, to speak of the child's "models" of language, in the plural, in order to
emphasize the many-sidedness of his linguistic experience. We shall try to identify the models of language with which the normal child is endowed by the time
he comes to school at the age of 5, the assumption being that if the teacher's own
"received" conception of language is in some ways less rich or less diversified it
will be irrelevant to the educational task.

We tend to underestimate both the total extent and the functional diversity
of the part played by language in the life of the child. His interaction with others,
which begins at birth, is gradually given form by language, through the process
whereby at a very early age language already begins to mediate in every aspect of
his experience. It is not only as the child comes to act on and to learn about his
environment that language comes in; it is there from the start in his achievement
of intimacy and in the expression of his individuality. The rhythmic recitation of
nursery rhymes and jingles is still language, as we can see from the fact that
children's spells and chants differ from one language to another: English
nonsense is quite distinct from French nonsense, because the one is English and
the other French. All these contribute to the child's total picture of language "at
work."

Through such experiences, the child builds up a very positive impression—
one that cannot be verbalized, but is nonetheless real for that—of what language
is and what it is for. Much of his difficulty with language in school arises because

he is required to accept a stereotype of language that is contrary to the insights he has gained from his own experience. The traditional first "reading and writing" tasks are a case in point, since they fail to coincide with his own convictions about the nature and uses of language.

Perhaps the simplest of the child's models of language, and one of the first to be evolved, is what we may call the INSTRUMENTAL model. The child becomes aware that language is used as a means of getting things done. About a generation ago, zoologists were finding out about the highly developed mental powers of chimpanzees, and one of the observations described was of the animal that constructed a long stick out of three short ones and used it to dislodge a bunch of bananas from the roof of its cage. The human child, faced with the same problem, constructs a sentence. He says "I want a banana," and the effect is the more impressive because it does not depend on the immediate presence of the bananas. Language is brought in to serve the function of "I want," the satisfaction of material needs. Success in this use of language does not in any way depend on the production of well-formed adult sentences; a carefully contextualized yell may have substantially the same effect, and although this may not be language there is no very clear dividing line between, say, a noise made on a commanding tone and a full-dress imperative clause.

The old *See Spot run. Run, Spot, run!* type of first reader bore no relation whatsoever to this instrumental function of language. This by itself does not condemn it, since language has many other functions beside that of manipulating and controlling the environment. But it bore little apparent relation to any use of language, at least to any with which the young child is familiar. It is not recognizable as language in terms of the child's own intentions, of the meanings that he has reason to express and to understand. Children have a very broad concept of the meaningfulness of language, in addition to their immense tolerance of inexplicable tasks; but they are not accustomed to being faced with language which, in their own functional terms, has no meaning at all, and the old-style reader was not seen by them as language. It made no connection with language in use.

Language as an instrument of control has another side to it, since the child is well aware that language is also a means whereby others exercise control over him. Closely related to the instrumental model, therefore, is the REGULATORY model of language. This refers to the use of language to regulate the behavior of others. Bernstein (1970) and his colleagues have studied different types of regulatory behavior by parents in relation to the process of socialization of the child, and their work provides important clues concerning what the child may be expected to derive from this experience in constructing his own model of language. To adapt one of Bernstein's examples, the mother who finds that her small child has carried out of the supermarket, unnoticed by herself or by the cashier, some object that was not paid for, may exploit the power of language in various ways, each of which will leave a slightly different trace or afterimage of this role of language in the mind of the child. For example, she may say *you mustn't take things that don't belong to you* (control through conditional prohibition based on a categorization of objects in terms of a particular social institution, that of ownership), *that was very naughty* (control through categorization of behavior in terms of opposition approved/disapproved), *if you do that again I'll smack you* (control through threat of reprisal linked to repetition of behavior), *you'll make Mummy very unhappy if you do that* (control through emotional blackmail), *that's not allowed* (control through categorization of behavior as governed by rule), and so on. A single incident of this type by itself has little significance, but such general types of regulatory behavior, through repetition and reinforcement, determine the child's specific awareness of language as a means of behavioral control.

The child applies this awareness, in his own attempts to control his peers and siblings, and this in turn provides the basis for an essential component in his range of linguistic skills, the language of rules and instructions. Whereas at first he can make only simple unstructured demands, he learns as time goes on to give ordered sequences of instructions, and then progresses to the further stage where he can convert sets of instructions into rules, including conditional rules, as in explaining the principles of a game. Thus his regulatory model of language continues to be elaborated, and his experience of the potentialities of language in this use further increases the value of the model.

Closely related to the regulatory function of language is its function in social interaction, and the third of the models that we may postulate as forming part of the child's image of language is the INTERACTIONAL model. This refers to the use of language in the interaction between the self and others. Even the closest of the child's personal relationships, that with his mother, is partly and, in time, largely mediated through language; his interaction with other people, adults and children, is very obviously maintained linguistically. (Those who come nearest to achieving a personal relationship that is not linguistically mediated, apparently, are twins.)

Aside, however, from his experience of language in the maintenance of permanent relationships, the neighborhood and the activities of the peer group provide the context for complex and rapidly changing interactional patterns which make extensive and subtle demands on the individual's linguistic resources. Language is used to define and consolidate the group, to include and to exclude, showing who is "one of us" and who is not, to impose status, and to contest status that is imposed, and humor, ridicule, deception, persuasion, all the forensic and theatrical arts of language are brought into play. Moreover, the young child, still primarily a learner, can do what very few adults can do in such situations: he can be internalizing language while listening and talking. He can be, effectively, both a participant and an observer at the same time, so that his own critical involvement in this complex interaction does not prevent him from profiting linguistically from it.

Again there is a natural link here with another use of language, from which the child derives what we may call the PERSONAL model. This refers to his awareness of language as a form of his own individuality. In the process whereby the child becomes aware of himself, and in particular in the higher stages of that process, the development of his personality, language plays an essential role. We are not talking here merely of "expressive" language—language used for the direct expression of feelings and attitudes—but also of the personal element in the interactional function of language, since the shaping of the self through interaction with others is very much a language-mediated process. The child is enabled to offer to someone else that which is unique to himself, to make public his own individuality, and this in turn reinforces and creates this individuality. With the normal child, his awareness of himself is closely bound up with speech: both with hearing himself speak, and with having at his disposal the range of behavioral options that constitute language. Within the concept of the self as an actor, having discretion, or freedom of choice, the "self as a speaker" is an important component.

Thus for the child, language is very much a part of himself, and the "personal" model is his intuitive awareness of this, and of the way in which his individuality is identified and realized through language. The other side of the coin, in this process, is the child's growing understanding of his environment, since the environment is, first of all, the "nonself," that which is separated out in the course of establishing where he himself begins and ends. So, the child has a HEURISTIC model of language, derived from his knowledge of how language has enabled him to explore his environment.

The heuristic model refers to language as a means of investigating reality, a way of learning about things. This scarcely needs comment, since every child makes it quite obvious that this is what language is for by his habit of constantly asking questions. When he is questioning, he is seeking not merely facts but explanations of facts, the generalizations about reality that language makes it possible to explore. Again, Bernstein has shown the importance of the question-and-answer routine in the total setting of parent–child communication and the significance of the latter, in turn, in relation to the child's success in formal education: his research has demonstrated a significant correlation between the mother's linguistic attention to the child and the teacher's assessment of the child's success in the first year of school.

The young child is very well aware of how to use language to learn, and may be quite conscious of this aspect of language before he reaches school; many children already control a metalanguage for the heuristic function of language, in that they know what a "question" is, what an "answer" is, what "knowing" and "understanding" mean, and they can talk about these things without difficulty. Mackay and Thompson (1968) have shown the importance of helping the child who is learning to read and write to build up a language for talking about language, and it is the heuristic function which provides one of the foundations for this, since the child can readily conceptualize and verbalize the basic categories of the heuristic model. To put this more concretely, the normal 5 year old either already uses words such as *question, answer* in their correct meanings or, if he does not, is capable of learning to do so.

The other foundation for the child's "language about language" is to be found in the imaginative function. This also relates the child to his environment, but in a rather different way. Here, the child is using language to create his own environment, not to learn about how things are but to make them as he feels inclined. From his ability to create, through language, a world of his own making he derives the IMAGINATIVE model of language, and this provides some further elements of the metalanguage, with words like *story, make up,* and *pretend.*

Language in its imaginative function is not necessarily "about" anything at all: the child's linguistically created environment does not have to be a make-believe copy of the world of experience, occupied by people and things and events. It may be a world of pure sound, made up of rhythmic sequences of rhyming or chiming syllables, or an edifice of words in which semantics has no part, like a house built of playing cards in which face values are irrelevant. Poems, rhymes, riddles, and much of the child's own linguistic play reinforce this model of language, and here too the meaning of what is said is not primarily a matter of content. In stories and dramatic games, the imaginative function is, to a large extent, based on content, but the ability to express such content is still, for the child, only one of the interesting facets of language, one which for many purposes is no more than an optional extra.

So we come finally to the REPRESENTATIONAL model. Language is, in addition to all its other guises, a means of communicating about something, of expressing propositions. The child is aware that he can convey a message in language, a message which has specific reference to the processes, persons, objects, abstractions, qualities, states, and relations of the real world around him.

This is the only model of language that many adults have; and a very inadequate model it is, from the point of view of the child. There is no need to go so far as to suggest that the transmission of content is, for the child, the least important function of language; we have no way of evaluating the various functions relatively to one another. It is certainly not, however, one of the earliest to come into prominence, and it does not become a dominant function until a much later stage in the development toward maturity. Perhaps it never becomes in any real sense the dominant function, but it does, in later years, tend to become the dominant *model.* It is very easy for the adult, when he attempts to formulate his ideas about the nature of language, to be simply unaware of most of what language means to the child; this is not because he no longer uses language in the same variety of different functions (one or two may have atrophied, but not all), but because only one of these functions, in general, is the subject of conscious attention, so that the corresponding model is the only one to be externalized. But this presents what is, for the child, a quite unrealistic picture of language, since it accounts for only a small fragment of his total awareness of what language is about.

The representational model at least does not conflict with the child's experience. It relates to one significant part of it, rather a small part, at first, but nevertheless real. In this it contrasts sharply with another view of language which we have not mentioned because it plays no part in the child's experience at all, but which might be called the "ritual" model of language. This is the image of language internalized by those for whom language is a means of showing how well one was brought up; it downgrades language to the level of table manners. The ritual element in the use of language is probably derived from the interactional, since language in its ritual function also serves to define and delimit a social group, but it has none of the positive aspects of linguistic interaction, those which impinge on the child, and is thus very partial and one sided. The view of language as manners is a needless complication, in the present context, since this function of language has no counterpart in the child's experience.

Our conception of language, if it is to be adequate for meeting the needs of the child, will need to be exhaustive. It must incorporate all the child's own "models," to take account of the varied demands on language that he himself makes. The child's understanding of what language is is derived from his own experience of language in situations of use. It thus embodies all of the images we have described: the instrumental, the regulatory, the interactional, the personal, the heuristic, the imaginative, and the representational. Each of these is his interpretation of a function of language with which he is familiar. . . .

Let us summarize the models in terms of the child's intentions, since different uses of language may be seen as realizing different intentions. In its instrumental function, language is used for the satisfaction of material needs; this is the "I want" function. The regulatory is the "do as I tell you" function, language in the control of behavior. The interactional function is that of getting along with others, the "me and him" function (including "me and my mummy"). The personal is related to this: it is the expression of identity, of the self, which develops largely *through* linguistic interaction; the "here I come" function, perhaps. The heuristic is the use of language to learn, to explore reality: the function of "tell me why." The imaginative is that of "let's pretend," whereby the reality is created, and what is being explored is the child's own mind, including language itself. The representational is the "I've got something to tell you" function, that of the communication of content.

What we have called "models" are the images that we have of language arising out of these functions. Language is "defined" for the child by its uses; it is something that serves this set of needs. These are not models of language acquisition; they are not procedures whereby the child learns his language, nor do they define the part played by different types of linguistic activity in the learning process. Hence no mention has been made of the chanting and repeating and rehearsing by which the child practices his language. The techniques of mastering language do not constitute a "use," nor do they enter into the making of the image of language; a child, at least, does not learn for the luxury of being a learner. For the child, all language is doing something: in other words, it has meaning. It has meaning in a very broad sense, including here a range of functions which the adult does not normally think of as meaningful, such as the personal and the interactional and probably most of those listed above—all except the last, in fact. But it is precisely in relation to the child's conception of language that it is most vital for us to redefine our notion of meaning, not restricting it to the narrow limits of representational meaning (that is, "content") but including within it all the functions that language has as purposive, nonrandom, contextualized activity. *

We are still very ignorant of many aspects of the part language plays in our lives. But it is clear that language serves a wide range of human needs, and the richness and variety of its functions are reflected in the nature of language itself, in its organization as a system: within the grammatical structure of a language, certain areas are primarily associated with the heuristic and representational functions, others with the personal and interactional functions. Different bits of the system, as it were, do different jobs, and this in turn helps us to interpret and make more precise the notion of uses of language. What is common to every use of language is that it is meaningful, contextualized, and in the broadest sense social; this is brought home very clearly to the child, in the course of his day-to-day experience. The child is surrounded by language, but not in the form of grammars and dictionaries, or of randomly chosen words and sentences, or of undirected monologue. What he encounters is "text," or language in use: sequences of language articulated each within itself and with the situation in which it occurs. Such sequences are purposive—though very varied in purpose—and have an evident social significance. The child's awareness of language cannot be isolated from his awareness of language function, and this conceptual unity offers a useful vantage point from which language may be seen in a perspective that is educationally relevant.

*Discussion of educational implications is omitted. [Eds.]

16

Catherine Garvey and Robert Hogan
Social Speech and Social Interaction: Egocentrism Revisited

Studies of young children's speech typically emphasize its egocentric, parasocial, or private quality (Kohlberg, Yeager and Hjertholm, 1968; Piaget, 1926; Vygotsky, 1962). According to these studies, the progressive decline in overt forms of private speech is accompanied by a growth in collaborative activity (Piaget, 1926), by the ability to recode or modify messages taking into account the informational needs of an interlocutor (Flavell, Botkin, Fry, Wright and Jarvis, 1968), or by the development of inner speech or thought (Vygotsky, 1962). The attention paid to the form, function, and fate of private speech rests in part on the assumption that the thought and behavior of children are initially egocentric and that with the passage of time their actions become increasingly social as a result of cognitive development and social experience. Such a viewpoint has unfortunately led social scientists to neglect children's early social interaction. Recent research suggests, however, that it may be useful to regard children as "sociocentric" essentially from birth (e.g., Borke, 1971; Ferguson, 1971; Stayton, Hogan and Ainsworth, 1971). Even the first stages of language acquisition may depend on the child's ability to discriminate the intent of others (cf. Macnamara, 1972); if so, then the view of the child as initially egocentric requires reexamination. A role-theoretical perspective (Sarbin and Allen, 1968) further suggests that language, the origins of social behavior, and the development of interpersonal understanding [in the sense suggested by Weber's term "meaningful behavior" (cf. Winch, 1958)] are all related. It may well be that a major function of early language use is social, in the sense of establishing and maintaining interpersonal contact. As such, children's talk could also serve as a vehicle for learning those concepts that underlie social intercourse (e.g., concepts of reciprocity, obligation, and complementarity).

Before the uses and forms of social speech can be understood, it is necessary to know how frequently and extensively such speech occurs and how it occurs in relation to other behaviors in a potential social interaction. Mueller (1972) found that among previously unacquainted children (ages $3\frac{1}{2}$–$5\frac{1}{2}$) in a dyadic play situation, the majority of utterances (62%) received a definite response. Only 15% of the utterances failed to elicit a response, while 23% attracted the listener's attention. The present paper examines the distribution of activity throughout the play sessions to determine the extent to which children engage in spontaneous interaction. It further inquires how extensively the interactions created by talk are sustained. Finally, the paper describes, as an example of the social use of speech, how a state of mutual engagement is created.

Method

SUBJECTS

Eighteen white, middle-class children in the $3\frac{1}{2}$–5 year age range served as subjects. These children were recruited from local nursery schools where the directors were asked to nominate children of English-speaking "professional" families. There were 11 girls and 7 boys.

PROCEDURES

Three children from the same school were brought at one time to the laboratory by their teacher. The triad was composed of both sexes and was either younger (age $3\frac{1}{2}$–$4\frac{1}{3}$) or older ($4\frac{1}{2}$–5). The children met the adult observers, saw the observation room, and then drew straws to see who would "play some games" and who would go as a dyad to the playroom. The child who drew the long straw went into the observation room with two adults where he was asked to choose objects which were "same" or "different." The dyad was left alone in the playroom where their activity was videotaped. The playroom contained toy telephones, a tool belt, a wooden car (big enough for two to sit on), dress-up clothes, a large stuffed snake, and fish, blocks, cars, trucks, an iron, and a broom. There were posters on the walls, a carpet, a couch, and curtains drawn back from the windows (one-way mirrors). The sessions lasted approximately 15 minutes and varied in length so that the children were not interrupted in the middle of a game. After each session the dyad was changed so that three dyads were formed from a triad. Thus, there were 6 younger dyads and 12 older dyads.

METHODS OF ANALYSIS

Verbatim transcripts were made of the audio material. All sessions were automatically timed at 15-second intervals and the speech was further divided into utterance units (UU)—stretches of one person's speech separated by pauses greater than 1 second or by another person's speech. The UUs were numbered and counted for both members of the dyad, and the mean length of the UUs in each dyad was calculated for each speaker. Rate of utterance for the dyad was determined by dividing the number of seconds in the session by the total number of UUs.

Judgments of mutual engagement, or focused interaction [e.g., a state in which the actions of members of a dyad are interdependent (cf. Goffman, 1963)], were made on the videotaped data of 12 dyads. Three independent judges indicated (anchoring their judgments to the nearest UU) when they thought the children moved into or out of a state of mutual engagement or focused interaction. The judges, following written instructions, could request replay of parts of the tape, and they indicated their decisions (in focus, out of focus, unsure) to the experimenter. Interjudge agreement was estimated using a random sample of 60 UU points from each dyad's session. Overall agreement was 82%. A major source of disagreement appeared to be the judges' inability to concur on the exact point of the beginning or ending of the two states of focused and unfocused interaction. The amount of time children were in focused interaction was calculated by dividing the time all three judges indicated was spent "in focus" by the total time of the session. This figure, then, was based on periods for which 100% agreement was obtained.

Social speech was defined as speech that is strictly adapted to the speech or behavior of the partner. To determine the extent to which the children's speech was social, each UU was coded according to its result. It was thus the interaction that was coded, rather than the speakers' intent, the nature of which, of course, the judges could only infer. Five categories of results, or consequences, of the UU were distinguished:

1. No apparent consequence (pause ensues, or speaker continues without response from listener, who may ignore him or may have failed to hear him)
2. Unrelated speech (listener speaks immediately after UU but speech is unrelated to UU)
3. Attending behavior (listener turns to speaker, watches or appears to listen)
4. Appropriate nonspeech behavior (listener performs action specified by UU)
5. Appropriate speech (listener replies to UU)

There obviously could be several immediate consequences of an UU, as in the case where a request, "Help me fasten this belt," was followed by compliance (appropriate nonspeech behavior) *and* another UU, "I'll try" (appropriate speech). To avoid multiple coding of an UU only the highest numbered relevant code was assigned, in this case, 5.

A sixth category (o) included those cases in which an action on the part of one child elicited a question or comment from the other. An UU coded 4 or 5 was said to form an exchange with its consequence, and an UU coded o an exchange with its antecedent. Thus, an exchange is formed of two component events, at least one of which must be an UU. An exchange conformed to a criterion of fixed order, that is, a change in order of the component events would destroy or change the meaning of the exchange. A series of UUs produced by one speaker was bracketed. Next, sequences of exchanges, which were formed from groupings of 4, 5, and o codes, were identified. A sequence could be broken by incidence of code 1 or 2 from the alternating speaker. However, if a code 1 was bracketed with a code 4 or 5, the sequence was not broken. Table 16-1 illustrates the coding categories, the bracketing, and the groupings of exchanges into exchange sequences.

A check of interjudge agreement in the use of the coding system showed that judges concurred in their codings of 89% of the total UUs. The coded UUs were tallied and the percentage of UUs which entered into exchanges was calculated. Sequences of exchanges were also tabulated.

Table 16-1. *Samples of Coding Categories, Bracketing, and Grouping of Exchanges*

UU number: Speaker A	UU number: Speaker B	Code	Number of exchanges
(Hums theme song from television show)		0	—
	127. We watch that.	5	—
128. Me, too.		5	—
	129. Isn't it funny?	5	—
130. I know, it sure is.			4
	176. My group got shot.	1⌉	—
	177. Did your group ever get shot?	5⌋	—
178. No.		5	—
	179. Well, mine did.	3	—
			2
180. Will you put this hammer in (tool belt) for me?		4	—
	(B puts hammer in)	0	—
			2
181. Thank you, I'll take it (tool belt) now.		1⌉	—
182. Oh, the phone's ringing.	(B glances at A, then	2	—
183. Hello?	moves away, picks up snake)	3⌋	—
	184. A snake can kill you.		
			0

Results

The analysis of rate of utterance and distribution of UUs by speaker indicated that the sessions contained a high level of verbal activity. The overall rate of utterance for 18 dyads was one UU every 4.6 seconds, and the average rates in the first and in the second half of the sessions were approximately the same. The rate of the younger dyads slightly exceeded that of the older. This does not mean that younger children spoke more rapidly; rather it means that their UUs were shorter. The overall rate was twice that reported by Mueller (1972) for his similar but longer observation sessions. The fact that the children in the present study were previously acquainted whereas Mueller's subjects were strangers may account for this higher rate of utterance. The overall mean and standard deviation for words per UU was 5.61 and 1.51; for younger dyads, 4.73 and 1.00; for older dyads, 6.04 and 1.65. The mean number of words and standard deviation per UU for younger girls were 5.05 and 1.28; for younger boys, 4.41 and 0.90. Among the older dyads, the mean number of words and standard deviation per UU for girls were 6.25 and 1.97; and for boys, 5.76 and 1.03.

The distribution of participation in the verbal activity was approximately equal for both members of each dyad. A dyad was said to be balanced in respect to relative participation if the percentage of UUs contributed by both members was equal or differed by 5% or less. Eleven of the 18 dyads were balanced. Of the remaining seven dyads, three showed differences of 20%; the remaining four showed differences of 12, 16, 16, and 18%, respectively. Sex did not account for the unbalanced participation since in the seven unbalanced dyads (all but two of which were composed of both sexes) three boys were dominant and two girls were dominant. Nor were there consistent individual tendencies to domination or subordination in respect to production of UUs. Only three individuals consistently participated less in relation to *both* partners in their respective triads, and no individual dominated in both dyads in which he or she participated.

The dyads used for the focus judgments were considered to be "in focus," or mutually engaged, for an average of 66% of each session. Bar graphs drawn of the judgments over each continuous session showed an alternation of focused and

Table 16-2. *Number of Dyads Producing Exchange Sequences of Varying Lengths and Numbers of These Sequences*

Length of sequences (exchanges)	Younger dyads (of 6) (N)	Total sequences (N)	Older dyads (of 12) (N)	Total sequences (N)
4	5	15	11	42
6	3	7	11	15
8	2	4	7	8
12 or more	1	2	5	6

unfocused periods. Periods judged "out of focus" were generally brief. Only one "out-of-focus" period exceeded 2 minutes, and this occurred at the beginning of a session. Many focused periods were also brief; however, each dyad showed sustained periods of mutual engagement. The basis for these sustained engagements included games and activity centered on toys or objects in the room, most usually with accompanying speech. More important, many periods of interaction included talk as the primary common focus of attention. In the following example the boy (A) and the girl (B) sat quietly, glancing occasionally at each other (this excerpt, composed of six exchanges, follows a sequence of exchanges concerning what A wanted to be when he grew up):

A. If I grow up my voice will change and when you grow up your voice will change. My mom told me. Did your mommy tell you?
B. No, your mommy's wrong. My voice, I don't want it to change. Oh, well.
A. Oh, well, we'll stay little, right?
B. What?
A. We'll stay little.
B. No, I don't want to. I *want* my voice to change. I don't care if it changes.
A. I care.

In summary, the children, though not continuously involved with one another, spent a considerable portion of their time in mutual engagement. The next question concerns the extent to which their speech was contingent on the speech or behavior of the partner.

The measure of the level of social speech was the percentage of UUs coded 4, 5, or 0, that is, those UUs that entered into a communicative exchange. The mean percentage of UUs that were coded 4, 5, or 0, that is, formed component events of exchanges, was 59%, $sd = 13.2\%$. Among the older children the means ranged from 48 to 77%; among the younger children, 21–64%. Single exchanges were by far the most numerous. All dyads, however, produced sequences of three exchanges, and the average number of such exchanges was nine per dyad. Sampling from the longer sequences, Table 16-2 presents the number of dyads who produced sequences of 4, 6, 8, and 12 or more exchanges and the number of such sequences produced by those dyads. A larger proportion of older dyads produced longer sequences, for example, 11/12 of the older dyads produced sequences of six exchanges, whereas only 3/6 of the younger dyads did so. Although sequences at the intervening lengths (e.g., 5, 7, 9, etc.) also occurred, the figures presented in Table 16-2 demonstrate that the children were capable of sustaining mutually adapted speech well beyond the simple exchange and also beyond the three-component conversations (which would be comparable to our sequences of two exchanges) described by Piaget (1926, p. 11).

The preceding analyses show that the children spent considerable time in social interaction, much of which consisted of talk. Such talk can be regarded as social behavior and as a means by which children enter into mutual engagement—a state that seems to be intrinsically satisfying to both partners. This is not to deny, of course, that social speech may serve many other functions or that some of these can be realized by nonverbal means. It is the case, however, that children consistently use speech to achieve and maintain contact with each other. The function (of securing attention and engagement) can, of course, be realized by nonverbal means. If a child wishes to initiate interaction with his partner he may wave a toy, make a loud noise, or perform a diverting stunt. Although these acts may attract the attention of his partner, such tactics will not necessarily assure his partner's engagement. There is a more powerful means to secure the involvement of the partner, a technique that illustrates children's use of talk to achieve social contact.

The summons-answer routine as a conversational opener in adult speech was described by Schegloff (1968). This simple but virtually invariable routine follows the following form. Move 1, speaker A summons B. Move 2, B answers: A, "Hey, Fred." B, "Yeah?" Further, with the summons, A commits himself to having something to say, a "reason" for the summons. With the answer, B indicates his availability for interaction. The third move is up to A; he must produce the "reason" for the summons. The routine thus creates a state of mutual committedness and obligation. Correct use of this three-move routine by children would provide substantial evidence of communicative intent and of the ability to use a conventional gambit to secure the involvement of the partner.

The transcripts of all dyads were examined to determine the incidence of this routine. A total of 23 well-formed instances occurred. Almost half of these opened a longer interchange. An example of the well-formed routine is: A. "You know what?" B. "What?" A. "Sometime you can come to my house." Move 1 was typically either an opener, for example, "Guess what," a personal name, or an ascribed role title, for example, "Father." Move 2, which followed on move 1 almost instantaneously, was represented primarily by "What?" Move 3 was, of course, quite varied in form.

Seven aborted routines were identified. In two cases move 2 was missing (B failed to answer). In five cases move 3 was missing (A failed to provide a reason): A. "Mother?" B. "What?" A. (Silence—then A moves away). The number of aborted routines is probably greater than would be expected in adult interaction, for adult speakers would seek to repair or provide an excuse for an imperfect performance of the routine.

Excluded from well-formed routines were cases in which move 1 was an exclamation, which though perhaps an attention getter might be construed as an expression of delight or surprise, and cases in which move 1 contained content in addition to the summons, for example, content anticipating the reason.

In one case a routine appeared to be headed for failure as A did not supply move 3. After a short pause, B repeated move 2. Then, to the surprise of the experimenter (and to the delighted astonishment of B), A played a verbal trick on B. After using the power of the routine to bring B into a position of social contact,

A pulled the rug out from under her by supplying a joking insult as the "reason." That the routine was intended was evident from the pleasure that the two children displayed in the joke. Here is the sequence in its entirety:

[A, male, and B, female, are playing independently]:

A. Do you know what?

B. What? [Pause, B turns to A and moves toward him]
    What? [Repetition is louder, with broader rising–falling intonation]

A. [A grins, then laughs before speaking]
    You're a nut.

B. What? What? What's a nut? What? [A and B laugh simultaneously,
    B dashes threateningly at A, shrieking the final "What?"]

[A and B drift apart after the laughter dies down]

The playful manipulation of the obligation contracted by the routine suggests considerable competence in the use of verbal means to achieve contact.

The successful routines described above have two features in common: first, they create a state of involvement; second, the "reason" always introduced a topic new to the interaction. If the routine is used competently, and if it has desirable consequences, then it seems likely that there would be a tendency to extend its use. A number of sequences, including the excluded cases, resembled well-formed routines but differed from these by occurring within an interchange, thus the element that corresponded to move 1 contained reference to a topic already introduced. In these sequences, move 1 was a request for response containing an indefinite pronoun or interrogative. Move 2 was a simple response in question form. Move 3 supplied the "reason" replacing the indefinite pronoun or interrogative of move 1. This sequence may be viewed as an extension of the summons-answer routine on the following grounds: (1) the form is similar, though move 1 is extended to include a topic; (2) the function is similar (move 1 requests B's attention to what A has to say, while A obligates himself to supply the reason underlying move 1). The major differences are that this variant occurs in the middle of an interaction rather than at the beginning and that the function changes from that of securing involvement to maintaining it. An example of this sequence which we can call the rhetorical gambit follows.

[A, male, B, female, playing together with tool belt]:

A. Hey, do you watch Horrible House?

B. No.

A. I watch Horrible House. Horrible House is silly.

B. O.K., gimme the flashlight. We gotta turn it on. [A hands flash-
    light to B.]

Move 1-A. Horrible House is funny. Do you know why?

Move 2-B. Why?

Move 3-A. 'Cause Branch always does silly stuff.

B. Unhuh.

[A goes on to describe what Branch does.]

The function of maintaining the partner's wavering attention is clear, for B is more interested in playing with the tools than discussing the television show.

Only five instances of the rhetorical gambit occurred, all of them among the older dyads. Given the small sample, it is improper to claim developmental significance for this finding. If, however, a routine is a series of reciprocal moves in fixed order with a specific function, then variation in the form and context of its use probably depends on learning the formally simpler variety in its basic function and simplest context (i.e., the discourse initial context rather than the embedded context). In adult speech, of course, the summons-answer routine usually serves as a first move in a more complex chain of sustained conversational interaction. Learning to converse may entail, at least in part, learning such short fixed routines, learning to extend or displace features or components of such sequences, and finally learning to combine the sequences and their variants.

Discussion

Our protocols, taken from children's free-play situations, included many instances of private (or egocentric) speech, for example, repetitions, monologuing, and collective monologuing (Piaget, 1926), as well as muttering, self-answered questions, and task self-guidance (Kohlberg et al., 1968). The data suggested, however, that the children were mutually engaged the majority of the time and that most of their utterances were mutually responsive, that is, adapted to the speech or nonverbal behavior of their partner. Social speech, as defined here, appeared in abundance, and all dyads were able to sustain mutually responsive speech beyond simple exchanges. Furthermore, both younger and older dyads used a conventionalized series of verbal moves to create a state of mutual involvement. It should be emphasized that the present results do not contradict earlier estimates of the incidence of private or egocentric speech or accounts of its gradual decline. This paper stresses, however, that genuinely *social* behavior does in fact occur between children in the age range of $3\frac{1}{2}$–5 years and that the spontaneous speech of this age may reflect the emergence of the social understandings that underlie such acts as invitations, requests, insults, and excuses. Further exploration of what is said and what is done in children's early social interaction is clearly warranted.

In his study of covert speech in children, Conrad suggested that (at ages 3–5 when overt speech is fluent) "children do not talk silently to themselves because they have nothing biologically useful to say" (1971, p. 403). This further emphasizes the fundamentally social nature of early speech. From a role-theoretical perspective one can argue that children are sociocentric from birth, but lack the skills and talents necessary to interact. As a consequence, interaction among children is initially centered on games concerned with manipulating the physical environment, in what appears to be parallel and egocentric play (cf. Piaget 1932). Language may then develop, as Bruner (1972) suggests, within this context of action and rule-governed play. We would argue, however, that early language serves, not only to coordinate the children's actions, but also to facilitate mutual engagement which has those actions as its focus. As children become able to sustain an interaction per se, play activity becomes less important as a vehicle for promoting these relationships; this development continues until children can interact solely by verbal means. We propose, then, that early activities that promote the acquisition and use of verbal forms of interpersonal contact are biologically useful, for they must precede those later derivations from basic dialogue which become monologue, inner speech or thought, writing, and, finally, adult dialogue.

Piaget found, in his study of children's ideas about causation, that in the period of precausality questions about psychological motives far outnumbered questions about causal explanation. This suggests that learning to detect and interpret verbal cues of intent would be a major skill developed during the period when children practice social communication. It should also be the case that a significant proportion of social communication at this stage is devoted to organizing and structuring the social situation itself. We hope to find further examples of behavior sequences that, with practice, will form the habitual repertoires on which more mature communication behavior depends.

17

David Furrow

Social and Private Speech
at Two Years

Investigators who have studied children's uses (functions) of language traditionally distinguish between speech that is directed to a social audience and speech
that is not (Dore, 1974; Piaget, 1926; Rees, 1978; Schachter, Kirshner, Klips,
Friedricks and Saunders, 1974; Vygotsky, 1962). Moreover, language use has
been examined in one of these contexts to the exclusion of the other. Bates,
Benigni, Bretherton, Camaioni, and Volterra (1977), Bruner (1975b), Dore
(1974), and Schachter et al. (1974) considered social speech while explicitly
excluding private speech (i.e., speech that occurs in social situations that is not
directed to other persons; Piaget, 1926). Halliday (1975) studied all speech as
social, ignoring the possibility of private speech. And Goodman (1981), Kohlberg, Yaeger, and Hjertholm (1968), and Rubin and Dyck (1980) conducted
detailed examinations of private speech with little or no attention to social
speech. None of these studies gives an overall view of the functions of both
children's social and private speech.

Current literature does not allow us to compare the two speech contexts
across studies because (1) no two investigators have used the same functional
classification scheme, and (2) functions have not been analyzed into categories
independent of their presumed intended audience. Rubin and Dyck (1980), who
studied private speech, and Halliday (1975), who considered social functions,
exemplify the variation among functional categories across studies. Rubin and
Dyck defined "material comments," "activity comments," "directions to self,"
and "question" categories, among others; Halliday wrote of "instrumental,"
"interactional," "regulatory," and "personal" speech functions, among others.

Abridged from "Social and private speech at two years" by D. Furrow, 1984, *Child Development*, 55,
355-362. Copyright 1984 by Society for Research in Child Development. Reprinted by permission of
publisher and author.

Interdependence between function and categories of presumed audience has existed because previous studies (Halliday, 1975; Kohlberg et al., 1968; Schachter et al., 1974) have made assumptions about the functions of inter- and intrapersonal speech that determined a priori whether some utterances were assigned a social or personal audience. Halliday's functional schema, which ignores the existence of private speech, is an obvious example here.

The present research looks at the functions of social and private speech using the same classification scheme for both in an attempt to determine empirically whether there are functional differences across contexts. Speech samples were collected from 2-year-old children in a free-play situation with an adult. Sessions were videotaped, and from videotapes the social behaviors that accompanied utterances were examined to make judgments about the audience to which utterances were directed; that is, an attempt was made to determine the social context of utterances. Three social context categories were defined—eye contact, other social, and private speech. Utterances were then classified as serving 1 of 12 functions using a taxonomy designed to have categorizing criteria orthogonal to those used in making social context judgments. Percentages of each context made up by each of the 12 functions were compared.

Method

SUBJECTS

Twelve children, 23–25 months of age, served as subjects. Equal numbers of males and females and of first-borns and later-borns were selected. Subjects were recruited from a listing of infants whose parents had responded favorably to an earlier general request for research subjects. All children were from graduate-student or middle-income families. Children's mean Stanford–Binet IQ score was 105 (sd = 21.47). Mean length utterances (MLUs) spanned Brown's (1973) early stage 1 to stage 3, ranging from 1.34 to 3.02.

PROCEDURE

Data were collected in a play setting in a child's home. One half hour of free play was videotaped on each of 2 days. The first day allowed the child to become acquainted with the experimenter, while data analyses were performed on day 2 data. A camera was mounted on a tripod and located approximately 8 feet from the child and a male experimenter who were seated opposite each other with toys placed between them. Adjustments in camera angle were made from the front; that is, while still seated near the child, the experimenter swiveled the camera in the child's direction. Excluding major disruptions (such as bathroom visits) during which taping was stopped, only 49 out of a total 2449 (or 2.00%) of children's utterances occurred off camera.

For both sessions, the experimenter visited a child at home during a time when mother felt the child would be awake and alert. Camera equipment was set up in a play area where a selection of the child's toys were available. Taping was begun when the child had adapted to the experimenter and the camera equipment (i.e., the child was willing to interact, and the mother judged the child to be exhibiting normal play behaviors), and 30 minutes of records were taken. Taping continued as long as the child remained in the same room with the camera. A session was unstructured, with the child primarily controlling the sequence of events, although sessions always included a variety of play activities. On day 1, mothers who chose to do so were allowed to participate in activities; on day 2, however, people other than the experimenter and the child were not welcomed in the play. On both day 1 and day 2, the experimenter was the child's primary social partner. He assumed the role of a socially responsive, active participant in the child's activities, but not that of the instigator of play topics or verbal interactions; children were primarily in control of the nature of the play and any utterances that occurred. For 2 of the 12 children, only one session was conducted because of scheduling problems; these children's mothers did not participate in the play session, and so videotaping conditions were identical to those of day 2.

Although the sessions were unstructured, they always included a variety of play activities. Sampling from several children, activities included play with dolls, trucks, blocks, and Tinker Toys. Speech topics covered these activities as well as objects present in the room (e.g., fireplaces, family photos) and objects or events not present in the room (e.g., oil deliveries, daddies).

Transcripts of children's and adult's speech were made from videotapes. Speech samples for each child were drawn from day 2 transcripts, using Brown's (1973, p. 54) rules, with the following modifications: (1) speech samples of 200 as opposed to 100 utterances were drawn (a modification in rule 1), (2) all comprehensible and incomprehensible speech utterances were included, as were other vocalizations with the exception of laughing, breathing, and effort noises (modifying rule 2), (3) no more than two, as opposed to all, direct repetitions of an utterance were included in a sample (modifying rule 3), (4) any child utterance that was a response to an adult question was excluded from the sample (an added rule), and (5) all utterances that occurred off camera were omitted (an added rule). For children who had speech samples taken from a first visit (the two children with 1 day only conducted and a third child who did not produce enough utterances on day 2), sampling began at a later point in the session (a further change in Brown's rule 1).

The data were obtained from videotaped records of sample utterances. The tapes were played to classify the social behaviors that accompanied an utterance into one of three social context categories (defined below). They were played again to classify utterances into 1 of 12 function categories (defined below). All classifications were made by an observer unaware of the concerns of this study. This observer (and the second observer) were trained on social context and functional coding by the experimenter, using videotapes of 2- to $2\frac{1}{2}$-year-old children who were not a part of this study. Observers were trained separately. The experimenter and an observer coded a child's speech and then compared categorizations and discussed differences. The first observer had coded at least 30 children's social contexts and functions prior to doing the analyses here; the second observer had experience with two transcripts.

SOCIAL CONTEXT

Three social context categories—eye contact, other social, and private speech— were defined to discriminate social from private speech. Briefly, the three contexts were (1) eye contact, where eye contact occurred during an utterance's expression or in the preceding or following 2 seconds, (2) other social, where no eye contact occurred during an utterance or in the preceding or following 2 seconds, but other social indicators did—for example, the child's behavior involved the adult, or the utterance was near other utterances with social signs, and (3) private speech, where no social markings accompanied an utterance and it was isolated from utterances with social markings. More detail on context follows.

An utterance was scored as occurring in an eye contact context if the child had sustained eye contact with an adult during its expression or in the 2 seconds preceding or following it unless such eye contact (1) occurred entirely during another utterance, (2) terminated just before the utterance began but had been prolonged eye contact that overlapped with a previous utterance and ended contiguously with it, or (3) began just after an utterance with the expression of a subsequent utterance. In these instances, the eye contact was scored for the adjacent utterance only.

An utterance was considered in the other social context if, during the interval circumscribed by the 2 seconds preceding and following it, (1) the child's behavior involved an adult (through physical contact or approach, or extension of arms toward the adult), or (2) an adult's behavior involved the child (through physical contact or an action attracting the child's gaze). Furthermore, if (3) an utterance contained a vocative, it was included in this category. The remaining criteria depended on the relationship between an utterance and surrounding ones. These included a child's utterance (4) having the same topic as a preceding adult utterance (one that ended no more than 2 seconds before the child's began), (5) being preceded or followed by a sequence in which the child responded to an adult question, or (6) occurring within 2 seconds of an utterance that had eye contact or any of the factors listed as 1–5 above associated with it. Finally, any utterance that occurred within 2 seconds of an utterance that had eye contact or any of the factors listed as 1–6 above associated with it was also included in the other social category.

All remaining utterances were classified as the private speech context. These utterances were not associated with eye contact nor with social interactive behaviors as defined above, and they were temporally isolated (more than 2 seconds) from utterances that did accompany such behaviors.

Second observer judgments were obtained for 100 randomly chosen utterances, and the percentage of agreement was determined. At first, the second observer watched the video portion of a tape and was not permitted to hear the utterances she rated. This required that the first observer listen to the tape and give a hand signal to delineate the interval in which a judgment was required. The observer was asked to categorize a child's behavior during the signaled interval in the eye contact category if there was behavioral interaction between adult and child. It was necessary to play the audio portion of the tape to the second observer to allow the remaining utterances to be sorted into other social and private speech contexts. Second observer categorizations of social context agreed 94% of the time with first observer judgments.

FUNCTIONS

Twelve exhaustive categories of functions were defined, based on functional distinctions drawn by Bruner (1975), Halliday (1975), and Kohlberg et al. (1968). An overview of the functional categories used and a general characterization of what they reflect is given below. Then, the procedure followed for utterance categorization is described.

The functional categories were:

1. Instrumental: An utterance refers to the child's wants, and/or an utterance is whined—for example, "I want it."
2. Regulatory: An utterance refers to an event that might be immediately carried out; another person is the specified agent, or there is no agent and the child does not perform the action herself—for example, "Go there."
3. Self-regulatory: An utterance refers to an event that might be immediately carried out; the child is the stated agent or there is no agent and the child performs the action herself—for example, "I put that there."
4. Attentional: An utterance refers to a sensory event that is ongoing or might be immediately carried out—for example, "Look."
5. Interactional: Utterance content is a conventional greeting—for example, "Hi."
6. Expressive: Utterance content is an evaluative opinion, an expression of an internal state, or a stock phrase that expresses feeling—for example, "I love you."
7. Referential: An utterance refers to a present object or a present event that does not involve the child—for example, "That."
8. Describing own activity: An utterance refers to an ongoing or just completed event in which the child was involved—for example, "Putting it."
9. Question: Utterance intonation contour resembles adult rising question

intonation and/or an utterance is syntactically a question—for example, "What that?"

10. Imaginary: An utterance is sung, is word play, or represents a transformation of real objects or events, whether present or not—for example, "That hat" (said of block on head).

11. Informative: An utterance refers to a nonpresent object or event—for example, "Daddy at work."

12. Incomprehensible: An utterance is unaudible or incomprehensible.

Utterances were classified into one and only one functional category. If an utterance contained more than one proposition, classification was based on the clause that was more elaborated or, if clauses were of equal length, on what the observer judged as the central proposition of the utterance. In classifications, first considered was whether an utterance was comprehensible or incomprehensible. Incomprehensible utterances were placed into a single category. Comprehensible utterances were further categorized (see below).

Second, intonation contour was used for classifications. If an utterance was made with what the observer considered to be question intonation, it was classified in the question category. If an utterance was whined, it was classified as instrumental. Singing made an imaginary utterance.

Third, certain utterance contents determined their classification. Use of "I want" or any request or demand for behavior that would be nurturant to the child were signs of an instrumental function. Evaluative opinions (usually yes or no) or other expressions of the child's feelings (determined by content or by one of the stock phrases that carry such meaning, such as uh-oh!) were called expressive utterances. Question syntax made an utterance a question. Standard interactional utterances (greetings, etc). were interactional. If a sensory verb (look, see, etc.) was central to an utterance and was used in the present tense, that utterance was attentional.

Fourth, the content of linguistic utterances and their relationship to the environment was considered. Utterances either referred to objects or events (action sequences). Utterances that named a location were classified with events if the location was or immediately became involved in an action; otherwise they were classified as objects. If an utterance named an object or an aspect of an object, then whether the object was present or absent was noted. If present, then the utterance was scored as referential. If absent, then the utterance was informative. If the object named represented a transformation of a present or absent object, then the utterance was imaginative.

If an event was referred to or described, more factors were considered than for objects. As with objects, presence or absence was noted, but also whether the event had just occurred (in the prior 2 seconds), was ongoing at the time of the utterance, occurred in the 2 seconds following it, or was capable of being immediately carried out by a present agent was considered. Moreover, whether the event referred to involved the child's own action was taken into account. An utterance was considered to be self-regulatory when it referred to an event that was just about to occur or potentially could and the child was the stated agent and/or the child immediately carried out the action. Such utterances were regulatory when the child was not the stated agent and did not carry out the action. An utterance telling of a more distant future event or past one was judged informative. An utterance that named an event that was occurring or had just occurred was describing own activity if the child was involved in the action, and it was referential if not. An utterance that described an unreal or fanciful event was imaginary.

Percentage agreement on functional categorization was determined by observations made by a second observer who was unaware of any of the other concerns of this study on 1000 randomly sampled utterances. Overall, first and second raters agreed 87% of the time on function classifications. Reliability within categories ranged from 71% (imaginary) to 95% (questions). Observers agreed over 75% of the time on all functions except imaginary and interactional (73%).

Functional categorization was independent of decisions about the social direction of an utterance; for example, both the self-regulatory function, which is traditionally defined as occurring in private speech, and the interactional function, which is traditionally thought of as an interpersonal function, can occur in any of the three social contexts. The distribution of functions across social contexts was determined empirically, not by category definitions.

Results

Overall, children's utterances were proportionately distributed among the three contexts, with 58.4 of 200 (29.2%) in eye contact, 70.4 (35.2%) in other social, and 71.2 or (35.6%) in private speech contexts. On the other hand, there was much variability among individuals in eye contact ($sd = 12.51$) and private ($sd = 12.90$) utterances, with other social ones being more constant from child to child ($sd = 4.20$). These data yielded a coefficient of egocentrism (the proportion of spontaneous utterances occurring privately; Piaget, 1926) of about one-third. Regarding overall functional use, the referential function was predominant [57.0 (28.5%) of all utterances].* A repeated-measures ANOVA was executed on context $\times$ function data, giving an $F(35,385) = 13.85$, $p < 0.01$. This showed that certain combinations of function and social context appeared more frequently than others.

Analysis of context differences in functions was performed post hoc, using methods suggested by Rodger (1975). So that differences in overall frequencies of the contexts would not contribute to differences among functions, comparisons were based on the percentages of each context made up of the different functions. Percentages were calculated for each child, and then averaged. These data appear in Table 17-1. A one-way repeated-measures ANOVA on percentage data

*Table omitted. [Eds.]

Table 17-1. *Percentages of Eye Contact, Other Social, and Private Speech Contexts Composed of the 12 Functions*

Function	Eye contact	Other social[a]	Private speech	Differences
Referential	28.8	28.9	29.0	
Incomprehensible	18.4	18.5	21.3	
Describes own activity	11.1	12.7	16.5	Private > eye, other
Expressive	5.4	11.9	6.8	Other > private > eye
Questions	8.2	6.3	7.6	Eye, private > other
Self-regulatory	4.1	4.3	10.3	Private > eye, other
Informative	10.1	4.8	1.7	Eye > other > private
Regulatory	5.3	5.2	2.1	Eye, other > private
Attentional	3.5	3.0	1.7	Eye > other, private
Imaginative	2.0	1.9	1.3	
Instrumental	1.4	1.7	0.9	
Interactional	1.7	0.9	0.8	

[a]This column of figures does not total exactly 100.0 because of rounding.

yielded an $F(35,385) = 14.71$, $p < 0.01$. Comparisons were done on these data using orthogonal contrasts. Six of these contrasts were significant, giving seven significantly different clusters of means. The ordering of functions within contexts is given below, using implied population means from the analysis (Rodger, 1975). All implied means are multiples of $\sigma\sqrt{1-\rho}$. In all three contexts, the referential function is predominant (1.90), and incomprehensible utterances are next most frequent (0.96), but thereafter distributions are different. In the eye contact context, in decreasing order come informative and describing own activity utterances (0.27), questions (−0.07), regulatory and expressive (−0.26), self-regulatory and attentional (−0.39), and finally imaginative, instrumental, and interactional (−0.62) functions. In the other social context, describing own activity and expressive functions are third most frequent (0.27), with questions and regulatory (−0.26), self-regulatory and informative (−0.39), and attentional, imaginative, instrumental, and interactional (−0.62) functions following. In private speech, describing own activity utterances are as frequent as incomprehensible utterances (0.96), followed by self-regulatory (0.27), questions and expressive (−0.07), and regulatory, attentional, imaginary, instrumental, informative, and interactional functions (−0.62). The implied means indicate that informative, regulatory, and attentional utterances make up a significantly greater percentage of the eye contact context than the private speech context, while the opposite is true for describing own activity and self-regulatory functions. For all of these five functions, their relative importance in the other social context is equivalent to that in the eye contact context (regulatory, describing own activity) or private speech context (attentional), or it lies between the two (informative). The expressive function is more represented in the private speech context as opposed to the eye contact context, but it is most important in other social speech. Finally, questions show no differences between eye contact and private speech contexts, but are a smaller percentage of the other social context. The final column of Table 17-1 reports these differences. No differences on referential, incomprehensible, imaginative, instrumental, and interactional functions were found.

Discussion

This study of 2 year olds' speech empirically demonstrated differences in the functions that occur in social and private contexts. Since eye contact and private speech categories best represent recent definitions of social and private speech (Bates et al., 1977; Goodman, 1981), differences in functions across these contexts are best related to previous literature. The other social context is considered below. In past investigations of social speech, attention has been paid to referential, instrumental, regulatory, and interactional functions (Bates et al., 1977; Bruner, 1975; Dore, 1974; Halliday, 1975), while informative and imaginative ones have also been studied (these are Halliday's terms). Table 17-1 shows that regulatory, informative, and attentional functions are a significantly greater percentage of social than private speech utterances. The self-regulatory function has dominated discussions of private speech. Kohlberg et al. (1968, p. 732) viewed it as the sole function of this speech form with word play, describing own activity, questions answered by self, self-guiding comments, and muttering as "different developmental levels of behavior with a common self-communicative functional significance." (For related descriptions of private speech, see Goodman, 1981; Rubin, 1979; Rubin and Dyck, 1980.) Fuson (1979) envisaged emotional/ expressive and imaginary as uses separate from the self-regulatory function of private speech. Table 17-1 shows that self-regulatory, expressive, and describing own activity functions are more predominant in private than social speech. Overall, empirical data from the present study support many of the assumptions made in previous investigations.

While there were differences in use of several functions across social and private contexts, these were statistical and not absolute differences. In some instances, where functions are predominantly in one context and nominally in the other (e.g., informative makes up 10.1% of the eye contact context, but only 1.7% of the private context), it is possible that measurement error is responsible for their dual appearance. In other cases, however, it is clear that a function appears in both contexts, although it is favored in one. For example, describing own activity is highly represented in both social and private contexts, although it makes up a greater percentage of the latter. If it is assumed that any functional percentage that fell into the least frequent group of functions could be considered measurement error, informative, attentional, and regulatory functions were exclusively social functions, while none were exclusively private. That uniquely social but no unique private speech functions were found for 2 year olds fits in well with the hypothesis given by Vygotsky (1962, p. 19) that "egocentric speech forms when the child transfers social, collaborative forms of behavior to the sphere of inner personal psychic functions." Investigations of other ages are needed to substantiate this hypothesis more generally.

Discussion thus far has focused on eye contact and private speech contexts, based on the assumption that eye contact was the strongest indicator that an utterance was directed to a social audience (Goodman, 1981) and that the absence of any social behaviors demonstrated the least amount of social intent. The two contexts theoretically define opposite poles of a dimension of "socialness" of utterances, with other social context presumably lying between the two extremes. Empirical findings support the hypothetical relationships among the three contexts, since 9 of the 12 functions studied made up percentages of the other social context that were between percentages for the eye contact and private speech contexts (see Table 17-1).

Given that functional differences among contexts have been empirically demonstrated, it is the task of future research to determine *why* differences exist. One possibility is that certain functions—such as regulatory—require social intervention before consequences will result from their use, whereas others—such as self-regulatory—do not. If it is assumed that social feedback to an utterance is usually associated with children's social signals, and not with their absence, then a bias toward social use of regulatory speech and private use of self-regulatory speech is expected because of children's past experience with using each function. This hypothesis needs empirical confirmation. Furthermore, assumptions about what consequences are associated with particular functions need to be examined. While the regulatory and self-regulatory utterances both have expected overt physical consequences (the performance of an action by another or by the self), it is less clear what consequences result from use of informative utterances, for example. Possibilities include (1) overt responses from another, (2) overt responses from the self, or even (3) internal cognitive consequences with *no* overt manifestations. Future research should specify consequences associated with each function type and demonstrate that these consequences predict context differences in functions. Finally, a child's age and speech setting may relate to the consequences that exist for any given function (and thus to functional differences across social contexts); therefore, these variables should be studied as well.

18

Jacqueline Sachs and Judith Devin

Young Children's Use of Age-Appropriate Speech Styles in Social Interaction and Role-Playing

It is well known that adult speakers have different speech styles for different situations, and one style that has received much attention recently is "baby talk" (speech modifications appropriate for young listeners). The focus of this paper is the use of this speech style in children. Observations were made of four children in five situations: talking to their mothers, to peers, to babies, to baby dolls, and pretending that they themselves were babies. Analyses of these observations provide at least partial answers to several questions about the children's ability to adapt their speech to listeners, both in social interaction and in role-playing. Four questions were addressed.

1. To what extent did each child use speech characteristics appropriate for babies? Until recently, it had been assumed, in line with Piaget's (1926) description of the child as "egocentric," that young children could not take account of listener characteristics in planning their speech. This assumption seems to be contradicted by reports of children's "code-switching" abilities (Weeks, 1971; Gleason, 1973). These reports were supported by the findings of Shatz and Gelman (1973): 4 year olds used shorter sentences, fewer complex constructions, and more attention-getting devices in speaking to 2 year olds than they did with their mothers or with peers. Shatz and Gelman pointed out that these modifications are also found in mothers' speech to young children. We were interested in learning more about the degree to which young children use mother-language characteristics when talking to babies and have analyzed several speech characteristics not studied by Shatz and Gelman.

2. Were the modifications observed in our samples the result of the com-

Abridged from "Young children's use of age-appropriate speech styles in social interaction and role-playing," by J. Sachs and J. Devin, 1976, *Journal of Child Language*, **3**, 81–98. Copyright 1976 by Cambridge University Press. Reprinted by permission of publisher and authors.

munication pressures of the immediate situation, or did the children have a "speech style" for babies? Mother-language characteristics can arise from at least two sources. First, when one talks to a baby or young child, the responses of the immature listener impose certain pressures on the speaker to simplify, to repeat, to use "colorful" speech, and so on. Second, most adult speakers, whether they interact with young children or not, seem to know that there is a speech style (or various elements that make up a style) considered appropriate for children. The elements of baby talk would appear to have their origins in communication pressures such as those just mentioned, but knowing a style might be thought of as a short-cut to learning to interact successfully with babies. For example, when Snow (1972) asked mothers and nonmothers to make tape recordings for children, the adults modified their speech in ways that were appropriate, even though the listeners were not present. In this study, we were interested in the extent to which young children have incorporated some sort of knowledge of an appropriate style for babies. The situation in which the children spoke to dolls provided information relevant to this question. Since there was no real listener, there would be no reason for the children to simplify their speech or use other mother-language characteristics, unless they had some more abstract appreciation of baby talk.

3. What did the children know about the speech of babies? Mother-language characteristics could be used by children talking to babies or dolls simply because they had heard mothers talk that way, rather than because they had some idea themselves of the limitations of babies' linguistic or cognitive abilities. The situation in which children role-played that they were babies gives some indication about what these children knew about babies' speech.

4. How accurate were the children in naturalistic role-playing situations? Piagetian theory and much of the child development literature has suggested that young children cannot role-play. On the other hand, it is common knowledge that even 2 year olds "pretend to be" various characters in their play. So far, there has been little systematic research on this type of natural role-playing, or on how accurately children's language reflects the roles they play. Our data seemed to offer some relevant evidence. Speaking to a doll and speaking as a baby is role-playing of a sort that often occurs spontaneously in the young child's speech.

The Speech Samples

Four children (3;9–5;5) were observed. The children all appeared to be normal in language and intellectual development. One had a younger sibling, who served as the "baby" listener, but the others were only children. The baby listeners ranged in age between 1;2 and 2;5, and all were using some speech. The children were tape recorded by their mothers at home in a number of situations. Whenever possible, spontaneous play and interactions were recorded. These observations were supplemented by sessions in which the mother made play suggestions (as will be described below). The listeners were all familiar to the children being observed. If a child did not readily participate in the interaction or role-playing situation when it was suggested, the child was not used. Two other children (one boy and one girl) would not talk to dolls or as babies when it was suggested, and were not included in the sample. The mean number of utterances for each child in each situation was 71. The total number of utterances analyzed was 1430.

The samples with real listeners, which will be referred to as *to mother*, *to peer*, and *to baby* consisted of spontaneous speech in a free play situation. The samples of speech to the baby doll (*to baby doll*) were either of the children's spontaneous speech to his or her own doll or speech generated after the mother had suggested that the child talk to the doll "who is a baby just learning how to talk." To elicit speech *as baby* the mother suggested that the child talk to her "like a baby just learning how to talk," except for one case in which the child spontaneously also spoke for the baby in the *to baby doll* situation.

The sample of speech *to mother* or *to peer* was collected first. Since the observations were made over several days, any increase in the complexity of the child's speech that came about by natural development would cause more complexity in the speech *to baby*, *to baby doll*, and *as baby*, contrary to the hypothesis. The sample of speech *to baby doll* was collected before the sample *to baby*, to avoid the possibility that the child would view the doll as the child with whom he or she had recently interacted.

The tape recordings were transcribed and the transcriptions were checked by another listener. For the planned analyses, described below, the data were coded independently by three judges, and cases of disagreement were either resolved by mutual agreement or omitted. The proportion of agreement for the various speech characteristics coded ranged from 0.92 to 1.00.

The Analyses

Before the samples were collected, predictions were made concerning a number of speech characteristics that had been reported in research on mothers' speech to children. We will first describe the mother-language characteristics and then give the predictions concerning them.

Some mother-language characteristics involve the simplification of speech. In this study, simplified speech could also come about because the child being observed was less comfortable in the *to baby*, *to baby doll*, or *as baby* situations. Therefore, simplification alone would not show that the children were using baby talk style. Other mother-language characteristics (such as the increased use of questions or speaking with a higher pitch) do not involve simplification, and finding these characteristics in the speech of young children to babies and dolls would strengthen the test of the hypothesis that the modifications are based on some sense of their appropriateness for the listener. We have adopted Ferguson's

(1964) term for the mother-language characteristics that do not involve simplification. He called them "clarification" characteristics. Such modifications of the input might help the child comprehend the meaning more easily, pay more attention, or notice the linguistic structure.

The simplification characteristics analyzed were:

1. *Mean length of utterance* (MLU). MLU is often used as a rough index of complexity in children's speech, and has also been used in most studies of mother's speech to children (e.g., Snow, 1972). The MLU in words was calculated following the coding procedure reported by Shatz and Gelman.

2. *Mean preverb length.* This is the mean number of words before the main verb in all clauses. This measure was used by Snow (1972) in assessing the complexity of mothers' speech to children, because she felt that it might give a more sensitive index for fairly complex speech than does MLU alone. The procedure reported in her paper was used.

3. *Tenses other than present.* Since the frequency of use of various verb tenses might also reflect complexity in speech, the proportion of utterances that used any tense other than present was calculated.

4–5. *Subordinate constructions and relative clauses.* Complex syntactic constructions such as these are less frequent in speech to young children (Snow, 1972). Also, Shatz and Gelman found that these constructions (among others) were less frequent in the speech of 4 year olds to 2 year olds. Shatz and Gelman's definitions were used for the analyses.

The clarification characteristics analyzed were:

1. *Names.* One finds more use of attention-getting devices in mother-language (Snow, 1972). One attention-getting device is to use the listener's name in the utterance. The proportion of utterances was calculated in which the listener's name (or name-substitute such as *mommy, little dolly,* or *baby*) was used.

2. *Repetitions.* Mothers often repeat utterances to young children, either exactly or maintaining the same general semantic content while changing the linguistic form (Snow, 1972). The proportion of exact or modified repetitions in the various situations was calculated. An utterance was counted as a modified repetition if it used some word(s) from the preceding utterance and maintained the same semantic intent. For example, a word or words might be added, as in *I wipe my tea, I wipe my tea up* or *I hurt my piggie. Becky, I hurt my piggie.* A word or words might be deleted, as in *Some more in there. In there* or *Don't put her foot in that little hole. Don't.* Occasionally, a word was substituted, as in *Drink your thing down. Drink your stuff down* or *Lookit the kitty. See the kitty.*

3. *Questions.* Adults use more questions when speaking to a young child (Snow, 1972). The proportion of utterances that were in interrogative form was calculated for each condition. The function of the question (e.g., a question serving as an imperative) was also determined according to the following definitions. (*a*) External-world (sought information about things external to listener, as in *Where is the fireman?*), (*b*) Internal-state (sought information about the listener's wants, needs, and likes as in *Do you want some?*), (*c*) Request (asked for something or for permission to do something, as in *Can I take some more?*), (*d*) Imperative (politely asked listener to do something or stop doing something, as in *Don't do that, O.K.?*), (*e*) attention-getting (directed listener's attention to interaction, as in *Know what?*), (*f*) Instruction (elicited answer to something that speaker knew, as in *Is it red?*), (*g*) Confirmation (sought approval from listener for statement or action, often with tag, as in *I'm putting it on, O.K.?*), and (*h*) Repetition (asked for repetition or clarification of listener's utterance, as in *Racket hair?*).

4. *Imperatives.* Mothers use more imperatives to their young children (Snow, 1972); therefore, the proportion of imperatives in each sample was calculated.

5. *Phonetic aspects.* Most researchers who have studied baby talk style have noted special prosodic and sound substitution features (e.g., Ferguson, 1964). Weeks (1971) found that even very young children used these "register markers." Instances of the use of register characteristics were noted on the transcripts. Although the cues to baby talk style have not been thoroughly described, we found that the coders were in good agreement as to whether this register was being used in a particular situation. The cues seemed to be primarily higher pitch and exaggerated intonation patterns. We have not quantified these results, but will report some observations.

The following predictions were made for the simplification and clarification characteristics:

1. Speech *to peer* and *to mother* would not differ significantly. This prediction was based on the findings reported by Shatz and Gelman.
2. Speech *to baby* would be simpler than speech *to mother* (and *to peer*), and would show more clarification characteristics.
3. Speech *to baby doll* would be simpler than speech *to mother* (and *to peer*), and would show more clarification characteristics.
4. Speech *as baby* would be simpler than speech *to mother* (and *to peer*). No prediction was made concerning clarification characteristics.

After the samples had been collected and the planned comparisons completed, other observations were made concerning the form, pragmatic function, and content of the children's speech in the various situations.

Results

The results will be presented for each child, first in terms of the planned comparisons and then in terms of the other observations about the speech samples.

Sally (Age 3;9)

As well as being the youngest child reported here, Sally had by far the most immature speech. She engaged in word play during the sessions, made many morphological errors or omissions in her speech (e.g., *Him don't have two of them, Daddy doing this*), and used other early sentence structures (e.g., *That not hold on*). She also gave us the smallest speech sample of the four children, using 239 utterances over the five situations.

The results of the planned analyses are summarized in Table 18-1. As hypothesized, none of the differences between *to mother* and *to peer* was statistically significant. However, if there were no difference between the two situations, we should expect to find some of the analyses revealing differences in one direction (i.e., more like speech *to baby*) and some in the other. In fact, for most of the analyses, the speech *to peer* differed from speech *to mother* in the direction predicted for speech *to baby*. This result is consistent with that found for the other children: *to peer* usually differed from *to mother* in the direction predicted for *to baby*.

To baby differed from *to mother* in the predicted direction for all but one analysis. There were significantly more Imperatives *to baby* ($t = 4.23$, $df = 128$,

Table 18-1. *Sally: Results of Analyses of Simplification Characteristics and Clarification Characteristics in the Various Situations*

Analysis	to mother	to peer	to baby	to baby doll	as baby
Mean length of utterance	4.35	3.84	3.98	3.35*	2.83
Mean preverb length	1.46	1.65	1.25	1.03*	1.00
Proportion not present tense	0.34	0.29	0.21	0.05**	0.00
Proportion subordinates	0.01	0.00	0.00	0.00	0.00
Proportion relatives	0.00	0.00	0.00	0.00	0.00
Proportion names	0.03	0.09	0.11	0.22**	0.00
Proportion repetitions	0.04	0.09	0.05	0.07	0.17
Proportion questions	0.11	0.16	0.09	0.16	0.00
Proportion imperatives	0.08	0.16	0.38**	0.20	0.00

*$p < 0.05$, compared with *to mother*.

**$p < 0.01$, compared with *to mother*.

$p < 0.001$). To *baby* was significantly different from *to peer* also in the use of imperatives ($t = 2.98$, $df = 128$, $p < 0.01$), but of the other analyses, only half differed in the predicted direction. Thus, *to baby* seems to contain elements of a different speech style from that used *to mother*, but could be the same style used *to peer*, based on these analyses. However, other characteristics of the *to baby* speech would distinguish it from *to peer*. To *baby*, Sally used endearments (e.g., *Becky poo*), attempted to elicit imitations (e.g., *Say "I won't," Say "Some more cookie"*), and appeared to use the child's name as a second-person pronoun substitute in some instances (e.g., *Becky did it, Becky got a cookie*).*

To *baby doll* was different from *to mother* in the predicted direction for all analyses, with four being statistically significant: MLU ($t = 2.52$, $df = 118$, $p < 0.05$), Preverb Length ($t = 2.34$, $df = 118$, $p < 0.05$), Tense ($z = 4.49$, $p < 0.001$), and Names ($z = 3.52$, $p < 0.001$). Comparing *to baby doll* with *to peer*, there were significant differences for Preverb Length ($t = 2.81$, $df = 101$, $p < 0.01$) and Tense ($z = 3.76$, $p < 0.001$). Certain routines that seemed typical of baby talk were found in Sally's speech *to baby doll*, such as *There you go* (said when giving the doll some food), *That's a big girl*, and *Tea make you big girl*. Here, again, were utterances that may involve substitution of the name for "you": *I give some to Raggy Ann, I give Raggy Ann some tea*. Although Sally did make many morpheme errors in her speech generally, one structure that did not appear *to mother* or *to peer* was found in the *to baby doll* situation. She used, with exaggerated intonation, utterances such as *I loves you, I gives you hug*. Comparable constructions were correct *to peer* (*I wipe it up, I get some, I had a lot of it*), and did not appear *to mother* because more complex structures were always used (*I can't, I will fall, I talking to Judy a lot, I can read it when I go* (to school). Such utterances *to baby doll* may have been examples of baby talk routines.

As *baby* speech yielded nonsignificant differences in the predicted direction in all cases. However, the role-playing was very difficult for Sally to maintain. After the role-playing was suggested to her, most of her speech continued to be directed to her mother (these utterances were not counted as *to baby*), and she prefaced each of the role-playing utterances with *Baby says*. Thus, Sally did not really seem to shift into the role, though she seemed to know something about the kinds of things a younger child might say. All of these utterances were short, simple, and used babyish phonetic characteristics. As *baby*, Sally said things such as *Do like, I want bottle, I want in the scooter, Cookie please*. The extent to

---

*These utterances, found in some of the children's speech, may be a reflection of pronoun substitution in mothers' language. However, at least two other possibilities exist to explain this speech characteristic. First, young children often accompany their play with a "narration" about what they are doing. Thus an utterance such as *Becky got a cookie* may not be addressed to Becky or to any other listener. Also, in our situation, there was always an adult somewhere in the room with the child. Although the adult was not interacting in the play, the child could have occasionally addressed statements to the adult about the ongoing events. We see no way at present to distinguish among these possibilities, but it should be noted that utterances of this sort only appeared in the *to baby* and *to baby doll* situations.

which her utterances were appropriate may reflect a general awareness of how babies act (dependent) and sound, rather than an awareness of the linguistic abilities of babies. Sally supplied the most limited sample of *as baby* speech, but we shall see that at least two of the other children had difficulties similar to Sally's in this situation.*

Peter (Age 4;0)

The analysis for Peter is based on 498 utterances. The results of the planned analyses are shown in Table 18-2. In all but two analyses, *to peer* differed from *to mother* in the direction predicted for speech *to baby*. *To peer* had significantly shorter Preverb length ($t = 2.44$, $df = 257$, $p < 0.05$) and more Questions ($t = 2.84$, $df = 257$, $p < 0.01$). There was, however, a higher proportion of Subordinate constructions ($z = 2.23$, $p < 0.05$).

To baby differed from *to mother* as predicted by having a significantly shorter Preverb length ($t = 2.57$, $df = 257$, $p < 0.05$) and more Imperatives ($z = 2.51$, $p < 0.05$). There were significantly fewer Questions *to baby* ($z = 2.54$, $p < 0.05$). Comparing *to baby* with *to peer*, none of the differences was significant in the predicted direction. Again, Questions were significantly different in the direction opposite to that predicted ($z = 4.31$, $p < 0.001$).

Further analysis of Peter's use of Questions revealed that there were not only large differences in the proportion of questions in the various situations, but large differences also in the functions that the questions served. Both *to mother* and *to peer*, Peter used many tag questions (17% of his questions *to mother* and 61% of his questions *to peer* were tags). The function of these questions seemed to be seeking confirmation of a statement or an action (*And cut it out, O.K.?*, *We could use yours, huh?*, *You can tell him, all right?*). To mother, Peter also used many other questions that were really "answers to questions" with a rising intonation contour. Peter seemed to be asking for confirmation with these questions also. They might be thought of as tag questions without the tags, as in *We're going with Grandma?*, *They need garbage pails?* One interpretation of the high proportion of questions is that they were a conversational device—a way of keeping the listener involved. Another possibility is that they reflect Peter's experimentation with the tag question form. No full syntactic tags appeared in his speech, and he used tags in situations that did not seem appropriate. For example, when asked if this was his lunch, he replied, *No, I had lunch before, huh?* To mother, other questions were either External-world (40%) or Requests (16%). To peer, questions that did not function for Confirmation were also usually External-world. The functions of Questions *to baby* were in sharp contrast to those described above, with little use of tag questions. Most questions concerned Internal-state (70%), such as *Want to see how much there is?* and *Did you like it on the horses yesterday?* These questions reflected the general tone of Peter's

---

*Data for one of the subjects are omitted. [Eds.]

interaction with the younger child. He helped her, instructed her (*See how much, Feel it. It's cold, You don't supposed to smoke cigarettes*), and directed her behavior (*Put it on your little plate*).

To *baby doll* differed in the expected direction with significantly shorter Preverb Length ($t = 2.47$, $df < 231$, $p = 0.05$), more Names ($z = 4.36$, $p < 0.001$), and more Imperatives ($z = 2.87$, $p < 0.01$). Questions again differed significantly in the opposite direction ($z = 3.17$, $p < 0.01$). Comparing *to baby doll* with *to peer*, the former contained significantly more Names ($z = 2.28$, $p < 0.05$). Questions again differed significantly in the opposite direction ($z = 4.79$, $p < 0.001$). Of the six questions *to baby doll*, four were Internal-world. One tag question was used (*You're gonna come with me, O.K.?*) and one that, according to our definitions, was External-world (*Did you drink your water?*).

In the speech of the four children we observed, we never found an External-world question *to baby* or *to baby doll* that asked for information the listener would not know. Information-seeking questions not involving wants and likes always were about a past event that the listener had been involved in. In contrast, when the children talked *as baby* (with the mother as listener), External-world questions were used in about the same proportion as they were *to mother* and *to peer*. All of the children seemed to have a very good sense of what different listeners should be expected to know.

As *baby* differed in the expected direction for all analyses as compared with *to mother*, with significant differences for MLU ($t = 4.05$, $df = 310$, $p < 0.001$). Preverb Length ($t = 2.06$, $df = 310$, $p < 0.05$), and Tense ($z = 3.54$, $p < 0.001$). Questions were used significantly less frequently *as baby* ($z = 5.62$, $p < 0.001$).

Table 18-2. *Peter: Results of Analyses of Simplification Characteristics and Clarification Characteristics in the Various Situations*

Analysis	to mother	to peer	to baby	to baby doll	as baby
Mean length of utterance	5.94	5.92	5.34	4.98	4.45**
Mean preverb length	2.01	1.62*	1.53*	1.54*	1.72*
Proportion not present tense	0.42	0.31	0.30	0.42	0.23**
Proportion subordinate	0.03	0.09*	0.02	0.02	0.00
Proportion relatives	0.02	0.01	0.00	0.00	0.00
Proportion names	0.03	0.06	0.03	0.20**	0.02
Proportion repetitions	0.02	0.02	0.07	0.04	0.02
Proportion questions	0.34	0.53**	0.17**a	0.12**a	0.07**
Proportion imperatives	0.05	0.10	0.16*	0.18**	0.02

[a]Significant difference which is inconsistent with relevant hypothesis.

*$p < 0.05$, compared with *to mother*.

**$p < 0.01$, compared with *to mother*.

Comparing *as baby* with *to peer*, there were significant differences for MLU ($t =$ 3.95, $df = 310$, $p < 0.001$), Subordinates ($z = 3.51$, $p < 0.001$), Names ($z =$ 2.03, $p < 0.05$), and Questions ($z = 7.39$, $p < 0.001$). It seems reasonable to conclude from these results that *as baby* was a different type of speech from that *to mother* or *to peer*. However, the source of the difference may be primarily that the linguistic content was limited in appropriate ways. Much of Peter's role-playing speech was about "babyish" things—he talked about bottles, food, crying, sleeping, and the problems of being little. He was similar to Sally and Stephanie in that his role-playing was not consistent. For example, he would often check with his mother about some characteristic of babies (*Do they like to eat food?*) or he would describe his actions (*They crawl around. Like I'm doing it right now*). All of these utterances were counted in the *as baby* analysis because there was no objective way to code which utterances were really in the role. Even the utterances that seem clearly to be in the role were not always syntactically appropriate (*Can I hold my bottle? I just wanna go to bed, They say I'm a cry baby*). As well as knowing something about topics relevant to babies, Peter made phonetic modification of his speech that did not appear in the other situations.

Naomi (Age 5;5)

The results for Naomi are shown in Table 18-3, and are based on a sample of 387 utterances. *To peer* differed in the direction predicted for *to baby* in seven of the nine analyses, with significantly more Names ($z = 1.98$, $p < 0.05$) and Questions ($z = 2.83$, $p < 0.01$). *To baby* differed from *to mother* in having significantly more Names ($z = 4.30$, $p < 0.001$). Comparing *to baby* with *to peer*, none of the differences were significant. *To baby* was a difficult interaction for Naomi. Her listener was quite unresponsive, and she became frustrated by her inability to control his behavior. For Naomi, the more "abstract" baby, a doll, elicited mother-language characteristics much more than did interation with the 2 year old.

To baby doll differed significantly in the expected direction for MLU ($t =$ 5.17, $df = 200$, $p < 0.001$), Preverb Length ($t = 3.97$, $df = 200$, $p < 0.001$), Names ($z = 6.67$, $p < 0.001$), Repetitions ($z = 2.59$, $p < 0.01$), and Imperatives ($z = 2.57$, $p < 0.05$). Comparing *to baby doll* with *to peer*, there were significant differences for Preverb Length ($t = 3.16$, $df = 85$, $p < 0.01$) and Names ($z =$ 2.79, $p < 0.01$). *To baby doll*, Naomi talked about feeding and sleeping (e.g., *Want some milk?*, *Like your milk?*, *Good baby*, *Go to sleep*). Almost all of her utterances *to baby doll* were said with high pitch and exaggerated baby talk intonation. Sometimes this intonation even turned into singing, as when she repeated *You're sound asleep* several times, turning it into a lullaby. Some of her utterances reassured her doll (*Baby, it's all right. Nothing will happen. I'm never gonna get hurt*), and others accompanied teaching the doll to climb on the swing (*Now reach up. Reach up. Put your leg in. Up you go. Up*).

All of Naomi's questions *to baby doll* were Internal-state (83%) or Attention-

Table 18-3. *Naomi: Results of Analyses of Simplification Characteristics and Clarification Characteristics in the Various Situations*

Analysis	to mother	to peer	to baby	to baby doll	as baby
Mean length of utterance	6.38	5.37	3.67	3.60**	3.16**
Mean preverb length	2.26	2.18	2.33	1.39**	1.76*
Proportion not present tense	0.38	0.36	0.00	0.50	0.00
Proportion subordinate	0.02	0.03	0.00	0.00	0.00
Proportion relatives	0.03	0.00	0.00	0.00	0.00
Proportion names	0.02	0.09*	0.33**	0.35**	0.04
Proportion repetitions	0.05	0.09	0.00	0.15*	0.45**
Proportion questions	0.14	0.34**	0.17	0.13	0.29*
Proportion imperatives	0.11	0.11	0.17	0.25*	0.02

*$p < 0.05$, compared with *to mother*.

**$p < 0.01$, compared with *to mother*.

getting (17%). In contrast, *to mother* she used 38% External-world questions, 25% Requests, 19% Internal-state, 12% Attention-getting, and 6% Confirmations. *To peer*, 45% were External-world, 45% requests for Repetitions, and the rest Internal-state.

As *baby* was simpler than *to mother* in each analysis, with two being significant: MLU ($t = 5.61$, $df = 192$, $p < 0.001$) and Preverb Length ($t = 2.12$, $df = 192$, $p < 0.05$). The other analyses show that Naomi's *to baby* speech used characteristics that we had classified as "clarifying" more frequently than did her speech *to mother*, with more Repetitions ($z = 7.36$, $p < 0.001$) and Questions ($z = 2.31$, $p < 0.05$). Comparing *as baby* and *to peer*, again all the simplicity analyses were in the predicted direction. Among the clarification characteristics, Repetitions were more frequent *as baby* ($z = 3.88$, $p < 0.001$).

Naomi's role-playing was the most consistent of the four children we observed. This may be because she was the oldest child, but could also be because the role-playing was spontaneous rather than the result of a suggestion from her mother. (When Naomi talked to her doll in the *to baby* situation, she supplied the doll's speech as well.) Since the other children spoke *as baby* to their mothers, their inability to maintain the role may have been due to a conflict in situational cues. In a sense, Naomi's situation was easier, because she controlled it completely rather than having to respond to what another person said. On the other hand, she had to constantly shift roles, which the others did not do.

Naomi's *as baby* speech was generally simpler than her other speech. Was it accurate? The most complex utterances were entirely out of the range that one would expect of a baby just learning how to talk. The "baby" Naomi was role-playing still used a bottle and slept in a crib, but said *Could you put my sweater on?*,

I wanna lay down, OK?, *Oh, I'm just resting*, and *Now you don't let me do that again*. Naomi's notions about baby syntax were clearly not correct. What accounts for the simplification found in our analyses is that most of Naomi's utterances were more accurately babyish, e.g., *What dat?*, *Hat on*, *Bottle*, *Blanket*, *Pamper*, *No touch*. She repeated many single words, and often simplified utterances as she repeated them, e.g., *Hat on. Hat.*, *No touching. No touch.*, *I want some milk. Milk.* Furthermore, the phonetic aspects of Naomi's *as baby* speech were dramatically different from her normal or *to baby* speech. *As baby*, her speech was slow and hesitant with many phonological substitutions, even in the complex utterances, e.g., /w/ for /r/ and /l/, /d/ for /t/ and /y/, /z/ for /j/, /d/ or/z/ for ð/, /š/ for /s/. The content of the *as baby* speech, as for the other children, focused primarily on food, sleep, and dependency.

Conclusions

The children observed did not talk to younger listeners in the same way they talked to their mothers or their peers. To some extent, each child used characteristics that have been found in mothers' speech to children. *To baby* was usually different from *to mother* in the predicted direction, with the largest differences in Preverb length, Names, and Imperatives. *To baby* was also usually different from *to peer* in the predicted direction. Other aspects of the speech, such as the use of endearments and certain baby talk routines, also differentiated *to baby* from *to mother* and *to peer*. One of the characteristics analyzed, Questions, consistently yielded results opposite to those predicted. All of the children used Questions less frequently *to baby* than *to peer*, and two of the four used a smaller proportion of Questions *to baby* than *to mother*. However, when Questions were described in terms of their speech functions, the various uses were appropriate for the listeners. *To baby*, most of the questions requested information about the Internal state of the child, whereas *to mother* and *to peer*, mostly External-world questions were used. This analysis seems to show the value of going beyond the standard syntactic categories when assessing the appropriateness of speech for various situations.

The changes the children made in their speech did not depend solely on the communication pressures encountered in interacting with babies. Modifications occurred for both the baby listeners and for baby dolls. Speech *to baby doll* was usually different from speech *to mother* in the predicted direction, with the largest differences being Preverb length, Names, Imperatives, MLU, and Tense. Comparing *to baby doll* with *to peer*, again the analyses were usually in the predicted direction, though the differences were smaller than when compared with *to mother*. Thus, the children seemed to know a "style," or elements of a style, for babies. On the other hand, the fact that they used some mother-language characteristics when talking to dolls does not mean that they knew everything about baby talk. First, children's speech to younger children or dolls may have a variety of sources. Some of the characteristics may reflect the child's knowledge about characteristics of babies (inattentiveness, cognitive limitations, and so on), some may come about because of the content that is believed to be appropriate, and some may simply be learned routines or stereotypes. More study is needed to separate out these various factors which affect the child's communicative ability. Second, in this study we have looked at only a few mother-language characteristics, but there are many others (e.g., expansions) that may or may not have been in the children's speech.

From the *as baby* analyses, it appears that the children knew something about the speech of babies, but not everything. The *as baby–to mother* comparisons were always as predicted for the simplicity characteristics. MLU, Preverb length, and Tense stood out as characteristics that differentiated the speech in these situations. *As baby–to peer* also was usually as predicted. Clarification characteristics were used more frequently *as baby* also, perhaps because they serve as attention-getting devices. However, none of the children used utterances that were entirely like those of a younger child. At least two factors seemed to contribute to the inaccuracy observed in the role-playing speech: (1) all of the children except the oldest were quite inconsistent about the role-playing, and (2) the frequent simple utterances were accompanied by some very complex ones (sometimes said with babyish prosodic characteristics), indicating that the apparent simplification may not have resulted from knowledge about a baby's syntactic limitations. On the other hand, all of the children were aware of certain phonological and prosodic characteristics of babies' speech.

The results of the two role-playing situations, *to baby doll* and *as baby*, suggest that traditional approaches to role-playing may have underestimated the child's abilities. By looking at language, we may gain a more sensitive means of assessing the child's knowledge about the people in his environment and his ability to take on different characteristics.

Age seems to be a very salient listener characteristic for the child. The awareness of age appropriateness in speech appears at a time when the general level of cognitive development, according to Piagetian theory, would imply insensitivity to listener characteristics. The fact that children can modify their speech for younger listeners may function to facilitate language learning in the younger child. In many cultures children have the speech of other children, not adults, as their primary linguistic input, and it would be well, in studying input, to consider the possible role of children as language transmitters.

Finally, these results suggest that the child's utterances should not be viewed simply as a sample of the output of his grammar: the utterances that occur in a particular situation are partly a result of the communication characteristics in that situation. Descriptions of the young child's linguistic ability must be rich enough to capture the developing awareness of appropriateness of speech for various communication situations. The problems involved in such descriptions will be similar to the problems encountered when working with adults' speech, but with an added serious complication. There are at least two sources for the variations in forms that one finds in a young child's speech. First, there are variations in form that are attributable to knowledge about appropriateness. This source of variability has been the focus of this paper. Second, there may be variations in form that come about because of the intrinsic instability of forms that are recent additions to the child's linguistic system. For adults language is a highly automatized behavior, but for children the control of forms seems much like the sort of control involved in learning to ride a bicycle. The skills gradually improve, but can be disrupted easily. In looking at a particular sample of child speech, it may be difficult to separate these two factors. For example, some children use regressive speech forms when they are stressed. This is often called "using baby talk," but we must ask whether it is the same type of baby talk that we find in role-playing. Do the regressive forms represent a style shift to speech appropriate for the child in the role of a younger, more dependent child? Or are the forms due to the fact that the child loses control of his more advanced speech when he is in a difficult situation? It seems essential that we develop a fuller understanding of the sources of linguistic variability in children's speech in order to understand the processes involved in language development.

19

Carole R. Beal and John H. Flavell
Young Speakers' Evaluations
of Their Listener's Comprehension in a
Referential Communication Task

In referential communication tasks young children have been shown to be inef-
fective speakers, often producing messages that are too general or idiosyncratic
(Asher, 1979; Glucksberg, Krauss and Higgins, 1975). On the other hand, they
are able to recognize when their listener appears not to understand. For example,
they can accurately interpret nonverbal cues to another person's state of comprehension. Even very young children respond to requests by a listener for more
information, although their responses may not be very effective in resolving the
communication problem (Garvey, 1979; Peterson, Danner and Flavell, 1972;
Wellman and Lempers, 1977; Wilcox and Webster, 1980).

Although attention to the listener is obviously important, it may at times
mislead a child speaker. The reason is that other people may not always provide
accurate feedback about their comprehension. Research in the area of comprehension monitoring has shown that child listeners often overlook problems in
inadequate messages and fail to report that they do not understand (Flavell,
Speer, Green and August, 1981; Markman, 1977). In addition, the Robinsons
(Robinson, 1981a) have found that adults usually do not provide explicit indications that they have not understood a child's message. Adults will often guess at
the child's intended meaning or ask a clarifying question, rather than saying to
the child "I don't know what you mean." Therefore, the child speaker, without
explicit feedback to the contrary, might mistakenly assume that the listener in
fact understands his message, even when the listener may not have been given a
sufficiently clear and specific message for adequate understanding to be possible.
For example, a child listening to game instructions described by another child

may interrupt too soon to report that she knows what to do, or indicate that she knows how to play the game after hearing an inadequate description of the rules.

The mature speaker must be able to evaluate the listener's true state of comprehension in order to plan subsequent messages accordingly. This estimate of the listener's comprehension should not be made entirely on the basis of the listener's feedback, since that feedback is often inaccurate. Yet previous studies have shown that young speakers are influenced by the behavior of the listener in referential communication tasks. The Robinsons have found that, when communication failure occurs, young children often blame the listener for selecting the wrong referent, rather than blaming the speaker for giving a poor message (Robinson, 1981b). Children are also more likely to rate the quality of a poor message as adequate if the listener succeeds in selecting the appropriate referent by chance than if the listener guesses incorrectly (Robinson and Robinson, 1977). They also give higher ratings of quality to ambiguous messages if the listener confidently selects a referent than if he refuses to pick one (Singer and Flavell, 1981).

However, in these studies the children were asked to evaluate the quality of the message itself, rather than to judge its effect on the listener's state of comprehension. It may be that children who are first made clearly aware of the quality of the message would be less susceptible to the influence of the listener's behavior when asked to estimate the listener's comprehension of the message. A mature speaker will know that a message that is incomplete or too general can effectively prevent the listener from understanding, even if the listener provides feedback to the contrary.

In the present study children were made aware of the quality of messages delivered to a puppet listener. After the puppet indicated either that he understood or did not understand the message, the children then evaluated the puppet's true state of comprehension. We hypothesized that young children might tend to rely more on the listener's feedback about his comprehension of the message than on their knowledge of its quality. Older children might have a more solid understanding that message quality can effectively determine how well the listener understands and be able to use that knowledge to detect mistakes in the listener's comprehension monitoring.

Method

SUBJECTS

The subjects were 18 preschoolers (mean age 59.5 months), 23 kindergartners (mean age 72.5 months), and 21 first graders (mean age 82 months), from predominantly white, middle-class schools. There were approximately equal numbers of boys and girls at each age level. Children whose primary language was not English were not included in the study.

MATERIALS

Two hand puppets, Mr. Popper the penguin and Charlie the dog, were manipulated by the experimenter. Half the children interacted with Mr. Popper in the first part of the procedure, and the other children saw Charlie first. A small, lidded box was used to isolate the puppet while the child practiced giving the directions before each trial.

An envelope containing eight index card drawings of different colored houses was used during the pretest.

Two identical maps were used for each trial; one map was given to the child and the second placed before the puppet. The maps consisted of simple roadways drawn in several colors on large sheets of white paper. Four different-colored houses were located at the ends of the paths. A set of four cards accompanied each set of maps and was used by the child to deliver the directions for each trial. The first card in each set showed the picture of the house that the puppet was to locate for that trial; each of the remaining three cards showed the color of the road next in the sequence of directions the child was to give to the puppet. To deliver the directions the child had to simply announce the color of each road on the card that the experimenter handed to the child. There were three types of directions: complete, because the three cards matched the three roads leading to the target house; incomplete, because the three cards led only to the point where two roads branched, each of which led to a house; and ambiguous, because the first two cards led to a branching point and the final card could refer to either of the two possible roads, which were the same color.

Two index cards were used by the puppet during the listener-response trials. On one card was printed "I know which house it is," and on the other "I don't know which house it is."

PROCEDURE

Pretest

The pretest was given to verify that the child was able to distinguish between "thinking you know something" and "really knowing it," and to demonstrate to the child that the puppet could be wrong in what he thought. In the pretest the experimenter and the puppet closed their eyes while the child chose and hid a card from the envelope set. The puppet was then asked if he knew which card the child had chosen, and he nodded yes. Then the experimenter asked the child if the puppet really knew which card the child had chosen, and if the puppet thought he knew. If the child answered incorrectly, the puppet made an incorrect guess, and the child was again asked if the puppet "really knew" and if he thought that he had known. The child had to correctly answer both questions to pass the pretest. Four preschoolers, two kindergartners, and one first grader were not included in the study because they failed the pretest.

Evaluation-Only (Practice) Trials

Three trials followed in which the child was given practice in evaluating the quality of directions given to the puppet. There were three types of directions: complete, incomplete, and ambiguous. The first trial was a complete message. The child was shown the first pair of maps and was asked to name the colors of the roads and to verify that the maps were identical. One map was then given to the puppet. The experimenter explained that the child would give directions to the puppet, who would listen, look at his map, and try to decide which was the target house for that message. It was stressed that the child and experimenter knew where the target house was, but that the puppet did not know.

The puppet was placed in the box on the table while the child practiced giving the directions with the cards. The experimenter and child used the first card to locate the target house on the child's map, and placed the card face down (so the puppet could not see it) near the child. The child was free to look at the card as a reminder of which house the puppet was trying to find. The experimenter then handed each remaining card to the child, who announced what color road was next in the sequence.

When the child understood how to deliver the directions the puppet was brought out. It was explained that the child should look at the cards carefully and decide if the puppet would be able to tell exactly how to get to the house, because the cards were sometimes wrong. The child then delivered the directions to the puppet, who listened attentively and looked at his map, without indicating any of the houses. The child was then asked, "What do you think? Does he really know which house it is, or doesn't he?"

On the remaining two evaluation-only (practice) trials, the child delivered incomplete and ambiguous directions, in that order due to intervention on the ambiguous message trial. Since ambiguity is especially difficult for young children to notice, if a child did not spontaneously detect the problem with the ambiguous direction the experimenter drew the child's attention to it, saying, "There are two blue roads here and this card has just a blue road on it; it doesn't tell which blue road is the right one."

Listener-Response (Test) Trials

In the next six trials, the child evaluated the quality of the directions, the puppet reported whether he had understood the directions, and the child evaluated the puppet's true state of comprehension. The second puppet was used for the listener-response trials in case the child had formed any expectations about the first puppet. The child was told that this puppet would decide if he knew or did not know which the target house was, and would select a card indicating his decision. The child was told, "What Mr. Popper [Charlie] says might be right, but sometimes he might be wrong. Sometimes he might make a mistake."

The two possible listener responses (the puppet knew the house location or did not know) were each paired with examples of complete, incomplete, and ambiguous directions. Thus, for three trials the puppet's response conflicted with the quality of the message given. For example, the puppet might indicate that he knew which house was meant after hearing an incomplete direction. Each message was paired with one listener response for half the children, and with the other for the remaining children. The six listener-response (test) trials were presented in counterbalanced orders, with the restriction that no more than two of the same listener responses could occur in a sequence.

For each of the listener-response (test) trials the puppet was placed in the box while the child practiced delivering the directions. The child was asked "Do these cards tell exactly how to get to this house?" as the experimenter pointed to the target house. If the child answered incorrectly the experimenter explained how the directions were actually clear, or not very clear, to ensure that every child knew the quality of each direction before its delivery. The puppet was then retrieved, and listened to the directions. The puppet held up one of two message cards to indicate his response and the experimenter read the card to the child as the puppet nodded that he knew (or did not know) which house it was. The child was then asked, "He says he knows [doesn't know] which house it is. What do you think, does he really know, or doesn't he?"

Ten college student volunteers were also tested in a slightly modified, adult-appropriate version of the procedure. They evaluated the quality of the directions and the accuracy of a hypothetical listener's feedback about his comprehension.

Results

For the evaluation-only (practice) trials, the percentage of children making correct evaluations on each trial was 87% for the complete message, 78% for the incomplete message, and 59% for the ambiguous message. McNemar tests for the significance of changes ($df = 1$, $p < 0.05$) showed that the children were more likely to say that the puppet knew the target house when the directions had been complete than when they had been incomplete or ambiguous. The only significant age effect for an individual message type was that the preschoolers more often said the puppet really knew the intended house when the directions had been incomplete, $\chi^2(2) = 9.6$, $p < 0.01$. In general, the younger children were less accurate than the first graders in their evaluations of the inadequate messages. However, the children's performance on these initial practice trials did not predict their performance on the subsequent listener-response (test) trials.

On the listener-response (test) trials children evaluated the quality of the directions before actually delivering them to the puppet. The mean number of trials, out of six possible, on which children incorrectly evaluated the directions' quality was 1.3 for the preschoolers, 1.1 for the kindergartners, and 0.95 for the first graders; these means were not significantly different. Most of these errors

Table 19-1 *Percentage of Subjects Saying the Listener Really Knew the Identity of the Target House*

| | Type of Directions and Listener Response | | | | | |
| | Complete | | Incomplete | | Ambiguous | |
Subjects	Knows	Does not know	Knows[a]	Does not know	Knows[a]	Does not know
Preschool	94	44	61	11	44	5
Kindergarten	82	39	39	8	52	17
First grade	95	62	28	0	23	19
Adult	90	100	0	0	20	0

[a]On these "inconsistent" trials the listener makes a comprehension-monitoring error.

occurred when the child said incomplete or ambiguous directions told exactly how to get to the target house.

The percentages of subjects at each age who said that the puppet "really knew" which was the target house on each of the six listener-response (test) trials are shown in Table 19-1. On three of the listener-response (test) trials (columns 1, 4 and 6 of Table 19-1) the puppet's report of his comprehension was consistent with the quality of the directions. On the other three trials (columns 2, 3, and 5) his response was inconsistent: that is, he reports that he does not know where the house is when the directions are complete and that he does know where it is when the directions are incomplete or ambiguous. As Table 19-1 shows, children at all age levels were quite accurate at evaluating the puppet's responses on the consistent trials.

On the three inconsistent trials an incorrect answer was to indicate that the puppet's report was accurate. Table 19-2 shows the percentage of subjects at each age giving incorrect answers on these trials. The younger children were more likely than the first graders to indicate that the puppet's report of his comprehension was accurate when his feedback was inconsistent with the quality of the directions provided, $\chi^2(2) = 9.8$, $p < 0.01$. The mean percentage correct on these three trials was 49.8% for the preschoolers and kindergartners and 70.3% for the first graders, with almost all of the younger children making some errors on the inconsistent trials. The χ^2 tests showed there were no significant age changes in the number of errors when the inconsistent trials were tested individually ($df = 2$).

As Table 19-1 shows, the adult subjects almost always used only the quality of the directions in deciding if the listener really understood (there were only three errors). Even in the case when the listener said he did not understand a complete message they were quite confident that he really understood. One subject explained, "He must just be saying what he is feeling without thinking about it."

Table 19-2. *Percentage of Subjects Making Errors on Trials When Listener Response Was Inconsistent with the Quality of the Directions*

Subjects	Errors (N)	
	0–1	2–3
Preschool	39	61
Kindergarten	39	61
First grade	81	19
Adult	100	0

Discussion

All the children in this study appeared to be interested in the puppet in his role as the listener as they delivered the directions to him and carefully observed his responses. Consistent with previous findings (e.g., Flavell et al., 1981), some of the children failed to detect the problems with the incomplete and ambiguous messages on the evaluation-only (practice) trials. These initial practice trials served to improve the children's ability to correctly evaluate the quality of the directions on the subsequent listener-response (test) trials. On the listener-response (test) trials even the youngest children were quite proficient at detecting the problems in the inadequate messages. On the rare occasions in which a child overlooked the problem in a message, the experimenter's intervention ensured, as much as possible, that the child was aware of the adequacy of the information given to the puppet before evaluating his response.

The children were also as aware as we could make them that the puppet could make mistakes in his comprehension monitoring. Only children who understood the distinction between "thinking you know" and "really knowing" were included in the study, and this pretest also served as a demonstration that the puppet could make a comprehension-monitoring error. The children were also specifically told that his monitoring might be unreliable.

The results indicate that young communicators must, in addition to being able to evaluate message quality, learn that message quality has a role in determining the listener's comprehension. Despite their knowledge that the directions given to the puppet were at times incomplete or ambiguous, the younger children still seemed to be influenced by his feedback when they evaluated his comprehension. "He says he knows, and I believe him," said one young child. The preschoolers and kindergartners did not clearly infer that an inadequate message made it impossible for the puppet to know the identity of the target house, and that if he said he knew he must be wrong. In contrast, the first graders, like the adults, seemed to realize that the quality of a message can effectively determine another person's comprehension, and they used this knowledge to decide when the puppet was overestimating or underestimating his comprehension. These results are consistent with previous work showing that young children do not clearly understand that the poor quality of a message can be responsible for their own comprehension difficulties (Beal and Flavell, 1982; Flavell et al., 1981; Robinson, 1981b).

There are several factors regarding estimates of a listener's comprehension that were not addressed in this study but that might be at work in more naturalistic communication situations. It is likely that a young speaker would not be as aware of the quality of his messages in everyday communication as he was in this task. Taken together with the fact that young children often believed the listener's feedback even when they knew the directions had been inadequate, this suggests that the tendency to rely on listener feedback may be even stronger in real communication situations. It should also be pointed out that in everyday communication the process of deciding if a listener actually understands can be more uncertain than it was designed to be in this study. For example, sometimes a listener may genuinely not understand a perfectly clear message, and it is important for the speaker not to ignore the listener's confusion. In fact, the first graders in this study did not consistently claim the puppet really understood complete directions when he reported that he did not. Several adults commented that in a less constrained conversation they would try to resolve a listener's misunderstanding, even if they were sure they had communicated adequately. Another possibility in actual conversations is for the speaker to expect the listener to use his own stored knowledge to fill in gaps in the message and resolve his own confusion. The task in this study was designed to minimize the possibility that the listener could use information other than that actually given in the directions to locate the target house. The first graders must have been more clearly aware than the younger children that the experimenter actually determined the puppet's responses, but they did not seem to believe the puppet's apparent comprehension of inadequate messages was due to actual knowledge of the target house location.

Although there were differences between the present communication situation and those typical of everyday life, both require a speaker skill that has not been previously examined, to our knowledge. That is, the speaker must be able to evaluate what the listener's state of comprehension could reasonably be at a given point in the conversation. The speaker must also be prepared at times to question or discount his listener's indications of comprehension if such feedback seems inconsistent with his evaluation of the quality of the communication. The results of this study suggest that young speakers tend to accept uncritically what a listener says about his comprehension, even when their accurate evaluations of the message quality ought to lead them to be skeptical of the listener's feedback. Young children seem susceptible to a mutual illusion of successful communication (see Piaget, 1926): the young listener often indicates that he understands when in fact he could not, and the young speaker often believes him.

IV

DISCOURSE:
CONVERSATION AND
NARRATIVE

Conversation and narrative involve rules, strategies, and schemata for initiating, maintaining, developing, and terminating extended discourse. Adult discourse has been the subject of spirited controversy among anthropologists and sociologists for some time and the study of narrative is a classic concern of literary critics, but psychologists have only recently attempted to understand the strategies and temporal patterning of children's conversations and stories.

In the 1960s, sociolinguists began to look at talk in social contexts in order to identify interrelations among speaker, hearer, message, social context, features of code, and other aspects of the total communicative act. Continuing in the tradition of examining real talk in everyday situations, sociologists (e.g., Sacks, Schegloff, and Jefferson, 1974) analyzed the formal structure of conversational interaction, examining mechanisms for initiating and terminating conversations, allocating "turns," and changing topics. At the same time that anthropologists and sociologists were delineating the social-communicative nature of discourse, philosophers began to emphasize the functions of speech and to describe the social knowledge that underlies the performance of "speech acts."

John Dore, trained as a linguist and influenced by speech act theory, was one of the first to conceptualize communicative intentions and attitudes of prelinguistic children as "illocutionary acts" (Dore, 1973, 1976). Dore argued that children's utterances express generic attitudes such as requesting, complaining, answering—pragmatic functions that become more explicit as they are linguistically codified in the course of development. In the selection reprinted in this section, **Dore** describes the theoretical grounds for his study of children's responses to questions, arguing that "pragmatic meaning" involves speakers' implicit communicative intentions, and the relation of utterances to other utterances and to the nonlinguistic context.

In addition to producing, comprehending, and responding to single utterances, speakers must connect utterances to form larger meaningful stretches of talk. In the controlled study of conversation included in this section, **Fine** analyzes the means of achieving cohesion both in conversation between speakers and within the extended discourse of a single speaker. Following the system developed by Halliday and Hasan (1976), Fine shows how 5- to 10-year old children use a variety of cohesive devices to pattern their conversations. Children become increasingly sensitive to the conversational status of the interlocutor and use cohesion devices differentially as a function of the person with whom they are communicating.

Another approach to the analysis of conversation, one originally used in the understanding of narrative is the *scriptal* approach (Schank and Abelson, 1977). Scripts are conceptual representations of temporally organized events or routines. Possession of scripts frees individuals from the constraints of the immediate perceptual situation, enabling them to predict the familiar and attend to the novel. In their examination of the structure and content of children's conversations during play, **Nelson and Gruendel** show how successful script enactment is a joint social enterprise that involves shared knowledge systems and collaboration among the speakers. The authors suggest a basis for both successful and unsuccessful play interactions and argue that conversational competence involves strategies for checking and appropriately adjusting background assumptions. Threats to conversational coherence, in which one partner departs on an egocentric tangent without considering the other's utterance, must be cooperatively repaired by both partners.

Many developmental studies of narrative deal with children's comprehension and recall of stories, often with greater emphasis placed on narrative structure than on thematic content. Influenced by Chomsky's efforts to write generative grammars of sentences, some investigators have tried to account for recall and production of stories on the basis of rules for sequencing and integrating the constituents. These efforts are directed toward describing the structure of "well-formed" stories (see, e.g., Thorndyke, 1977; Mandler and Johnson, 1977). In the section of her article reprinted in this volume, **Mandler** presents her theoretical approach to narrative (see also Mandler, 1984). The notion that individuals grasp and retain a meaningful structural skeleton rather than individual sentences has been the basis for Mandler's concept of story grammar. Mandler suggests that narrative event structure has an ideal form and hypothesizes that stories which deviate from this abstract order are more difficult to process and retrieve than well-formed stories.

Stein, like Mandler, seeks to understand the knowledge structures underlying children's narrative skills. She sees story telling as the integration of two kinds of knowledge: social-personal knowledge and knowledge about the discourse system. Arguing that various functions of story-telling should be differentiated, Stein identifies the "representational" function as especially important in the early school years, in that stories help children solve problems and understand the world. In the article selected for this volume, Stein proposes a hierarchical structural scheme for analyzing stories and presents evidence for a developmental progression in children's story concepts. Stein also examines the thematic content of narrative, and her inquiry into the specific kinds of goals, obstacles, and resolutions in children's texts leads her to conclude that stories serve as important vehicles of interpersonal exploration for young children.

20

John Dore
"Oh Them Sheriff":
A Pragmatic Analysis of
Children's Responses to Questions

How do we know when an answer to a question is appropriate? Why is it that when a 2 year old was asked, *Put the truck where?* his answer, *Put truck window,* was considered appropriate; but when the same child was asked, *Which is right, "two shoes" or "two shoe"?* his response, *Pop goes the weasel!* was considered a non sequitur? These examples are from a study by Brown and Bellugi (1964) who were concerned with children's acquisition of syntax and the experimental techniques necessary to get at it. Since that time a great deal has been found out about the development of syntax, but very few studies have asked, much less found out, what makes an answer appropriate. An exception was Ervin-Tripp's work (1970), which provided the necessary first step toward explaining appropriateness. She described the development of "grammatically appropriate" answers to "*Wh* questions," that is, answers that "are appropriate from the standpoint of grammatical category." And, apart from this formal "category agreement," she pointed out that other relevant aspects of answering, among them that "some semantic interpretation is made of a question, unless it is merely a routine. In addition, a pragmatic interpretation may be required" (p. 80). Children's pragmatic interpretation of questions is the focus of this present chapter.

The data presented here are from a study of the spontaneous responses by 3-year-old children to questions addressed to them. While many of their responses were grammatically matched, the majority were not; these responses were, however, "pragmatically appropriate" in various ways. The primary purpose of this chapter is to characterize the notion of pragmatic appropriateness, or more specifically, of "contingency relations" between questions and answers; another purpose is to propose the form of interpretive rules underlying children's responses. This will be accomplished first by briefly describing what is taken to be the domain of linguistic pragmatics and then by discussing the results of our study of children's illocutionary acts in general and their responses to questions in particular.

The Domain of Linguistic Pragmatics

Some philosophers of language have discussed the distinction between grammar and pragmatics. Stalnaker (1972), for example, claims that

> Syntax studies sentences, semantics studies propositions. Pragmatics is the study of linguistic acts and the contexts in which they are performed. There are two major types of problems to be solved within pragmatics: First, to define interesting types of speech acts and speech products; second, to characterize the features of the speech context which help determine which proposition is expressed by a given sentence. (p. 383)

To illustrate these kinds of problems, I will take an example from Grice (1975). He has been developing a theory of the **full signification** of an utterance, which involves not only **what is said**, but also **what is meant** and **what is implicated**. For example, if a speaker of English hears the utterance *He is in the grip of a vice*, Grice claims that he would know that **what was said** was "about some particular male person or animal and that at the time of the utterance (whatever that was) either (1) that x was unable to rid himself of a certain kind of bad characteristic, or (2) that some part of x's person was caught in a certain kind of tool or instrument." Notice that one knows this much about the utterance, without knowing anything about the context, by virtue of knowing the grammar of standard English. However, Grice adds that "for a full identification of what the speaker had **said** one would need to know (*a*) the identity of x, (*b*) the time of the utterance, (*c*) the meaning, on the particular occasion of utterance, of the phrase "in the grip of a vice" (a decision between (1) and (2) above" (p. 6). These aspects of saying are pragmatic: (*a*) and (*b*) require knowledge about the particular context, and (*c*) depends upon whether the speaker intended his utterance metaphorically. Knowledge of the context and of another's intentions cannot be handled in the grammar (cf. Katz and Langendoen, 1976).

Similarly, Grice's notion of conversational implication is also pragmatic. He would claim, I think, that if *He is in the grip of a vice* followed the question *Do you think he is the right man for the job of Archbishop?* then, on the "bad characteristic" reading, **what is meant** by the utterance may be that he is not the right man; if it followed the command *Tell him to come in here immedi-*

ately! then, on the "tool" reading, **what is meant** might be that he cannot come. *

To Grice's account of **what is said grammatically** and **what is said pragmatically** can be added the following kinds of **what is done.** In saying *He is in the grip of a vice* one performs the **act of referring** to some male and to some characteristic or tool, and one performs the **act of predicating** some characteristic or situation of this male. On another level of doing, the speaker is **describing** a situation or a location (on the "tool" reading) or he is **attributing** a certain internal state to the male (on the "characteristic" reading). Furthermore, if the utterance follows the *Archbishop* question, we might want to say that the speaker is **denying** (albeit obliquely) the proposition in the question; if it follows the command, we would say that the speaker is **explaining** why *the man* cannot come. Notice that these responses do not overtly answer the question or acknowledge the command, at least in the sense of providing the most expected or predictable information; they are nonetheless appropriate, if oblique, responses. Finally, there are other contexts in which this utterance might be produced where we would call it a joke.

In summary, the acts of referring and predicating are **parts** of speech acts, describing, attributing, denying, and explaining **are** speech acts, and jokes **are** probably what Stalnaker means by "speech products." The point of explicating **what is done** is to show that the acts performed by a given utterance are not determined by its grammar, although the grammar may constrain the kinds of acts that can be performed by a given utterance. I take it, then, that **what is said grammatically** is in this sense independent of pragmatic phenomena such as **what is said pragmatically, what is meant conversationally,** and **what is done.** In this view, everything that a speaker knows about the utterance, except the phonological, syntactic, and semantic knowledge of the sentence type, can be treated as the pragmatic, as distinct from the grammatical, component of the utterance. For the purpose of discussion, we can assume that "semantic meaning" has to do with the reading of the proposition while "pragmatic meaning" has to do with the intentions of the speaker, the relations of utterance to contexts, and conversational skills.

Searle (1969) describes the speech act as containing two components: a proposition (defined in terms of a predicating expression taking one or more referring expressions as its arguments) and an illocutionary force (which indicates how the speaker intends his utterance to be taken). The proposition conveys the

---

*I realize that Grice's example is artificial to the extent that in actual conversation hearers rarely, if ever, perceive utterances such as *He is in the grip of a vice* as ambiguous. But, apart from the fact that such utterances must almost always be interpreted metaphorically, the example suits Grice's theoretical purpose. Moreover, my juxtaposition of the utterance with the preceding utterances is even more artificial. Yet in this section I am solely concerned with distinguishing the theoretical boundary between grammar and pragmatics. The following sections report results from empirical studies that provide sufficient examples of actual occurrences of utterances that are "functionally equivocal" (if not structurally ambiguous).

conceptual content, while the illocutionary force indicates whether the utterance should count as an assertion, promise, question, and so on. Illocutionary acts are those performed in producing certain utterances. They were distinguished by Austin (1962) from "a locutionary act, which is roughly equivalent to uttering a certain sentence with a certain sense and reference" and from "perlocutionary acts: What we bring about or achieve by saying something, such as convincing, persuading . . ." (p. 108). The following discussion of children's language is restricted to illocutionary acts.

Dore (1976) argued that the primary determinant of the illocutionary force of an illocutionary act is the speaker's **communicative intention** (CI). This is an intention to induce in the hearer two specific effects: (1) the **expected illocutionary effect**—that the hearer recognize the illocutionary status of the utterance, and (2) the **expected perlocutionary effect**—that the hearer recognize what the speaker expects him to do or believe as a consequence of recognizing the utterance's illocutionary status. For example, if I ask *What's your name?* I will have achieved my expected illocutionary effect if you recognize that I have asked you a certain kind of information question; I will have achieved my expected perlocutionary effect if you recognize that I expect you to tell me your name. The clearest evidence of my success, of course, would be your actually telling me your name. Unlike other notions of intention, a CI must be linguistically marked. That is, it must be conveyed by utterances of certain grammatical forms, and the illocutionary acts determined by CIs must be conventionally governed by rules for the use of utterances in contexts so that hearers automatically recognize speaker's CIs.

However, it is important to note that form alone cannot determine pragmatic function. The hearer's recognition of the speaker's CI depends upon several factors that operate independently of the grammar. This claim is supported by the results of both of the following studies, although the two studies approach the nonisomorphism of form and function differently. In the first study, the purpose of which was to identify the array of illocutionary acts performed by children, utterances were **initially coded for intention.** Thus, one child's utterance of *Why don't you sit in the seat behind?* was coded as a **Request for Action** on the basis of the evidence yielded by the methodology employed. In the second study, which focused on the children's responses to questions, that same utterance was **initially identified on the basis of grammatical form** as an information question; the analysis of the hearer's response—the hearer replied with *Alright* and sat in the seat behind the speaker—indicated that he interpreted the question as an **Action Request**. Therefore, although the procedures for initially categorizing utterances were different in the two studies, the results of both led to the same conclusion: It is not the grammar that conveys illocutionary intent.

Children's Illocutionary Acts

Four boys and three girls of middle-class backgrounds attended a nursery 2 hours a day, 3 days a week, over a period of 7 months, and their interactivity was videotaped about 2 hours a week. A wide variety of situations (including structured activities like snack time and arts and crafts as well as free play) were systematically sampled. Although the nursery school teacher was almost always present, she was as unobtrusive as possible regarding child-initiated activities. Consequently, the children appeared to engage in relatively unrestrained, spontaneous conversations and more than half of their speech was addressed to other children. The following corpus comes from videotapes of 1-hour sessions per month for the last 4 months of the study. The children ranged in age from 2;10 to 3;3 years at the first of these four sessions. The corpus consists of almost 3000 child utterances, each of which was coded for illocutionary act.

The decision procedure for coding utterances as illocutionary acts was to determine, in the following order:

1. The literal semantic reading of the primary proposition of the utterance, on the basis of its logical subject, predicate, adverbial phrases, and other constituents (according to Katz, 1972).
2. The grammatical and prosodic operators on the proposition.
3. The new, or focused, information; new in relation to both conversation and context (Halliday, 1970).
4. The speaker's related utterances and nonlinguistic behavior.
5. The reciprocal and contingent behavior, both verbal and nonverbal, of his interlocutors (Garvey, 1975).
6. The contextual features directly relevant to the pragmatic status of the utterance (Lewis, 1972).

Let me exemplify the steps in this procedure. The vast majority of the children's utterances were propositional in structure (although sometimes elliptical), consisting of at least a subject and predicate; for example, the *I* and *am painting* (respectively) in *I am painting*. Numerous kinds of grammatical operators applied to propositions: Word order converted a proposition to a Yes–No question (for example: *Are you painting?*), and a grammatically determined intonation pattern did the same (as in *You're painting?*), and an interrogative pronoun converted it to a *Wh* question (*What are you doing?*). The new information in an utterance may be new in relation to the conversation (*Nothing* might be the *Wh* answer to the above *Wh* question), or information could be new in relation to what was already given in the context (*He likes to* would be an **Attribution** about the above "painter's" internal state relative to painting).

The single most important evidence for determining the illocutionary act is the speaker's utterances that are contingently related to the target utterance being coded. For example, one boy said to a girl, *Hey, don't sit there!*, which was coded as a **Protest**; then he said *I was sitting there* which was contingently related to his first utterance by stating his right to make a **Protest**. The remarks of addressees often indicate how they interpret the speaker's intention; children often reply with *Okay* to a speaker's **Action Request** in order to verbally encode their **Compliance**. And a third source of evidence for identifying illocutionary acts is the teacher's remarks that were, though often unsolicited, contingently related to a child's utterance to another child. For example, one boy tried to make an **Action Request** appear to be a genuine **Protest** by raising his fist and saying, in an abrupt rising–falling intonation contour, *Get out of here* to a girl. The teacher immediately asked *Why does she have to?*, thereby questioning the boy's right to issue a **Protest**. The girl did not leave.

The context is often crucial in determining an illocutionary act. Contextual features, in fact, often override the literal meaning of a proposition: Instead of an **Event Description**, *I am painting* would be coded as role-playing if the child were merely waving his arms in the air as he said it. The utterance *We painted the windows* would be coded as a joke if the participants in the conversation respond with laughter because they know that it is obviously untrue, and even unreasonable. In general, the coding of individual illocutionary acts is determined by both "internal" grammatical factors, and "external" discourse-relation and contextual factors. Most often, the relations among sequences of utterances define the status of individual utterances in the sequence.

Thirty-two types of illocutionary acts were performed by the children in the study. Table 20-1 lists the types and gives the code, the definition, and an example of each type. We achieved a reliability of better than 82% for all sessions for classifying utterances into illocutionary act types; this was measured in terms of the initial agreements of two experienced coders who scored independently. Given the state of our knowledge about children's pragmatic processing of speech, it would be premature to argue that the illocutionary act categories we postulated have an absolute validity or even that the categories are arranged in the most descriptively adequate way. However, this initial phase of the research enabled us to group together utterances of roughly the same illocutionary value, based on definitions available in the literature and on our own intuitions. Fortunately, of all illocutionary types, questions are the easiest to identify because of their distinct grammatical form. *

Table 20-1. *Definitions and Examples of the Communicative Intentions We Identified as Underlying the Children's Illocutionary Acts*[a]

REQUESTS . . . solicit information, actions, or acknowledgment	
RQYN	*Yes–no questions* . . . solicit affirmation or negation of the propositional content of the speaker's utterance, e.g., *Is this a birthday cake?*
RQWH	*Wh-questions* . . . solicit information about the identity, location, or property of an object, event, or situation, e.g., *Where's John?*
RQAC	*Action requests* . . . solicit a listener to perform, not to perform, or cease to perform an action (process, etc.), e.g., *Give me some juice!*
RQPM	*Permission requests* . . . solicit a listener to grant permission for the speaker to perform an action, e.g., *Can I go?*
RQRQ	*Rhetorical questions* . . . solicit a listener's acknowledgment to allow the speaker to continue, e.g., *You know what I did yesterday?*

*The rest of the chapter, reporting findings, is omitted. [Eds.]

Table 20-1 *continued.*

RESPONSES . . . directly complement preceding utterances

RSYN   *Yes–no answers* . . . complement yes–no questions by affirming, negating, or otherwise answering them, e.g., *No, it isn't.*

RSWH   *Wh- answers* . . . complement *Wh* questions by providing information about the identity, etc., requested, e.g., *John's under the table.*

RSAG   *Agreements* . . . complement previous utterances by agreeing with or denying the content, e.g., *That isn't a car.*

RSCO   *Compliances* . . . complement requests by complying with or refusing to comply with them, e.g., *I won't wash my hands.*

RSQL   *Qualifications* . . . complement utterances by qualifying, clarifying, or otherwise changing their content, e.g., *But I didn't do it.*

DESCRIPTIONS . . . represent observable (or verifiable) aspects of the environment

DSID   *Identifications* . . . label an object, person, event, or situation, e.g., *That's a house.*

DSPO   *Possessions* . . . indicate who owns or temporarily possesses an object, e.g., *That's John's egg.*

DSEV   *Events* . . . represent the occurrence of an event, action, process, etc., e.g., *I'm drawing a house.*

DSPR   *Properties* . . . represent observable traits or conditions of objects, events, or situations, e.g., *That's a red crayon.*

DSLO   *Locations* . . . represent the location or direction of an object or event, e.g., *The zoo is far away.*

STATEMENTS . . . express facts, beliefs, attitudes, or emotions

STRU   *Rules* . . . express rules, conventional procedures, analytic facts, definitions, or classifications, e.g., *You have to put it there first.*

STEV   *Evaluations* . . . express impressions, attitudes, or judgments about objects, events, or situations, e.g., *It looks like a snowman.*

STIR   *Internal reports* . . . express internal states (emotions, sensations, etc.), capacities, or intents to perform an act, e.g., *My leg hurts.*

STAT   *Attributions* . . . express beliefs about another's internal state, capacity, intent, etc., e.g., *He doesn't know the answer.*

STEX   *Explanations* . . . report reasons, causes, and motives for acts or predict states of affairs, e.g., *He did it cause he's bad.*

CONVERSATIONAL DEVICES . . . establish, maintain, end, or otherwise regulate interpersonal contact and conversations

CDBM   *Boundary markers* . . . initiate or end contact or conversation, e.g., *Hi,* and *Bye.*

CDCA   *Calls* . . . make contact by soliciting attention, e.g., *Hey, John!*

CDAC   *Accompaniments* . . . signal closer contact by accompanying a speaker's action: e.g., *Here you are.*

CDRE   *Returns* . . . acknowledge the listener's preceding utterance or fill in to maintain the conversation, e.g., *Oh.*

CDPM   *Politeness markers* . . . make explicit the speaker's politeness, e.g., *Please* and *Thanks.*

Table 20-1 *continued.*

PERFORMATIVES . . . accomplish acts by being said

ROLE   *Role-plays* . . . establish a fantasy, e.g., *This is a train.*

PROT   *Protests* . . . object to the listener's previous behavior, e.g., *No, don't touch that!*

JOKE   *Jokes* . . . produce a humorous effect by a nonliteral, playful remark, e.g., *I throwed the soup in the ceiling.*

GAME   *Game markers* . . . initiate, continue, or end a game, e.g., *You can't catch me.*

CLAI   *Claims* . . . establish facts by being said, e.g., *I'm first.*

WARN   *Warnings* . . . notify the listener of impending harm, e.g., *Watch out.*

TEAS   *Teases* . . . annoy the listener by being provocative or taunting, e.g., *You can't come to my house.*

MISCELLANEOUS CODES

UNTP   *Uninterpretable* . . . for unintelligible, incomplete, or incomprehensible utterances.

DOUB   *Double coded* . . . for utterances receiving two of the above codes.

---

[a]Each definition begins with ". . . is an intention to induce in a listener the recognition that the speaker wants his utterance to be taken as . . ."; following the ellipsis is a specification of the speaker's expectation.

21

Jonathan Fine

Conversation,
Cohesive and Thematic Patterning
in Children's Dialogues

The investigation of conversation has recently taken several directions including speech act analysis, examination of the linguistic structure used in conversation, and the ethnomethodological approaches of conversational organization. Each of these approaches focuses upon different segments of a conversation, and yet one must suppose that these various approaches probably interact in very subtle ways. If one focuses entirely upon *uncontrolled* natural conversations, there are too many factors that one can point to that probably affect the language— physical distance of the speakers from each other varies, the number of speakers can vary over different segments of the conversation, the locations may vary as the conversation unfolds, and so on. Given the rather primitive level of our understanding of the factors that can influence conversational structure, one can argue in favor of using partly controlled conversations in order to facilitate finding which parameters are the most important determinants of conversational patterning. This was the motivation for the current study.

Design

In this study the number of participants, their ages, status (as student or teacher), sex, the location of the conversation, and to some extent the artifacts in the recording location have all been controlled. The topic of the conversations was not controlled since informal observation suggested that conversations on a prede- termined topic are more formal and less spontaneous, holding other situational factors constant, than conversations without a predetermined topic (see Hands-combe, 1969, for a study of topics used spontaneously by a group of children slightly older than those in the present study).

Students from 5 to 9 years old were chosen since this span covers the first years of formal education. The students are learning to interact in an environment different from the immediate family setting. They are learning to use different varieties (Gregory, 1967) of language in situations that are new to them.

The conversations analyzed in this study were drawn from a larger corpus taped in the first few months of 1972 in Toronto, Canada. Thirteen classes in two elementary schools were used as sources for subjects from kindergarten to grade four. For each of the three age levels, eight conversations are analyzed. Four of the conversations are dialogues (D) between two students and four are conversations between two students and their classroom teacher (TD). Thus, the two sets of conversations do not have an equal number of speakers. It would be desirable to equalize the number of speakers in future research, a procedure not possible in the current study which is based on data gathered for an earlier investigation.

Six students (three male, three female) were selected randomly from each class. For the dialogue situation, the students each selected a friend from their own class as a partner. For the teacher–dialogue situation, students from the original set of six were paired and combined with their classroom teacher. Since one student was recorded with different partners in the two situations, the sample of 24 conversations comprised 36 students and 12 teachers. In each age level there were six male and six female students. The 5-year level consisted of 12 students aged 5;1 to 6;3 with a mean of 5;6 (males 5;7, females 5;5). The 7-year level consisted of 12 students aged 7;3 to 8;4 with a mean of 7;9 (males 7;7, females 7;10). The 9-year level consisted of 12 students aged 8;4 to 10;3 with a mean of 9;5 (males 9;2, females 9;8). In this study sex is not used in the analysis of conversations.

The recordings were made in small rooms within the school (a small kitchen in one case and the nurse's room in the other). The presence of the tape recorder was evident, and the students were asked not to touch the microphone nor to talk directly into it, but to talk to each other. The setting was informal with the microphone being attached to the back of an extra chair (at the appropriate height) so that a very "technical" atmosphere was avoided. Identical tape recorders had been given to the teachers for classroom use a month before the data collection began, in order to accustom the students to the recorders.

The language gathered in the two controlled situations is not a perfect sample of the speech of the students. Each prearranged situation must affect the language used. However, by comparing how different students use language in the same situation and how the same students use language in different situations some valid conclusions can be drawn (see *Five to Nine*, 1972, p. 4).

Each 5-minute conversation was transcribed into standard orthography by pairs of experienced transcribers. Most of the procedures accord with the suggestions developed independently by Williams and Legum (1970). The transcripts were coded on the level of the turn, the clause, and the cohesive unit with a total of over 150,000 pieces of information being placed in computer files.

Scoring Conventions and Results for Cohesion

The different types of cohesion within a text and exophoric reference to nonlinguistic information give directions to the hearer of how to interpret the language of the speaker. Cohesion relates one stretch of language to another, whereas exophoric reference implies a search command to the hearer to find the information needed for interpretation outside of the language spoken. Almost all occurrences of exophoric references in the conversations analyzed are first- and second-person pronominal and adjectival forms (e.g., *you* and *your* in *Do you have your books?*).

The system of cohesion used in this study is taken almost directly from Halliday and Hasan (1976). The cohesive system in English is more complex than this outline describes. However, the level of detail presented is suitable for a study relating cohesion to other aspects of conversation. . . .

For this study, six main types of cohesion are analyzed: anaphoric reference, ellipsis, lexical cohesion, substitution, conjunction, and cataphora. In addition, exophoric reference is coded so that it can be compared to the "search within the text" instruction of anaphoric reference.

Anaphoric reference

This is coded into three categories: personals, demonstratives, and comparatives. Personals include *he, him, his; she her, hers; it, its; they, them, their, theirs*. Demonstratives include *this, these, here; that, those, there, then, the*. The list of demonstratives illustrates the important principle of cohesion: the mere presence of an item from one of the lists does not necessarily establish a cohesive bond. For example, *the* is cohesive only when it is anaphoric (referring backward to previous language). Possessive pronominal forms (e.g., *his* in *Did you find his?*, *Is his yellow?*) are coded as both personal reference and ellipsis of the noun that the possessive form could modify (e.g., *bicycle*). Two search commands are implied by the possessive pronouns: "find the element which supplies the identification of the person" and "find the noun which is omitted." The double coding captures the possibilities of redundancy (if the two searches lead to the same antecedent nominal group) or ambiguity (if the two searches lead to different nominal groups).

The items *it, you, they*, and *we* can be interpreted as referring to an institutional entity and thus may be noncohesive. Examples of these uses are *you never know, we don't do that sort of thing here, they're fixing the road out there*, and *it's snowing* (Halliday and Hasan, 1976, p. 53). These institutional instances of exophora do not require the verbal context nor the nonverbal situation for their interpretation.

Complete lists cannot be drawn for comparative reference, but the defining principle is to look for the bonds needed to supply information to interpret the language. Comparative reference supplies information about the similarity of one part of the text to another, with or without respect to a particular quantity or quality (Halliday and Hasan, 1976, pp. 76–77). Examples of items that can establish comparative reference cohesive bonds are the following (Halliday and Hasan, 1976, pp. 333–334): *same, identical; similar, such; different, other, else; more, less.*

Ellipsis

This is divided into three categories: nominal, verbal, and clausal. In cases of nominal ellipsis the typical head of the nominal group, a common noun, is missing and the function of head is taken over by a deictic (e.g., *this*), numerative (ordinal, cardinal, or indefinite, e.g., *Do you want the first/five/some?*), epithet (e.g., superlative, comparative, e.g., *I prefer the biggest/bigger*), or classifier [e.g., a noun used as a modifier as in *I've got the cotton (shirt)*] (Halliday and Hasan, 1976, pp. 147–153).

Lexical cohesion

This is classified into the categories of same item, synonym, superordinate, and general word. For example, *animals* would be coded as a superordinate of *frogs* and *snakes* in *I like frogs and snakes and all sorts of animals. Thing* would be coded as a general word cohering with *pencils, paper, ink, erasers* in *Get the pencils, paper, ink, and erasers and put those other things away.* Lexical cohesion is the most difficult type of cohesion to code because language is only loosely organized with respect to lexis. It is sometimes difficult to determine if two lexical items are synonymous or not, or whether a lexical item is, or is being treated as, a superordinate of another lexical item. However, in practice, most instances could be coded quickly and with little doubt. Reiterated lexical items occur with a reference item (e.g., *ball* being a repetition in *Where's the ball?*). However, even when there is no referential connection, lexical cohesion is achieved by the continuity of lexical meaning—a continuity established by the relation between lexical items.

There are difficulties in coding even lexical repetition. For example, are repetitions of *to* with the infinitive forms of verbs to be regarded as lexical repetitions? Although a series of infinitives (e.g., *I like to eat breakfast, to play with my friends, to go to school*) creates cohesion by parallel grammatical structures, there is little semantic content in items from such closed grammatical systems. Similarly, prepositions may be used with little semantic content (e.g., *for* in *What did you do that for?*). The coding procedure avoided coding as lexical repetitions such frequent items from relatively closed grammatical sets.

Substitution

This establishes a cohesive bond by supplying an item of the same grammatical class as the item necessary for interpretation. Substitution may be nominal, verbal, or clausal. The nominal substitutes are *one, ones, the same, so;* verbal ones are *do, be, have, do the same/likewise; do so, be so; do it/that, be it/that;* clausal ones are *so, not.* Again, it is not just the occurrence of one of these substitutes that is cohesive. Rather, the use must establish a bond to other parts of the conversations.

Conjunction

This, like lexical cohesion, is not well defined. The categories for this study are additive, adversative, causal, temporal, and other. "Conjunctive elements are cohesive not in themselves but indirectly, by virtue of their specific meanings; they are not primarily devices for reaching out into the preceding (or following) text, but they express certain meanings which presuppose the presence of other components in the discourse" (Halliday and Hasan, 1976, p. 226). Additive elements like *and,* adversative elements like *yet, but, although,* temporal elements like *then, soon, next time,* and causal elements like *therefore, consequently* presuppose other elements for their interpretation and for the interpretation of some further (usually following) stretch of language.

Cataphora

Cataphoric bonds are relations in a text that direct the hearer to coming elements of the text for the information needed to interpret an element. *This, these, here,* for example, can refer forward cohesively. For example, in describing procedures *this* is often used cataphorically: *This is how to build a cabin: first get. . . .*

In coding some types of cohesion the antecedents are indeterminate and in some cases it is indeterminate whether the reference is to another stretch of language (endophoric) or to something outside of language (exophoric). Part of the indeterminacy lies in the analyst's attempt to understand the conversation in its extralinguistic situation and part lies in the sometimes indeterminate way language is used. However, with a structured experimental situation and by considering the conversation as a whole (thus noting the reactions of participants) most of this type of difficulty can be eliminated. In cases of indeterminacy an arbitrary dummy code is used and these cases are eliminated from this study.

The speaker of the antecedent information for each cohesive bond is identified as the same student (SS), another student (SO), or the teacher (T) for the teacher dialogues. When the teacher's language has a bond to the teacher's own language the code T is used and SO represents a bond from the teacher's language to that of one of the students.

Cohesive bonds are coded to the *nearest possible* antecedent. That is, if there is a chain of cohesive bonds, the antecedent is taken to be the *closest* term in the chain (in all cases but cataphora it is the closest earlier term). This procedure emphasizes local cohesive bonds and is appropriate for studying the interaction of cohesion with the locally organized patterning of conversational turns described below.

As outlined, the different types of cohesion establish different kinds of linguistic links. From the position of the hearer, the difference is the kind of task set up by the cohesive relations. Each case of anaphoric cohesion in the data is coded to indicate the speaker of the antecedent stretch of language to which it is linked. By examining whose speech contains the antecedent for each type of cohesion, a description is obtained of both linguistic patterning and speakers' attention to the language of conversation. A separate analysis of substitution is omitted because of its infrequency. Substitution constitutes no more than 3% of the cohesion for any age group.

Ellipsis directs the hearer to some earlier stretch of language without providing an overt structural place-holder (as in the case of substitution). It is thus a link in the text that must be made by the hearer to interpret the stretch of language containing the ellipsis. For example, in the first clause of the second turn there is ellipsis of the verbal head (*quitting*) and consequently the hearer must recover the semantic information from the preceding turn.

F: She she's quitting.
M: Is she? What's she going to do?

RESULTS FOR ELLIPSIS

The teacher directs the hearer to the teacher's own language by ellipsis much more frequently (61% of ellipsis) than students direct hearers to their own language by ellipsis (12 to 26%). For each of the groups of children the percentage of their ellipses referring to the student's own language (SS) and to the teacher's (T) is given in Table 21-1.

Table 21-1. *Percentage of Their Ellipses Referring to Student's (SS) and Teacher's (T) Language*[a]

	5 years	7 years	9 years	
SS	12	26	25	(49)
T	40	27	33	(83)
	(53)	(33)	(46)	

[a]The numbers in parentheses indicate the actual number of cases in the data.

The youngest students used a higher proportion of ellipses linked to the teacher (40 vs 27%) and a lower proportion linked to their own language compared to other students (the rate of linking to *other students* is fairly constant for the students and varies betwen 41 and 45%). This tendency indicates that the youngest students are primarily orienting their speech to the structure of the teacher's language to a greater extent than the older students, since ellipsis assumes that the necessary structure is recoverable from some earlier stretch of language. The hearer is then also required to attend to the structure of the teacher's language to a high degree in order to interpret the student's language.

RESULTS FOR LEXICAL COHESION

Lexical cohesion creates a continuity of meaning either by repetition of lexical items (the most frequent type by far), or by the use of synonyms, general words, or superordinates. The repetition of *grandmother* in the third turn below helps indicate that the speaker is talking about the same thing.

> M: Does your grandmother speak English?
> F: No.
> M: No just just Italian just Italian. I think your grandmother would miss you.

This type of cohesion does not necessarily direct the hearer to some earlier text for its interpretation but it does signal a continuity of meaning. The percentage of lexical cohesion tied to the student's own language and to the teacher's language is given in Table 21-2.

As with ellipsis, the youngest group of children has a slightly higher proportion of lexical linking to teachers (17 vs 11%) and a lower proportion of lexical linking to themselves (52 vs 56%). The 5 year olds tend to use lexical cohesion to orient to their teacher's language more than the other students, just as they used ellipsis. The teachers have the highest rate of lexical linking to themselves. Compared to the rates for ellipsis, the students' relative rate of linking to themselves is much higher for lexical cohesion and their rate of linking to the teachers is much lower. This finding indicates that the continuity signaled by lexical cohesion (often extending to several links as a field of discourse is built up; see

Table 21-2. *Percentage of Lexical Cohesion Tied to Student's (SS) and Teacher's (T) Language[a]*

	5 years	7 years	9 years	Teacher	
SS	52	56	55	—	(1027)
T	17	11	11	63	(658)
	(353)	(366)	(542)	(424)	

[a]The numbers in parentheses indicate the actual number of cases in the data.

Gregory, 1967) tends to be used by students to link their own language. Ellipsis, on the other hand, usually involves only one link, depends on structural clues, and is used more by students to link their language to the language of their teachers. For the hearer, this difference between lexical cohesion and ellipsis indicates that the appropriate approach for interpreting students' language is to attend to ellipsis in order to relate the language to the structure of the teacher's language and to attend to the lexical characteristics of student's language to relate them to earlier lexical selections by the same student. These generalizations indicate only a difference in proportion of the use of one strategy or another rather than a fundamental contrast in cognitive tasks.

RESULTS FOR CONJUNCTION

The percentage of conjunction referring to a student's own language (SS) to another student (SO) and to the teacher (T) is given in Table 21-3. Conjunction shows the *highest* rate of linking to the speaker's own language of all types of anaphoric cohesion. It is generally used within turns. An example of adversative conjunction is *or* in

> Yea, is it near the kitchen or down in the cellar?

As with ellipsis and lexical cohesion the youngest children link their own language to that of the teacher at a slightly higher rate than the two older groups of children.

The gloss on conjunctive cohesion, and thus the direction to the hearer for interpretation, is "interpret what follows [in a particular way for each conjunctive particle] with respect to what precedes." This meaning of conjunction taken with the way it is used suggests that students compare meanings of stretches of language primarily within their own speech. Furthermore, the tendency is for older students to refer progressively more to their own language and less to other students and teachers. Unlike ellipsis and lexical cohesion, older students use conjunction to link less to both other students and teachers, rather than less only to teachers.

Table 21-3. *Percentage of Conjunction Referring to Student's (SS), Another Student's (SO), and Teacher's (T) Language[a]*

	5 years	7 years	9 years	Teacher	
SS	73	85	91	—	(707)
T	10	4	4	82	(148)
SO	16	10	5	14	(98)
	(280)	(229)	(330)	(114)	

[a]The numbers in parentheses indicate the actual number of cases in the data.

Table 21-4. *Percentage of Anaphoric Reference Linking to a Student's (SS), Another Student's (SO), and a Teacher's (T) Language*[a]

	5 years	7 years	9 years	Teacher	
SS	48	66	76	—	(544)
T	24	8	6	53	(265)
SO	25	19	14	44	(290)
	(258)	(159)	(381)	(301)	

[a]The numbers in parentheses indicate the actual number of cases in the data.

Conjunction, then, seems less independent of the social difference between students and teachers than ellipsis and lexical cohesion. That is, conjunction, which relates meaning to meaning by adding a meaning relation (exactly how the second stretch of language is to be interpreted, i.e., additive, causal, temporal, or adversative), is more sensitive to social differences of the speakers of the first stretch of language than ellipsis or lexical cohesion, which create links without adding a direction of how the second stretch of language is semantically related to the first.

RESULTS OF ANAPHORIC REFERENCE

The percentage of anaphoric reference linking to a student's own language (SS), to another student (SO), and to the teacher (T) is given in Table 21-4. In the following turns M is a teacher and C is a 5-year-old student.

M: Where are you moving? Where are you going?
C: In Mississauga.
M: Mississauga. Have you been to see the house? What's it look like?
C: It's big.

It in the third turn is linked to *house* in the same turn. The teacher is making an anaphoric link to her own language. In the fourth turn the student's use of *it* links the turn to the teacher's turn. Although there is not as high a level of linking to the speaker's own language as for conjunction, the pattern of increasing linking by older students to their own language and decreasing linking to the teacher's and to that of other students is the same for reference as for conjunction. The student's use of these two types of cohesion is sensitive to the same features of development with age and to the relative social status of the other speakers in the conversations. The relatively low rate by teachers may indicate that their social role of encouraging and reacting to the students is associated with more linking to the language of those students. Further studies are needed to provide more detailed evidence.

DISCUSSION OF COHESION RESULTS

The similarity in the linguistic and psychological function of conjunction and reference is that a meaning relationship is established and this relationship requires the use of meaning from earlier in the text. Ellipsis and lexical cohesion, on the other hand, are relations set up between linguistic structures and items themselves, rather than essentially between the meanings of those items. That is, ellipsis and lexical cohesion (which is overwhelming lexical repetition) are more formal relations than semantic ones. The development pattern in the conversations examined is that students from ages 5 to 9 are becoming sensitive to the social relations among speakers in conversation. They use those types of cohesion that tend to relate meanings to other meanings differentially according to the speaker of the earlier relevant meaning. Development of sensitivity to the speaker is thus demonstrable for aspects of meaning relationships but not for more formal relations in language. This result is to be expected in viewing language as a tool for communication that children learn to use in social situations to convey meaning. Children are learning to communicate meaning to others, not how to manipulate undifferentiated linguistic symbols in mechanical ways.

In combining anaphoric reference and conjunction the data indicate that the youngest children use a higher rate of cohesive links that directly involve meaning relationships (anaphoric reference and conjunction) when linking with the language of other speakers. Although there is proportionately less such cohesion used by the older children, this finding does not contradict the conclusion that these particular cohesive relations are the ones most sensitive with respect to social relationships among speakers.

In summary, older children use different types of cohesion to link their language to others. The older children, compared to the 5 year olds, tend to use the more formal types (ellipsis and lexical cohesion) when linking their language to others. However, it is the more meaning-oriented types of cohesion (conjunction and anaphoric reference) that are used by the older children in a manner that is sensitive to the social identity of the speaker that they are linking their language to.

Most characteristics of language are not all-or-none phenomena in actual usage. Rather, there is variation as other factors influence a particular pattern in language. Proportions of the different types of cohesion are investigated so that relative levels of usage can be compared across different age groups and situations. Factors such as the different absolute amounts of cohesion are thus controlled. Excluding exophora, the types of cohesion are different means of creating semantically coherent stretches of language (see the discussion of "textness" in Halliday and Hasan, 1976, and in Halliday, 1977). From the position of the hearer these types of cohesion along with exophora give directions for interpreting the language being spoken. The study of proportions thus gives a description of the balance of these directions. For the hearer, this

Table 21-5. *Percentage of All Types of Cohesion*[a]

		5 years	7 years	9 years	Teacher	
Meaning relations (anaphoric reference, conjunction)	D	30	21	32	—	(839)
	TD	39 (550)	27 (403)	42 (733)	28 (429)	(1276)
Formal relations (ellipsis, substitution, lexical)	D	39	46	47	—	(1307)
	TD	38 (636)	43 (631)	45 (929)	47 (741)	(1630)

[a]Raw frequencies are in parentheses.

balance can indicate the most efficient set of expectations for interpreting the language of the speaker.

It was found in analyzing the speaker of antecedent information that the cohesive types tending to establish meaning relations in a text (conjunction and anaphoric reference) are sensitive to sociolinguistic changes whereas the cohesive types setting up more formal links (ellipsis, lexical cohesion) are not sensitive to those changes. It is also the former type of cohesion that is used differentially by the various groups of speakers in the coding of given and new information in the clause (see Fine, 1977, Chapter 5 for details and discussion).

The percentage of all types of cohesion represented by meaning relations and formal relations of cohesion is given in Table 21-5 for each age group and for the two experimental situations: D—dialogue, TD—teacher dialogue. In this analysis substitution has been added to ellipsis and lexical cohesion as a more formal cohesive relation.

As with the analysis of the speaker of the antecedent of the cohesive link, the types of links involving meaning more directly are those aspects of cohesion that are varied as the situation changes. The more formally based links (of ellipsis, substitution, and lexis) are almost constant in their respective proportions of all cohesive links.

The lack of variation in the level of more formally established cohesive links in the two situations may indicate that these types of cohesive links are influenced by factors other than the number and social status of the speakers in a conversation. There is also a small but progressive change in the level of these cohesive links with age, in the direction of the teachers' level of usage. On the other hand, the teachers' level of usage of cohesive links more clearly involving meaning relations (conjunction and anaphoric reference) differs distinctly from the students' levels in the same conversations. . . .[*]

---

[*]Section on the structure of turn-taking is omitted. [Eds.]

General Discussion

Language in conversation is organized both grammatically and in terms of conversational organization. This study has used systemic grammar and the analysis of low-level conversational sequencing to investigate the patterning in children's conversations. The findings include patterns of linking one speaker's language to the language of others. The identity of the speaker of the antecedent language and the type of turn being related to are shown to fall into specific patterns. Conjunctive words (such as *and, however, furthermore*) and anaphoric reference (such as third person pronouns and adjectives, e.g., *he, hers, they*) set up cohesive links with some preceding stretch of language. In this study of the speech of 5, 7, and 9 year olds it is found that the younger children link their own language to that of the teacher more than do the older children. Furthermore, certain types of cohesive links and the pattern of exophoric reference (reference to outside the language of the conversation, e.g., *here* in *Come here immediately!*) vary according to the number and identity of the speakers in a conversation. In addition, only certain classes of cohesion, those more directly involving meaning relations, are sensitive to such sociolinguistic variables as the speaker of the antecedent language, the age of the speaker of the cohesive item, and the type of conversation. As well as being related to conversational organization and the situation the language is used in, cohesion is distributed into specific parts of the clause as defined by thematic and information organization in the clause. Cohesive items coded as "given" in the clause (following a theory of systemic grammar) more frequently set up a link to a turn that is not part of a conversationally defined set of question–answer–confirmation or imperative–response. The "given" location in the clause, then, tends to build connections between turns when the turn-taking structure of the conversation does not supply a strong functional connection between the turns.

The approach of combining different kinds of analysis to study conversation must be explored further. Work on one or another component of conversation must eventually be combined with the study of other aspects of conversation in order to move to more comprehensive understanding. In addition, such combined studies can shed light on the separate components of conversation.

22

Katherine Nelson and Janice M. Gruendel
At Morning It's Lunchtime:
A Scriptal View of
Children's Dialogue

For many years, children's speech to other children was viewed as egocentric or noncommunicative, both in terms of its pragmatic function and its cognitive intent. Variously described as "parasocial" (Vygotsky, 1962), "egocentric" (Piaget, 1926, 1962), or "private" (Kohlberg, Yeager, & Hjertholm, 1968), noncommunicative speech has been reported to account for between 30 and 60% of all the language that occurs when young peers get together. A frequently cited example of such nondialogic language behavior was reported by Kohlberg et al. (1968, p. 693). The speakers are $3\frac{1}{2}$-year-old boys:

CONVERSATION (1)

> Brian: I'm playing with this.
> David: A what's, a what's.
> Brian: Oh nuts, oh nuts.
> David: Doodoodoo, round, round up in the sky. Do you like to ride in a (toy) helicopter?
> Brian: OK. I want to play in the sandbox.
> David: Much fun. Do you want to ride in the helicopter?
> Brian: I'm going outside.

This excerpt exemplifies the typical noncontingent, self-oriented, often playful aspects of children's speech. Although the exchange reveals the regularity of turn-taking essential to dialogue, and also contains mechanisms (e.g., "Okay") that appear to link alternate contributions, in actuality each participant links his

Abridged from "At morning it's lunchtime: A scriptal view of children's dialogues" by K. Nelson and J. Gruendel, 1979, *Discourse Processes*, **2**, 73–94. Copyright 1979 by Ablex. Reprinted by permission of publisher and authors.

utterance to his own prior utterance and not to those of his partner, thus producing what Piaget (1926) labeled "collective monologue."

Recently, the pendulum has swung in the opposite direction with a growing
consensus that early language is essentially social with roots in the prelinguistic
mother–child communication system (Bates, 1976; Bruner, 1975; Greenfield
and Smith, 1976). The essentials of dialogue—turn-taking, reciprocity, intent—
are reported to be established early (Schaffer, 1978), and several authors have
viewed conversation as both the goal of mothers (Snow, 1977) and the outcome
for children (Halliday, 1975) during the child's second year. . . .

While the recent emphasis has been on the social and communicative
functions of children's speech, the existence of a substantial number of noncommunicative exchanges among preschool children, as in conversation (1), continues to demand an explanation. Under what conditions does communicative
rather than noncommunicative speech arise? When do turn-taking exchanges
become dialogue and when collective monologue?

The Structure and Function of Dialogue

To address the questions we need some basis for identifying the structure, function, and content of dialogues as compared to nondialogic exchanges. Most of
the emphasis in recent research has been on structural aspects. Among these,
alternating turns is universally identified as a feature of conversational structure.
Turn-taking has been observed among mother and child pairs in prelinguistic
vocalizing exchanges and infants very early appear to acquire this aspect of the
language game (Bruner, 1975b; Lewis and Freedle, 1973; Schaffer, 1978; Stern,
1974). But although turn-taking is necessary to the establishment of dialogue, it
is clearly not sufficient, for even when children follow an alternation rule,
dialogue in the sense of topic sharing does not follow automatically, as is evident
in conversation (1) quoted above.

Other aspects of dialogic structure are less widely agreed upon but tend to
implicate function and content more strongly than does turn-taking. For example,
the notion of reciprocity involves obligations on the part of each participant to
exchange listener and speaker roles, and the interpretation of intent requires the
appropriate interpretation of the speaker's message by the listener. Some recent
attempts to analyze mother–child exchanges in terms of message content have
focused on contingent responding (e.g., Bloom, Rocissano, & Hood, 1976; Cross,
1977), that is, the semantic or syntactic links between the two turns. While this is
an important step, it is a limited one. Contingent responding involves one exchange
between speaker and listener; in contrast, dialogue implies an extended series of
turns during which a single topic or set of related topics is sustained or changed
according to conversational rules. The ability to maintain topic reference over a
single turn is clearly necessary but not sufficient for the maintenance of dialogue.

A way must be found to describe the developing ability of both speakers to maintain shared reference over a full conversational exchange.

It is our claim that a proper dialogic analysis demands a description of the knowledge systems that each participant brings to the conversational exchange. This claim is based on the assumption that the ability to engage in dialogue requires two types of knowledge: first, general knowledge of the rules of conversational structure, and second, a wide range of content knowledge that enables and, indeed, results in conversational relevance. Importantly, however, the key to the actualization of truly dialogic exchanges lies in the fact that both types of knowledge must be *shared* by both participants (cf. Keenan and Schieffelin, 1976; Rommetveit, 1974). In conversation (1), for example, it is obvious that while both children apparently shared knowledge about turn-taking, they appear not to have had access to shared content knowledge useful in their object-focused exchange, and dialogue did not result. Indeed, much of the earlier work on peer speech has tended to focus on children observed in interaction with objects where the object itself was the focus of the children's interest and the structural quality of the exchange was the focus of the investigator's interest. But as content interacted with structure, true dialogic behavior was displayed only to a low degree.

In brief, our general argument states that when both conversational structure and content knowledge are shared by young participants in a language situation, dialogue may be expected to occur. Consider, as an example, a conversation between two 4-year-old children audiotaped while they were talking with toy telephones in the housekeeping corner of their nursery school:

CONVERSATION (2)

> Gay: Hi.
> Daniel: Hi.
> Gay: How are you?
> Daniel: Fine.
> Gay: Who am I speaking to?
> Daniel: Daniel. This is your daddy. I need to speak to you.
> Gay: All right.
> Daniel: When I come home tonight, we're gonna have . . . peanut butter and jelly sandwich, uh, at dinner time.
> Gay: Uhmmm. Where're we going at dinnertime?
> Daniel: No where. But we're just gonna have dinner at 11 o'clock.
> Gay: Well, I made a plan of going out tonight.
> Daniel: Well, that's what we're gonna do.
> Gay: We're going out.
> Daniel: The plan, it's gonna be, that's gonna be, we're going to McDonald's.
> Gay: Yeah, we're going to McDonald's. And, ah, ah, ah, what they have for dinner tonight is hamburger.
> Daniel: Hamburger is coming. OK, well, goodbye.
> Gay: Bye.

In contrast to the earlier example of conversation (1) which is best described as collective monologue, this example is, we claim, dialogic. Turn-taking is evident in both examples, and while objects were present in the settings of both conversations, the focus of the second conversation was not on the telephone objects themselves but on the reenactment of an event presumably well known to both children, the telephone exchange in which dinner plans are resolved. No doubt these children had seen or heard their parents making dinner plans, perhaps over the telephone, and probably had participated directly in a telephone experience themselves. They may have even seen similar telephone behavior on television.

This example illustrates the important point that to sustain a dialogue the participants must each assume a shared topic context within which that dialogue is structured. This shared context determines such things as what is expressed and what is left to inference, the particular answers that follow from a given question, and the particular semantic and syntactic links that will be established between utterances. Shared context may derive from two primary sources—the immediate situation, including objects and people present, and background knowledge about the topic of the discourse. Either or both of these may serve to cement the individual contributions to the conversation. Both are evident in the telephone exchange. Indeed, this particular conversation reveals a multiply-embedded structure that relies upon shared context at several levels.

First, a pretend-play context is established within which a conversational exchange then takes place. The contextual focus of the conversational exchange, the telephone context, itself invokes a particular type of dialogue that in the real world is independent of visual cues. In fact Daniel and Gay obeyed this constraint in their pretend realization, but we do not know whether this was intentional or not. Finally, the primary dialogic context of mother and father making dinner plans is then invoked. Thus the levels involved may be represented in the following embedded structure:

(Pretend (Conversation (Telephone (Dinner plans))))

Each of the embedded levels may be seen to involve its own structural characteristics and to rely on substantive event knowledge, all of which are shared by the young participants. Shared context in this exchange thus goes far beyond the immediate here and now that initially helps to ensure that conversational exchanges are held "on track."

The assumption of shared context is essential to all conversation. Where it is in doubt, adults have ways of establishing it, for example, "Have you met the new chairman?" "What was that again?" "Oh, that's not how I understood it." Much adult conversation, in fact, may be viewed as sharing information that then serves as background for further exchanges. Educated and sophisticated adults are so adept at establishing and shifting contexts that the importance of this assumption is quite easily overlooked. Young children, however, are in the process of mastering knowledge of their first few differentiated contexts and cannot be expected to adapt their viewpoints and their conversations so readily. We would like to suggest, in fact, that what has been generally termed egocentrism in the young child is a misplaced assumption of shared context by either or both participants in a dialogue. By "misplaced" we mean an assumption made either without a check on validity or without sufficient direct experience in different contexts to adjust it automatically. A misplaced assumption of shared context also may result if the child lacks the conversational strategies that enable a context adjustment, such as repetition, questioning for clarification, or disagreement. In brief, our hypothesis is that for the preschool child, when the assumption of shared context is correct, dialogue will occur; when it is misplaced, the characteristics of egocentric speech will emerge. Since both participants make such assumptions, one may be adjusted and the other not. Thus we can expect to observe a number of different types of interaction that may vary according to both the substantive knowledge and contextual adjustment strategies of both participants.

Social Script Structures

We noted above that the structural aspects of dialogue begin to be established very early in mother–child exchanges (e.g., Schaffer, 1978). It is equally evident that young children are developing knowledge representations for everyday events in which they participate or observe. Even the 12 month old anticipates the day's routines and learns to follow them by, for example, responding to verbal and nonverbal cues that breakfast, a walk, and bath occur in that order and that each event involves the child in a specific sequence of behaviors. Indeed, it is around these well-practiced sequences that early verbal exchanges become established. "Bath?" says mother. "Ess," says baby toddling off to the bathroom to take off her clothes, (Church, 1966). An example reported by Schank (Schank and Abelson, 1977, p. 225), suggests just how early children have acquired knowledge of routine events on which they rely for interpretation of action: "Joshua, at age four months, showed a clear knowledge of certain scripts. One day when we returned home from shopping, instead of opening the door, putting the stroller with Joshua in it and then returning for the groceries, I reversed the order, putting the groceries in the house first. Joshua became extremely upset at this."

The term "script," as used here refers to the conceptual representation of Joshua's knowledge of the *coming home from shopping* routine. In more general terms, a script can be defined as a conceptual structure that describes appropriate sequences of events in a particular context. "A script is made up of slots and requirements about what can fill those slots. The structure is an interconnected whole, and what is in one slot affects what can be in another" (Schank and Abelson, 1977, p. 41). Scripts may represent any number of routine, sequential events, such as going to bed, attending a birthday party, eating at a restaurant, taking a bath, or having a telephone conversation. Each script includes a minimum set of actors and players, each assuming a certain role. The script is constructed from the point of view of one of the players; in the case of the young child, from his point of view, which may differ in important ways from that of the adult or of another child. Scripts are stored as part of a person's long-term memory and are instantiated, that is, activated as part of conscious mental processing, in an appropriate verbal or situational context. Scripts are of considerable functional importance to the individual by enabling him to predict what, when, and who in familiar situations and to monitor predictable details while actively attending to novel elements of the event (Nelson, 1977; Schank and Abelson, 1977).

It is our claim that the development of topic relevant dialogue structure may profitably be viewed as a function of building up of shared social scripts that specify the structure and content of familiar events in the child's experience. In fact, the conversational structure may itself be viewed as one kind of very general social script. As we have already seen, young children early develop *conversational scripts* based on the shared focus of mother–child interaction. As we have also already noted, when the knowledge underlying the language situation is shared—as in event-based exchanges—the topic is held on target, but when it is not, the contributions of each speaker tend to be unconstrained and to stray in noncommunicative directions. It is our thesis that a well-understood script whose content and structure is shared by its two young participants can help the children extend their conversational skill beyond the point where what should be said is determined by the immediate situation to the point where dialogue may be free of immediate context, in play or in the exchange of knowledge.

Our recent research on how young children build up scripts (e.g., Nelson, 1978b) is based on the belief that they are a basic organizing structure for the young child's knowledge system. In our view, scripts are useful to the child for predicting the sequence of routines, anticipating who will act and how, recognizing alternative slot fillers, and in general operating as an expert on the passing scene. It is the well-known scripts for baths, feeding, and other home activities that enable the child to take an active part in the action as well as in the conversation about the action, even when out of the context of the immediate situation. Home-based scripts deriving from the shared experiences of mother and child are limited, of course, in their generality. They may be shared to a greater or lesser extent by members of the family other than mother and child, depending upon the care-taking arrangements, but often in our culture each home script is somewhat idiosyncratic and specific to a particular dyad. Thus, at the outset the young child has limited potential for shared knowledge situations both in terms of contexts and in terms of possible sharing partners. For this reason, mothers may be able to engage their children in far more sophisticated dialogue than strange adults or other children are able to do. Parents are, of course, more practiced at interpreting the child's intentions as well.

In our research thus far we have given special attention to children's scripts for the lunch situation at the day care center and have found that for most children interviewed the script consists of a set of sequenced basic events— playing, eating, napping—plus less important, more specific, or optional events, such as washing hands, getting food, spilling milk, having dessert, and throwing away plates. An important outcome of this study is the finding that playing and eating are very general script components for young children. If pressed, they will mention what you play and what you eat, but their usual reference to the event is the general event term itself, a strategy that leaves open the possibility of filling in the details with context-specific slot-fillers. In other words, the child's script is revealed as a general structure, not a particular one. It is this general character that enables the child to instantiate a script on all appropriate occasions and to use it for predicting the sequence of general components. Specifics would be a hindrance to this usefulness. Generality is also useful when the script is to be used as a basis of shared knowledge in play and dialogue. It is not that the child does not have knowledge about appropriate slot-fillers, but that these unspecified slot-fillers provide open opportunities for variation within a common frame.

A second important outcome of the analysis was the finding of a high level of agreement on the basic event sequence across children. Such commonalities of the social script for routine events is an obvious support for the usefulness of shared script knowledge in the interactions of young children.

Use of Scripts in Dialogues

In order to examine the use of script knowledge in young children's conversations, we have taped a number of children at play in day care centers. Conversation (2) quoted earlier was one example. These conversations are presented here with no claim as to their representativeness. Rather, they have given us the beginnings of an understanding of the relation of script knowledge to variation in conversational structure.

To see how a script may be used as a framework for a dialogue, let us examine a conversation between two girls (G-1 and G-2, aged 4;4 and 4;8, respectively) who are cutting cookie shapes out of play dough. The numbers to the left of the transcript refer to one exchange, consisting of two turns. We have divided the dialogue into parts to facilitate the discussion of its structure.

CONVERSATION (3)

Part I

    (1) G-1: And also, at night time, it's supper time.
            G-2: Yeah, at night time, it's supper time. It is.
    (2) G-1: It's morning.
            G-2: At morning, it's lunch time! [emphatic]
    (3) G-1: At morning, we already had breakfast. Because at morning, it's lunch time!
            G-2: RIGHT! [emphatic]
    (4) G-1: Yeah, at morning, it's lunch time.
            G-2: At morning, it's lunch time.

Part II

   (5) G-1:   But, FIRST comes snack, then comes lunch.

        G-2:   Right. . . . Just in school, right?

   (6) G-1:   Yeah, right, just in school.

        G-2:   Not at home.

   (7) G-1:   Well, sometimes we have snacks at home.

        G-2:   Sometimes.

   (8) G-1:   Sometimes I have snack at home.

        G-2:   Sometimes I have snack at my home, too.

   (9) G-1:   Uh-hum. Because when special children come to visit us, we sometimes have snack. Like, like, hotdogs, or crackers, or cookies or, or something like that.

        G-2:   Yeah. Something. Maybe cake. (Laughs)

  (10) G-1:   Cake.

        G-2:   Cake. Yeah, maybe cake.

  (11) G-1:   Or maybe, uh, maybe, hotdog.

        G-2:   Maybe hotdog.

Part III

  (12) G-1:   But, but, but, Jill and Michael don't like hotdog. Don't you know, but, do you know Michael and Jill?

        G-2:   I know another Michael.

  (13) G-1:   I know, I know another Michael.

        G-2:   No, I know just one Michael. I just know one Michael.

  (14) G-1:   Do you know Flora?

        G-2:   NO! But you know what? It's a, it's one, it's it's somebody's bro . . . it's somebody's brother.

Part IV

  (15) G-1:   Are you eating your dinner? (Laughs) but not for real.

        G-2:   Not for real.

  (16) G-1:   Because at morning, it's lunch time.

        G-2:   Right, at morning it is lunch time.

  (17) G-1:   Right, at morning it is lunch time.

While the conversation here is loosely tied to food, and thus may be seen to be related to the play activity, the play activity is not itself the subject of the dialogue as it was in Conversation (1). The dialogue rather involves the sharing of script information about meals. In this sense we have an event script serving as the subject of the conversation as well as providing structure to the conversation. The overall structure consists of four parts, each beautifully reflecting the alternation of turns and strategies for topic elaboration and agreement. Part I consists of the first four exchanges and ends with the agreement "At morning it's lunch time." Part II consists of exchanges 5 through 12, ending with the topic-shifting "but Jill and Michael don't like hotdog." Part III runs through exchange 14 in the discussion of the identification of Michael. Part IV is a reprise of Part I.

Parts I, II, and IV all involve script knowledge in different ways. Part I establishes agreement as to which meals belong in which segment of the day. Notice that each participant adds a bit of knowledge to the accumulation of the shared day script. The repetition of the almost poetic "At morning it's lunch time" seems to reflect mutual satisfaction with this sharing. It is interesting to note in this conversation how repetition, which has been identified as a mechanism for maintaining structure in the face of inadequate means for making a substantive contribution (Keenan, 1977), is used here as a means of establishing agreement on shared knowledge. It seems probable that repetition serves two purposes—one structural—to maintain the dyadic flow—and the other substantive—to affirm understanding and resolve uncertainty and disagreement. Both no doubt occur also in adult speech under appropriate conditions. It does not seem that one use is more primitive than another but rather that one would expect them to appear in different types of exchanges.

In the discussion of snack in Part II of this dialogue, there arises the first uncertainty. G-2, when faced with the proposition that snack comes before lunch, tries to pinpoint the differentiation of home and school scripts, which up to that point had not apparently been necessary. She asserts that snack takes place only in school. At first G-1 agrees, but then shifts on her turn 7. Agreement is apparently highly important in this exchange, and one might surmise that, since general knowledge is being shared, it is important that it be agreed upon. Common knowledge—truth in the eyes of the young child—is not subject to dispute. G-2 therefore agrees in her turn that sometimes she has a snack at home. (It seems possible that the difficulty here occurs as G-2 realizes that she does not have a snack before lunch at home, but this fine point gets lost in the ensuing conversation.) Having agreed on the occurrence of snack at home, G-1 proceeds to list some of the possible food items or slot-fillers (hotdogs, crackers, cookies, cake). Again there is agreement. However, mention of hotdog leads G-1 to note an exception to the general situation, that is, to a particular detail that constrains the generality of the script: Jill and Michael, two of the "special children" who might come to visit, do not like hotdogs! This observation in turn leads to the digression about the identification of Michael. Note that agreement in this case is not necessary—the girls are content to recognize that they might know different special children. Finally, with a joke (Are you eating your dinner?) which seems to refer to the established script for ordering mealtimes and not the play situation, the girls return to the main theme: at morning it's lunch time. The theme has lasted over 18 exchanges or 36 individual turns.

This spontaneous dialogue shows not only the existence and depth of script knowledge, but also the way in which the children are able to use it to sustain the conversation. Without the script structure in mind it might appear that the shifts we have identified were a type of chain association. For example, when G-1 on Turn 12 says, "But Jill and Michael don't like hotdog," we can see that this poses a problem for the script that has been established as the central topic, because Jill and Michael are special children and hotdog is one of the foods that has been specified as appropriate for that slot. The script leads to the repetition of agreed upon general elements conjoined with the independent introduction of optional details that are not necessarily agreed upon.

Note another interesting aspect of the conversation that we have also found in our previous studies of scripts: the young child is able to move backward as well as forward within them. This is apparent at Turn 5 when G-1 says, "But FIRST comes snack." Thus, within this type of temporally organized structure based on scriptal knowledge, cognitive reversibility is possible for the child, and at a much younger age than one usually finds it in more cognitively oriented, less familiar tasks.

Consider next the case of two girls (3;5 and 3;7) whose shared script knowledge serves as a basis for fantasy play. A toy model of a school room and people toys are used as props. In this dialogue individual turns are numbered rather than exchanges in order to facilitate the analysis of links, which follows.

CONVERSATION (4)

Part I

		(Rings the bell)
(1)	G-1:	Stop!! The school is open! (rings bell) School is open. Walk, walk, walk, walk, walk in. Whoops!
(2)	G-2:	You shut up this end. (Closes the front flap of the school house.)
(3)	G-1:	Yeah, shut up this end and let's get all these things ready.
(4)	G-2:	Yeah, it's night-time. We have to go home now.
(5)	G-1:	Yep. Now where's the other person? Put it, put it on, now, yeah. (Brings people out of school) Now close this up.
(6)	G-2:	They have to go home! Why do you think they have to stay in school! They have to go home!
(7)	G-1:	(Laughs)
(8)	G-2:	And the teacher has to go home, too. What do you think she's in there. She likes to sleep in a school. Nobody sleeps in a school.
(9)	G-1:	Nooo.

Part II

(10)	G-2:	OK. Here's her house and she's sleeping right here. She's in here. OK. Here comes . . . She's right next to the school (walks Teacher to school) Right here. She doesn't have to walk too far.—
(11)	G-1:	(Rings bell) School's open!
(12)	G-2:	Ding, ding! Go in.
(13)	G-1:	Having snack.
(14)	G-2:	(Rings bell loudly)
(15)	G-1:	Having snack, no. I want to ring the bell for snack. (rings it)

(16) G-2: Here, here.

(17) G-1: What's that?

(18) G-2: In case she sits right there. (?) (Puts people in chairs at tables)—

(19) G-1: Whoops. School is closed.

(20) G-2: All the people out. (Moves them out) Out.

(21) G-1: School is closed. (Rings the bell)

(22) G-2: Walking home! Walking home! (Both sing-song this way as they move F-P people around the room.)

(23) G-1: Back at school, back at school! (Rings the bell)

(24) G-2: Walking home, walking home.

Part III

(25) G-1: School is ready.

(26) G-2: School is ready! Uh-oh, ba-sketti-oh!

(27) G-1: The door's closed, because it's not locked up. But you can walk in this door. (Walks person in) And, but no one there has a (?). Not snack time, yet. First, you take your coat off.

(28) G-2: Here I come to school, walk. The TEACHER! (Walks teacher into school)

(29) G-1: THEN, then you play, then you play.

(30) G-2: This is the teacher. This is the teacher. She's looking out the window.

(31) G-1: These guys are playing outside now. Now people are playing outside.

(32) G-2: No, they're taking a nap now. Put 'em in! They're going to take a nap now. Teacher, the teacher's rubbing her back. The teacher's . . . rubbing . . .

(33) G-1: She . . . this is the teacher, and she's walking outside to get something from her car. Ba-doop, ba-doop (walks teacher to pretend car). Get something out from her car. Laughs. Walk back inside. OK.

(34) G-2: Her mother's car is broken, so let's ride in the teacher's car.

(35) G-1: Yeah. Rubbing your back, rubbing your back. (Makes teacher rub children's backs) Ooops, school's closed!

(36) G-2: School's closed! Wake up everybody. Time to go outside, time to go outside. WHEEE!!! (Everyone is moved outside the school)—

In this sequence of 18 exchanges the topic clearly depends upon the play activity, and the activity, in turn, is derived from a script of the school day. Thus both activity and dialogue are dependent upon the shared school script. Note, however, that the script is critical in a way that it would not be if real rather than play activity were involved. That is, in cases where the exigencies of real-life

Part I

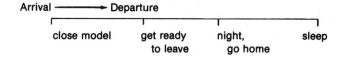

Part II

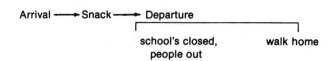

Part III

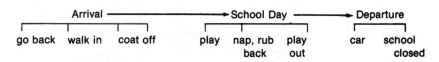

Fig. 22-1. *Cycles of script events: Conversation 4.*

goal-directed action require a certain response the situational script is helpful but not necessary. However, in play—where the activity is dependent upon situational knowledge—the script itself is essential to initiate and direct both action and its accompanying dialogue.

Like the previous one, this dialogue is also characterized by highly regular turn-taking and a preference for agreement as reflected in the introductory "yeah's" and "yep's," even in cases where the apparent action is not in agreement. Note also the highly general, indeed, skeletal enactment of the school day: you come (by walking or by car), you play, snack, the teacher rubs backs at nap, you wake, go outside, and then go home. Both the absence of detail and the repeated cycles of coming and going are striking, for both tend to ensure agreement among participants. Interestingly, the three cycles of arrival to departure are expanded by the children from the beginning of the dialogue to its end, through the inclusion of first one, then several intermediate event components in different parts of the script structure (see the skeletal cycle frame in Fig. 22-1). . . .

Although there are numerous instances within this conversation in which the children are at the same points in the sequence of mentioned events, there is also an extended set of turns in which each child runs off a different part of the script.* Note especially the sequence beginning with turn 23. In contrast to earlier points in the dialogue where there is much agreement and coordination, in this sequence, the children move through their own scripts more or less

*One table and one figure omitted. [Eds.]

independently. This gives the exchange some of the hallmarks of egocentric language, and at one point it leads to a threatened dispute (turn 32), where child G-2 says, "No, they're taking a nap now. Put 'em in!" The shared script that previously directed and supported the joint conversation and active play also allows the two to proceed within the script independently of one another without noting the independence until there is an actual conflict over the placement of the props. Such tying of one's utterance to one's own prior turn rather than to partner's turn has been observed in adult conversation under conditions of topic conflict as well, and is referred to as *skip-connecting* (Coulthard, 1977). Note how the structure of repair is revealed here at turns 31 through 36 after the two children have been running through their own individual scripts and come to disagree. G-2 incorporates information about the teacher's car, while G-1 goes back to pick up the "rubbing back" component introduced by G-2 on turn 32. Thus the dialogue converges again and ends in agreement.

Another use of a script, in planning situations, was illustrated in Conversation (2), introduced earlier. As noted above, in this case we find a series of scripts embedded within each other. The telephone conversation invokes a plan for dinner, and the plan calls up one slot-filler for the dinner script (peanut butter and jelly), but Gay introduces an alternative path for the meal script—going out. As in at least one form of the real-life situation that is simulated here, Daniel readily accepts and expands it to suggest McDonald's. Note that invoking McDonald's necessitates in turn a change of menu choice—that is, a slot-filler— from peanut butter and jelly to hamburgers. . . .*

Each of the conversations considered here have demonstrated the basic realization of the *conversational script*, involving turn-taking and a focus on a common topic. In each case the temporal routine script of well-understood events adds a common knowledge structure relating to the common topic and thus allows the participants to proceed smoothly within it.

Further systematic analysis is needed to substantiate our claim that, in addition to the focus on a common topic, shared knowledge about that topic is needed to sustain a dialogue, and that the form of that knowledge for the young child is typically that of a script for routine events. We are currently investigating situations in which we can specify in advance whether or not two children share similar scripts and thus can be expected to engage in dialogue on a topic.

There are many other identifiable functions of the script structure besides that of providing support for the establishment of dialogues. As illustrated in the examples given above, the script provides a temporal structure within which temporal terms can begin to be understood and used ("But FIRST we have snack"). It provides a structure in which general concepts—play, eat, snack— stand for specific slot-fillers comprising a list of optional possibilities, for example, cookies, cake, hotdogs—in much the same way that general terms such as food and furniture stand for alternative specific items. It provides for the specification and understanding of basic roles to be played within the routine event. By

---

*Conversation (5) and discussion are omitted. [Eds.]

internalizing the script the child is internalizing knowledge about the roles of others, enabling him thereby to take on those roles when necessary or convenient (as in play). This is clear in the case of Conversation (2) in which the "daddy" and "mommy" roles are played out.

Conclusion

Let us then summarize the argument we are presenting. First, when knowledge is shared it provides a structure within which interaction can take place—where people can understand each other. This is, we generally hope, our normal situation. When it is not the case, we usually strive to find some common ground for understanding or we abandon the conversational effort altogether; that is to say, dialogue depends on shared assumptions and particularly on the assumption of shared topic. This assumption can be right or wrong. When it is wrong—when there is no shared topic or script—the person doing the assuming, of whatever age, appears egocentric since he or she proceeds within his or her individual structure oblivious to the fact that the other is operating along a different tack. This may be as true of congressional debate or of the teacher in the elementary or college classroom as it is of the preschool child. However, preschool children are at a particular disadvantage because they have built up few routine scripts and therefore have few to share. In addition, they may not recognize the signs that others do not share their own understandings. The more sophisticated, the more interpersonally sensitive, the more linguistically skillful person will recognize the signals of a lack of shared knowledge, while the less well-equipped person in these respects will evidence symptoms of egocentrism. Sharing social scripts for how things are done, what to expect next, who plays what role, can serve to overcome this apparent egocentrism, and we therefore believe that learning scripts provides an essential foundation for much of the child's social, cognitive, and linguistic development.

The other side of the coin, however—that is, recognizing when the person to whom one is talking does *not* share one's knowledge or point of view—probably requires some minimum amount of experience with a number of differentiated scripts involving people in different roles, experience which the preschool child is unlikely to have. This results in the phenomenon of the preschool child who follows her own script, oblivious to the discrepancies between her own behavior or speech and that of the person with whom she is sharing the situation. It is worth emphasizing again, however, that the dialogues we found were almost always well-structured from the point of view of alternation and commonality of topic. This basic alternating structure is probably built up in the turn-taking routines of mother and child in the preverbal and early language learning period, as noted above. In these exchanges the mother understands and interprets the child's role and reference even when the child's speech is ambiguous. Thus learning the structure of conversational exchanges takes place within a context in which the child's assumption of shared knowledge is justified, that is, the child's emerging knowledge of events and routines is shared by, and indeed often directed by, the mother. It is, in fact, this shared knowledge that enables the pair to talk about past and future events, events displaced in time and space, rather than being confined to the immediate present. We would go beyond this to suggest that it is within the support offered by contexts shared between mother and child that the child learns not only the turn-taking aspect of conversational structure but also the semantics and syntactics of conversational contingencies, such as topic sharing and contingent responding. It is in this respect that the content and structure of the child's knowledge system take on importance for the establishment of structural properties of dialogue.

However, as we have clearly seen, when the child meets with other people—teachers and peers, for example—the assumption of shared knowledge may *not* be justified. When this occurs and there is no commonality of topic context—no shared script—teachers are usually better at providing corrective signals and asking redirective questions than are peers, who are operating within their own limited scriptal understanding. This no doubt explains why egocentric speech has often been observed among peers but less frequently with parents or other adults. Later, the child will begin to verify and expand her own knowledge through interactions with peers. This is the kind of exchange that we saw in Conversation (3), involving checks, agreements, and explanations. On the other hand, where scripts are in conflict and there is no recognition of the need for reconciling the discrepancies, we find disorganization and disagreement.

We have used the script notion thus far as an aid to understanding under what circumstances egocentric exchanges will occur, that is, to establish a taxonomy of children's conversations. However, as the analysis of Conversations (2) through (4) has shown, the construct has implications for structural analysis as well. Through the use of an underlying script structure with its obligatory and optional events, objects and roles, its temporal, spatial, and causal links, one may identify places within the dialogue where links to a previous utterance—one's own or another's, immediately past or more remote—are evident where they would not be with a less explicitly knowledge-based analysis. Such analysis, of course, demands that one be able to specify independently of the dialogue itself the particulars of the script as they are understood by each individual participant. In the present case we believe that the scripts are reasonably transparent; nonetheless there are many points at which others might well disagree with our interpretations. Our present research is directed toward the establishment of these more controlled situations with a view toward a more systematic structural analysis of the resulting dialogues than we have presented here.

In the interim, we conclude on the basis of our exploration thus far that understanding children's dialogues necessarily involves understanding structures and functions of their general knowledge systems. Similarly, children's ability to engage in dialogue depends upon their ability to establish and maintain a shared context based on their mutual understanding of situation and script.

23

Jean M. Mandler
A Code in the Node:
The Use of a Story Schema
in Retrieval

A major advance in our understanding of discourse processes has come from the recent attempts to characterize the structure of various kinds of prose. Much of this work has concentrated on the structure of stories (e.g., Kintsch, 1977; Mandler and Johnson, 1977; Rumelhart, 1975; Thorndyke, 1977). Each of these attempts has shown that stories have suprasentential structure, that subjects are sensitive to such structure, and use it to guide both comprehension and recall. For example, Thorndyke (1977) and Kintsch (1977) have shown that stories presented in scrambled order are less well recalled than those presented in normal order. Rumelhart (1977a) has shown that rules governing the formation of summaries of stories may be derived from rules describing the underlying structure of stories. The present study explores in more detail some of the ways in which subjects use their knowledge of story structure to guide retrieval.

Many of the attempts to describe the structure of stories have been cast in the form of grammars, consisting of sets of rewrite rules capable in principle of generating well-formed stories or of breaking down a well-formed story into its constituent units. Mandler and Johnson (1977), following work by Rumelhart (1975) and earlier work by Propp (1968) and Colby (1973), characterized the underlying structure of simple stories as a set of basic nodes in a tree structure, each of which is either causally or temporally connected to other nodes in the tree. The rules governing the sequencing and connection of nodes were found to be adequate to parse a fairly large set of stories, including both single and multi-episode stories of several types.

Once a structural description of stories has been decided upon, there re-

Excerpted from "A code in the node: The use of a story schema in retrieval" by J.M. Mandler, 1978, *Discourse Processes*, 1, 14–35. Copyright 1978 by Ablex. Reprinted by permission of publisher and author.

mains the yet more difficult task of specifying how people use such structure in encoding and retrieving the information in a story. Mandler and Johnson (1977) assumed that the structure of a story influences comprehension and recall because of the operation of story schemata. That is, the set of grammatical rules which specify whether or not a story is well formed is intended to represent expectations which a listener has incorporated in the form of a cognitive schema. Story schemata are acquired through experience with listening to stories as well as experience with typical kinds of causal and temporal event sequences in the world. Thus, story schemata consist of sets of expectations about stories, about the units of which they are composed, the way in which those units are sequenced, and the types of connections between units that are likely to occur.

The Use of A Story Schemata During Encoding

The cognitive schemata reflected by the grammar serve several functions during encoding. They provide a limited set of frameworks within which incoming material will be structured. They help the listener to know which aspects of the material are apt to be important or relevant. They also tell the listener when some part of the story is complete and can be stored or that some proposition must be kept in working memory because related material is yet to come.

Although some schema must be activated at the time of encoding if the material is to be comprehended, the selection process is guided by the details of the actual input. "Once upon a time" or some other aspect of the Setting of a story, for example, alerts listeners to expect a sequence of statements different from those they would hear if listening to a news report, a recipe, or a multiple-choice test. However, people have heard many different kinds of stories and can draw upon a variety of schemata to fit them. It is perfectly possible for subjects to "change their minds" as a story proceeds, to decide that they have gotten off on the wrong track, and to revise their notions of what the story is about. Reorganization can occur even after a story is finished (Spiro, 1977).

Mandler and Johnson (1977) described an explicit set of rules governing the structure of episodes in various kinds of stories, indicating which categories or nodes must be present and in what order. We were less explicit as to how a listener knows when one node is complete and the next begun. That is, we relied on an intuitive understanding of the characteristics of basic story categories. Although precise definitions remain to be formulated, it will be helpful to the following discussion to give an informal description of the basic nodes in an episode and some of their characteristics which people use to decide when a particular node has been completed and a new one begun.

The first basic node in a story is a Setting, usually consisting of stative information about one or more characters, and often including information about the time and locale of the story. The Setting is often signaled by the use of formalisms, such as "Once upon a time . . ." The Setting is followed by one or more episodes, but only a single episode story will be considered here. The first basic node in the episode is a Beginning, which may be any sort of event. The clue to the listener that the Setting is complete and the Beginning node has been entered is usually a shift from a state description to an event description; the transition is often signaled by a formalism such as "Now, one day . . . ," which indicates a shift to the time frame of the events in the first episode.

The listener exits from the Beginning and enters the next node, the Development, when there is a shift to a Reaction of a character. The shift is from an external to an internal event, at least implicitly connected by a casual relation, i.e., the event just described causes a character to react. By definition the reacting character becomes the protagonist of the episode. Thus, the Reaction node is central to the formation of an episode.* Typically, the Reaction node consists of two parts: a Simple Reaction, specifying the emotional response or what the protagonist thinks about the Beginning event, and a Goal, in which the protagonist formulates a plan to deal with any problem the Beginning may have created.

At this point the listener is set to hear about a Goal Path, necessary to complete the Development. A Goal Path consists of an Attempt to reach the Goal and the Outcome of that attempt. The Attempt node must involve the protagonist in an effort to achieve the explicitly stated or implied goal and consists of a series of actions by the protagonist. The Outcome node is entered by some statement indicating whether the Attempt resulted in success or failure. Goal Paths are recursive, and if the Outcome was not successful, the listener should be prepared for either another Goal Path, or an Outcome-embedded episode (which will not be discussed here), or for the Ending node.

The Ending is difficult to describe informally because there are several options. In general, it consists of some further consequences, less directly connected to the Attempt than the Outcome. Frequently the Ending has the emphatic character of a resolution to a series of events. It often refers back to one or more previous nodes in the episode, and may also include a reaction on the part of another character. If the story contains more than one causally connected episode, the reaction of another character may signal the creation of a new protagonist, and thus the Ending of one episode may commence a new episode.

We assume that a set of general rules of this sort enables a listener to structure incoming propositions while listening to a story. In some cases there are no choicepoints, as in the case of an Outcome following an Attempt. In others, particularly nodes at which new causally connected episodes may begin, there are several alternate routes that may be followed and the listener must keep previous nodes in mind until one or more subsequent nodes have occurred in order to organize all of the information into an appropriate structure. There are obviously a number of places even in a well-structured story where the listener may go wrong. If any nodes are omitted or are displaced from the ideal order, the

---

*All footnotes omitted. [Eds.]

chances of confusion or of encoding the information in terms of an unstable novel structure increase.

The Use of a Story Schema During Retrieval

At the time of retrieval, subjects have at their disposal a set of ordered categories, whose approximate form is known independently of the details of the content. The schema serves as a code which operates in three ways during retrieval. First, it tells the subject what general sort of information is to be retrieved; that is, it points to a general area of memory. Second, it provides a temporal sequence to find specific content, telling subjects which address to move to next. Third, if the exact content of a category in the sequence cannot be retrieved, the schema allows the subject to generate an approximation, based on the structure of the schema itself, before moving on to the next address.

The operation of a story schema should produce specifiable characteristics of recall. For example, it accounts for certain kinds of additions and distortions. When the exact content of a node is not retrievable, the schema indicates that something is missing and provides a guide to the structural characteristics of the material to be substituted at that point. Similarly, the schema directs a particular output order of events. In the normal situation, the input and output order will be identical, but if the story has been presented in an irregular fashion, the output should be more likely to maintain the ideal order rather than the order actually heard. . . .

24

Nancy L. Stein

The Development of
Children's Storytelling Skill

The purpose of this paper is to describe the knowledge and skill that are used when children make up and tell their own stories. Storytelling is a complex activity and requires the integration of different types of knowledge. Although the prototypic idea of storytelling is associated with an experience that entertains, delights, and entrances the listener, stories serve a variety of functions in addition to pure entertainment. In most instances, entertainment is a secondary outcome of the narration process.

Stories, by nature and definition, are reflections of the social values, beliefs, and goals that underlie and motivate human interaction. At the heart of the story lies a sequence of events that chronicles the dilemmas people encounter and the methods by which these dilemmas are resolved. Normally, most stories begin with events or sets of conditions that alter the ability of an animate being (i.e., the protagonist) to attain important goals. The major function of this initiating event is to make the protagonist aware that a lack state exists and that a valued goal needs to be achieved. After focusing on the desire to attain a particular goal, a protagonist then constructs a plan of action and carries it out in the hopes of successful goal attainment. Thus, storytelling involves a concerted effort to maintain or achieve highly valued goals (Stein, 1982, 1983; Stein and Glenn, 1982; Stein and Policastro, 1984; Stein and Trabasso, 1982).

Since stories reflect the structure and content of personal and interpersonal knowledge, it becomes increasingly important to understand the relationship between the development of social knowledge and the development of good

The present paper serves as a summary of a joint project, *The Development of Discourse Competence: Evidence from Children's Stories*, completed in collaboration with Tom Trabasso. Portions of this paper were presented at the Eleventh Annual Boston University Child Language Conference, October 17–19, 1986.

storytelling skills (Stein, 1982, 1983). Although storytelling is dependent upon knowledge of the social world, knowing how to tell a good story entails more than an ability to understand and relate social experience. The story is a form of discourse, serves particular functions, and contains themes related to important beliefs, values, and goals of a particular social group. The storyteller must choose from a rich store of social knowledge and be able to combine this information with knowledge about discourse forms and functions, taking into account how the process of narration will affect the listener's understanding and reactions (Stein, 1986).

Although young children have acquired substantial amounts of knowledge about social contexts and the structure of personal and physical causality (Bretherton and Beeghley, 1982; Hood and Bloom, 1979; Huttenlocher, Smiley and Charney, 1983; Stein and Levine, 1986; Trabasso, Stein, and Johnson, 1981), they may not have acquired enough knowledge to understand many of the features associated with the adult conception of a good story. Storytelling is a product of the development of shared communication systems. Acquiring expertise in this domain requires exposure to many different discourse contexts. The fact that young children are proficient at understanding many core concepts associated with personal and physical causality does not guarantee an elaborated understanding of the story concept. In fact, children's astute understanding of certain social contexts may result in an overestimation of their knowledge about causality, discourse forms, and functions (Stein, 1986; Stein and Salgo, 1984).

Thus, an investigation of children's knowledge about stories seems warranted. In particular, an examination of the following four aspects of stories is pertinent:

1. the function of stories,
2. the definition of a story,
3. the types of conflicts and resolutions that occur in stories, and
4. the types of themes used to integrate story events.

The remainder of this paper is devoted to a discussion of these different types of knowledge. The data presented are the results of a study that investigated children's skill at constructing their own stories. Children who participated in this study were from middle-class suburban elementary schools in Chicago and St. Louis. Eighteen children from each of three grade levels (kindergarten, third, and sixth) participated in the study. All children were asked to generate "good" stories about the following three topics:

1. a fox who lived in a forest,
2. a girl named Alice, who lived by the seashore, and
3. a boy named Alan who had lots of toys.

The provision of topic stems allowed a systematic examination of changes in the structure and content of children's stories. Each topic stem served to constrain the types of knowledge accessed and used during narration. Thus, when telling stories about a fox, the themes, conflicts, and resolutions should be related to children's knowledge about foxes, what these animals do, and how these animals relate to other animals around them.

In spite of the constraining effect of the stem, a wide degree of latitude still existed in framing and producing a story. Children had to draw on their knowledge about the reasons for telling stories; they had to consider the dimensions that define a story; and they had to evaluate the adequacy of their knowledge about conflict resolutions in order to construct solutions to the hypothetical problems they posed during narration. Thus, providing children with a topic stem still required an effort to coordinate and integrate different types of knowledge. Therefore, both individual and developmental variation could be assessed.

A concern that influenced the design of this study was related to the demands that storytelling puts on working memory. Because of the complexity involved in integrating different types of knowledge during narration, working memory is often overloaded. Under these conditions, storytellers often resort to finishing the story in the quickest manner possible with little regard for the finished product. Thus, production studies often underestimate the amount and complexity of knowledge children have acquired about the story. Therefore, two procedures were used to ensure that the results from this study accurately reflected children's concept of a good story.

First, all children were asked to evaluate the goodness of their stories at the end of each session. If children rated any of their stories as poor examples of a story, they were given a chance to revise them and to make them correspond to a good story. If children stated that they could not revise their stories to conform to a good story, they were not included in the study. Of all the participants in the study, only one child in kindergarten, two in third grade, and five in fifth grade requested (and were granted) a revision of their original stories. No children were excluded from the study on these grounds.

A second precaution was taken to ensure that generated narratives represented children's concept of a good story and not their inability to tell a good story. The week after the storytelling task was completed, children were told two folktales that had been used in the Stein and Glenn (1979) study. Each story had at least two episodes, with one episode embedded in another. In order to participate in the study, children were required to recall each story and to include at least 40% of all category statements appearing in the original text of the stories. Furthermore, children had to answer correctly at least 60% of a set of probe questions related to each story. Only three 5 year olds and two second graders had difficulty completing these requirements. These children were replaced with others who succeeded.

The results and implications of this study are organized according to the four types of knowledge previously outlined: functions of storytelling, the definition of a story, the use of different conflict resolution schemes, and an analysis of the thematic content of the stories.

Functions of Storytelling

Storytelling serves two primary functions (Stein, 1982, 1983; Stein and Policastro, 1984). The first is a communicative one and the second is a representational one. Classically, storytelling is conceived of as an art through which the culture and heritage of a society are transmitted. Most cultures have constructed tales that explain the origins of the world, how human beings were created, and the role humans play in relationship to nature and other human beings. These stories convey information about important events that have shaped the beliefs and values of a particular society (Stein, 1982; Stein and Policastro, 1984). The stories are often told to change the beliefs and behavior of those who listen. The persuasive element is rarely hidden in the act of storytelling, and the goals of explaining, teaching, and imparting moral information are important motives for the storyteller.

Stories are also told in order to understand social events more fully. During the process of narration, a person frequently comes to understand better the conditions that constrain or facilitate a successful solution to a particular problem. For example, storytelling can result in a better understanding of the feelings, beliefs, and values that regulate people's behavior in different social contexts. Storytelling also allows an individual to work out plans that lead to a successful problem solution or to the discovery of the negative consequences of certain actions and events. Thus, the act of storytelling is often related to the act of learning and restructuring what is already known.

Although the present study does not focus directly on the role of different functions of storytelling, I will argue shortly that most storytelling experiences in the early preschool and elementary school years are oriented toward learning about people and about the conditions that lead to successful problem solutions. Although persuading and explaining may underlie certain storytelling experiences, children rarely use the story to teach, moralize, or create serious explanations for phenomena that would otherwise remain incomprehensible to the listener. Understanding what happened to a person, sharing feelings, figuring out possible motivations that underlie action, and understanding the consequences of actions are the primary goals of the young child. Not until a later time does the child realize the full persuasive import of narration.

The Definition of a Story

The teller's conception of a story critically influences decisions about the structure and content of a narrative. Almost all formal definitions of a story constrain the types and forms of social information that can be included in a text (Stein, 1982; Stein and Policastro, 1984). Accordingly, a text will not be considered a story unless certain features are included, even though the discourse contains information about social situations.

The degree of correspondence between different types of social discourse and different formal definitions of a story is illustrated in the tree diagram outlined in Fig. 24-1. The diagram contains a descending tree structure that gradually includes the central dimensions of several different definitions of a story. Although we tend to think that a culture would have just one shared definition of a story, this is not the case. The formal definitions vary in terms of those dimensions that must be included in order to call a piece of discourse a story. The tree diagram (Stein and Policastro, 1984) represents the way that formal definitions vary dimensionally. Moreover, the diagram can be used to illustrate how a narrative can increase in complexity and correspond to different definitions of a story.

The first dimension that is included in a story is an animate character,

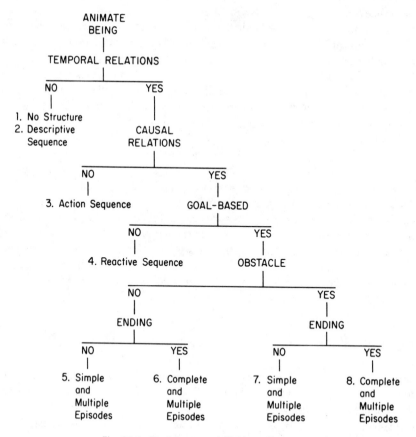

Fig. 24-1. *Decision tree: definitions of a story.*

found in almost all story definitions. The second dimension refers to the possibility of including temporal relationships to link the events in a story sequence. Although most formal definitions of stories require that both temporal and causal relationships connect events, it is possible to generate "stories" without either type of relationship. Table 24-1 contains examples of children's stories that correspond to each level in the tree diagram. Examples 1 and 2 in Table 24-1 illustrate children's stories that contain neither temporal nor causal relationships. The narrative in example 1 is simply a repetition of the two-line topic stem provided at the beginning of each storytelling session. Example 2, which was called a descriptive sequence, is similar to the Setting Category that is used to begin a story. The descriptive sequence contains information about the personality and physical characteristics of a fox. Temporal or causal connections could not easily be inferred to link events in this sequence.

If temporal relationships are used to connect events, then two possible variations in the text can be created. A text sequence can contain events that are temporally but not causally related or the text can contain events that are both temporal and causal in nature. If a text is generated so that only temporal relationships connect the events, a narrative similar to the third example in Table 24-1 is generated. This type of narrative is labeled an action sequence. Here, the routine day in the life of a fox is described. Clearly, one action follows another, but causal relationships do not necessarily connect any two of the events in the sequence.

If causal relationships are used to link the sequence of events, the resulting narrative can either exclude or include goal-based action. The fourth set of examples in Table 24-1 represent stories that have causal sequences but no goal-based action.

If goal-based action is included, the storyteller can construct a sequence of events that does not include an obstacle blocking goal attainment. Alternatively, a sequence can be constructed in which an obstacle must be overcome to succeed in attaining a goal. Examples 5 and 6 are stories that contain goal-based action and the protagonist does not have to overcome an obstacle to attain the desired end state. The two examples differ only in that example 6 has an ending category and example 5 does not. Endings include mainly two types of information: internal state reactions evaluating the success or failure of goal achievement or a moral that summarizes a general principle that has been learned by pursuing a particular plan of action. Often the inclusion of an ending to a story indicates that the teller has made a series of inferences that connect the story in a more coherent manner. Thus, an ending represents an additional dimension that makes the story concept more elaborated.

The inclusion of an obstacle serves to further elaborate the concept of a story. Examples 7 and 8 are representative of children's stories in which an obstacle has been included in the sequence of events. In example 7, however, there is no ending included in the story. In example 8, both an obstacle and an ending are included.

Table 24-1. *Examples of Passages at the Eight Different Levels of the Definition of a Story Outlined in Fig. 24-1*

1. No structure

    Once there was a boy named Alan
    who had lots of toys.
    He had lots and lots of toys.

2. Descriptive sequence

    Once there was a big gray fox
    who lived in a cave.
    He was mean and scary, really scary.
    He had big giant eyes
    And a bushy tail that hit people in the face
    And he ate little rabbits.

3. Action sequence

    Once there was a big gray fox
    who lived in a cave.
    In the morning, he came out of his cave.
    Then he went for a swim.
    Then he played with his friends.
    Then he found some nice berries.
    Then he laid in the sun.
    Then he picked up some rocks.
    Then he went home
    And went to bed for the night.

4. Reactive sequence:I

    Once there was a girl named Alice
    who lived down by the seashore.
    Alice was in the water,
    floating on her back,
    when along came a shark,
    and Gulp, Gulp,
    that was the end of Alice.

    Reactive sequence: II

    Once there was a fox
    who lived in a cave near the forest.
    One day there was a big storm,
    that came and washed away everything
    that the fox owned,
    including the nice juicy fish he loved.
    The fox was so sad
    because his food was lost.
    All he could do was sit down and cry.

5. Goal-based episode: no obstacle, no ending

    Once there was a big gray fox
    who lived in a cave near the forest.
    One day, he decided that he was very hungry
    and that he needed to catch something for dinner.
    So he went outside
    and spotted a baby rabbit,
    caught him,
    and had him for dinner.

6. Goal-based episode: no obstacle, ending included

> Once there was a big gray fox
> who lived in a cave near the forest.
> One day he decided he was hungry
> and that he needed food very badly.
> So he went to his favorite stream,
> dipped his hand down in the water,
> and came up with a great big fish.
> He was so happy
> that he ran home to tell his mother
> he caught it all by himself.

7. Goal-based episode: obstacle, no ending

> Once there was a fox
> who lived in a cave near a forest.
> He wanted some food for dinner,
> and went out looking for something.
> He looked and looked,
> but nothing.
> Suddenly he saw a rabbit hopping by.
> He ran real fast and tried to catch him,
> but he kept missing
> cause the rabbit was smarter than the fox.
> So he didn't get any dinner.

8. Goal-based episode: obstacle and ending included

> Once there was a big gray fox
> who lived in a cave near the forest.
> One day the fox got sick
> and wanted someone to come and visit him.
> He looked outside,
> but nobody came.
> So he got up,
> which he could hardly do,
> and went outside
> and put up a sign saying
> "Come in and visit me."
> And then everyone came in,
> except that none of them came out
> 'cause he ate 'em all up.
> He was a pretty smart fox
> and they were pretty dumb.

Table 24-2 contains a summary of adult story concept judgments from the Stein and Policastro (1984) study. These data show whether or not adults judge each type of narrative described in Fig. 24-1 and Table 24-1 to be stories. The data indicate that adults make significant distinctions between the different types of narratives and will label only some of them stories. Noncausal sequences are clearly not rated as stories.

Within the group of narratives that were causally structured, further distinctions were made among the texts. Even though non-goal-based texts were consid-

Table 24-2. *Proportion of Adult Subjects Who Rate Each Passage Type as Belonging to the Story Category*[a]

Passage type	Mean proportions
1. No structure	0.00
2. Descriptive sequence	0.11
3. Action sequence	0.42
4. Reactive sequence	
a. Conforming to Prince's definition	0.75
b. Conforming to Mandler and Johnson's definition	0.70
5. Goal-based: no obstacle and no ending	0.86
6. Goal-based: no obstacle but ending included	0.86
7. Goal-based: obstacle but no ending	0.92
8. Goal-based: obstacle and ending included	0.95

[a]From Stein and Policastro (1984).

ered to be stories, more adults rate the goal-based texts as stories than the non-goal-based sequences. When asked to judge how "good" or "prototypic" each narrative was, goal-based texts were always judged to be better examples of stories that were non-goal-based texts. Similarly, goal-based sequences with obstacles were always judged as better examples of stories than those without an obstacle.

For the moment, then, let us assume that a goal-based story with the inclusion of an obstacle and an ending is the ideal form of a good story for an adult. Our next question concerns the degree of correspondence between the adult concept and children's concepts, as judged by their stories. Have children acquired the same kind of knowledge about the story as an adult or does their knowledge differ from an adult's? If their knowledge differs, what is the nature of the difference?

Children's stories were scored for the inclusion of five different dimensions, and Table 24-3 contains the results of these analyses. First, the data indicate that the appearance of goal-based stories increased from 48% in the kindergarten group to 80% in the 10-year-old group. Older children are much more likely to impose a causal structure on their narratives, they include more goal-based action, and they elaborate their plots with the inclusion of obstacles more frequently than younger children. They also include endings more frequently than do younger children. Thus, the development of narrative skill involves many different levels of complexity. The development of complexity in children's narratives is also reflected in the analysis of two other dimensions: the number of episodes in the narrative and the type of connector used to link episodes. Older children's stories always included more episodes than younger children's stories. Even when the number of episodes in a story was controlled, older children were more likely than younger children to tell stories with causally embedded episodes. The fact that older children included more obstacles in their stories almost ensured that this would be the case. Telling a story in which the protagonist

Table 24-3. *Proportion of Stories with Each of the Five Dimensions Included in the Narrative*

	Grade level		
	K (N = 54)	3 (N = 54)	5 (N = 54)
Dimension included			
1. Non-goal-based	0.49	0.28	0.19
2. Goal-based without obstacles	0.40	0.11	0.18
3. Goal-based with obstacle	0.11	0.61	0.63
For goal-based stories	(N = 28)	(N = 39)	(N = 41)
4. Endings included	0.39	0.54	0.68
5. Two or more episodes	0.20	0.62	0.71
6. Episodes connected by cause relationship when two or more episodes included	0.22	0.77	0.74

initially fails to achieve a goal almost always guarantees a continued course of action in which the protagonist attempts to generate a new solution to the original problem. Thus, a failed goal in the first episode directly precipitated a course of action in the second episode.

Because younger children were less likely to include obstacles in their stories, their multiple-episode stories were different in structure from those generated by older children. Younger children were more likely to allow their character to succeed in the first episode, and therefore the course of action in the second episode was not related to that in the first, even though the sequence of events in each separate episode was causally coherent. Thus, failure to include obstacles in a narrative affected both causal and structural properties of the narrative.

Knowledge about Conflict Resolutions

Table 24-4 includes data on an entirely different set of analyses carried out on these children's stories. Just as the concept of a story is important in guiding the generation process, so is knowledge about the various types of goal conflicts that occur in stories. Three different analyses were carried out to determine the types of obstacles children included in their stories, whether or not they allowed their protagonist to be successful at goal attainment, and the means (plan of action) that a protagonist used to overcome an obstacle.

The data at the top of Table 24-4 illustrate that children use the story most frequently to talk about interpersonal conflict. This result is similar across the

Table 24-4. *Proportion of Stories with Different Obstacle Types, Different Problem Resolutions, and Different Means of Overcoming Obstacles*

	Grade level		
	K	3	5
A. Obstacle type	(N = 28)	(N = 39)	(N = 41)
1. Interpersonal	0.59	0.52	0.64
2. Environmental	0.41	0.33	0.26
3. Intrapersonal	0.00	0.15	0.10
B. How is problem resolved?	(N = 28)	(N = 39)	(N = 41)
Protagonist succeeds in fulfilling original goal	0.78	0.59	0.75
C. Means used to overcome environmental obstacles	(N = 12)	(N = 13)	(N = 11)
1. Direct attempt	0.50	0.36	0.60
2. Verbal appeal to other	0.50	0.27	0.30
3. Unsolicited third party enters	0.00	0.27	0.10
4. Goal abandonment	0.00	0.10	0.00
D. Means used to overcome interpersonal obstacles	(N = 16)	(N = 26)	(N = 30)
1. Threaten or use force	0.75	0.26	0.30
2. Escape threat	0.12	0.30	0.00
3. Assertion of authority	0.00	0.12	0.12
4. Deception or counterattack	0.13	0.32	0.48
5. Verbal persuasion or compromise	0.00	0.00	0.10

three age groups. Environmental obstacles (e.g., mountains to climb, oceans to swim) are also placed in the path of a protagonist, but not nearly as frequently as interpersonal obstacles are. The least frequently occurring obstacle is the intrapersonal conflict in which a protagonist has two goals, and the attainment of one precludes the attainment of the second. Thus, as many researchers have claimed, the story is the basic forum for interpersonal conflict resolution.

The second part of Table 24-4 shows that in most children's stories, the protagonist succeeds in attaining the original goal set forth in the beginning of the story. That children have a strong desire to see stories end in a positive fashion has been noted by others, namely Brian Sutton-Smith (1975). The results of this analysis tend to add support to his hypothesis.

The third part of Table 24-4 contains the means used to overcome obstacles put in the path of a protagonist. When the obstacle was environmental in nature, two types of strategies predominated. Either the protagonist made a direct attempt to generate another plan to overcome the obstacle or the protagonist appealed to another person for help in overcoming the obstacle. It should be noted that when environmental obstacles were put in the path of a protagonist, more cooperation between story characters was found than in interpersonal situations. The environmental obstacle served as an outside force with which to unite characters in the pursuit of a common goal. Interestingly, there were few reliable developmental differences in the methods children used to overcome environmental obstacles.

The means used to overcome interpersonal obstacles, however, were very different in kind, and significant developmental differences were found in the types of strategies children invented for their protagonists. The most common strategy used by kindergarten children was one of direct threat or actual use of force. As the success rate of attaining a goal with this strategy indicates, most protagonists experience a positive outcome. The third and fifth graders, however, begin to use very different strategies in the face of interpersonal conflict. Although threat was used by some, the assertion of authority by appeal to reason and strategies involving deception and counterattack began to emerge. The counterattack strategies were used most frequently by the fifth graders. It is interesting to note that the notion of compromise or verbal persuasion rarely emerged in these stories.

Thematic Analyses

A final set of analyses focused on the themes children used to organize their narratives. A theme is defined differently, depending upon the researcher completing the analysis. In our story work (Stein and Trabasso, 1982), a theme represents the type of goal that guides the majority of a protagonist's actions throughout an episode. Table 24-5 contains the distribution of themes that occurred in each of the three stories told by the children.

The themes could be classified into three major categories:

1. those related to interpersonal goals,
2. those related to goals concerning objects or events,
3. those related to personal goals, and
4. those related to everyday habitual activities of a character.

The fourth category refers to script-like action, in which the narrator runs through the everyday activity of a protagonist, from sunrise to sunset.

Table 24-5 contains the distribution of themes in the three different stories. For two of the stories, Alice and the Fox, interpersonal themes were the most prevalent. In fact, in the Fox stories, 82% of the themes were interpersonal in nature, with destruction by and harm to the protagonist being the most common goals. Similarly, in the Alice story, threat of physical harm was the most common problem Alice had to overcome. However, the themes were more varied in the Alice story. Many children focused their attention on the difficulties Alice had in either maintaining valuable relationships or in attaining material objects. And the Alan story clearly focused children's attention on the problems associated with keeping valuable objects (e.g., remember that Alan had lots of different toys).

Table 24-5. *Distribution of Themes by Topic Stem*

Theme categories	Story stems		
	Alice (N = 54)	Fox (N = 54)	Alan (N = 54)
Protagonist—other			
Acquisition of valued relationship	0.14	0.00	0.15
Destruction of other by protagonist	0.02	0.12	0.03
Threat of physical harm to protagonist	0.32	0.33	0.03
Hunger/destruction of other	0.02	0.37	0.00
Protagonist—object			
Maintaining or protecting valued object	0.15	0.05	0.44
Protagonist—internal state Adventure—curiosity	0.03	0.01	0.02
Competence—mastery	0.03	0.03	0.05
Script—scenario	0.22	0.04	0.25

The results of the thematic analysis showed that the topic stem had a considerable constraining effect on the content of the story. Just the mention of a valuable object was enough to prompt many children to tell long elaborated stories about problems associated with protecting and keeping a valuable possession. However, the importance of interpersonal considerations was never far from the focus of children's attention. In order to protect his valuable toys, Alan often had to overcome major interpersonal obstacles (e.g., jealousy on the part of other children or selfishness on the part of Alan). Thus, we can see how children weave interpersonal knowledge throughout the narrative sequence, independent of the topic stem.

Conclusions

The results of this study focused on several important developments in children's storytelling skill. When stories were examined for features that corresponded to different story definitions, older children's stories were found to be more elaborated than younger children's narratives. In particular, older children told more goal-based stories, included more obstacles, and included more endings evaluating the protagonist's actions in the story. Because older children included more obstacles, the episodes in their stories were more tightly connected. When the protagonist failed to attain a goal the first time, a reinstatement of the goal almost always occurred in the second episode, thereby embedding the second episode in the first.

From studies investigating children's and adults' concept of a story (Stein and Kilgore, 1985; Stein and Policastro, 1984; Stein and Salgo, 1984), we know that the complexity of generated stories corresponds closely to children's definition of a "good" story. Although young elementary school children are quite capable of generating episodically based stories with obstacles included in them, these children do not make distinctions between goal-based stories and other types of narratives that include animate characters. For example, 5- and 7-year-old children think a descriptive sequence, an action sequence, and a reactive sequence are good stories, rating these text types as highly as episodic narratives. Adults, however, make clear distinctions between those narratives that are causally structured versus those that are not. Moreover, adults make further distinctions among the texts considered to be stories. Those stories containing goal-based action and obstacles are considered to be better stories than those that do not include these dimensions. Thus, there is a clear progression of elaboration that occurs in the conceptual representation of a story as a form of discourse. This representation is distinctly separate from children's ability to remember and recall elaborated stories.

Under certain conditions, with the appropriate topic stem, even 5-year-old children can generate goal-based narratives with obstacles included. As an example, almost all of the kindergarten children generated episodically structured stories in response to the fox stem. The majority of stories generated in response to the other topic stems, however, were not episodically structured. The consistency with which children include specific features in their narratives is thought to be related to their conceptual understanding of stories, rather than to be tied to contextual conditions that might predispose children to include certain dimensions during the process of narration.

Even when younger children included obstacles in their stories, the methods used to attain goals are distinctly different from those used by older children. These differences were especially prevalent in stories containing interpersonal conflicts. In particular, younger children relied on direct aggressive tactics to solve their problems, either by the use of threat or by the use of force. Older children, however, began to use verbal appeals to authority, argumentative reasoning, and deception or counterattack strategies to solve problems.

The use of these strategies was frequently related to children's explicit reference to the consequences of not using these methods for solving problems. Older children frequently stated that their protagonist would be defeated if they did not use deception or counterattack. Thus, the appearance of certain means for solving problems appears to be a direct function of the knowledge of the consequences and obstacles encountered in using other means for solving a problem. If children's knowledge of obstacles had been probed more directly, a clear relationship between their obstacle knowledge and the choice of strategy in storytelling contexts should have been found.

Several findings in this study were similar over the three age groups. All children used the story as a vehicle for elaborating upon interpersonal conflict situations. Conflicts with the environment were mentioned, but not with the regularity and frequency of interpersonal conflicts. Moreover, even when older children began their stories with an environmental problem (e.g., how Alan would be able to maintain and protect his favorite toys), their knowledge of environmental problems was almost always linked to their knowledge of interpersonal conflict. Other people were seen as vehicles for both opposing and facilitating goals children have with respect to the environment.

Interestingly, the story was not used as a vehicle to explore intrapersonal conflict situations. Children did not consider many situations in which conflicts between two important goals within the protagonist were the major source of tension in the narrative. Moral tales were rarely the topic of narration, and when evaluation did occur, it was used to illustrate how smart and clever the protagonist was in carrying out a particular course of action (see example 8 in Table 24-1 for an illustration of this type of evaluation).

The absence of the moral tale or the tale told for teaching or historical purposes does not mean that children are deficient in the skill and strategy necessary to tell these types of stories. The focus on problem solving may represent the first step in the narration process. In order to teach or persuade, the nature and structure of the problem has to be well conceived and represented. When children tell stories under conditions in which they are constructing the tale for the first time, by necessity they are constrained to constructing a coherent problem solution. After this step has been accomplished, they can then consider the moral and teaching functions of a narrative. Alternatively, children might be able to generate narratives for the explicit purpose of teaching someone else about the importance of a particular social value if the original requirements for storytelling were focused on these functions. These issues need to be explored more fully in future studies of the storytelling process.

Finally, it was clear that few children used the narrative to explore internal states, motivations, and thinking of their story characters. Although older children were more apt to include explicit references to internal states of characters, even these children did not use internal states and beliefs to explain the nature of individual differences in social behavior or to explore the nature of conflicts between two people. Again, these results must be interpreted cautiously. Children were not asked to explicitly use the narrative as a mode of explanation for interpersonal actions. The results suggest, however, that the narrative mode of discourse is not being used as broadly as it might be.

The story is an excellent vehicle for understanding historical events and explanation. Thus, storytelling can facilitate the development of explanatory skill, especially in regard to the nature of social action and human motivation. Understanding the relationships between beliefs, motives, and actions is central, and narration serves this purpose. Given that children already focus on the interpersonal nature of conflicts and that they rapidly assess the conditions that lead to successful problem solutions, focusing attention on the relationships between beliefs and action should not be difficult. This strategy might directly affect their ability to use the narrative more elaborately across a variety of contexts.

V

METAPHOR AND
METALINGUISTIC
PROCESSES

Metaphor may be defined as a use of language in which a term (or phrase) customarily applied in one domain is transported across conventional category boundaries and applied in another. Metalinguistic ability refers to the ability to reflect upon language and includes monitoring one's own linguistic productions, making spontaneous repairs, and otherwise showing awareness of language in itself as a medium of expression comprising sounds, words, and sentences.

The modern era in the study of children's metaphoric abilities began with Asch and Nerlove's (1960) investigation of children's comprehension of terms such as "sweet" and "hard," which, in the adult language, refer both to physical characteristics of objects and to psychological characteristics of persons. Asch and Nerlove found that very young children do not understand the "double function" or dual reference of such terms, and that understanding develops through a series of phases; older children not only understand dual reference but can explain the relationship between the two applications. The findings of this study raised questions about relationships among the production, comprehension, and explication of metaphor that continue to structure inquiries of metaphoric language in childhood.

In the study included here, **Winner, Rosenstiel, and Gardner** seek to elucidate relations between metaphor comprehension and explication by presenting subjects (ranging in age from 6 to 14 years of age) with two different kinds of tasks—one requiring the choice of a paraphrase, and the other an explanation of the metaphor's meaning. In addition to using psychological–physical metaphors of the kind employed by Asch and Nerlove, these investigators used cross-sensory metaphors. Categorizing responses in terms of type of reasoning, Winner et al. are able to show qualitative shifts in the ways metaphors are understood and explained, as well as an overall discrepancy between the comprehension and explication of figurative language.

What is the basis of early spontaneous metaphor? Some investigators view such expressions—often occurring as the playful renaming of objects—as category mistakes, overextensions that transgress conventional boundaries of which the child is not aware. Other researchers (see Winner, 1979) suggest that many such crossovers are deliberate, based on perceptual and action similarities between objects. The study by **Billow** bears directly on this controversy. Observations of children in preschool settings yielded many instances of nonliteral uses of terms, such as referring to the observer's hair as "grass" in the course of play. Interviews were designed to find out if preschool children could differentiate literal and figurative applications of terms they had used, and whether they could explain the grounds of their metaphoric usage. On the basis of his findings, Billow suggests that even very young children deliberately transgress category boundaries, but only older preschoolers can begin to explain the basis of their figurative renamings.

According to **Vosniadou, Ortony, Reynolds, and Wilson,** children's comprehension of metaphor can be conceptualized in terms of conditions that determine the difficulty of processing information, such as familiarity and predictability. In the excerpt from their article reprinted here, Vosniadou et al. propose that probable (or predictable) metaphoric endings to stories will be much more readily understood than less probable endings. Using story enactment rather than verbal explication as the measure of comprehension, they found that even their preschool subjects showed a high degree of comprehension for probable metaphoric endings phrased in nonliteral terms. Furthermore, they found no difference among preschool, first graders, and third graders in the understanding of such story endings. The findings cast doubt on the view that comprehension of metaphor requires at least concrete operational thinking (in Piaget's terms) and that, as Asch suggested, there is a sequence of stages from literal interpretation to genuine metaphoric responding.

Current research suggests that under some conditions preschool children spontaneously produce metaphors and also demonstrate understanding of metaphoric language. Just as Billow showed that genuine metaphors may be evoked in concrete play contexts, so Vosniadou et al. have demonstrated metaphoric comprehension in children as young as 4, given response measures involving enactment and supportive story contexts. Evidence does suggest, however, that explication of the grounds of similarity between literal and nonliteral referents involves metalinguistic abilities beyond the capacity of preschool children and may rest on further developments in the cognitive domain.

The investigation of metalinguistic functioning has followed several distinct paths since the field was delineated as an area of inquiry about 10 years ago. Much of the early work was concerned with the child's ability to detect semantic and syntactic anomalies in sentences and to supply corrections. Other research was concerned specifically with the child's ability to analyze the flow of speech into syllables or words. Many verbal explication tasks have been interpreted as involving metalinguistic functioning. In addition, some researchers have seen the child's early play with language as related to awareness of language as a medium.

Horgan focuses on one young child's early jokes in terms of what they reveal about the child's exploration and understanding of language. The reports of the child's play with the sound patterns of language are reminiscent of Weir's (1962) account of her son's bedtime monologues, but here the play occurs in the communicative context of mother–child exchange. The jokes involving changes in established meaning patterns bear some similarities to the "topsy-turvies" reported by Chukovsky (1968). Horgan argues that these spontaneous occurrences attest to very early awareness of central aspects of language. But the relation between such early playful activity and later metalinguistic functioning remains controversial.

The question of young children's understanding of word–object relations was conceptualized by Piaget in terms of "nominal realism," a term intended to capture the child's supposed tendency to regard the name of an object as an intrinsic object attribute rather than a label established by convention. Other early developmentalists (Werner, 1978; Vygotsky, 1962) were also interested in this phenomenon. In the study included here, **Rosenblum and Pinker** aim to disentangle the often confounded factors of children's understanding of questions phrased as counterfactuals ("Can you call a dog a cat?") and their ability to manipulate names, as indicated by their performance on renaming tasks. Controlling for children's ability to accept counterfactual statements, Rosenblum and Pinker found that both monolinguals and bilinguals in the age range 4 to 6 show greater understanding of word–object relations than previous investigations suggest. The two groups differ not so much in their awareness of the word–object relation, but in how they justify renamings—with bilinguals giving far more attention to the social-communicative context.

In the final article in this section, **Litowitz** provides an analysis of children's approaches to word definition. As she suggests, asking children to define words is one method of studying concept formation; it is also a metalinguistic task that calls on the child's ability to operate on a purely verbal plane, to use language to talk about language. Litowitz analyzes the responses of her 4- to 7-year-old subjects in terms of five levels, designed to capture qualitative differences in progress toward the Aristotelian form of definition which involves providing both genus and species (e.g., "A fork is a tool or instrument used for eating"). She proposes that two lines of progression are evident in the children's responses: from more concrete to more abstract (as Anglin, 1970, and others have suggested), and from individual/personal to socially shared meanings. Finally, Litowitz suggests that the kinds of responses given on definition tasks depend on the subject's interpretation of the task, which in turn rests on knowledge of the appropriate form of definitions and underlying semantic organization.

25

Ellen Winner,
Anne K. Rosenstiel, and Howard Gardner
The Development of Metaphoric Understanding

There is an apparent paradox concerning the development of metaphoric sensitivity in children. It has been argued, on the one hand, that the capacity to understand metaphoric figures of speech develops only during late childhood and early adolescence (Asch and Nerlove, 1960; Elkind, 1969; Schaffer, 1930). This contention is consistent with the view that metalinguistic skills (the ability to perform operations on language itself) develop only in the final stages of language acquisition (Inhelder and Piaget, 1958).* On the other hand, studies focusing on the child's ability to produce figurative language have repeatedly documented the spontaneous use of metaphors, similes, and other figures of speech by preschool-age children (Carlson and Anisfield, 1969; Chukovsky, 1968; Gardner, 1973; Gardner, Kircher, Winner and Perkins, 1975; Weir, 1962). In addition, pre-schoolers have been shown to be able to match words to elements from other sensory modalities in a metaphor-type paradigm (Gardner, 1974).

A resolution to this apparent conflict may be achieved if the components of metaphoric capacity are disentangled. For the most part, those making claims about metaphoric sensitivity have not adequately differentiated kinds of metaphoric skill. Yet there may be a wide divergence between the spontaneous production of figures of speech, the comprehension of metaphor, and the metalinguistic awareness that makes possible an explication of the metaphor's rationale.

In what follows, *metaphor* refers to a figure of speech that illuminates one dimension of a particular object by drawing attention to its similarity to an object from another realm of experience that normally is viewed as dissimilar (Black,

*All endnotes are omitted. [Eds.]

Abridged from "The development of metaphoric understanding" by E. Winner, A.K. Rosenstiel, and H. Gardner, 1976, *Developmental Psychology*, **12**, 289–297. Copyright 1976 by American Psychological Association. Reprinted by permission of publisher and authors.

1962; Goodman, 1968; Richards, 1965). Such a trope is effected by transporting a word from a customary to a novel, but appropriate, context. Both the recognition of separate realms and the ability to capture in language a relation between them are thus prerequisites of metaphoric production and comprehension.

To be sure, natural language categories themselves display relatively "fuzzy" boundaries (Labov, 1973), and the interpretation of any term or sentence is highly context dependent. It is therefore difficult to specify a single criterion for distinguishing between literal and figurative language (Black, 1962). Yet, as a practical matter, it is usually possible both to isolate certain expressions as metaphoric and to indicate which realms are involved in the metaphoric transfer. Moreover, empirical investigations of metaphor depend upon such a procedure.

Beyond these general considerations, it is necessary to indicate the dimensions along which metaphors may vary. First, the length of the unit within which the metaphor is captured may range from an individual term to an entire proposition (Black, 1962). Moreover, the syntactic structure of the metaphor may take any form (Black, 1962). Finally, metaphoric comparisons may involve any number of realms (Goodman, 1968). Insufficient attention to these and other possible sources of variation has diluted the significance of early studies and has highlighted the need for careful attention to the linguistic form of specific metaphors.

Whereas both the ability to produce metaphor (Chukovsky, 1968) and the capacity to reflect upon the processes of metaphoric production and comprehension (Asch and Nerlove, 1960) have been investigated, surprisingly little is known about the process of comprehension itself. In those few studies concerned with comprehension (Asch and Nerlove, 1960) the metaphors used have not, for the most part, been drawn from everyday language or from literary sources, but have instead been single words or phrases out of context. Furthermore, the procedures of these studies have not elicited the child's underlying strategies and reasons. Metaphoric understanding has been regarded as a capacity that is either totally present or wholly absent; as a result, possible steps in the development of metaphoric understanding remain to be documented.

The purpose of the present study was to test in children a form of metaphoric comprehension crucial for apprehending conversation and literary works: the understanding of linguistic metaphors embedded in complete sentences. That form of metaphor captured in a proposition linking two nouns and an adjective (An X is an adjective Y) was examined because it is common and lends itself readily to explication. Of the many metaphoric figures that could be produced from such a sentence, two were selected: the psychological–physical metaphor, which illuminates a psychological experience by appealing to an event in the physical domain (Fernandez, 1972), and the cross-sensory metaphor, which illuminates an experience in one sensory modality by referring synesthetically to another sensory modality (Gardner et al., 1975). Both types of metaphor allow, and frequently include, dual-function adjectives (e.g., *hard*), which have a primary, physical meaning and a secondary meaning acquired through metaphorical extension (Asch and Nerlove, 1960). The secondary meaning may be psychological (e.g., a *hard* man) or may make reference to a different sensory modality (e.g., a *hard* sound). The use of such adjectives was thought to be desirable for school children: Because they make explicit part of the resemblance between the two nouns, the dual-function adjectives might facilitate comprehension.

Two tasks were used to investigate comprehension of these types of metaphor: a multiple-choice task, in which subjects were offered different paraphrases of metaphors, and an explication task, in which subjects' own metaphoric interpretations were obtained. The study focused on the question of whether a regular sequence of understandings (or misunderstandings) precedes a full comprehension of metaphor.

When presented a metaphoric sentence in the cited form (e.g., "The prison guard was a hard rock"), in which the two nouns are drawn from distinct categories of experience, the adult knows that direct predication of class membership is not an acceptable solution and that the sentence is intended metaphorically; he or she must find a way in which X is like Y. Seeking and discovering this similarity constitutes mature metaphoric understanding. In contrast, young children may either not recognize such a sentence to be intended metaphorically or may be unable to perceive X and Y as both similar and dissimilar (Inhelder and Piaget, 1964). Although the appropriateness of a "stage theory" of metaphoric understanding needs to be empirically demonstrated, the kinds of reasoning observed by previous investigators (Asch and Nerlove, 1960; Billow, 1975; Gardner, 1974; Gardner et al., 1975) suggested three steps preceding the attainment of mature metaphoric understanding.

First, children might directly predicate class membership: The sentence would be accepted at face value and a magical world invented in which X can be Y (Piaget, 1929). The statement "The prison guard was a hard rock" would be interpreted as the transfiguration of person into stone. Such an interpretation was termed magical.

Second, somewhat older children might invent a situation in which the two terms of the metaphor may sensibly be juxtaposed. The sentence is not taken at face value but is instead read as "X is associated in some way with Y;" the link between the two terms of the metaphor is transformed from one based on identity to one based on contiguity. Such a transformation involves a radical shift to an interpretation based on metonymy (Jakobson and Halle, 1971). The above-mentioned metaphor could come to mean that the guard worked in a rocky prison, a solution here termed metonymic.

Third, older children might discard the magical and metonymic modes in favor of the metaphoric, but their early metaphoric interpretations might be somewhat primitive. Such children might find it easier to posit a similarity if both terms of the metaphor could be understood as belonging to the same realm: A focus upon an incidental aspect of one of the terms would likely lead to such an understanding. For instance, in the prison guard metaphor, if one focuses upon the guard solely as a physical object, no comparison need be made between the physical and the psychological domains: The sentence can be taken to mean that the guard is muscular and thus, like the rock, physically hard. In a cross-sensory metaphor, such as "Her perfume was bright sunshine," if one focuses only upon the color of the perfume, no comparison need be made between the sensory modalities of smell and color, and the sentence is interpreted to mean that the perfume was, like the sun, a bright yellow hue. Such interpretations, which were based on aspects within the same modality, were termed primitive metaphoric.

In the most sophisticated genuine-metaphoric response, the aspects of the two terms that are compared are drawn from different domains or modalities. Such a metaphoric interpretation depends upon finding the appropriate dimension that is shared by the two terms of the metaphor. Thus, in the prison guard metaphor, a psychological property is likened to a physical one, and the metaphor is interpreted to mean that the guard was resistant to the prisoners. Analogously, the perfume metaphor is understood to mean that the perfume was pleasing.

In sum, in the present study two tasks were used to observe the course of development of metaphoric comprehension. These results, considered in conjunction with earlier findings, could clarify the ontogenetic relations among the abilities to produce, comprehend, and explain metaphor.

Method

SUBJECTS

One hundred and eighty subjects, equally divided between females and males at each of six age levels (both modal and median ages 6, 7, 8, 10, 12, and 14 years, rounded to the nearest year) participated in the study. Subjects were selected at random from their classrooms, although, by prearrangement, a few children with known learning disabilities were eliminated from the selection procedure. Social class background was predominantly lower-middle class. Each child was seen individually by one experimenter in a quiet room for about 20 minutes. Because of the concentration required, experimental sessions for the 6 and 7 year olds were divided into two 10-minute sessions.

MATERIALS

Half of the subjects were given a metaphor explication task in which they were required to supply their own interpretation to orally presented metaphoric sentences. The other half were given an orally presented multiple-choice task in which each metaphoric sentence was followed by four possible interpretations: magical, metonymic, primitive metaphoric, and genuine metaphoric. The alternatives were randomly ordered and matched, as far as possible, in length. Both tests used the same 16 metaphoric sentences. The items were equated, insofar as possible, in length and word frequency. There were eight psychological–physical and eight cross-sensory metaphors.

PROCEDURE

Subjects in the explication group were told:

> Stories sometimes have different meanings and people don't always agree
> about what they mean. I am going to read you a short story and I want you to
> tell me what you think the story means.

When children responded to only part of the sentence or merely repeated the
words, nondirective probes were used, for example, "Can you tell me a little
more about that?"

Subjects in the multiple-choice group were told:

> Stories sometimes have different meanings, and people don't always agree
> about what they mean. I am going to read you a story and then I will read
> you four different things that some people think that the story might mean. I
> will read them twice and I want you to tell me which one you think that the
> story means.

When appropriate, instructions were repeated or paraphrased. Subjects were not
allowed to respond by saying "the second one" or "the last one," but were
required to paraphrase their choice. If they proved unable to do so, the four
interpretations were repeated.

Practice items were used to ensure understanding, and no subject was
included in the study if he or she was unable to understand the procedure.
Except for difficulty experienced by some of the 6 year olds on the multiple-
choice task, the procedure posed no problems. Buffer items—syntactically equivalent, nonmetaphoric sentences with one obviously correct interpretation—were
interspersed among the test items as an unobtrusive means of reminding subjects
of the task. For the 6 and 7 year olds, who were tested in two sessions, an
additional practice item was included at the beginning of the second session.

SCORING

Subjects' choices were recorded as either magical, metonymic, primitive metaphoric, or genuine metaphoric, and the total number of each type was computed. Initially, reliability was established on a subset of items (82% agreement
was obtained). Thereafter, two judges scored all the items: Whenever there was a
disagreement, the particular response was discussed until accord was reached.
The explications were scored in such a way that performance could be compared
with the multiple-choice task (as either magical, metonymic, primitive metaphoric, or genuine metaphoric). To account exhaustively for all explications,
however, it was necessary to include two additional categories: incomplete and
inappropriate metaphoric. Sample items (one psychological–physical and one
cross-sensory), along with an example of each type of response and the guidelines
by which they were scored, are presented in Table 25-1.

Table 25-1. *Responses to Sample Metaphors*[a]

Name	Example	Definition and guidelines for scoring
Magical	The king had a magic rock and he turned the guard into another rock. Her perfume was made out of rays from the sun.	A paraphrase is offered that maintains the literal meaning of the sentence. Plausibility is achieved by inventing a magical world in which the laws of the natural world do not apply.
Metonymic	The guard worked in a prison that had hard rock walls. When she was standing outside in the bright sun she was wearing perfume.	The sentence is rephrased so that the two terms of the metaphor can both be interpreted literally without defying realism. Plausibility is achieved by relating the two terms through contiguity rather than through identity.
Primitive metaphoric	The guard had hard, tough muscles. Her perfume was a bright yellow color like the color of the sun.	Through a focus on an incidental aspect of the first term, the dual-function adjective retains its primary meaning in the modification of both terms of the metaphor. No comparison is made between the physical and psychological domains or between the sensory modalities.
Genuine metaphoric	The guard was mean and did not care about the feelings of the prisoners. Her perfume had a wonderful smell.	A central aspect of the first term is noted; the dual-function adjective thus achieves its secondary meaning in the modification of both terms of the metaphor. An implicit comparison is accordingly effected between the physical and psychological or between two sensory modalities.
Inappropriate metaphoric	The guard was old. Her perfume had a funny smell.	Based on an incorrect secondary meaning of the dual-function adjective, a central property is missed and the wrong psychological or sensory dimension is grasped.
Incomplete metaphoric	It was a big rock. There was some perfume.	(a) No intepretation. (b) verbatim repetition, or (c) description of only one term of the metaphor is given.

[a]The sample metaphors were "After many years of working at the jail, the prison guard had become a hard rock that could not be moved" and "The smell of my mother's perfume was bright sunshine."

Results

MULTIPLE-CHOICE TASK

Aseries of nonindependent 6 (Age) × 2 (Sex) analyses of variance were performed on the number of magical, metonymic, primitive metaphoric, and genuine metaphoric responses chosen by subjects. There were significant effects of age for

Table 25-2. *Percentage of Response Types at Each*
Age Level on Metaphor Multiple-Choice Test

Age (in years)	Magical	Metonymic	Primitive metaphoric	Genuine metaphoric
6	20	34	25	23
7	35	24	20	22
8	15	20	30	34
10	5	7	17	71
12	0	1	11	88
14	2	0	6	92

each type of response: magical, $F(5, 78) = 16.23$, $p < 0.001$, metonymic, $F(5, 78) = 22.26$, $p < 0.001$; primitive metaphoric, $F(5, 78) = 9.23$, $p < 0.001$, and genuine metaphoric, $F(5, 78) = 46.85$, $p < 0.001$. There were no significant main effects for sex or Group × Sex interactions.

In order to compare the older and younger subjects, a comparison was made between the lower ages (6, 7, and 8 years) and the upper ages (10, 12, and 14 years). As can be seen from Table 25-2, magical, metonymic, and primitive metaphoric responses were more frequent among the younger subjects, and genuine metaphoric responses were more frequent among the older subjects. Chi-square tests were computed to compare the number of subjects choosing between 0 and 4 of each response type with those choosing between 5 and 16 for the two age groups. Magical, $\chi^2(1) = 26.69$, $p < 0.001$, metonymic, $\chi^2(1) = 20.07$, $p < 0.001$, and primitive metaphoric, $\chi^2(1) = 8.94$, $p < 0.01$, choices were greater among the younger subjects, and genuine metaphoric choices were greater among the older subjects, $\chi^2(1) = 37.79$, $p < 0.001$.

To analyze further the differences obtained in the analyses of variance, Newman–Keuls post hoc comparisons of means were performed. Only those significant differences ($p < 0.05$) that further delineate the pattern described above are reported here.*

MAGICAL. The greatest number of magical responses was made by the 7 year olds, who had significantly more responses than did 6 and 8 year olds.

METONYMIC. The 6 year olds had significantly more metonymic responses than 7 year olds; however, 7 and 8 year olds did not differ significantly.

PRIMITIVE METAPHORIC. Primitive metaphoric responses reached a maximum among the middle ages. Specifically, 8 year olds chose significantly more

---

*Footnote specifying results of the post hoc tests are omitted. [Eds.]

Table 25-3. *Percentage of Response Types at Each Age Level on Metaphor Explication Test*

Age (in years)	Incomplete	Magical	Metonymic	Primitive metaphoric	Inappropriate metaphoric	Genuine metaphoric
6	25	12	26	27	5	5
7	10	8	35	26	7	14
8	8	7	12	33	10	30
10	1	2	7	28	14	48
12	2	1	3	18	9	76
14	2	0	2	8	9	79

primitive metaphoric responses than did children of all the other ages except 6 year olds. In addition, 10 year olds provided significantly more such responses than 14 year olds.

GENUINE METAPHORIC. Significantly more genuine metaphoric choices were made by 10 year olds than 8 year olds, and 12 year olds made more than 10 year olds.

EXPLICATION TASK

Analyses of variance like those for the multiple-choice task were computed. In addition, analyses were also computed for the two categories (1) incomplete and (2) inappropriate metaphoric. There were significant effects of age for magical, $F(5, 78) = 9.60$, $p < 0.001$, metonymic, $F(5,78) = 16.18$, $p < 0.001$, primitive metaphoric, $F(5, 78) = 5.37$, $p < 0.001$, genuine metaphoric $F(5, 78) = 60.51$, $p < 0.001$, and incomplete, $F(5, 78) = 8.98$, $p < 0.001$, interpretations, but not for inappropriate metaphoric interpretations.

Table 25-3 shows a pattern of responding similar to that for the multiple-choice task. Chi-square analyses like those for the multiple-choice task showed that magical, $\chi^2(1) = 6.54$, $p < 0.02$, metonymic, $\chi^2(1) = 17.10$, $p < 0.001$, and primitive metaphoric, $\chi^2(1) = 13.38$, $p < 0.001$, explications were greater among the younger subjects than the older subjects; genuine metaphoric explications were greater among the older subjects, $\chi^2(1) = 45.60$, $p < 0.001$.

Newman–Keuls post hoc tests were computed, and those differences ($p < 0.05$) that amplify the reported results are presented. *

INCOMPLETE. Six year olds had significantly more incomplete responses than children of all other ages.

---

*Footnote specifying results of the post hoc tests are omitted. [Eds.]

METONYMIC. Among the younger ages, both 6 and 7 year olds had more metonymic explications than did 8 year olds. There was no significant difference between 8 year olds and any of the upper ages.

PRIMITIVE METAPHORIC. Eight year olds were most likely to supply primitive metaphoric explications, and they provided significantly more responses than did children at ages 12 and 14.

GENUINE METAPHORIC. As in the multiple-choice task, there was a steady increase with age in the number of genuine metaphoric explications.

There were three significant effects of sex in the explication task. Boys were more likely to give magical responses, $F(1, 78) = 5.44$, $p < 0.003$, than were girls; girls were more likely to give genuine metaphoric explications, $F(1, 78) = 5.01$, $p < 0.03$; and there was a significant Sex × Age interaction for genuine metaphoric explications, $F(5, 78) = 2.68$, $p < 0.03$. Whereas 14 year old males were more likely than females to offer genuine metaphoric explications (male $M = 13.57$; female $M = 11.75$), the opposite proved true for ages 8, 10, and 12 years.

EFFECT OF TYPE OF METAPHOR ON METAPHORIC RESPONSES

To analyze the effect of the two types of metaphor, separate, nonindependent 6 (Age) × 2 (Item Type) repeated measures analyses of variance were performed for each category of metaphoric choices and explications, with age as a between-subject variable and item type as a within-subject variable. In the multiple-choice task, cross-sensory items elicited more genuine metaphoric choices, $F(1, 84) = 4.11$, $p < 0.05$, than did psychological–physical items; moreover there was a significant Group × Item interaction, $F(5, 84) = 6.22$, $p < 0.001$. The difference between the two types of metaphors was greater at the two youngest age groups than at the other ages.

Cross-senosory items elicited more genuine metaphoric explications than did psychological–physical items, $F(1, 84) = 32.46$, $p < 0.001$. Again, there was a significant Group × Item interaction, $F(5, 84) = 51.52$, $p < 0.001$. Cross-sensory items were easier for subjects in age groups 7, 8, and 10 years, but not for the youngest or the oldest subjects.

FURTHER ANALYSES OF EXPLICATIONS

In addition to the scoring of different types of responses, the subjects' individual comments were categorized, wherever applicable, according to the kinds of strategies associated with a particular response. These observations are noted below.

Discussion

Results of both the multiple-choice and explication conditions supported the hypothesized sequence of steps and clarified the relationship between two types of metaphor. Primarily metonymic and primitive metaphoric responses were offered by 6, 7, and 8 year olds. Although no age group favored magical interpretations, children between 6 and 8 years had more magical responses than did older children: Those who gave magical responses did not take the sentences to be literal descriptions of the "real" world, but rather as descriptions of a fairy-tale world. However, there was evidence that these subjects were not entirely happy with this solution. One subject, for instance, said, "People can't become rocks! That's impossible!"

The conflict posed by rejecting the logical absurdity of a magical interpretation and at the same time honoring only the literal meaning of individual words was solved metonymically by many of the children, who altered the expressed relationship from one of identity to one of contiguity. By 8 years of age, subjects chose genuine metaphoric responses as often as primitive ones; and by 10 years of age, subjects strongly favored genuine metaphoric interpretations. The observed shift from metonymic to metaphoric interpretations may reflect the same processes that underlie the established trend in children from syntagmatic to paradigmatic word association (Entwisle, Forsyth and Muuss, 1964).

Although 10 year olds demonstrated a basic understanding of metaphor, they were often either unable to explain their interpretations or they had recourse to metonymic or primitive metaphoric justifications. Similarly, these children sometimes offered a genuine metaphoric interpretation, followed immediately by a primitive one, suggesting the ease with which metaphoric thinking gave way to less sophisticated reasoning. An interesting (although not statistically significant) observation at this age was that 10 year olds offered the highest number of inappropriate metaphoric interpretations. Thus, these children exhibited the operations of metaphor before they could use words with precision.

A higher level of metaphoric understanding emerged in early adolescence. Whereas the 10 year olds saw only one similarity between the two terms of the sentence, 14 year olds could characterize the metaphoric relation in a variety of ways. For instance, a 10 year old said that "The taste was a sharp knife" meant simply, "It was spicy," but a 14 year old responded, "The taste was a shocking flavor, hitting all of my senses at once."

A comparison of the two types of items revealed that cross-sensory metaphors posed less difficulty than psychological–physical ones. The relative difficulty of the psychological–physical metaphors for younger subjects may have been due to an unfamiliarity with psychological domains; alternatively, the psychological–physical leap may be a comparatively greater one because the elements of cross-sensory metaphors are still both within the physical domain.

Whereas the developmental trends are relatively clear, it is more difficult to establish the strategies that led to the adoption of the various responses. Whether the "premetaphoric" understandings were due to an inability to interpret words on multiple levels (a linguistic immaturity), to an inability to perceive similarity between disparate objects (a cognitive deficit), to an insensitivity to cues indicating that a sentence is intended metaphorically (a problem of pragmatics), or to some amalgam of these factors is a question open to further investigation.

The strategies that enabled children to adopt a metaphoric approach are also in need of clarification. The inclusion in each sentence of a dual-function adjective meant that part of the resemblance between the two terms was explicit. Thus, the adjective *hard* may have served as a clue in finding a similarity between the prison guard and the rock; alternatively, the children may have ignored the reference to rock and simply found a way for the guard to be *hard*. Although both of these achievements culminate in a metaphorical response, the former is undoubtedly the more sophisticated.

Taken together with results of prior research on metaphor, these findings suggest that spontaneous production occurs first, followed by comprehension and then by the ability to explain the rationale of a metaphor. The spontaneous metaphors produced by young children are most often visual comparisons prompted by stimuli in the environment. In contrast, the comprehension of another's metaphor typically demands not only that both terms be imagined but also that properties other than perceptual ones be taken into account. Finally, the ability to explicate the workings of a metaphor involves a distance from the processes of both metaphoric production and comprehension as well as that metalinguistic awareness that only arises in preadolescence.

26

Richard M. Billow

Observing Spontaneous Metaphor in Children

Metaphor has been defined as a figure of speech that relates two disparate words or larger sentence elements to each other in terms of a similarity dimension or analogical relationship. Since the basis of the similarity or analogy to which attention is called by the metaphor is not usually noticed, some tension is created in the comprehender of the metaphor who is forced to create a basis for relationship.

For example, the similarity of a horse and a pony is obvious, since the two objects are from a similar semantic domain or category of meaning. However, the similarity of a soul and an enchanted boat, as used by Keats in *Prometheus Bound*, is less obvious, and from two relatively unrelated semantic categories. The reader of the metaphor is required to establish a relation (the ground) between the two categories in order to dissipate the tension created by comparing souls (the topic) to boats (the vehicle) (cf. Richards, 1965). Thus, to say that a soul is an enchanted boat is to create a metaphor while to say that a horse is a pony is more likely to create a controversy.

It is possible that metaphoric processes function quite early in the child's life and contribute to his or her cognitive development. Evidence of nascent metaphoric productive competence in young children would attest to the possible contribution of metaphor not only to the extension of vocabulary, but to the growing mastery of reality, as claimed for it by many theorists (Cassirer, 1946; Langer, 1948; Searles, 1965; Sharpe, 1968).

In effect, metaphor functions as a bridge between different realities (such as an object and its signifier), different levels of meaning (such as literal and ab-

Abridged from "Observing spontaneous metaphor in children" by R.M. Billow, 1981, *Journal of Experimental Child Psychology*, **31**, 430–445. Copyright 1981 by Academic Press. Reprinted by permission of publisher and author.

stract, or real and make-believe), and different realms of experience (inner or psychological reality vs outer or "empirical" reality). . . .

Recently developmental psychologists have become interested in the nascent figurative productive capacity (Gardner, 1974; Gardner, Kircher, Winner, & Perkins, 1975; Gentner, 1977; Kogan, Connor, Gross, & Fava, 1980; Pollio and Pollio, 1974; Winner, 1979) and comprehension (Asch and Nerlove, 1960; Billow, 1975; Cometa and Eson, 1978; Gardner, 1974; Malgady, 1977) in children. The experimental paradigms of these studies have involved giving children words or pictorial stimuli to apply to metaphoric situations, or giving them metaphoric words or sentences to interpret. Relatively little attention has been given to whether children spontaneously produce metaphors. The latter phenomenon, however, has been noted in an anecdotal collection of child sayings (Chukovsky, 1968) and in several clinical case studies not primarily concerned with metaphor (Carlson and Anisfeld, 1969; Gardner, 1973; Piaget, 1962; Weir, 1962; Werner and Kaplan, 1963).

Chukovsky (1968) characterized the child from 2 to 5 as a "linguistic genius" and held that this age period represented "a special, heightened sensitivity to the materials of speech" (p. 9). He stressed the contribution to linguistic advancement which spontaneous metaphoric expressions represented. Chukovsky believes, however, they were based on accident, unintended error of fact, word usage, or analogy (p. 25). . . . Matter and Davis (1975, p. 322) more recently argue in the same vein:

> In early stages of language acquisition children produce categorical errors and mistakes that can be taken as metaphorical expression but are not. The child is in the process of learning to recognize and correct perceptual, cognitive, and conceptual "error" . . . As these "errors" are corrected, children develop a highly literal linguistic behavior. In this intermediate stage, children are getting their categories straight . . . Following the literal stage, children again enter the world of category mistakes intentionally . . . they discover metaphor. (Cited in Ortony, Reynolds, Arter, 1978)

In partial contrast to Chukovsky and to Matter and Davis, Piaget (1962) sees the child as recognizing a "pretense" (p. 227) or nonliteral aspect to such verbalizations. Yet he has stressed that the expressions are far from fully deliberate. At age 3;6, on noting the effect of ocean waves on ridges of sand, Piaget's daughter remarked that "It's like a little girl's hair being combed" (pp. 227–228). The striking verbalization, Piaget argues, was a "mere image," deficient as a true concept since the principle for classification was only partially determined by logical transformations involving objective qualities of the stimulus. Other determining factors include the child's immediate activity, internal imagery and feeling state, as well as fluid and changing linguistic and classificatory principles.

Several recent investigators have emphasized the young child's possible underlying competence. Carlson and Anisfield (1969) believe that their preschool subject was aware of both appropriate and inappropriate semantic extensions. . . .

Gardner (1973, p. 125) saw in his 20-month-old daughter's reference to her cookie as a "boat" a deliberate symbolic transformation. Furthermore, he feels that there was communicative intent, an effort to make a novel object "acceptable to herself and to other persons" (p. 125). He does not feel that all such figures of speech are deliberately selected, however. In reviewing a protocol of one young speaker, he estimated that perhaps one-half of the figures involved "a deliberate effort to play with a word's sound or reference to achieve a desired meaning or effect" (p. 145). Winner (1979) has recently analyzed the same protocol. In her meticulous analysis, the preponderance of apparently nonliteral utterances was credited as metaphor, rather than as semantic overextensions.

The present study attempts to answer the question of whether spontaneous apparent metaphors are a frequent part of child language and whether the child recognizes the metaphoric relation created. It is conceivable that metaphors, if they occur, are instances of semantic serendipity and that children do not realize the similarity or analogy dimension involved. It is conceivable, as well, that children do recognize the relationship involved, but remain unable to verbalize it. Some evidence of nascent figurative understanding would be forthcoming should these children be capable of evidencing knowledge of the literal name of their metaphorically named object. Stating a ground of comparison would be further support of a hypothesis of underlying metaphoric awareness. Therefore, the child was assessed as to the level of metaphoric awareness. Verbalized knowledge of conventional denotation or a statement that the figure was "just pretend" was each considered a criterion of nascent figurative competence. Stating a ground of comparison, i.e., a metaphoric rationale, indicated more advanced understanding.

Naturally occurring utterances were observed and recorded. The children were then questioned about their apparent metaphoric creations to determine their awareness and understanding of their utterances.

The data were examined for developmental trends in the age range from 2 to 6 years. Also analyzed were the content areas of the children's figures. As an example of symbolization, metaphors hypothetically may give some clue, via analysis of "tenor" (Richards, 1965) or underlying meaning, to pervasive thoughts and interests of children (cf. Jones, 1950; Sharpe, 1968; Wellek and Warren, 1969).

Finally, to make inferences regarding possible underlying cognitive processes, possible grounds underlying the verbal constructions of the children were analyzed. It is likely that all metaphor is overdetermined and multileveled, and that careful scrutiny would reveal a number of bases or grounds for the particular expression at that particular time in the speaker's life (cf. Wellek and Warren, 1969, for example). In the present study, the major grounds of each verbalization were placed in one or more nonexclusive categories. Four categories seem prominent: (1) logical level of the expression, (2) the activity of the child, (3) visual image, and (4) feeling.

1. *Logical level.* Billow (1975, 1977) has called attention to two possible

logical levels of metaphoric grounding on the basis of *similarity analogy* or of *proportional analogy.* "Similarity metaphor," such as "He is an old fox," involves a matching operation. A "proportional metaphor" has the form of two sets of things, each set internally related in a similar manner to the other. Hence, a proportion is created, such as in Keats' lines (cited in Henle, 1966, p. 176):

> When by my solitary hearth I sit
> and hateful thoughts enwrap my soul in gloom

In the former, the attribute of slyness is the basis of the similarity matching, or ground, between the topic "He" and the vehicle "fox." In the latter there are four elements proportionally related: something (e.g., a web) is to a person's body as hateful thoughts are to a person's soul. The ground is the match between relationships, not among individual members of the relationships.

2. *The activity of the child.* In his brief discussion of early metaphoric-like utterances, Piaget (1962) emphasized how the young child's "immediate activity," rather than primarily the child's mediated activity, contributes to the ground of the verbalizations. Other researchers as well have provided evidence of the role of action in the child's early namings (e.g., Luria and Yudovich, 1971; Winner, 1979).

3. *Visual image.* Chukovsky (1968) and Piaget (1962) implicated the mental image as a perpetrator of the young child's cognitive confusion leading to metaphoric-like verbalizations. As discussed earlier, Piaget tended to dismiss such verbalizations by referring to them as "mere images." The role of mental imagery in metaphor production and comprehension is far from established (Paivio, 1979). It seems worthwhile to consider how such imagery is used by very young children in their creation of metaphor.

4. *Feeling.* Osgood (1953) seems to be the first psychologist to systematically analyze metaphor in terms of empirically derived underlying affective reactions (Paivio, 1979). From quite a different perspective, psychodynamic theorists (e.g., Jones, 1950; Sharpe, 1968), also have emphasized that there are affectual linkages which ground metaphor.

Method

SUBJECTS

Seventy-three children, 39 girls and 34 boys, were observed. They ranged in age from 2;7 to 6;0 and were approximately evenly distributed in sex per age group sampling. The group consisted mainly of white middle-class children.

THE SETTING

The children were observed in a child care center (47 children, ages 2;7–6;0), a nursery school (8 children, ages 3;0–5;3), and a kindergarten (18 children, ages 5;0–6;0).

The three settings were similar in physical as well as in educational–emotional atmosphere. The educational philosophies shared tolerance, even encouragement, for spontaneous child play. Children were able to interact freely with each other, with the teachers and aides (including males), and with the play materials. A sex × setting analysis of variance revealed no statistically significant effect for sex or setting on production of metaphors.

PROCEDURE

The observers were one male and three female graduate students trained under the author's supervision. Each separately observed individual children for one-half hour during free play. All possibly "figurative" expressions of each subject were recorded. That is, whenever the child referred to an object (including a person), feeling, or event by a term which would not ordinarily be used for that referent, the observer wrote down the verbalization and its context. After the observation period, the observer questioned the child as to whether he or she knew the correct denotation for the object, event, or feeling. If possible, the observer continued to question in an attempt to understand the child's basis for the verbal substitution. An example follows:

> Child (age 3;5): "It's going for a walk in the forest (taking little rubber animal and gliding it around observer's back) and it's going to eat some grass (animal reaches observer's hair)." (at 23 minutes of observation)
> Observer: (After 7 minutes) "Where's the grass?"
> Child: (Points to a green rug)
> Observer: "What's this?" (observer's hair)
> Child: "Grass."
> Observer: "What's this?" (pointing to observer's hair again)
> Child: "Hair."

An effort was made to observe each child for two one-half-hour periods, at least 1 month apart. There was a total of 134 observations, 122 of which were in paired units.

SCORING FOR METAPHOR

Each word or phrase uttered by the child which ordinarily would not be used to describe the particular object, feeling, or event was considered a metaphor, unless excluded as indicated below. Thus, in the above example, both the words "forest" and "grass" were scored as metaphor. Neither word is ordinarily used to refer to parts of a person's body. Hair, rather than another part of the person's body, is used as grass because there is a similarity in shape, texture, configuration, etc., between the two substances. The hair is used as the vehicle, which illuminates one or more dimensions of a particular substance (grass), by drawing attention to the similarity (the ground) between the two which are ordinarily viewed as dissimilar. The hair rather than another available object or substance is used just because of the similarity relationship. The concreteness of this example may reflect the conceptual level of the child but it takes little away from the metaphoric relationship created.

Finally, to ascertain developmental trends at each age level, the number of protocols containing one or more metaphors was compared to the number of protocols containing none. Hence, statements relating to metaphoric activity at a particular age level sometimes refer to the number of protocols containing metaphor, rather than to the raw number of metaphors produced. An alternate method of quantifying findings was established to avoid false elevation of an age group's performance based on a single subject's heightened productivity. As occasionally happened, one child produced atypically two or more metaphors in an observation while, on the average, the other members of the age category produced fewer than one.

INTERSCORER RELIABILITY

On eight occasions, two examiners simultaneously observed the same child and carried out separate inquiries with the child. The recorded verbalizations were virtually identical on each occasion. Only minor differences appeared in responses to questioning. These are understandable as reflecting both differences in questioner's style and differences elicited by consecutive inquiries.

Each observer submitted data scored for metaphor and for other types of verbal expression (e.g., misnomer, overextension, etc.). The author independently scored the protocols in the same manner. The level of agreement between scorers was 90%. Occasional differences of opinion between author and observers were resolved or the ambiguous verbalization went uncredited as metaphor.

Results

The observers recorded 83 metaphors in 134 half-hour observations. Metaphors appeared in a total of 48 out of 134 observations. If a child produced a single metaphor in an observational period, more than a third of the time (39%), that child was likely to produce another within that same half-hour observation.

Table 26-1 presents the frequency with which metaphors were observed in the spontaneous speech of the children as a function of age (in years and months). Out of 28 half-hour observations of the youngest children (2;7 to 3;6), one or more metaphors appeared 50% of the time. The number of observations in which one or more metaphors appeared, dropped to 39% in the age group 3;7 to 4;6. With the 4;7 to 5;6 age group, 33% of the observations contained meta-

Table 26-1. *Percentage of Observations in Which Metaphors Appeared*

Age[a]	Number of children	Total number of observations	Percentage of observations in which metaphors appeared	Range of metaphors per observation
2;7–3;6	16	28	50	0–4
3;7–4;6	22	41	39	0–4
4;7–5;6	18	36	33	0–5
5;7–6;0	17	29	20	0–7

[a]Years and months.

phor, while in the 5;7 to 6;0 age group, only 20% of the observations contained such a verbal expression. . . .*

Although the data fell into a striking pattern of decline with age, the paucity of observations reduces the power of the χ^2 to the point that the overall effect does not reach statistical significance ($\chi^2 = 5.37$, $p > 0.05$). However, a comparison of the youngest age group with the oldest group does reach statistical significance ($\chi^2 = 5.37$, $p < 0.05$), with the younger children more likely to produce metaphor.

CONTENT OF THE FIGURES

An effort was made to identify the underlying themes by grouping the metaphors in categories according to their possible central "tenors" (Richards, 1965), or meanings. Thus, one tenor of "I'm going to scoop up ice cream" (age 2;11, playing with water) would relate to *food*. One tenor of "I go mister" (age 4;5, one girl to another who was blocking pavement of the bicycle rider) would refer to *interpersonal* or role relationship (e.g., the sex-stereotypical notion of "ladies first"?). Interpersonal metaphors were credited when a person is given a new name, e.g., calling a girl "mister," or when a nonliteral utterance accompanied role play, e.g., (to O, S playing in sand) "You're in jail." The most frequent themes referred to food or interpersonal relationships, with 34% of all responses accounted for under the former category, another 26% accounted for under the latter, and the remaining 40% being miscellaneous content areas, not reliably classifiable.

Comparing the younger (age 2;7–4;6) and older age (4;7–6;0) children in their production of the two classifiable types of metaphors, a developmental trend emerges. The younger children were more likely to use food-related metaphors, and the older children were more likely to use role-related metaphors ($\chi^2 = 4.49$, $p < 0.05$). In terms of total metaphor production, 32% of the younger children metaphors were food related, while only 19% were role related. In contrast, the older children produced only 15% food-related metaphors, while 35% were role related.

*Figure omitted. [Eds.]

THE GROUNDS OF THE METAPHORS

There were no clear age differences in any of the following categories.

Logical Level

An attempt was made to classify metaphors into those which evidence either similarity or proportional type of thinking. In every case in which a child volunteered or was coaxed to offer a metaphoric rationale (See Table 26-2), he or she verbalized a similarity relation between vehicle and topic. For example, in "Get the bomb!" (age 4;7, picking up ball), the child volunteered that the ball was a bomb because they were "both round." The point of resemblance between substituted word and denoted object is shape.

A few of the metaphors seemed possibly of the proportional type, where an analogous relationship between two sets of elements is implied. In "We're gonna go a choo choo train" (age 4;6, heading line of children), analogous part–whole relationships between the line and the train seemed implied. However, when interviewed, the child expressed interest in the visual similarity of the two lines, not in the analogous relationship of their elements. The response was "Because we make a line like a train."

Not surprisingly, given the subjects' age range, questioning revealed in each case of possible proportional metaphor a concrete or preconcrete operational level of explanation. Of course, it is quite possible that the child created the expression using more developmentally advanced schemata than he or she was able to bring to explanation. But, since no evidence was forthcoming confirming proportional reasoning processes, it must be concluded that the spontaneous metaphors seem to resemble most closely similarity metaphors in underlying logical construction.

The Activity of the Child

About half (53%) of the metaphors occurred during periods of heightened motor activity and this may be interpreted as at least partially being "motivated" by the

Table 26-2. *Percentage of Levels of Metaphor Explanation*

Ages[a]	Raw number of metaphors	Conventional denotation (%)	Mention of "pretend" (%)	Metaphoric rationale (%)	One or more types of explanation (%)
2;7–3;6	27	35	4	4	38
3;7–6;0	56	33	12	19	46
2;7–6;0 (combined)	83	34	10	14	43

[a]Years and months.

child's "immediate activity" (Piaget, 1962). For example, it is conceivable that one of the grounds in "It's a blanket" (age 3;2, shaking cloth) is a "physiognomic" (Werner and Kaplan, 1963) similarity between the feeling of shaking a blanket and of shaking a cloth. It is possible that a "functional need" accompanying motor activity stimulated the implicit comparison of wooden blocks to furniture in the expression "We've got to put more furniture in here" (age 4;0, putting blocks in truck).

Visual Image

In many instances, however, an action context was absent or seemed secondary in terms of the motivation for the verbal expression. In 10% of the sample, similarities between an internal image or representation and denoted object (Piaget's "mere image") seemed prominent. For example, in "A porcupine" (age 2;11, scooping and splashing water with a can), neither the child's action nor the action of the water seems similar to the animal denoted. The ground of similarity turns on the visual resemblance between the jagged splash of water and the jagged covering of an imaged porcupine. Again, in "A dead tree" (age 4;4, referring to a slanted bean bag), there seems to be no action context. The child appeared to be suddenly struck by the visual resemblance of the shape of a fallen tree to that of the slanted bean bag.

Feeling

When Romeo calls Juliet the "sun," one ground of the comparison is similarity of feeling, certainly not that of shape or other visual likeness. With the young subjects of the present study too, evidence was forthcoming that some metaphors were partially grounded in similarity of feelings toward topic and vehicle. It is quite possible that there remains an affective link, in all metaphor (see Sharpe, 1968, for example). However, in three cases (4%), the child verified an affective basis for his or her expression. When asked about the phrase, "I'm the mommy," the child (age 3;1) responded, " 'cause I love Jessica and I'm the mommy." The child's rationale suggests that whereas on a surface level the metaphor's topic is "I," a deeper tenor refers to the speaker's positive feelings toward Jessica which are compared to the feelings a mother has toward her child. The ground of the metaphor is the similarity between a mommy who loves and the subject who loves.

The other two cases are as follows. "The lost dog is going inside" (age 4;5, crawling about miniature house, with a playfully sad expression). When questioned about the response, the child responded with the appropriately sad affect, "I'm the lost dog 'cause I don't have any parents but I pretend." Here again, a shared feeling, sadness, seems to ground the topic ("I"), to the vehicle (lost dog). Finally, from a little boy (age 4;7, covering a discarded, disfigured doll with dirt): "This is a dead doll, no it's a dead girl. We killed Amy-Sue." When asked about his phrase, the child responded, " 'Cause we hate Amy-Sue. She's a girl." In the latter example, the vehicle, dead girl, replaces the topic, Amy-Sue, the ground being a similarity in bad feeling toward the two "discards."

CHILDREN'S JUSTIFICATIONS OF THEIR METAPHORS

In response to inquiry, children supplied evidence of metaphoric awareness 43% of the time. Evidence comprised one or more of the following: knowledge of conventional denotation, spontaneous mention of "pretend," or provision of an adequate rationale for the verbal substitution. As Table 26-2 reveals, even the youngest children (ages 2;7 to 3;6) possessed some understanding of the substitutive aspect of their metaphoric verbalizations. They were able, for example, to provide conventional denotations in place of 35% of their metaphors. Michael (age 2;8) for example, pointing to a cup with sand in it, exclaimed to the observer: "Look what I found: (what?) Tea!" After the half-hour observation period, the observer then pointed to sand not in the cup and asked what it was. This question established whether the child knew the conventional term for the substance. He correctly responded with "sand." However, in response to a further question concerning the term for what was in the tea cup, the child persisted with "tea," then delightedly spilled the sand back into the sand pile. The observer did not persist in questioning since it seemed clear to her that the boy was simply having fun, even if at her expense, and no confusion, misnaming, or accident motivated the expression.

At a rate almost identical to younger children (33%), those older than age 3;6 supplied conventional denotations to their metaphors. However, this group was more likely to articulate further the meaning of the metaphors. In an additional 12% of the inquiries, the child spontaneously assured the examiner that his or her choice was "just pretend." When Dana (age 4;6) said "Good night, husband," for example, she answered the examiner's request to identify her husband with "My husband? My husband pretend."

In 11 cases, or 19% of the inquiries addressed to the children older than age 3;6, accurate rationales were provided for metaphors. Thus, when asked why a bench was his "bed," a 5 to 6 year old quickly replied, "You can sleep on it." In addition to this single instance of a rationale based on functional similarity, one rationale was based on affective similarity, the aforementioned " 'cause I love Jessica and I'm the mommy," one rationale was based on similarity in cause and effect (as well as in affect), "I'm the lost dog 'cause I don't have any parents but I pretend," and eight rationales invoked physical resemblance such as shape or size.

THE ROLE OF SEMANTIC ERROR

The observers noted surprisingly few verbal "accidents," although they were alerted to include all such examples in their observations. Fewer than 6% of the total number of recorded expressions were based on possible errors of denotation. The several borderline cases include referring to a thumbtack in the carpet as "That's the pin that pinched me" (scored as a misnomer), and referring to crayons as "sticks," then defining them as "nails, don't know," and refusing further questioning. Three clear cases of misnomer or grammatical error were recorded, representing 3% of the verbalizations recorded as possible metaphor. . . .

Discussion

The results present clear evidence that preschool children between the ages of 2;7 and 6;0 do make consistent use of metaphoric language. While the child's language is a reflection of his or her cognitive status and, therefore, the vehicles are rather mundane and often related to topics of immediate objects, events, and emotional situations, there are, nonetheless, obvious uses of words and phrases in a metaphoric manner. These metaphoric constructions involve the use of words with referents not designated by the literal or ordinary use of these words, but drawing attention to similarities between the word referent and the contextual referent at hand. . . .

The findings argue against a view of spontaneous metaphor as motivated by linguistic accident, that is, by faulty or immature understanding of semantic or grammatical principles (Chukovsky, 1968; Ervin and Foster, 1960; Matter and Davis, 1975; Piaget, 1962). In fact, it appears that the very young child deliberately rather than accidentally uses words and objects to stand for other quite different objects, and that the use involves a dimension of similarity which is clear and fitting. . . .

Matter and Davis (1975; see also Ervin and Foster, 1960) describe a developmental period in which metaphoric activity decreases. The present study reveals a decreasing occurrence of spontaneous metaphor with advancing age. However, there are explanations other than "error correction" and "getting their categories straight" that would conform better to the data of this study. Gardner (1973), who also described a similar developmental trend, has suggested that there might be a functional pleasure which spontaneous metaphor produces in the practice of linguistic schemas. By 5 years old, the schemas are interiorized and hence call for less practice. Gardner is implying that spontaneous metaphors decline partially due to an "habituation effect" of functional pleasure in making them.

The decline of spontaneous metaphors may be considered from a more purely cognitive–structural point of view, rather than from a linguistic perspective. Increased cognitive structuralization may make verbal spontaneity just one of a rapidly increasing number of mental options available to the developing child. If this were true, the option of spontaneous metaphor should remain available to the child. Indeed, other investigations suggest that the developing child has an underlying and increasing capacity to produce metaphor when called for by a task's demand (Gardner, 1974; Kogan et al., 1980; Pollio and

Pollio, 1974). Thus, in a composition task without specific instructions or cues to produce metaphor, a steadily decreasing rate of spontaneous production appeared in the written productions of children in grades 3, 4, and 5 (Pollio and Pollio, 1974). When "permission," "cueing," or external structure is provided to children, production of metaphor continues to increase with age.

Such findings, along with those reported here, suggest that whereas spontaneous metaphor production decreases with age, the capcity for spontaneous metaphor production increases along with other cognitive capacities. It is possible, then, that spontaneous metaphor decreases only in terms of its outward manifestation, i.e., in terms of verbalizations, but continues as unverbalized, mental activity and/or capacity. Such activity may remain out of the immediate awareness of the subject, but may be called forth into awareness and outward productivity "on demand."

As Piaget emphasized, early spontaneous metaphors seem to be examples of preoperational classifications on the basis of similarity. However, Piaget underestimated the cognitive accomplishment such verbalizations represent because he believed that they arose from the child's excited, momentary confusion of a new object with a mental image of a remembered object, e.g., his daughter's gleeful comparison of the action of ocean waves on ridges of sand with combing hair. The data simply do not support a conclusion of confusion or cognitive failure. What the very young child lacks are the cognitive and linguistic tools to fully explain the bases of his or her spontaneous utterances. But even here, at times the child evidences impressive nascent metalinguistic understanding and competence in verbalizing such understanding.

It is quite possible that one wellspring of metaphoric creation is indeed the momentary and novel link between an image (not necessarily visual) and an object, idea, or situation. Piaget relegates such "ludic" (imaged) thinking to a vestigial role in advanced thinking (with few exceptions, e.g., geometry, cf. Piaget and Inhelder, 1971).

In contrast, Werner and Kaplan (1963), similarly to the psychoanalysts (e.g., Jones, 1950; Sharpe, 1968), theorize that imaginal (multisensory) experience maintains a positive and pervasive influence on symbol formation, throughout the life span. According to Werner and Kaplan (1963, p. 18), imagery in the broad sense of composing "affective, interceptive, postural, (visually) imaginal elements" sets in motion the very mental operations involved in symbol formation. Rather than only confuse symbol formation, "organismic" (Werner and Kaplan, 1963), i.e., "bodily" (Jones, 1950; Sharpe, 1968) experience also may infuse symbol formation, hence, language with meaning.

A word needs to be said about the relationship of spontaneous metaphor to play in general, particularly role play. Whereas spontaneous metaphor often accompanied and was expressive of role play, this does not suggest that such metaphor is merely role-play verbalized. It is equally likely that role-play emerges from underlying metaphoric activity. Role-play, like spontaneous metaphor, requires the capacity to create similarity in the midst of difference. It would seem then, that a capacity to think metaphorically would precede both metaphoric verbalizations and role-play. It is worth reminding the reader that the observations of the children took place in play situations; this may explain partially the link between play and verbal play in this study. . . .

The present study suggests that metaphoric processes exist much earlier in the child's life than hitherto empirically investigated. Nascent metaphoric competence may be observed at preoperational age levels. Evidence deduced from the observation and questioning of children supports the view that spontaneous metaphors are often deliberate and used appropriately. Finally, on some occasions the child is capable of articulating the rationale for the verbal substitution.

27

Stella Vosniadou, Andrew Ortony,
Ralph E. Reynolds, and Paul T. Wilson

Sources of Difficulty in the Young Child's Understanding of Metaphorical Language

Existing research reveals conflicting findings about the ability of children to understand metaphorical language. While research directly investigating children's comprehension of metaphor tends to show that metaphor comprehension does not occur until late childhood or early adolescence (Asch and Nerlove, 1960; Billow, 1975; Cometa and Eson, 1978; Winner, Rosenstiel and Gardner, 1976), there is other evidence that even preschool children have some basic metaphoric competence. For example, Gardner (1974) found that, given a pair of adjectives (hard/soft) and a pair of sounds, colors, or faces, $3\frac{1}{2}$-year-old children could sometimes match such adjectives with an appropriate sound, color, or face. Gentner (1977) also showed that preschool children can perform analogical mappings from the domain of the human body to pictures of mountains or trees as consistently as adults.

Further support for the idea that young children have some basic metaphoric competence comes from observations that preschool children are very creative in their use of language, making sophisticated comparisons that involve the ability to see similarity between things that, at a superficial level, seem very dissimilar (Billow, 1981; Carlson and Anisfeld, 1969; Chukovsky, 1968; Gardner, Winner, Bechhofer and Wolf, 1978; Piaget, 1962; Winner, McCarthy and Gardner, 1980b). Of course, the fact that children produce utterances that appear metaphorical from the adult point of view does not establish that the children themselves are aware of the distinction between metaphorical and literal similarity. However, in a recent study, Vosniadou and Ortony (1983) found that

Abridged from "Sources of difficulty in the young child's understanding of metaphorical language" by S. Vosniadou, A. Ortony, R.E. Reynolds, and P.T. Wilson, 1984, *Child Development*, 55, 1588–1606. Copyright 1984 by Society for Research in Child Development. Reprinted by permission of publisher and authors.

by 4 years of age children are able to distinguish comparisons based on metaphorical similarity from those based on literal similarity.

In our view, the incompatibility between claims that young children do not understand metaphorical language and reports that they produce metaphors or have some fundamental metaphoric competence is partly due to certain methodological problems with the empirical research upon which some of these claims are based. Developmental work on metaphor comprehension often suffers from one or more of three common problems. First, failure to understand metaphors is sometimes confounded with lack of background knowledge. For example, the failure to correctly interpret a metaphor such as "The prison guard was a hard rock" (see Winner et al., 1976) might be the result of inadequate knowledge about prison guards and/or about the particular personality traits to which "hard" can be applied metaphorically (but see Winner, Wapner, Cicone, & Gardner, 1979).

Second, metaphorical utterances are often presented to children in the absence of any reasonable linguistic or nonlinguistic context. However, in real life children are not usually exposed to metaphors out of context. Thus, to test metaphor comprehension in this way puts the child in an unrealistic situation. Lack of an appropriate context can often lead to comprehension difficulties or errors even in an adult's comprehension of literal language, let alone in the child's understanding of metaphorical language.

Finally, children's comprehension of metaphor is frequently measured in terms of the quality of a paraphrase or explanation. Although the ability to paraphrase and explain metaphors is worth investigating, paraphrase and explanation may not be valid indices of metaphor comprehension. They require the ability to reflect on one's comprehension and therefore impose cognitive demands in addition to those required for comprehension alone (Brown, 1980; Flavell, 1981). Thus, while appropriate paraphrases and explanations certainly suggest successful comprehension, inadequate paraphrases and explanations cannot be taken as evidence of comprehension failure.

Corroborating this last point are the results of studies not requiring verbal explanations of metaphors. For example, Winner, Engel, and Gardner, 1980a) found that children do better in multiple-choice tasks than in tasks in which they must state the grounds of the metaphor themselves. Reynolds and Ortony (1980), using a four-alternative forced-choice task and the context of a short story, found that 7 year olds showed evidence of metaphor comprehension. And, in the context of proverb comprehension, Honeck, Sowry, and Voegtle (1978) found that 7-year-old children could understand proverbs when they had to match a proverb to one of two pictures—a nonliteral correct interpretation of the proverb and a foil. Yet even tasks such as these have their limitations: they do not give the child the opportunity to respond spontaneously, and they still impose additional cognitive demands.

We believe that the processes underlying the understanding of metaphorical uses of language are fundamentally the same as those involved in the comprehension of literal uses of language. Thus we see no reason, in principle, why metaphorical language should present children with an insurmountable comprehension problem. In both literal and metaphorical uses of language the meaning of a linguistic input is derived rather than given. The derivation of this meaning is achieved under the constraining influences of the already established context and of characteristics of the input itself. In other words, comprehension involves the interaction between top-down and bottom-up processes (Rumelhart, 1977b). Within this general framework, the difficulty of a comprehension task can be conceptualized in terms of the interaction of two interrelated but independent difficulty sources: (1) the predictability of the meaning for a linguistic input with respect to the already established context (a predominantly top-down component), and (2) the complexity of the linguistic input itself with respect to its derived meaning (a predominantly bottom-up component). Both of these factors contribute to the difficulty of the comprehension task, presumably because of the nature and complexity of the underlying processes involved. When the difficulty of the comprehension task (i.e., deriving a meaning for the linguistic input) reaches some point, which we call the *difficulty limit*, comprehension failures result.

This account appears to apply to both literal and metaphorical instances of language use. However, while predictability of meaning is independent of the literal/metaphorical distinction, the complexity of a linguistic input is not. Other things being equal, one might expect metaphorical uses of language to be more difficult to understand than literal uses because additional processing is necessary to determine the referents of the terms used metaphorically. However, this does not mean that all metaphorical inputs need be harder to understand than any literal input. Nor does it mean that the additional difficulty resulting from metaphorical inputs always and necessarily results in a total level of difficulty that is close to or exceeds the difficulty limit for young children. Therefore, we are skeptical about general claims that metaphor comprehension develops much later than the comprehension of literal language (e.g., Cometa and Eson, 1978), and that it follows a literal stage (e.g., Winner et al., 1976). Rather, it appears to us that, to a large extent, the success or failure of comprehending metaphorical uses of language depends on the overall difficulty of the comprehension task, conceptualized in terms of the interactive effects of different sources of difficulty, rather than on metaphor per se.

The purpose of the present research was to investigate the young child's understanding of metaphorical language within the theoretical framework we have outlined. Both of the two potential sources of comprehension difficulty, that is, the predictability of the meaning of the linguistic input with respect to the established context, and the complexity of the linguistic input itself, were investigated. All three experiments manipulated predictability by using metaphorical sentences representing more likely or less likely outcomes of the same story. In addition, Experiments 2 and 3 examined the effects of the complexity of the linguisitic input. This was accomplished by changing the verb of the metaphorical sentences (literal vs nonliteral verb) and by manipulating the explicitness of their comparative structure (simile vs metaphor). *

The present experiments used metaphorical sentences that compared items that were expected to be relatively familiar to young children. Also, the experimental paradigm adopted required children to act out the actions described in the stories, including the actions implied by the metaphors. Children did this by manipulating objects in a specially constructed "toy world." Metaphor comprehension was measured on the basis of "enactments." This "enactment" paradigm provides a measure of metaphor comprehension that does not depend on metalinguistic skill or linguistic ability, and that still leaves the child free to respond to the task in his own way. In addition, acting out the entire story forces children to process the story's content, making it more likely that they will use this content to understand the metaphor. Research (e.g., Markman, 1977; Paris and Lindauer, 1976) has shown that children do not always engage in sufficient cognitive processing of verbal information in experimental settings. Having children act out the stories helps to avoid this problem.

Experiment 1

One variable with obvious potential for influencing the difficulty of the comprehension task is the degree to which the idea expressed by a linguistic input is predictable from some already established context. The main purpose of this experiment was to investigate how the predictability of the idea expressed by a metaphor (its implied meaning) affects its comprehension. Metaphors were presented in the context of a story and differed with respect to the predictability of their implied meanings. It was hypothesized that if predictability influences the difficulty of the comprehension task, then better performance should result from metaphors representing more probable story endings than from those representing less probable endings.

METHOD

Subjects

Subjects were 90 children: 30 preschoolers, ranging in age from 4;0 to 4;11 years (mean age, 4;5), 30 first graders, ranging in age from 6;0 to 6;11 years (mean age, 6;5), and 30 third graders, ranging in age from 8;1 to 8;11 years (mean age, 8;7). The children attended a nursery school or an elementary school in a rural town in Illinois. In each group, approximately half of the children were girls and half were boys.

---

*Only the first experiment is included. [Eds.]

Design and Materials

The design was a 3 (grade: preschool vs 1 vs 3) × 2 (predictability level: more probable vs less probable) factorial design with between-subject measures on both factors. In addition, there were two control groups, a literal-ending group, and a no-ending group. There were eight subjects in each group, with the exception of the literal control group which had six subjects.

The task consisted of listening to seven short stories (a practice story and six experimental ones) and acting them out with toys. For the experimental group all stories ended with a metaphorical concluding sentence that described a story outcome and that also had to be acted out with toys. Comprehension was assessed on the basis of the children's enactments of the metaphorical concluding sentences.

Two types of concluding sentences were constructed for each story. They differed with respect to the likelihood of the story outcomes they described, given the story content. Those describing actions that represented relatively likely outcomes of the stories will be referred to as *more probable*. Those describing actions that represented relatively less likely story outcomes given the story's content will be referred to as *less probable*. The degree to which the actions described by the concluding sentences represented more or less probable story outcomes was operationally defined in terms of the likelihood that children would enact the ending described by the concluding sentence given only the preceding context information. These likelihoods were originally determined in a pilot study, and in this experiment were confirmed on the basis of the enactments of the no-ending control group.

The no-ending control group was run concurrently with the experimental group at each age level. The children in this group heard the stories without a concluding sentence and were asked to act out their own endings. Of the endings provided, 55% were the same as the actions described by the more probable concluding sentences, while only 27% matched the actions described by the less probable concluding sentences. The remaining 18% of the endings did not agree with either one of the existing concluding sentences.

The literal-ending control group was included to ensure that children were able to understand and act out the particular story endings when expressed in literal language and thus to exclude the possibility that failure to correctly enact the metaphors was caused by factors unrelated to the experimental manipulation. In the literal control group the concluding sentences were "translations" of the metaphors in the sense that they induced similar enactments to those induced by a correct interpretation of the metaphors. The literal concluding sentences had the same syntactic form as the metaphorical concluding sentences. All concluding sentences are given in the Appendix.

The stories varied in length from 90 to 110 words and described situations familiar to, or easily imaginable by, young children. The following is an example of one of the stories together with its various endings:

Billy invited some of his friends to his house, so his mother baked some cookies. She told Billy not to eat the cookies before his friends arrived and she sent him to his room to play. Then she put the cookies in the cupboard and went out to the backyard. After his mother left, Billy came down. He opened the cupboard and found the cookies. He was ready to eat the first cookie when he heard his mother coming back in.

More Probable Concluding Sentences
Metaphorical: "Billy was a squirrel burying the nuts."
Literal: "Billy was a child hiding the cookies."

Less Probable Concluding Sentences
Metaphorical: "Billy was a squirrel heading for his tree."
Literal: "Billy was a child running to his room."

The children acted out the stories with toy figures that were set up on a 4 × 5-foot rectangular board. Seven miniature buildings were placed on the long sides of the board, and one center piece was placed in the center of the board, facing the child.

The seven side buildings were the same in all stories and represented a constant environment in which the children enacted the stories. The buildings were made of wood, were roughly to scale, and on average were about 10 inches high. They were painted by an artist in a realistic way.* The side buildings represented (starting from the right) a hospital, a school, a toy store, a church, two houses, and a McDonald's restaurant. There were four different center pieces. One depicted a park with a playground, another, the interior of a house, a third piece represented a football field (used as a practice item), and, finally, one represented a circus.

Procedure

Each child was tested individually by two experimenters. Testing took place in a quiet room in the school and lasted from 35 to 40 minutes. Children were randomly assigned to the experimental group or to one of the control groups. Each child was first asked to identify the various buildings. In the few cases in which a building could not be identified, the building was named by the experimenter. The child was then instructed to listen carefully to the stories and to act them out with the available toys. Children in the experimental group were told to pay particular attention to the ending of each story "because the story's ending will not say exactly what happens." They were instructed to use the toys to act out what they thought the ending of the story meant. Children in the no-ending control group were asked to act out their own endings to the stories. For all groups, one story was used as a practice item and was always read first. No specific feedback was provided, and, in particular, the children were never told

---

*Photographs of materials are omitted. [Eds.]

what a correct enactment of a concluding sentence was like. The order of presentation of the other stories was random for each child.

One of the experimenters read the stories, stopping at prearranged positions to give the child time to act out the described actions. If the child could not act out the concluding sentence, the instructions were repeated and the sentence was reread. If this did not help, the experimenter proceeded to the next story. When all the stories were read, the experimenter asked the children in the experimental condition to justify their enactments of the concluding metaphorical sentences of the last three stories. The children were asked to try to explain what the metaphors meant.

The second experimenter recorded all the enactments on a map that corresponded to the story, and noted all relevant verbalizations. All sessions were audiotaped, and two children in each group were videotaped.

Scoring

Upon examining the children's responses, it became apparent that one story with its corresponding metaphorical sentences was particularly difficult for all children to enact. This was because, for both the more probable and less probable endings, the nature of the physical setup made the intended metaphorical interpretation either too unlikely or inappropriate. For example, one of the endings required a small figure to "bully" a much larger figure. Children were reluctant to act this out under any circumstances. The data from this story were discarded, reducing the number of stories analyzed from six to five. Responses on the first (practice) story were not scored.

The children's enactments in the metaphorical-ending groups were coded by two independent judges. The few cases (2%) of disagreement were easily resolved after brief discussion. The following four categories of enactments were employed:

1. Unrelated enactments covered cases in which a child performed an action apparently unrelated to that implied by the metaphor. If, for example, given the sentence *Billy was a squirrel burying the nuts*, a child made Billy's mother spank Billy, the response would be coded as an unrelated enactment. Those instances in which a child failed to respond to the metaphors at all were also placed in this category.

2. Literal enactments covered cases in which a child tried to enact the metaphors literally. If, for example, given the sentence *Billy was a squirrel burying the nuts*, a child pretended that Billy was a squirrel and that he was burying some pretend nuts outside his house or in the floor of the kitchen, the response would be coded as literal.

3. Composite enactments, which fell between literal and correct enactments (to follow), were the cases in which a child acted out the implied meanings of the metaphors partly literally and partly correctly. Again, if,

given the sentence *Billy was a squirrel burying the nuts,* a child made Billy try to bury the cookies in the kitchen floor like a squirrel, it would be coded as a composite enactment. In this example a child would have correctly interpreted *nuts* to refer to the *cookies,* but would have tried to enact *burying* literally.

4. Correct enactments were those in which an action clearly corresponded to the implied meaning of the metaphors. Thus, if given the sentence *Billy was a squirrel burying the nuts,* a child made Billy hide the cookies either back in the cupboard or somewhere else, the response was coded as correct.

The children's enactments in the literal-ending control group were also examined. Each response was marked as correct if it represented an accurate enactment of the actions described in the literal concluding sentence.

RESULTS

Results from the literal control group revealed that the children had no problem understanding the stories or enacting the endings when these endings were stated literally. The mean proportion of correct enactments was 1.00 for all age levels with the more probable endings. With the less probable endings, this proportion was 1.00 for the third-grade children and 0.93 for the preschool and first-grade children. Thus, the predictability of the concluding sentence, given the preceding context, seemed not to have affected the enactments in any significant way. This was not the case for the metaphorical concluding sentences.

Table 27-1 shows the mean proportion of responses in each of the four enactment categories for the more probable and less probable metaphorical concluding sentences in the three age groups. As the last column shows, the mean

Table 27-1. *Mean Proportion of Enactments in the Four Enactment Categories of the Metaphorical Concluding Sentences*

Grade	Enactment categories			
	Unrelated	Literal	Composite	Correct
More probable ending				
Preschool	0.07	0.03	0.05	0.85
First	0.00	0.05	0.05	0.90
Third	0.00	0.00	0.07	0.93
Less probable ending				
Preschool	0.45	0.25	0.07	0.23
First	0.20	0.17	0.18	0.45
Third	0.17	0.00	0.15	0.68

proportion of correct enactments was high for all age groups in the case of the more probable metaphors, but it decreased dramatically, especially for the younger children, in the case of the less probable metaphors. This decrease was accompanied by an increase in all other enactment categories, with the exception of literal enactments, which disappear in the third-grade group.

It should be mentioned here that the data were quite consistent across children. For example, given the more probable concluding metaphors, only 1 of the 24 children in the three age groups scored less than four out of five correct. In the less probable condition, only one preschooler (out of eight) produced more than two correct enactments, only one first grader produced more than three, while only one third grader produced less than three.

A 3 (grade) × 2 (predictability level) analysis of variance was performed on the proportion of correct enactments to the stories containing metaphors. The unrelated, literal, and composite enactments were not included in this or in any of the other analyses reported in this or subsequent experiments. Also, because all ANOVAs were performed on proportional data having a binomial rather than a normal distribution, an angular or inverse sine transformation was applied in all cases. The grade × predictability level analysis showed main effects for grade, $F(2,42) = 6.49$, $p < 0.01$, and for predictability level, $F(1,42) = 62.27$, $p < 0.001$. Although an inspection of Table 27-1 would lead one to expect a significant interaction between grade and predictability (and analyses using the untransformed data confirmed this expectation), the grade × predictability interaction was not significant with the transformed data ($F < 1$).

In order to determine whether the performance of the experimental group exceeded the performance of the no-ending control group, two additional analyses were performed. First, the enactments in the no-ending control group that

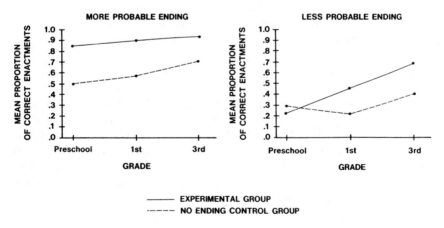

Fig. 27-1. *Mean proportion of correct enactments for the experimental and no-ending control groups.*

agreed with the actions implied by the more probable metaphors were compared to the correct enactments of these metaphors in a 3 (grade) × 2 (group: metaphor vs control) analysis of variance. The analysis showed a main effect for group, $F(1,42) = 28.93$, $p < 0.001$. The upper graph of Fig. 27-1 presents the mean proportion of correct responses in the two groups. It shows that the children could all easily enact the implied meaning of the metaphors representing the more probable story endings, and that they did so much more often than did children in the no-ending control group.

Then the enactments in the no-ending control group that agreed with the action implied by the less probable metaphors were compared to the correct enactments of these metaphors in another 3 (grade) × 2 (group) analysis of variance. This analysis showed a main effect for group, $F(1,42) = 6.10$, $p < 0.01$, a main effect for grade, $F(2,42) = 6.50$, $p < 0.01$, and a grade × group interaction, $F(2,42) = 3.14$, $p < 0.05$. The mean proportions of correct enactments in these two groups appear in the lower graph of Fig. 27-1. As can be seen, there was no difference between the experimental and no-ending control group in the case of the preschool children. First- and third-grade children, however, did better in the experimental group than the no-ending control group.

Examination of the verbal protocols revealed, as expected, that the older children provided better and more complete explanations of the metaphors than did the younger children. It was not until third grade that children began to systematically provide explanations that related the two domains analogically (e.g., "It meant like a squirrel is frightened when somebody gets near them and I thought it meant him darting up the stairs and going to bed so that his mom wouldn't know that he was in the kitchen trying to get the cookies"). Of the children who gave literal responses (preschoolers and first graders), most explained them mainly in terms of "pretend" actions. That is, Billy was not a real squirrel but he pretended to be one; he acted like a squirrel by running fast on four legs, digging, and burying the cookies. There were few "magical" types of responses such as those discussed by Winner et al. (1976).

DISCUSSION

The results of this experiment suggest that under certain circumstances even preschoolers show evidence of understanding metaphorical language. This in itself is a new finding. It seems that children can and do draw inferences from the information provided by the linguistic and situational context in which the metaphor occurs—inferences that help them understand the metaphor's implied meaning. The decrease in the performance of, especially, the younger children on the metaphors that represented less probable story endings also indicates that the context in which the metaphorical language occurs is an important variable in metaphor comprehension.

It might be argued that the younger children did not really understand the more probable metaphors that they enacted correctly, but that they simply acted out the actions invited by the linguistic and situational context. This argument is not, however, supported by the data. The fact that the more probable metaphor group performed significantly better than the no-ending control group shows that the presence of the metaphorical sentences contributed to the number of correct enactments over and above the contribution of the context. Still, all the children, and particularly the younger ones, found it difficult to use the meaning conveyed by the metaphor to revise their original hypotheses based on contextual information alone. This is shown by their low performance with the less probable metaphors. It seems that difficulties arose for these children not from the presence of metaphorical language per se, or from the unpredictability of the ending per se, but from the conjunction of the two. This conclusion follows (1) from the fact that the more probable endings expressed metaphorically constituted no serious problem for the children, (2) from the fact that the correct enactments of these metaphors were more likely to be produced given the context *and* the metaphor than given the context alone, and (3) from the fact that there was no effect of unpredictability when literal concluding sentences were used.

These arguments do not, of course, exclude the possibility that factors other than the predictability of the ending might account for the low level of performance on the less probable metaphors as well as the high level of performance on the more probable metaphors. Indeed, there is reason to believe that such additional factors were at work. Consider first the low level of performance on the less probable metaphors. A closer examination of the metaphorical sentences revealed that most of the less probable metaphors had an additional feature that may have increased their difficulty relative to the more probable metaphors. While four of the five more probable metaphors contained a verb that could be interpreted literally (e.g., Kenny and Andy were puppies *following* their master), three of the five less probable metaphors contained either a verb that required a metaphorical interpretation (e.g., Sally was a bird *flying* to her nest), or an abstract verb that could not easily be interpreted literally (e.g., Billy was a squirrel *heading* for his tree). For the sake of brevity, we shall refer to this difference between the verbs as a difference between *literal* and *nonliteral* verbs. Metaphorical sentences containing a nonliteral verb might have been more difficult to understand than ones with literal verbs because of the need to make the additional metaphorical substitution. This additional source of difficulty in the less probable metaphors may well have resulted in a lower level of performance than would otherwise have been the case.

Turning to the performance on the more probable metaphors, two things are noteworthy. First, the absolute level of performance was high, and second, there was no effect of age. However, it does not follow from the fact that children at all ages were producing the same correct enactments that the processes they employed in doing so were the same. In fact, it appears that the correct enactments of the more probable metaphors could have been produced even if the children had not processed all of the concluding sentence. In particular, children might have been employing some procedure such as the following: (1) ignore the predicate in the first part of the sentence (e.g., "were puppies"), (2) interpret the verb (i.e., "following") as applying literally to the actors involved (e.g., Kenny and Andy *followed* someone), and (3) use contextual information and the meaning of the last noun phrase (i.e., "their master") to generate an action (e.g., Kenny and Andy followed mother).

Such a "short-circuiting" procedure would only require one metaphorical substitution, namely, that of the object noun phrase. Its use would lead to correct enactments of metaphorical sentences with literal verbs, but would tend to result in composite, literal, or incorrect enactments of the sentences with nonliteral verbs. Given that the less probable metaphors were the ones containing the majority of the nonliteral verbs, the observed increase in the number of composite, literal, and incorrect enactments with the less probable metaphors is certainly compatible with the hypothesis that particularly the younger children used some such simplifying procedure.

Convincing evidence for the additional difficulty of the less probable metaphors and for the use of some sort of simplifying procedure could not be culled from the data because verb type (literal or nonliteral) and predictability were confounded, and the design thus did not afford enough degrees of freedom to explore this hypothesis with any certainty. . . .

General Discussion

. . . Our findings have some interesting implications for a developmental theory of metaphor comprehension. Regardless of how rudimentary the preschoolers' understanding of metaphor is, the fact that there are some conditions under which they can understand metaphorical language is inconsistent with efforts to relate metaphoric understanding to Piagetian theory, and especially to the claim that formal, or at least late concrete operational, thinking is a necessary prerequisite for metaphor comprehension (Billow, 1975; Cometa and Eson, 1978; Elkind, 1970). It might be objected here that some of the preschool children were already performing at a concrete operational stage, and that these were the children who enacted the metaphorical sentences correctly, the remaining ones failing. This argument cannot, however, account for the fact that the data were very homogeneous, with most of the preschoolers correctly enacting the metaphorical sentences when the difficulty of the comprehension task was low, but failing to do so as the difficulty of the comprehension task increased. The Piagetian position as commonly interpreted by investigators of metaphor is incapable of explaining both the high performance of most of the preschoolers in some of the tasks and the observed decline in this performance as the complexity of the metaphoric input increases or its relation to the linguistic context becomes less predictable.

Although the present experiments contradict claims that concrete operations are a necessary prerequisite for metaphor comprehension, they do not necessarily invalidate the notion that the young child's classification abilities are related to metaphor comprehension. However, together with other research that has challenged many of Piaget's claims about the emergence and development of the young child's classification skills (e.g., Rosch, Mervis, Gray, Johnson, & Boyes-Braem, 1976; Mandler, 1982; Markman and Siebert, 1976), they do show that the Piagetian position, at least as it is usually interpreted, provides a limited perspective from which to view the development of metaphoric understanding and the nature of the cognitive mechanisms that underlie it (see also Vosniadou and Ortony, 1983).

Our findings are also inconsistent with the position that the development of metaphoric understanding follows a clearly identifiable sequence of stages, which starts with literal responses first, and only later follows with more mature types of metaphoric understanding (e.g., Asch and Nerlove, 1960; Winner et al., 1976). Very few children in our experiments adopted only literal interpretations of the metaphorical expressions, suggesting that they are not bound to one particular way of interpreting metaphorical language. On the contrary, as revealed in this study, children's metaphoric thinking seems to be more flexible than generally believed.

It might be argued that literal enactments of the metaphors were unlikely in these studies because materials necessary for such enactments (e.g., a toy squirrel and toy nuts) were not provided. While we agree that the provision of such materials would have increased the number of literal enactments, we believe that it would have decreased the ecological validity of the task. It is unusual for the literal referents of terms used metaphorically in ordinary communicative situations to be present in those situations. It would be confusing if, speaking figuratively, one were to announce while in sight of a bridge, "We'll cross that bridge when we come to it." Our concern in this research was with the comprehension of metaphors, not with the comprehension of puns, or the recognition of humor!

The arguments against the notion of a literal stage as a necessary prerequisite to nonliteral interpretations of metaphors are not meant to belittle the fact that there is a tendency in young children, which decreases with age, to opt for a literal interpretation of the metaphor when its correct meaning is elusive. In our experiments, these literal interpretations were justified on the grounds that they represented a pretend-play situation. Considering the amount of time a 4 year old spends in pretend play, this interpretation of the metaphors must seem very natural to them, in spite of its inappropriateness as far as the general story context is concerned. Thus, while symbolic play has been thought of as a precursor to metaphor (Verbrugge, 1979; Winner, McCarthy and Gardner, 1980b), which might very well be the case, we also see that the naturalness of pretend games might stand in the way of more mature metaphorical thinking in the young child.

One question that this study leaves unanswered centers around children's difficulty in correctly enacting metaphors involving nonliteral verbs. Is it simply that children find it hard to make the additional metaphoric substitutions, or are verbs more difficult to understand than nouns when used metaphorically? It has been argued that relational similarity is harder to understand than descriptive similarity (see Billow, 1975). However, even the simplest metaphorical expressions used in our experiments involved an implicit comparison of two objects (nest/house, repair shop/hospital, nuts/cookies) whose shared similarity was not of a physical/perceptual nature but of a relational nature. Thus, the success of the preschoolers in the present experiments, even with those metaphors and similes that involved only metaphorical nouns, shows a more sophisticated understanding of similarity and higher level of metaphoric competence than that shown by other studies (e.g., Billow, 1975; Malgady, 1977; Vosniadou and Ortony, 1983), where the metaphors compared objects for which the primary basis of similarity was perceptual.

Finally, it must be acknowledged that in these experiments the manipulation of "predictability" was rather heavy handed. For the purposes of the present experiments this manipulation was adequate, since its main purpose was to show that contextual predictability is an important variable in metaphor comprehension. A more careful examination of the contribution of context to the comprehension of metaphors would require a more thorough conceptual analysis of the notion of predictability.

Appendix

METAPHORICAL CONCLUDING SENTENCES

More probable:

1. Billy was a squirrel burying the nuts.
2. Mary was a car being taken to the repair shop.
3. Kenny and Andy were puppies following their master.
4. Sally was a tiger walking toward the jungle.
5. Jack was a child being sent to his room.
6. Paul was a horse heading for his barn.

Less probable:

1. Billy was a squirrel heading for his tree.
2. Mary was a pony being taken to the stable.
3. Kenny and Andy were puppies barking at their master.
4. Sally was a bird flying to her nest.
5. Jack was garbage being thrown in the trash.
6. Paul was a rabbit heading for the wolf.

LITERAL CONCLUDING SENTENCES

More probable:

1. Billy was a child hiding the cookies.
2. Mary was a girl being taken to the hospital.
3. Kenny and Andy were children following their mother.
4. Sally was a girl walking toward the school.
5. Jack was an elephant being sent to his cage.
6. Paul was a boy running home.

Less probable:

1. Billy was a boy running to his room.
2. Mary was a girl being taken home.
3. Kenny and Andy were children yelling at their mother.
4. Sally was a girl going to her car.
5. Jack was an elephant being thrown out of the circus.
6. Paul was a child fighting the bad boy.

28

Dianne Horgan

Learning to Tell Jokes: A Case Study of Metalinguistic Abilities

Most of the recent literature on children's humor looks at school-age children's responses to humorous stimuli, emphasizing the role of cognition. Much less is known about very early humor, particularly spontaneous jokes and their linguistic structure. When linguistic aspects of humor are discussed, it is usually with respect to fairly sophisticated elements such as ambiguity. This note will examine earlier spontaneous jokes (between ages 1;4 and 4;0) and will analyze them in terms of the metalinguistic abilities they represent.

The Piagetian-cognitive perspective provides a framework from which to view these data. Toward the end of the sensorimotor period children begin symbolic play. According to Schultz (1976), humor and symbolic play are closely related in the beginning, but become more differentiated as the child develops. In symbolic play, a child reproduces a motor schema outside of its normal context. That is, a child begins to be able to pretend. Children at this age pretend to be reading, sleeping, eating, putting on make-up, etc. Symbolic play can be viewed as self-constructed incongruity. Support for the relationship between symbolic play and humor comes from the fact that symbolic play is almost always accompanied by laughter: the child thinks it is funny to pretend to sleep, eat, put on make-up. McGhee (1979) describes what happens after the development of make-believe play. McGhee's stages are reflections of cognitive development and correspond to Piaget's descriptions of cognitive acquisitions. Stage 1 consists of incongruous actions toward objects, such as Piaget's child pretending a leaf was a telephone. Stage 2 consists of incongruous labeling of objects and events, such as calling a hand a foot. The absence of action toward the object characterizes the increase in cognitive ability. Stage 1 and 2 jokes are seen mostly during the preschool years. Stage 3 may start around 3 years. This stage involves conceptual incongruity, which entails violating one or more aspects of a concept. McGhee describes examples of word play during this stage. Children's humor first approaches adult humour in Stage 4 with an appreciation of ambiguity. This begins around age 7 with attainment of concrete operations, and is the stage most systematically studied. Children now can understand riddles. Research such as McGhee (1979) and Fowles and Glanz (1977) clearly demonstrates the relationship of humor to both cognition and metalinguistic abilities at this stage.

Relatively little is known about metalinguistic knowledge before age 7. Gleitman, Gleitman & Shipley (1972) presented evidence that some children as young as 2 displayed metalinguistic knowledge. By metalinguistic knowledge we mean the capacity to view language as an object. Many of the examples of metalinguistic abilities cited by Gleitman et al. are also early attempts at humor. In one such example the experimenter is trying to elicit a correction of a deviant sentence. She says *Allison, mailbox fill!* Allison, demonstrating a sense of humor as well as sophisticated metalinguistic knowledge, replies *We don't have any mailbox fills here.* Allison demonstrates her abstract knowledge of compound nouns. Gleitman et al. do not suggest that such metalinguistic ability is present in all 2 year olds and are reluctant to speculate on its origins. But they go on to discuss the precocious metalinguistic abilities of one 7 year old who, in their words, "had had a good deal of exposure to language games." Slobin (1978) has written about the precocious metalinguistic abilities of his daughter, and speculates that exposure to foreign languages may have focused her attention on relevant aspects of language. She, too, was exposed to language games. Many of Slobin's metalinguistic examples appear to be attempts at jokes.

This paper will present some longitudinal data from another somewhat atypical child. Kelly, the first-born daughter of a philosopher and a psycholinguist, was also exposed to language games from an early age. As part of a longitudinal study of her language development, I have collected a number of her spontaneous jokes. Most of these are closely related to her developing language skills and demonstrate early metalinguistic abilities. They offer additional insights into very early humor and its relationship to developing metalinguistic skills. We will look at Kelly's jokes in the context of her overall language system and see what they tell us about her knowledge of language. I have categorized her jokes into four types. Although they emerged in a sequential order, the earlier types continued. Thus, her development consisted of adding additional types of jokes and producing increasingly complex versions of old types.

VIOLATIONS OF SEMANTIC CATEGORIES

These included examples from McGhee's stages 1, 2, and 3. At 1;4, when Kelly had a vocabulary of less than 20 words, she learned the word *shoe*. Several days later, she put her foot through the armhole of a nightgown, saying *Shoe*, accompanied by shrieks of laughter. Later that day, she put her foot into a tennis ball can, saying *Shoe* and laughing. It is hard for me to believe that this is a case of overgeneralizing the word *shoe* based on its function. She was telling a joke. It was as though she was saying "Look, a shoe is something you put on your foot; a nightgown is NOT something you usually put on your foot, but I did!" She had violated the semantic category—shoes can be boots, sandals, and other perceptually distinct items, but there are things that can be put on feet that are NOT shoes. As soon as she could put two words together, she formed similar jokes by violating semantic restrictions—*Bed cry* would be accompanied by laughter. Throughout her development, the acquisition of a new word would stimulate a joke attempt of this type. When she was 1;11 I told her I was proud of her. She correctly surmised that only people are proud of you. She used a joke to "show off" (and to test) her new knowledge: *Daddy's proud of you. Grandma's proud of you. Uncle David's proud of you. Hamburger NOT proud of you. Ha, ha.* Of course, sometimes her analyses were incorrect and her jokes failed. After asking me why men could not wear dresses and contemplating my response about customs, she concluded that customs were something only men had. *Daddy has a custom. Uncle David has a custom. Mommy has a custom! Ha, ha, mommies can't have customs! The clock has a custom! Ha, ha, clocks can't have customs!*

This sort of joke telling is a very effective strategy for a language learner: you hear a new word, make a hypothesis about the semantic restrictions, and test your hypothesis by violating those restrictions. Thus, Kelly learned from our responses that she had correctly analyzed *proud*, but had incorrectly analyzed *custom*.

PHONETIC PATTERN GAMES

These are characteristic of McGhee's stage 3. This general category of jokes consisted of phonetic pattern games. At 1;8, she said *Cow go moo. Mommy go mamoo. Daddy go dadoo. Ha ha.* These jokes, like the violations of semantic categories, became more sophisticated as she got older. For example, at 3;3 she began starting the last syllable of every content word with a [t] and stressing that syllable: *banana* became *bana*TA, *dinner* became *din*TER, *strawberry* became *strawber*TEE, *Kelly* became *Kel*TEE, *Mommy* became *Mom*TEE, etc. Her special way of talking was always accompanied by much giggling.

CHANGING ESTABLISHED PATTERNS

These are more complex types of McGhee's stage 3 jokes. This third general kind of joke involved changing established patterns. Thus at 2;3 we heard that *Little Bo People had lost her steeple* and that *Rudolph the red-nosed reindeer, you'll go down and get a hamburger*. At 2;3 she invented the following rhyme:

> Five socks. Pick up stocks.
> Seven ox. Close the gox.
> Nine tens. Start agains.

At 2;9, the following song occurred:

K: Mommy, listen. Somebody come and play with me (*a Sesame Street song*).
Somebody come and play with I.
M: Oh, that's silly. It's supposed to be "me."
K: Somebody come and play with I—van! Ha, ha.
Somebody come and play with pee.
Somebody come and play with Pee—ter! Ha, ha.
Somebody come and play with cheese.
Somebody come and play with Cheez—Whiz! Ha, ha.

At 2;4, she was fascinated with Dr. Seuss's *There's a Wocket in my Pocket*, and tried to do her own versions:

M: (*trying to have a serious conversation*): Mommy has a baby in her tummy.
K: Yeah, and a wocket in her pocket!
M: No, really, there's a baby in there.
K: Mommy's got a deer in her ear, too!

RIDDLE-LIKE QUESTIONS

Early jokes in this category are characteristic of McGhee's stage 3. We can see the transition to stage 4 in this group of jokes. At 2;6, Kelly began making up her own riddles. As far as I know she had never heard an actual riddle—it is not a joke form used by her parents and she did not play with older children or watch TV. We did, however, frequently ask stylized questions that were structurally similar: *How does a cow/frog/cat/horse/etc. go?* or *What's daddy's name?* One of her favorite language games at this age involved questions about names of relatives, for example *What's mommy's mommy's name?* She became very adept at these. Even *What's Kelly's Daddy's brother's name?* would only cause a momentary delay. At 2;6 she initiated similar riddle-like games:

K: What does Jennifer have named Sheila?
D: I dunno. What does Jennifer have named Sheila?
K: A doggie named Sheila. What does Mary have named Alice?
D: I dunno. What does Mary have named Alice?
K: Does she have a pussycat named Alice?
D: Does she have a pussycat named Alice?
K: Yeah.

Slightly later, riddles that were further removed from the *What's the name* game appeared:

K: How do aspirins make?
M: Huh?

> K: How do aspirins make?
> M: I dunno, how do aspirins make?
> K: They make you feel better.

and

> K: What did Mommy woke?
> D: I dunno. What did Mommy woke?
> K: Up.

By 2;7, these riddle-like jokes had evolved even further; now like the distorted *Somebody come and play* song, Kelly deliberately set up a linguistically misleading context.

> K: Do we kick Mary?
> M: No, we don't kick Mary!
> K: Do we kick Jennifer?
> M: No, we don't kick Jennifer!
> K: Do we kick the swimming pool?
> M: No, we don't kick the swimming pool!
> K: We kick IN the swimming pool. Ha, ha!

Another such example came at 3;0:

> K: Mommy, do you love me?
> M: Yes.
> K: Do you love me TO HIT you? Ha, ha!

What can we conclude from these examples? We see a developmental progression for the appearance of different types of jokes. Each kind of joke seems to reflect increased cognitive complexity. The jokes in each stage exhibit the same kinds of cognitive skills described by McGhee. The metalinguistic knowledge represented by each can be summarized as follows.

> I. *Violations of semantic categories*. The child must realize that certain words can be applied to a CLASS of objects. That is, the child must be able to recognize categories such as animate versus inanimate in order to be able to violate the restrictions purposefully.
> II. *Phonetic pattern games*. To be able to alter the phonetics of a word to make a rhyme or to fit a more general rule demands that the child see the words as arbitrary symbols for the objects and not as essential properties of the objects. The child must, in some rudimentary sense, appreciate the arbitrariness of words.
> III. *Changing an established pattern*. This is a more sophisticated version of II. In II, the child is tinkering at the phonetic level. In III, the child is altering the pattern by changing words. In order for these jokes to work, the child has to choose a related word (e.g., *peep/people; sheep/steeple*), then fit it into the proper place, preserving the syntax and

something of the semantics. So the move from II to III would involve acquiring the ability to change item x to y where both x and y make sense, over and above the ability to change x to y where y is objectively recognizable as a permutation of x. This requires a broader range of linguistic knowledge than does changing the phonetic patterns of words.

IV. *Riddle-like questions.* Here the child sees the joke as having a set structure. Thus, Kelly told many jokes that started with the same structure: *How do* NOUN VERB? According to Piaget, symbolic play develops into stylized games with rules. The development of humor may follow a similar course. Kelly's early riddles followed a "formula" or a rule. She had to match her joke to the riddle format. Thus, at this point, Kelly's jokes not only revealed metalinguistic ability, but also metajoke ability.

How do these results fit with the various theories of humor? They certainly support the cognitive-perceptual model of humor; all the jokes deal with incongruity or ambiguity, reflect Kelly's increasing cognitive capacity, and fit Mc-Ghee's stages. We also have support for Freud's progression from mere "nonsense," or unresolvable incongruity, to jokes with meaning. Some jokes after 2;4 had motives reflecting conflict over sex, aggression, or siblings, but certainly not all of Kelly's jokes (and not the earliest jokes) resulted in any reduction of tension or anxiety. In none of the situations in which jokes occurred was Kelly in a state of noticeable anxiety.

Perhaps the most interesting questions raised by this study revolve around the reasons for Kelly telling jokes. One is certainly cognitive development; also, some jokes were motivated by sexual and aggressive drives. But what makes some children tell jokes and others not? We have hinted at a few possible factors. Kelly was exposed to and reinforced for language games. Her metalinguisitc knowledge was advanced. Her symbolic play was unusually imaginative and elaborate. Fowles and Glanz (1977) suggest three factors that are involved in humor: (1) cognitive ability, (2) familiarity with jokes, and (3) attention to language. The latter they consider a talent. Kelly had these factors as well. Brodzinsky (1975) found that reflective, as opposed to impulsive children develop a sense of humor earlier. Kelly is a reflective child. Two other aspects of her personality appear related: she has a high tolerance for degraded stimuli and she focuses attention on patterns.

Kelly's tolerance for degraded stimuli has been striking throughout her development. While most children expect the signifier (the inappropriate object that is to undergo the make-believe action) and the signified (the normal object that would normally undergo the real action) to share some perceptual features, Kelly would accept almost any object to stand for another. For example, at 2;8 she was looking for an umbrella for her play. She settled, quite happily, on a little plastic "G." At this age, I observed Kelly playing with several children of about the same age. I invariably found I could easily infer the theme of the other children's play from their props. With Kelly it was much harder. For example, Kelly and another child were playing with a toy stove, pots, and pans. The other child was realistically "cooking." I was unable to figure out what Kelly was doing. She responded to my queries with *It's not really a stove, but actually it's a computational stove and potty chair.* Kelly's tolerance for degraded stimuli may be related to her willingness to "degrade" or alter established patterns.

The other aspect of Kelly's general cognitive and linguistic style that seems to be related to her humor development was her unusual attention to patterns and the social context of language. In the child language literature (i.e., Nelson 1973, Bloom, Lightbown & Hood 1975, Horgan 1980) we find two general approaches to language. They have been given different labels by different researchers, but one type of child—the "referential"—seems to concentrate on the semantic content of the message and the individual words, while the other type—the "expressive"—concentrates more on the personal-social context and the patterns of language—the "gestalts." Kelly was an expressive type. She, like other expressive speakers, saw language not as a system to refer to objects, but more as a social game. In all her behavior, Kelly was a seeker of patterns. It was important to her that breakfast consist of Wheat Chex on top of Cheerios and not the other way around. At 1;4 we took her to Churchill Downs. She quickly extracted the pattern of the social ritual: when in a crowd of people, stand up and yell "Go!" That is exactly what Kelly did whenever she was in a crowd for months thereafter. Her obvious attention to patterns and to the social context was no doubt a contributing factor in her development of jokes. In her jokes she first attended to the pattern, then altered it in some way while preserving the rhyme or the cadence. She saw jokes as a form of social exchange. Questions for Kelly were rarely a means of seeking information, but more often were a means of initiating social interaction. Her riddle-like questions are an excellent example of this.

Kelly was very sensitive to the form of language as evidenced by her frequent "corrections" of our speech:

M: You're a good cook.
K: Sorry. I'm a good cookER!

and

M: I need to cut your hair.
K: Hairs! Sorry!

At 3;2 a neighbor told me she was having a friend for dinner. Kelly "corrected" her by pointing out that you can't eat friends. Kelly was also aware of multiple meanings for the same phonetic sequence, when she observed *There are two jeans: Jessica's mommy named Jean and jeans to wear.*

All of these factors no doubt contributed in some way to Kelly's spontaneous joking. Future research needs to examine such types of individual variation and their relationship to humor. So far most research has concentrated more on what makes children laugh than on what makes some children comedians.

29

Tamar Rosenblum and Steven A. Pinker

Word Magic Revisited:
Monolingual and Bilingual Children's
Understanding of the Word–Object
Relationship

One of the more intriguing claims that have been made about children's lack of metalinguistic awareness is that they cannot grasp the arbitrary nature of the word–object relation. Piaget (1929) observed that preschool children answer questions about why objects have the names they do as if they believed that the word is "magically" connected to the object or that the word is an intrinsic property of the object, like its size or color (a phenomenon he called "nominal realism"). In the same vein, Vygotsky (1962) noted that children give idiosyncratic answers to questions calling on them to manipulate names, such as "Can you call this dog a *cow?*" and "Can this 'cow' give milk?" (e.g., they would assent to the latter).

If preschool children have difficulty appreciating that words and objects are related by convention only, it would be natural to expect that bilingual children, who know two words for most objects, would come to appreciate this fact at a younger age. Indeed, diary studies (Leopold, 1949; Slobin, 1978) contain reports of bilingual children making precocious observations about words and their properties (though, of course, these may have been precocious children in general). Observations of groups of monolingual and bilingual children have shown that bilinguals often are more willing to refer to an object by a nonsense or unconventional name (e.g., Ben-Ze'ev, 1977; Feldman and Shen, 1971; Ianco-Worrall, 1972) or to articulate the principle that words and objects are related by arbitrary convention (Cummins, 1978). However, these differences in answers to questions have not always translated into behavioral differences (e.g., Cummins,

1978; Ianco-Worrall, 1972), and occasionally no differences have been found in tasks of understanding the word–object relation (e.g., Pinker, 1979).

In any case, we would like to argue that neither hypothesis—that preschoolers believe words to be intrinsic properties of their referents and that bilingual children are disabused of this notion earlier, when they learn two names for an object—receives unambiguous support from these data, even if the data were perfectly consistent. We see three problems of interpretation concerning these studies.

1. Children's interpretation of the questions: There is reason to believe that children's answers to the experimenter's questions in Piagetian tasks may not always reflect their cognitive abilities accurately (see Siegel, 1978). This could affect the interpretation of children's metalinguistic judgments in several ways. First, preschoolers do not seem to understand fully the words for linguistic entities and relations such as *word, say, means, sounds like*, and so on (Slobin, 1978). Furthermore, children (Osherson and Markman, 1975) and adults in preliterate cultures (Cole and Scribner, 1974) often answer logical questions or hypothetical questions as if the questions referred to empirical states of the world rather than to the necessity, possibility, or impossibility of the premise itself. Thus the somewhat bizarre question "Can you call a cow a tree?" may be interpreted as the far more plausible "Is the English word for a cow 'tree'?" (see Markman, 1976); therefore, the children's answers in the negative may not be as anomalous as they would first appear. This might be so because children are incapable of entertaining counterfactual information of any sort or because they choose not to interpret the question in its hypothetical sense owing to the bizarreness of that interpretation in the discourse context (see Grice, 1975). On this interpretation, if the children were "set" to attend to counterfactual information in that context, they might indeed answer the name-switching question in an adult-like way.

2. Variables confounded with bilingualism: Bilingual children may differ from monolinguals in more ways than simply knowing another language. In any given sample they may be brighter, higher in socioeconomic status (SES), more likely to entertain counterfactuals, or simply more talkative in an experimental setting (in which case they might give "better" answers to open-ended questions simply because they are willing to proffer an extended answer, whereas shyer children would answer in monosyllables, if at all). Interestingly, in each of the studies reporting differences between monolingual and bilingual children, one or more of these factors were not equated (e.g., intelligence for Feldmen and Shen, 1971; SES for Ianco-Worrall, 1972; talkativeness and comprehension of counterfactuals in all the studies), and in the studies that failed to find statistically significant differences (Pinker, 1979), both intelligence and SES were equated.

3. Interpreting differences—semantic versus pragmatic knowledge: It is not really true that monolingual children hear a single name for an object; consider, for example, *Sparky, dog, poodle, pet, animal,* and *living thing*. What differenti-

ates the bilinguals' experience from the monolinguals' is that, when a monolingual child hears a new word for an object (synonyms aside), the new word will differ semantically from the known name (e.g., *animal* refers to any animate creature, whereas *dog* refers only to those with a muzzle, fur, a bark, etc.). In contrast, when a bilingual child hears a new word for an object, often the new word will differ in that it is used in a different social context (e.g., in school vs at home; when speaking to mother rather than to father). Thus, monolinguals may learn that an object is referred to by two or more names by virtue of its individuality and its physical properties, whereas bilingual children learn that an object is referred to by two or more names by virtue of those attributes as well as its use in different discourse contexts. As a result, in an experimental setting, bilinguals might be more likely to agree to dubbing an object with a new name precisely because the experiment *is* a different social setting from that in which the regular name applies; the differences would be in the children's knowledge about when and why an object can have a second name, rather than whether it can have a second name or any other possible misconceptions about nominal realism or word magic. Simply obtaining a child's assent or dissent to switching names (e.g., Ben-Ze'ev, 1977; Feldman and Shen, 1971) will not settle this issue; at the very least, one would need the children's rationales for their assent or dissent to see if they referred to an object's properties, the social setting, or both.

This study was designed to address these three objections to the conclusion that monolingual, but not bilingual, children are susceptible to nominal realism. To address the objection about children's interpretation of the question, we presented the children with a nonlinguistic example of a counterfactual scenario and assessed whether they could entertain and comprehend the scenario. This serves three purposes. First, if all the children fail this test, we could attribute any subsequent general failure in a name-switching task to an inability to consider counterfactuals rather than to a metalinguistic deficit per se. Second, if bilinguals could pass the test but monolinguals could not, any subsequent differences between groups in the metalinguistic task could be attributed to this general cognitive difference. Third, if both groups would ordinarily balk at name switching but would agree to it only if "set" to attend to counterfactuals seriously, this test would provide the appropriate set and, if all children passed it, would give us more confidence that any subsequent failures in the name-switching task reflected metalinguistic deficits.

In addition, we ensured that our groups were equivalent in education and socioeconomic status by using Hebrew–English bilingual children of Israeli emigrants (who, unlike many bilingual groups, tend to be above average in parental education and SES); we also assessed the children's nonverbal IQ, their vocabulary development, and their general talkativeness. Finally, to assess whether differences are in semantic or pragmatic knowledge, we recorded the children's reasons for their answers on several name-manipulation tasks rather than simply the answer itself.

Method

SUBJECTS

The subjects of the study were 12 English monolingual and 12 Hebrew–English bilingual preschoolers of equivalent age, sex, nonverbal intelligence, and socio-economic status. The subjects ranged in age from 4;0 to 5;10; the monolingual group's average age was 4;9, and the bilingual group's average age was 5;1, $t(22)$ = 1.25, N.S. In each group, seven subjects were girls and five were boys.

Nonverbal intelligence was evaluated by two performance tests from the Wechsler Preschool and Primary Scale of Intelligence (Wechsler, 1963). The "Animal House" subtest, which requires the child to associate one of four colored pegs with each of four animal pictures, was chosen because it is a visual analog to the name-learning and usage tasks. The mean for the monolingual children on this subtest was 12.8; for the bilingual children, it was 13.1, $t(22)$ = 0.30, N.S. In addition, the Block Design subtest, which requires the child to arrange blocks so as to reproduce geometric patterns from models and pictures, was chosen because it is relatively language independent and, unlike Animal House, does not have a parallel in the interview procedure. The means for the monolingual and bilingual children were 14.0 and 14.4, respectively, $t(22)$ = 1.27, N.S.

All subjects were children of professionals or university affiliates and were enrolled in English-language child-care centers in the Boston area. All of the bilinguals were children of either Israeli Hebrew-speaking families who had moved to the United States but still spoke Hebrew in the home or (in two of the 12 cases) American English-speaking families who returned from an extended stay in Israel with their Israeli-born Hebrew-speaking child. One of these children spoke Hebrew at home; the other spoke English. Their data were comparable to those of other children in the bilingual group. The monolinguals were also all children of professionals; four of the 12 were known to be Jewish.

Bilingual subjects were selected according to three criteria. First, each of the bilingual subjects used both languages daily in different settings: Hebrew with family at home, and English with peers in the day-care center. We sought a reasonable balance between proficiency in the two languages, which we assessed by speaking with the child in both languages and interviewing the parents about the child's language history. Finally, if a child satisfied both these criteria, the Peabody Picture Vocabulary Test (PPVT) was administered in both its English standardized form and in a Hebrew nonstandardized translation. For the bilingual children, half the PPVT items were administered in one language, then the other half were administered in the other language; which half set was given in which language was counterbalanced across subjects. The first language tested was always the language in which the interview was conducted (see below). To tabulate the PPVT scores based on half the test questions, the basal and ceiling items were established as usual, but twice the number of correct responses between the two points were added to the basal score to compensate for the halved number of test items. We chose a 50-point difference between English and Hebrew PPVT scores as the maximum allowable disparity for inclusion in the bilingual group. Using these criteria, we selected 12 children from the 16 originally tested.

Monolinguals scored significantly higher than the bilinguals on the English PPVT—monolingual $\overline{X} = 116.5$, bilingual $\overline{X} = 89.1$, $t(22) = 4.75$, $p < 0.001$. The Hebrew scores cannot be compared directly with the English scores because the translated version is not standardized. Lower PPVT scores were expected for the bilinguals; their vocabulary development in each language tends to lag somewhat behind that of their monolingual counterparts until the middle school-age years, presumably because the bilingual child has exposure to fewer words or a reduced amount of exposure to any word in a given language than the monolingual has (see Ben Ze'ev, 1977; McLaughlin, 1978).

PROCEDURE

Each child was interviewed individually by the first author in a quiet room. All the monolingual children were tested in day-care centers; four of the bilinguals were tested in day-care centers, and eight in the child's home. Each session lasted approximately 40 minutes and was tape recorded. For the bilingual children, the choice of language in which the interview was to be conducted was left to the subject. All four bilinguals interviewed in the day-care center chose to speak English, and six of the eight children tested in their homes chose to speak Hebrew; therefore, it turned out that half of the bilinguals were tested in English, and half of them were tested in Hebrew.

After getting acquainted with the child, the experimenter administered the test of comprehension of counterfactuals, the test of volubility, and the name-manipulation test (which had five parts), followed by the WPPSI Animal House subtest, the PPVT, and the WPPSI Block Design subtest.

Counterfactual Test

The experimenter put on a blue-haired puppet and explained that "Mr. Blue" was from a "faraway country, where everyone has blue hair [turns puppet around to show its blue hair], walks on their hands [demonstrates], and rides tricycles to work." The experimenter then offered the puppet to the child, who then assumed the role of Mr. Blue. The experimenter prompted the child to have Mr. Blue repeat his story in the first person. At this point the experimenter ceased prompting and asked the child three questions: "Is your hair the color of the earth or of the sky?" (correct answer: sky); "When you go for a walk, do you put your shoes on the part of your body that has fingers or that has toes?" (correct answer: fingers); and "Do the grown-ups ride to work on something that has three wheels or that has four wheels?" (correct answer: three). The order of mention of the two alternatives in each question was counterbalanced across children. Note that the form of these questions is similar to the form of questions on the name-switching tasks: first the child is asked to accept some counterfactual; then he or she is asked to deduce some implication of the counterfactual.

Test of Volubility

Each child was first asked to name five common toys (boat, giraffe, horse, table, truck), then the experimenter asked two questions: "Which one do you like best?" and "Which two of these are most alike?" The number of content words in the child's response (nouns, adjectives, and main verbs other than *to be*, which has no present tense form in Hebrew) were recorded. Because these content words correspond one to one in English and Hebrew, this measure may be used to assess whether monolingual and bilingual children are equally voluble or shy in the experimental setting.

Name-Manipulation Test

The experimenter began the interview itself by addressing two hypothetical questions to the child—"Can you call this table a *shig?*" and "Can you call this boat a *cow?*"—and then asked the child to justify his or her responses.

The experimenter next administered three "renaming" tasks. First, the experimenter said "Let's call this table a *shig,*" referred to the object by that name in two requests ("Hand me the *shig*" and "Put the *shig* next to the truck"), and asked for a justification with the question, "Why can we now call the table a *shig?*"

Second, the child was taught a different name, but one already existing in the child's language, for another of the objects on the table (e.g., *cow* for boat), responded to requests as before, and, in addition, answered questions about the object's characteristics ("Does this 'cow' have legs or a smokestack?"; "Does it walk or does it sail?"; order of alternatives was counterbalanced). As before, the child was asked why the renaming was or was not possible.

Third, the child learned to call an object by the name of another object on the same table (e.g., *truck* for giraffe). As before, the child was asked to manipulate the object as referred to by its new name, was asked whether it had wheels or eyes and whether it drives or eats, and was asked why the renaming was or was not admissible. In addition, in this case the child was asked, "If that's a *truck,* what is this?" A larger but otherwise identical toy giraffe was shown, giving the children the opportunity to generalize from the name they had learned in the interview framework to another instance of the same object.

Results

COMPREHENSION OF COUNTERFACTUALS

All children tested answered the three questions correctly with ease, with the exception of the question, "Does he put his shoes on the part of his body that has fingers or that has toes?" Two bilingual and one monolingual subject (out of the 24) answered this question incorrectly. In view of the success of the other 21 children, and of these children with the other two items, it seems reasonable to conclude that our children, both mono- and bilingual, had little difficulty processing information introduced in counterfactual situations.

CONTROL FOR VOLUBILITY

There was no significant difference between the mean scores of the two groups in volubility. The mean number of content words for both questions for the monolinguals was 12.3, and for the bilinguals was 10.5, $t(22) = 1.11$, N.S.

On the basis of these two controls and the measures reported in the Subjects section, it can be concluded that any differences in the performance of the two groups on the name manipulations are unlikely to result from differences in the groups' socioeconomic status, ability to accept counterfactual situations, nonverbal intelligence, or volubility, but from the group's knowledge of a second language per se.

NAME-MANIPULATION TEST

The first two questions were hypothetical inquiries into whether calling an object by a nonsense name or by a different name was acceptable or unacceptable. The number of bilinguals and monolinguals who agreed and disagreed with the possibility of calling a table a *shig* was identical [7 out of 12, $\chi^2(1) = 0$]. Seven bilinguals and four monolinguals assented to calling a boat a *cow*, a nonsignificant difference, $\chi^2(1) = 1.51$, N.S. These results show that neither group was significantly more influenced than the other by so-called word magic.

There were also no differences between the monolingual and bilingual groups' performance on all three of the name-learning tasks. All 24 subjects successfully responded to commands to manipulate the objects when they were referred to by a nonsense name (*shig* for table), a different name (*cow* for boat), and a switched name (*truck* for giraffe, when a truck was also present). All children chose the correct property for an object over a property associated with the referent of its new name, except for one monolingual child and one bilingual child when asked about the object with the switched name. Only on the third task—the generalization from one instance of a newly learned switched name to another ("If this is a *truck* what is this?")—did some of the subjects have difficulty. Four of the monolinguals and three of the bilinguals treated the giraffe as a second instance of the learned name *truck*, but the remaining children did not make that generalization and called it a *giraffe*. None of these small differences between monolinguals and bilinguals was statistically significant.

Although all of the subjects performed similarly in their ability to give the correct answers in the name-manipulation tasks, the two groups differed significantly in their explanations for their performance when responding to the two questions "Why can/can't you call this X a 'Y'?" or the three questions "Why can/can't we now call this X a 'Y'?" following the name changes. The subjects' reasoning about the possibility of name manipulation was assessed in the following way. We excluded any putative explanation that simply mentioned the name of the object (e.g., "You can't call it a *shig* because it's a table") or that made no sense (e.g., "You can't call it a *shig* because it's nothing," or "It's not a *shig*, it's a pig, oink! oink!"). If a child could give an interpretable reason for his or her answer, it was then assigned to one of two subcategories that we found, post hoc, to account for most of the reasons: reasons based on objects' *attributes* ("because they're both green"/"because it doesn't have green on it," or "because it has four legs"), or reasons based on the experimental, situational, or personal *context* in which the name transfer was acceptable (e.g., "because it's in our game," or "because you told me and I know . . . I know what it is and you know what it is," or "because it's not true in life," or "because the kids [downstairs] wouldn't know . . . because we didn't tell them"). In addition, in the last task (calling an object by the name of another on the table), five of the children (four monolinguals and one bilingual) gave reasons based neither on the context nor attributes but on the ambiguity that would arise from having "two trucks." These responses were assigned to a third category and excluded from the analysis described below.

The Hebrew responses were all translated into English, and all the responses were typed on slips of paper, which were given to a naive rater, unlabeled as to source and in a random order. The rater then assigned them to "context" and "attribute" categories, agreeing in 95% of the cases with the first author's judgments. The second author, unaware of the group from which the child came, scored the responses on the remaining 5% of the answers.

Two findings emerged from this analysis. First, in all five tasks, bilinguals offered more reasons for their behavior than monolinguals. More interestingly, the monolingual and bilingual children differed in the types of reasons they gave: monolinguals referred to the attributes of the object more often than to the context of the naming exercise in all five questions, whereas bilinguals referred to the context more often than to the attributes in four of the five questions. This interaction can be tested in two ways. First, a child can be categorized as "context" if the majority of his or her reasons were based on reference to the context and "attribute" if the majority of reasons were based on the object's attributes. Nine of the 12 monolinguals based their reasons predominantly on the object's characteristics (categories were tied for two children), whereas 8 of the 12 bilinguals based their responses predominantly on the context, $\chi^2(1) = 5.04$, $p < 0.05$. Second, one can perform a t test on the mean scores of each group, where each subject was scored on the number of reasons based on context (out of five possible) minus the number of reasons based on attributes (also out of five) across the interview questions. Out of a possible score of $+5$ (all five answers were reasoned on the basis of context) to -5 (all five answers were reasoned on the basis of attributes), the monolingual mean score was -1.17, and the bilingual mean score was 1.17, $t(22) = 2.05$, one-tailed $p < 0.05$. This difference remains significant even when the scores are adjusted for age in an analysis of covariance, $t(21) = 1.88$, one-tailed $p < 0.05$.

Discussion

Our results show that middle-class preschoolers are not necessarily seduced by word magic, do not necessarily treat an object's name as inseparable from its attributes, and do not necessarily fail to realize that an object can be given a new arbitrary name. All 24 of our subjects were able to identify a familiar object when it was referred to by a new, nonsense name and by a name ordinarily used for a different object; 22 of the 24 were even able to understand a new name that referred to another object currently in view. These children were also able, in similar proportions, to answer questions about a renamed object's attributes without imbuing the object with the properties of the new name's conventional referent. Even in the hypothetical questions demanding more reflection on the part of a child ("Can you call this table a *shig/cow?*"), which children allegedly deny, about half of our subjects responded "yes" (58% and 46% for the nonsense name and the new name, respectively). And it is possible that the children who answered these questions in the negative may have done so not because of word magic, but for the reasons outlined in the introduction—that is, the question may have been construed as being about the object's true name in English. (In fact, the ideal adult response to the question would be something like "You could, I suppose, but that's not its name," and if one was speaking to a person learning English, even that response would be inappropriate. In an informal survey of six Stanford students and staff, we found that all six thought that the "correct" answer to the question is "no.")

We cannot be certain why our results differ from previous ones. It could be, as we proposed in the introduction, that our questions about hypothetical situations set the child to entertain questions and requests concerning counterfactuals; alternatively, our children could have been more precocious (they were all children of professionals), or our procedure more congenial to the child, than those used in the past.

Our second conclusion is that there is little evidence for a difference in awareness of the word–object relation between monolingual and bilingual children when confounding factors such as nonverbal intelligence, SES, volubility, and willingness to entertain counterfactuals are controlled. Our two groups were equally likely to assent to the possibility of calling an object by a new, nonsense name, were equally able to learn new nonsense, different, and switched names for an object, were equally able to identify an object's intrinsic properties despite a distracting name change, and were equally unlikely to generalize a new name to a similar object. Although there may be small quantitative differences between mono- and bilingual children that our measures, many of which were at ceiling, were incapable of detecting, there does not seem to be a dramatic difference in susceptibility to word magic, with monolingual children utterly incapable of considering alternatives to the conventional name for an object.

The third conclusion from this study is that there indeed does seem to be a difference between monolingual and bilingual children's awareness of the word–object relation, even if that difference is not that one group is aware of the nature of the relationship and the other group is not. Rather, it is that the two groups articulate different aspects of that relationship. Monolingual children are more likely to refer to the physical properties of an object when justifying or denying a new name for it (e.g., you can call the giraffe a *truck* because it has four legs and the hooves look like wheels, or you can't call a boat a *cow* because it doesn't have legs), whereas bilingual children were more likely to refer to the social context of naming or the shared knowledge that results (e.g., you can call it a *cow* "because it's in our game"). These responses are perfectly consistent with what the child must deduce about word meanings when he or she learns words. For a monolingual child, objects are given several names, which are distinguished by virtue of the properties of the objects in their extensions [e.g., *Sparky* may be used to refer only to the dog with a specific appearance, behavior, and domicile; *dog* may be used as a name for any creature within a far wider range of appearance and behavior, including attributes that Sparky may lack; *animal* may be used as a name for a class of creatures possessing a still wider class of attributes; and so on (see Anglin, 1977; Carey, 1978a; Clark, 1973; Macnamara, 1982)]. As a result, a monolingual child might come to the conclusion that any object can have a variety of names, each being appropriate to the object only when certain of its properties, the ones specified by the word's meaning, are to be emphasized. In fact, such "attribute" responses are not necessarily wrong or silly; the following hypothetical adult dialogues, for example, have a plausible ring to them: "Can you call garlic a *vegetable?*"/"Yes, because it is an edible plant/No, because it is too small and pungent to be eaten alone"; or "Can you call this computer an *engine?*"/"Yes, because it is mechanical and runs automatically/No, because it doesn't move."

Bilingual children clearly must share this experience with monolinguals; in fact, they provided similar numbers of answers referring to attributes as did the monolingual children (1.4 vs 1.7 reasons). However, the far greater number of reasons they offered referring to the naming context (2.5 vs 0.5 reasons) probably reflects their experience with a different set of contingencies about names. A bilingual child must learn that he or she can give a dog the name *dog* when addressing a certain person or type of person or when in a particular situation, but that that beast must be given the name *chien* when addressing other people or in a different setting. As a result, a bilingual child may realize that objects can have two different names by virtue either of various subsets of its attributes or by virtue of the various social contexts in which the object is named. The justifications the children gave for renaming an object in this study reflect just that knowledge.

30

Bonnie Litowitz
Learning to Make Definitions

Children must learn to define words in terms of other words. After the initial stages of language acquisition where the child verbally codes perceptual experience, often by asking "What's *that?*" (plus gesture), he must focus on language itself by asking "What's a *caterpillar?*" In both cases, the request and response are verbal; verbal information is being sought and given ("*That's* a caterpillar," plus gesture; "A *caterpillar* is an insect that turns into a butterfly"). In the first instance, the word *caterpillar* is a comment on the subject *that* whereas in the second case the word is subject, and the definition its comment (Bierwisch and Kiefer, 1970, p. 65). Bierwisch and Kiefer (1970) speak of the two functions of definitions: to paraphrase information already present (analytic/equivalence definitions, $x = y$) or to introduce new information (introductory/implicative definitions, $x \supset y$). However, in natural languages, this functional distinction is not formally expressed in language structure. The structures which serve these functions evolve throughout the development of the child. It is these evolving structures that are examined in this paper.

The obvious importance of these functions for determining what a child already knows and also for teaching a child new information can be seen by the fact that a definitional subsection is part of many standardized tests of intelligence [e.g., Weschler Preschool and Primary Scale of Intelligence (WWPSI), Weschler Intelligence Scale for Children–Revised (WISC-R), Binet]. These tests seek to establish the maturational age and intelligence quotient of the child, based in part on the child's ability to define words by means of other words. This paper is an attempt to describe the task of definition and offer an analysis of definitional

Abridged from "Learning to make definitions" by B. Litowitz, 1977, *Journal of Child Language*, 4, 289–304. Copyright 1977 by Cambridge University Press. Reprinted by permission of publisher and author.

responses by children aged 4;5–7;5 to definitional subsections of the WPPSI and WISC-R. . . .

As Vygotsky has pointed out (1962, pp. 52–53) there are three methods for studying concepts: (1) the method of definition, (2) the method of sorting by perceptual traits, and (3) the method of nonsense word. Vygotsky, as well as Werner and Kaplan (1950), preferred the third, but many researchers have preferred the second [e.g., Piaget's classificatory tasks, and the semantic feature analyses of Clark (1973b) and Andersen (1975)]. Few have used the first method (Luria and Vinogradova, 1959) outside of ethnoscience, a branch of linguistic anthropolgy, and especially not with children or within a developmental approach [see, however, Bever's suggested technique (1971, p. 271)].

The present paper represents this first method, which has the following drawbacks according to Vygotsky (although these drawbacks make it highly suitable for our needs). "It investigates the already formed concepts . . . the finished product of concept formation; it disregards sensory perceptual material, forcing the child into an uncharacteristic purely verbal plane; it divulges the relationship in the child's mind between previously formed families of words" (1962, pp. 52–53). It is precisely this verbal information on the organizational level of concept formation that is being sought and that is routinely tested in the definitional sections of standardized tests. In the past, however, perhaps because research on definitions, like word associations (with which they are often related), has been focused on the stimulus and response words alone, it is precisely this information that has been "thrown away" by researchers using methods (2) and (3) above (e.g., Andersen, 1975, pp. 96–97; Harris, 1975, pp. 148–149). . . .

Framework of Analysis*

DEFINITION: TASK DESCRIPTION

What is the definition of a definition? What are we asking when we say "What is (a) ——?" or "What does —— mean?"

First, we are asking for a verbal statement, that is, words in a certain ordered form. The minimal requirements of this outward form are that at least some of the words are not semantically empty and that the word on the left in the definition cannot appear on the right (the definiens must differ from the definiendum).

Second, we are asking for a verbal statement that passes information in a very particular sense. Amount of information is usually measured by novelty, i.e., improbability of occurrence. However, in defining, too great a novelty is not appropriate. Therefore we are asking for an abstraction from the individual experi-

---

*First part of this section is omitted. [Eds.]

encing of a lexical item in terms of (1) class inclusion or membership and (2) salient attributes or properties. As it happens, these are the . . . Taxonomic and Modification relations . . . that . . . organize meanings.

For example, a donkey is (T) an animal that (M) says "hee-haw." The first relation (T) is that of class inclusion/class membership and the second is that of the attributes/properties (M) that differentiate this member of the class from others (like a horse, a mule, etc.). These are of course the relations that constitute the exact form of an Aristotelian definition in terms of *genus-differentiae*.

Data: Analysis of Responses

What are the strategies that children use to answer the definitional questions on the WPPSI and WISC-R? The data are from 17 children, ages 4;5 to 7;5 (italicized words below are from tests; actual responses are to their right). The strategies these children use will be discussed, in the light of the above theoretical considerations, in terms of levels of "competency," i.e., their ability to match the proper definition of a definition—a verbal statement in Aristotelian form comprised of abstracted, social meanings.

LEVEL 1. A *nonverbal statement or a verbal statement that is semantically empty.* The most severe example of this level would be pure gesturing, such as the acting out of the stimulus word or pointing (ostensive definition). Ostensive definition is a kind of definitional form in that the pointing is a response to the request for a definition, although it is ambiguous inasmuch as pointing serves other functions, e.g., "I want that." Another form, more commonly found, is the language which accompanies gesture—pure deictic language:

snap   like this (+gesture)

This language cannot pass any information since it is composed exclusively of elements that operate on semantic entities and relations that are here given *without* those very semantic entities and relations. These responses are then completely semantically empty even though verbal.

LEVEL 2. *Word associations to the original stimulus word.* These responses generally show evidence that a semantic field has been activated but that no ordered form has been applied to that field. These responses, while verbal and not semantically empty, lack an ordered form. Unlike the earlier level, it is as though the respondent understands that a *verbal* statement with a certain outward form (i.e., minimally, the words on the right cannot be the same as the stimulus word and they cannot all be semantically empty) is called for but he has no idea how to proceed:

> *shoe* sock
> *bicycle* the man, a lady
> *hat* head*

One could easily "flesh out" these associations to form definitions by supplying the functors (connectives) needed, e.g., "A shoe is worn over a sock"; "The man or a lady own/ride a bicycle"; "Hat goes on the head." These fuller statements are purely speculative, however, for we could also say that "a shoe and a sock are both worn on the foot" or " . . . articles of clothing." Like all telegraphic speech where functors have been neglected, these statements are multiply ambiguous. It is not clear from the associations given as definitions what connection is intended. Most likely *no* connection is intended, since multiple ambiguity is communicationally very useful to the young child learning language.

LEVEL 3. *Concrete example of actual experience associated as a predicate to the stimulus word.* Here a more complete semantic listing is present and coded into words. The problem is that the experience is an idiosyncratic meaning, not a social meaning. The focus is on an original instance of the word and not on the shared semantic aspects of the word. One can compare this level of definitional ability to Vygotsky's level, in which the word is seen as an attribute of the experience. (This will later reverse for the child.)

> *knife* when you're cutting carrots
> *clock* when it rings it's time to wake and eat and get dressed and go to school

Some of these definitions show transitional phases between the second and third level in the form of *predicate linkings*: either the stimulus word is repeated with a predicate, or the stimulus word sets up an association that in turn becomes a stimulus to another response. Examples are

> *diamond* someone's ring—the mother's ring—blue or pink or red
> *clock* time—time to read
> *bicycle* ride with it—on the road

In some transitional phases, i.e., between second and third levels or between third and other levels, there is a listing of attributes. This listing can occur singly, e.g.,

> *knife* sharp
> *nail* on your finger

which is somewhere between associations and the concrete experience as attribute. Or the listing can occur like predicate linkings in which the attributes, which are often nothing more than kinds of possible predicates, are strung out

---

*Here and subsequently, some examples are omitted. [Eds.]

(e.g., *diamond*—blue, pink, red). Sometimes when experiences are still primary and words serve only as attributes, the experiences will be strung out as possible predicates:

> *bicycle* it's got wheels, a chain, handlebars
> *join* wants you to come to party or join a clubhouse

Occasionally, the attribute given will be an evaluative or affective marker of the original experience.

> *nuisance* when people are bad

Level 3, then, is characterized by a beginning awareness of what a definition requires in form but where the informational content is still idiosyncratic and experiential.

LEVEL 4. *Some awareness of a definitional form (a set predicate) and a beginning abstraction from the individual experience toward general social information.* The earliest set predicate used for definitions by children seems to be

> "you could ——."
> or
> "when you ——."

These may be omitted or only partially present in surface form:

> *knife* a knife is when you cut with it
> *letter* use for spelling

(or see transitional examples of Level 3 above).

Characteristic of this level is the attempt to modify the individual personal experience into a hypothetical situational form by using the general pronoun *you* (an anlage of *one*) and the conditional mode (*could*) or the indefinite temporal adverb (*when*) [cf. Brown (1973, p. 334) on the use of hypothetical statements in play]. These terms are all familiar to the child from his normal everyday language. They are enlisted to function as definitional forms because the child realizes that a set form is called for but does not yet know what it is.

Although we are accustomed to refer to a general developmental progression from concrete to abstract (Anglin, 1970, p. 98), Brown (1958, p. 286) reminds us that there is both abstraction before differentiation and abstraction after differentiation. In the case of definitions, earlier abstraction takes the form of common or shared predicates and hypothetical predicates (Anglin, 1970, p. 110), while later abstraction takes the form of more abstract categories and attributes (cf. Nelson, 1974). The mixed-level definitions, often marked by so-called hypothetical markers (e.g., *you*, *when*, *could*) show transitional stages in this progression from concrete to abstract as well as in the progression from individual/personal to socially shared.

An early approximation of the specialized definitional form is the classic functional definition of children. Children and some uneducated adults share a preference for functional definitions and completive (i.e., syntactic/contiguity) responses to word associations. (Adults favor paradigmatic/associative/similarity responses.) Here again we see the "adult" preference is for the Aristotelian notion of classes and categories (Ervin-Tripp, 1961; Anglin, 1970, pp. 13–28, 94–101) while children, on the other hand, as we have seen, prefer actual predicates (from experience) or probable/possible predicates (this hypothetical phase) in their definitions.

The form of the child's functional definition is

"an x is for y ing"

or

"an x is to y with"

(where y is a functional predicate of x).

The form of the adult Aristotelian definition is

"an x is *something* (class) that (*attribute*) or (*property*) (somewhere) (somehow). . ."

[If x is a verb, we can say: "x is a (*process*) that . . . "]

There is a mixed or transitional form of this fourth level and the fifth (that is the Aristotelian):

bicycle something you ride
shoe a thing you put on your foot

In this transitional phase the form appears to be

$$\text{"an } \underline{x} \text{ is } \begin{bmatrix} \text{(some)} \\ \text{(a)} \end{bmatrix} \text{ thing (that) } \begin{bmatrix} +\text{hypothetical definition} \\ +\text{functional definition} \end{bmatrix}\text{"}$$

letter a thing that you read
castle something a king lives in

LEVEL 5. *Pure Aristotelian definition.*

"an $\underline{x}$ is (a kind of) *class name* that *specific defining attribute or property* that exemplifies $\underline{y}$ "(y is a kind of x).

There are no examples in the data of full Level 5 definitions, but the following shows an approximation to this level.

donkey an animal
hero people save some people's lives—Superman and Spiderman

Discussion

The difficulty in attaining Level 5 for children seems to be the shallowness of their taxonomies. Between *knife, shoe, castle,* and *something* there is no elaboration. Thus "a knife is a kind of thing" is less informative than "knife is a kind of instrument/weapon/utensil" . . . "a castle is a home for a king." However, it seems that a child must learn the highest, nonspecific level of "something" before he can fill in the various taxonomies. This very general, all-purpose class of "things" is quickly nonproductive of information but is an early step in learning the formulation of definitions.

An example such as

fur   the very soft on an animal

illustrates the experience of "furriness" without the form to express it. One could say "fur is the very soft part or skin or hair on an animal." As taxonomies become fuller and more developed, other relations fill in as well, e.g., for animals, fur is synonymous to hair for people. This information presupposes two fields of elaborated taxonomies and interconnections between the two.

Similarly

knife   something you could cut with—a saw is like a knife

illustrates all the necessary information for a good definition lacking the elaborated taxonomies:

"Knife is an instrument used for cutting.

Among tools, a saw is $\begin{bmatrix} \text{a kind of} \\ \text{like a} \end{bmatrix}$ knife."

Earlier struggles with this form are seen in these examples:

castle   live in it. Mansions are sort of like castles.
chisel   sometimes make things tighter

That is, "a chisel is a kind of tool." In response to the question, "Who lives in a castle?," one child said

King Kong, kings and queens.

That is, "King Kong is a kind of king."

Incomplete taxonomies or improper form result in various similarities to schizophrenic speech [cf. syllogistic thinking in Werner et al. (1975), syllogistic reasoning in Riegel (1970), metaphorical thinking in Rubenstein (1972), palaeological thinking in Arieti (1955)], e.g.

tools sometimes make things tighter
chisels are tools
∴ chisels sometimes make things tighter

kings live in castles
King Kong is a king
∴ King Kong lives in a castle

However, there is a difference between complete semantic listings in which movement through these listings is faulty [as in the so-called thought disorders, but also including dream formation (Litowitz, 1975)] and the incomplete or shallow semantic listings. The former is a communicational disorder [see Bateson (1972), on schizophrenia as a discourse disorder] whereas the latter is a semantic deficiency. Furthermore, it would seem to follow from this view that different methods of teaching would be indicated depending upon the depth of taxonomies existing for the child being tested. As Premack (1970, p. 118) has stated: "Teaching a concept and mapping one that already exists are different enterprises." In the first case, semantic listings have been formed but the general communication strategies of (in this case) giving definitions have not been learned. These strategies are superimposed on the semantic information for the explicit purpose of passing a definite kind of informational content in a definitive form (Norman, 1973). For those children who have sufficiently deep taxonomies, one could teach the progressively more adult/mature forms of defining. Also one might want to investigate levels of other communicational abilities, e.g., play, storytelling capacities, role-taking, etc. In the second case, in which taxonomies are not developed, one would want to develop a semantic ability by helping these children code experience into the verbal mode. Consequently, investigational preference would focus on performance (action) levels and on examining any difficulties in translating from action experiences into verbal meanings. . . .*

CONCLUSION

Standardized tests that utilize vocabulary subsections measure breadth of vocabulary. The scores reflect maturational levels. Although these subsections are part of intelligence tests (e.g., WPPSI, WISC-R, Binet), Wolman and Barker (1965) have found that the ability to define by essence (vs by use) is not correlated with intelligence or sex, but rather with age and number of words known. They also found that the transition from functional to synonymic definitions is gradual and slow, not occurring all at once due to a major restructuring (cf. Piaget's formal operational stage). Even adults who can define in the mature form utilize the functional definitional form in situations in which either the Aristotelian form is not demanded, due to their understanding of the communicational situation (e.g., in a conversation with a friend, not as a definitional task on a test), or where the Aristotelian form is not possible, due to insufficient depth (e.g., new concepts, unfamiliar terms, unknown objects). Masters, Mesibov & Anderson (1970)

*Section on research possibilities is omitted. [Eds.]

have shown that speakers have to learn when to give paradigmatic or syntagmatic responses to word associations. Even adults who normally favor paradigmatic responses will produce syntagmatic responses under instructions to be as original as possible. The authors conclude that either associative hierarchies contain syntagmatic responses (= functional definitions) superseded by paradigmatic responses (= equivalent or synonymic definitions) or that speakers learn "response-type criteria" (p. 210). The two conclusions are not mutually exclusive. Our data show the earliest definitions to be functional (really prefunctional) and syntagmatic (i.e., actual or possible predicates), and they show also that a particular response-type, namely how to define words by means of other words, must be learned.

These findings are compatible with the ideas presented in this paper, that language experience (the ability and facility, through language experience, to code perceptual information into the verbal mode) will be reflected in the definitional form. Also reflected is the structural depth of this information in semantic memory and the ability to respond to the definitional task by restating the retrieved verbally coded information in a task-appropriate form.

Bibliography

Anderson, E. (1975). Cups and glasses: learning that boundaries are vague. *Journal of Child Language*, **2**, 79–103.

Anglin, J. (1970). *The growth of word meaning*. Cambridge, MA: M.I.T. Press.

Anglin, J.M. (1977). *Word, object, and conceptual development*. New York: Norton.

Antinucci, S., and Volterra, V. (1979). Negation in child language: A pragmatic study. In E. Ochs and B.B. Schieffelin (Eds.), *Developmental pragmatics*. New York: Academic Press.

Arieti, S. (1955). *Interpretation of schizophrenia*. New York: Brunner.

Aristotle (1951). Poetics. In S. Butcher (Ed.), *Aristotle's theory of poetry and fine art*. New York: Dover.

Aronoff, M. (1976). Word formation in generative grammar. In *Linguistic inquiry*, Monograph Supplement No. 1. Cambridge, MA: M.I.T. Press.

Asch, S., and Nerlove, H. (1960). The development of double function terms in children: An exploratory study. In B. Kaplan and S. Wapner (Eds.), *Perspectives in psychological theory*. New York: International Universities Press.

Asher, S.R. (1979). Referential communication. In G.J. Whitehurst and P.J. Zimmerman (Eds.), *The functions of language and cognition*. New York: Academic Press.

Austin, J.L. (1962). *How to do things with words*. Oxford: Clarendon Press.

Barrett, M. (1982). Distinguishing between prototypes: The early acquisition of the meaning of object names. In S. Kuczaj (Ed.), *Language Development*, Vol. 1. Hillsdale, NJ: Erlbaum.

Bates, E. (1976a). *Language and context: The acquisition of pragmatics*. New York: Academic Press.

Bates, E. (1976b). Pragmatics and sociolinguistics in child language. In D.M. Morehead and A.E. Morehead (Eds.), *Language deficiency in children*. Baltimore: University Park Press.

Bates, E., and MacWhinney, B. (1982). Functionalist approaches to grammar. In E. Wanner and L.R. Gleitman (Eds.), *Language acquisition: State of the art*. Cambridge, MA: Cambridge University Press.

Bates, E., Benigni, L., Bretherton, I., Camaioni, L., and Volterra, V. (1977). From gesture to first word: On cognitive and social prerequisites. In M. Lewis and L. Rosenblum (Eds.), *Origins of behavior: Communication and language.* New York: Wiley.

Bates, E., Benigni, L., Bretherton, I., Camaioni, L., and Volterra, V. (1979). *The emergence of symbols.* New York: Academic Press.

Bateson, G. (1972). *Steps to an ecology of mind.* New York: Ballantine.

Beal, C.R., and Flavell, J.H. (1982). Effect of increasing the salience of message ambiguities on kindergartners' evaluations of communicative success and message adequacy. *Developmental Psychology, 18,* 43–48.

Bellugi, U. (1967). The acquisition of negation. Unpublished doctoral dissertation. Cambridge, MA: Harvard University.

Bellugi, U., and Brown, R. (Eds.) (1964). The acquisition of language. *Monographs of the Society for Research in Child Development, 29* (Serial No. 92).

Benedict, H. (1979). Early lexical development: Comprehension and production. *Journal of Child Language, 6,* 183–200.

Ben Ze'ev, S. (1977). The influence of bilingualism on cognitive strategy and cognitive development. *Child Development, 48,* 1009–1018.

Berko, J. (1958). The child's learning of English morphology. *Word, 14,* 150–177.

Bernstein, B. (1970). A critique of the concept "compensatory education." In S. Williams (Ed.), *Language and poverty: Perspectives on a theme.* Madison, WI: University of Wisconsin Press.

Bever, T.G. (1970). The cognitive basis for linguistic structures. In J. Hayes (Ed.), *Cognition and the development of language.* New York: Wiley.

Bever, T.G. (1971). The word and its referent: General discussion. In R. Huxley and E. Ingram (Eds.), *Language acquisition: Models and methods.* New York: Ballantine.

Bever, T.G. (1982). Some implications of the nonspecific bases of language. In E. Wanner and L.R. Gleitman (Eds.), *Language acquisition: State of the art.* Cambridge, MA: Cambridge University Press.

Bierwisch, M., and Kiefer, F. (1970). Remarks on definitions in natural language. In F. Kiefer (Ed.), *Studies in syntax and semantics.* Dordrecht: Reidel.

Billow, R. (1975). A cognitive developmental study of metaphor comprehension. *Developmental Psychology, 11,* 415–423.

Billow, R. (1977). Metaphor: A review of the psychological literature. *Psychological Bulletin, 84,* 81–92.

Billow, R. (1978). Review of H. Pollio, J. Barlow, H. Fine, and M. Pollio. *Psychology and the poetics of growth. Bulletin of the Menninger Clinic, 42,* 454–456.

Billow, R. (1981). Observing spontaneous metaphor in children. *Journal of Experimental Child Psychology, 31,* 430–445.

Black, M. (1962). *Models and metaphors.* Ithaca, NY: Cornell University Press.

Bloom, L. (1970). *Language development: Form and function in emerging grammars.* Cambridge, MA: M.I.T. Press.

Bloom, L. (1973). *One word at a time: The use of single word utterances before syntax.* The Hague: Mouton.

Bloom, L. (1978). The semantics of verbs in child language. Invited address, E.P.A.

Bloom, L., and Lahey, M. (1978). *Language development and language disorders.* New York: Wiley.

Bloom, L., Hafitz, J., Tackeff, J., and Gartner, B. (n.d.). Complex sentences: Complementation in child language.

Bloom, L., Lifter, K., and Hafitz, J. (1980). Semantics of verbs and the development of verb inflection in child language. *Language*, **56**, 386–412.

Bloom, L., Lightbown, P., and Hood, L. (1975). Structure and variation in child language. *Monographs of the Society for Research in Child Development*, **40** (Serial No. 160).

Bloom, L., Rocissano, L., and Hood, L. (1976). Adult-child discourse: Developmental interactions between information processing and linguistic knowledge. *Cognitive Psychology*, **8**, 521–552.

Bolinger, D.L. (1977). *Meaning and form*. London: Longmans' Linguistics Library.

Borke, H. (1971). Interpersonal perception of young children: Egocentrism or empathy? *Developmental Psychology*, **5**, 263–269.

Bowerman, M. (1970). Learning to talk: A cross-linguistic study of early syntactic development with special reference to Finnish. Unpublished doctoral dissertation. Cambridge, MA: Harvard University.

Bowerman, M. (1974). Learning the structure of causative verbs: A study in the relationship of cognitive, semantic and syntactic development. *Papers & Reports in Child Language Development*, **8**, 142–178.

Bowerman, M. (1976). Semantic factors in the acquisition of rules for word use and sentence construction. In D. Morehead and A. Morehead (Eds.), *Directions in normal and deficient child language*. Baltimore, MD: University Park Press.

Bowerman, M. (1977). The acquisition of rules governing "possible lexical items": Evidence from spontaneous speech errors. *Papers & Reports in Child Language Development*, **13**, 148–158.

Bowerman, M. (1982). Reorganizational processes in lexical and syntactic development. In L. Gleitman and E. Wanner (Eds.), *Language acquisition: The state of the art*. London and New York: Cambridge University Press.

Bowerman, M. (1982). Evaluating competing linguistic models with language acquisition data: Implications of developmental errors with causative verbs. *Quad Semantica*, **3**, 5–66.

Braine, M.D.S. (1963). The ontogeny of English phrase structure: The first phase. *Language*, **39**, 1–14.

Braine, M.D.S. (1976). Children's first word combinations. *Monographs of the Society for Research in Child Development*, **41** (Serial No. 164).

Brainerd, C. (1978). The stage question in cognitive-developmental theory. *The Behavioral and Brain Sciences*, **2**, 173–213.

Bretherton, I., and Beeghley, M. (1982). Talking about internal states. The acquisition of an explicit theory of mind. *Developmental Psychology*, **18**, 906–921.

Brodzinsky, D.M. (1975). The role of conceptual tempo and stimulus characteristics in children's humor development. *Developmental Psychology*, **11**, 843–850.

Brown, A.L. (1980). Metacognitive development and reading. In R.J. Spiro, B.C. Bruce, and W.F. Brewer (Eds.), *Theoretical issues in reading comprehension*. Hilldale, NJ: Erlbaum.

Brown, R. (1957). Linguistic determinism and the part of speech. *The Journal of Abnormal and Social Psychology*, **55**, 1–5.

Brown, R. (1958). *Words and things*. New York: The Free Press.

Brown, R. (1973). *A first language: The early stages*. Cambridge, MA: Harvard University Press.

Brown, R., and Bellugi, U. (1964). Three processes in the acquisition of syntax. *Harvard Educational Review*, **34**, 133–151.

Brown, R., and Fraser, C. (1963). The acquisition of syntax. In C. Cofer and B. Musgrave (Eds.), *Verbal learning and verbal behavior*. New York: McGraw-Hill.

Brown, R., and Hanlon, C. (1970). Derivational complexity and order of acquisition in child speech. In J. Hayes (Ed.), *Cognition and the development of language*. New York: Wiley.

Brown, R., Cazden, C., and Bellugi, U. (1969). The child's grammar from I to III. In J.P. Hill (Ed.), *Minnesota symposium on child psychology*, Vol. 2. Minneapolis: University of Minnesota Press.

Bruner, J.S. (1972). Nature and uses of immaturity. *American Psychologist*, **27**, 687–708.

Bruner, J.S. (1973). The organization of early skilled action. *Child Development*, **44**, 1–11.

Bruner, J.S. (1975a). From communication to language: A psychological perspective. *Cognition*, **3**, 255–287.

Bruner, J.S. (1975b). The ontogenesis of speech acts. *Journal of Child Language*, **2**, 1–19.

Bruner, J.S. (1983). *Child's talk: Learning to use language*. New York: Norton.

Bruner, J.S., Caudill, E., and Ninio, A. (1977). Language and experience. In R.S. Peters (Ed.) *John Dewey reconsidered*. London: Routledge & Kegan Paul.

Bühler, K. (1934). *Sprachtheorie*. Jena: Fischer.

Bullowa, M. (Ed.) (1977). *Before speech*. Cambridge: Cambridge University Press.

Carey, S. (1978a). The child as word learner. In M. Halle, J. Bresnan, and G. Miller (Eds.), *Linguistic theory and psychological reality*. Cambridge, MA: M.I.T. Press.

Carey, S. (1978b). Less may never mean "more." In R.N. Campbell and P.T. Smith (Eds.), *Recent advances in the psychology of language*, Vol. 4A. New York: Plenum.

Carey, S. (1985). Are children fundamentally different kinds of thinkers and learners than adults? In S. Chipman, J. Segal, and R. Glaser (Eds.), *Thinking and learning skills*, Vol. 2. Hillsdale, NJ: Erlbaum.

Carey, S., and Bartlett, E. (1978). Acquiring a single new word. *Papers & Reports in Child Language Development*, **15**, 17–29.

Carlson, P., and Anisfeld, M. (1969). Some observations on the linguistic competence of a two-year-old child. *Child Development*, **40**, 565–575.

Carter, A. (1975). The transformation of sensorimotor morphemes into words: A case study of the development of "more" and "mine." *Journal of Child Language*, **2**, 233–250.

Carter, A. (1979). The disappearance schema. In E. Ochs and B.B. Schieffelin (Eds.), *Developmental pragmatics*. New York: Academic Press.

Cassirer, E. (1946). *Language and myth*. Berkeley: University of California Press.

Cazden, C.B. (1965). Environmental assistance to the child's acquisition of grammar. Unpublished doctoral dissertation. Cambridge, MA: Harvard University.

Chafe, W. (1970). *Meaning and the structure of language*. Chicago: University of Chicago Press.

Chomsky, C. (1969). *The acquisition of syntax in children from 5 to 10*. Cambridge, MA: M.I.T. Press.

Chomsky, N. (1957). *Syntactic structures*. The Hague: Mouton.

Chomsky, N. (1959). Review of B.F. Skinner's "Verbal Behavior." *Language*, 35, 26–58.

Chomsky, N. (1964). Formal discussion of Wick Miller and Susan Ervin. The development of grammar in child language. In U. Bellugi and R. Brown (Eds.), The acquisition of language. *Monographs of the Society for Research in Child Development*, **29** (Serial No. 92), 35–40.

Chomsky, N. (1965). *Aspects of the theory of syntax*. Cambridge, MA: M.I.T. Press.

Chomsky, N. (1975). *Reflections on language*. New York: Random House.

Chomsky, N. (1981). *Lectures on government and binding*. Dordrecht: Foris.

Chukovsky, K. (1968). *From two to five*. Berkeley: University of California Press.

Church, J. (1966). *Three babies: Biographies of cognitive development*. New York: Random House.

Clark, E.V. (1970). How young children describe events in time. In G.B. Flores d'Arcais and W.J.M. Levelt (Eds.), *Advances in psycholinguistics*. New York: American Elsevier.

Clark, E.V. (1973a). How children describe time and order. In C.A. Ferguson and D.I. Slobin (Eds.), *Studies of child language development*. New York: Holt, Rinehart & Winston.

Clark, E.V. (1973b). What's in a word? On the child's acquisition of semantics in his first language. In T.E. Moore (Ed.), *Cognitive development and the acquisition of language*. New York: Academic Press.

Clark, E.V. (1978). Discovering what words can do. *Papers from the parasession of the lexicon*, 34–57. Chicago: Chicago Linguistic Society.

Clark, E.V. (1982). The young word-maker: A case study of innovation in the child's lexicon. In E. Wanner and L.R. Gleitman (Eds.), *Language acquisition: The state of the art*. New York: Cambridge University Press.

Clark, E.V. (1983). Meanings and concepts. In J.H. Flavell and E.M. Markman (Eds.), *Cognitive development*, Vol. 3 of P.H. Mussen (General Ed.), *Handbook of child psychology*. New York: Wiley.

Clark, E.V., and Clark H.H. (1979). When nouns surface as verbs. *Language*, 55, 767–811.

Clark, E.V., and Hecht, B.F. (1982). Learning to coin agent and instrument nouns. *Cognition*, 12, 1–24.

Colby, B.N. (1973). A partial grammar of Eskimo folktales. *American Anthropologist*, **75**, 645–662.

Cole, M., and Scribner, S. (1974). *Culture & thought: A psychological introduction*. New York: Wiley.

Cometa, M.S., and Eson, M.E. (1978). Logical operations and metaphor interpretations: A Piagetian model. *Child Development*, **49**, 649–659.

Conrad, R. (1971). The chronology of the development of covert speech in children. *Developmental Psychology*, 5, 398–405.

Corrigan, R. (1978). Language development as related to stage 6 object permanence development. *Journal of Child Language*, 5, 173–189.

Coulthard, M. (1977). *An introduction to discourse analysis*. London: Longman Group Unlimited.

Cromer, R. (1974). The development of language and cognition: The cognition hypothesis. In B. Foss (Ed.), *New perspectives in child development*. Harmondsworth: Penguin.

Cromer, R.F. (1976). Developmental strategies for language. In V. Hamilton and M.D. Vernon (Eds.), *The development of cognitive processes*. London and New York: Academic Press.

Cross, T.G. (1977). Mother's speech adjustments: The contribution of selected child listener variables. In C.E. Snow and C. Ferguson (Eds.), *Talking to children*. Cambridge, MA: Cambridge University Press.

Cummins, J. (1978). Bilingualism and the development of metalinguistic awareness. *Journal of Cross-Cultural Psychology*, **9**, 131–149.

Darley, F.L., and Winitz, H. (1961). Age of first word: review of research. *Journal of Speech and Speech Disorders*, **26**, 272–290.

Denney, N. (1974). Evidence for developmental changes in categorization criteria for children and adults. *Human Development*, **17**, 41–53.

Denney, N., and Ziobrowski, M. (1972). Developmental changes in clustering criteria. *Journal of Experimental Child Psychology*, **13**, 275–282.

De Villiers, P.A., and De Villiers, J.G. (1972). Early judgments of semantic and syntactic acceptability by children. *Journal of Psycholinguistic Research*, **1**, 299–310.

De Villiers, J.G., and De Villiers, P.A. (1973a). A cross-sectional study of the development of grammatical morphemes in child speech. *Journal of Psycholinguistic Research*, **2**, 267–278.

De Villiers, J.G., and De Villiers, P.A. (1973b). Development of the use of order in comprehension. *Journal of Psycholinguistic Research*, **2**, 331–341.

Dockrell, J.E. (1979). Acquiring new words in two contexts. Unpublished paper. Stirling, U.K.: University of Stirling.

Donaldson, M., and Wales, R.J. (1970). On the acquisition of some relational terms. In J.R. Hayes (Ed.), *Cognition and the development of language*. New York: Wiley.

Dore, J. (1973). The development of speech acts. Unpublished doctoral dissertation. New York: City University of New York.

Dore, J. (1974). A pragmatic description of early language development. *Journal of Psycholinguistic Research*, **4**, 423–430.

Dore, J. (1975). Holophrases, speech acts and language universals. *Journal of Child Language*, **2**, 21–39.

Dore, J. (1976). Children's illocutionary acts. In R. Freedle (Ed.), *Comprehension and production*. Hillsdale, NJ: Erlbaum.

Dore, J. (1978). Concepts, communicative acts and the LAD. Paper presented at the Boston Child Language Meetings, Boston MA, September 29–30.

Dore, J. (1985). Holophrases revisited: their 'logical' development from dialog. In M.D. Barrett (Ed.), *Children's single-word speech*. New York: Wiley.

Downing, P. (1977). On the creation and use of English compound nouns. *Language*, **53**, 810–842.

Elkind, D. (1969). Piagetian and psychometric conceptions of intelligence. *Harvard Educational Review*, **39**, 319–337.

Elkind, D. (1970). *Children and adolescents: Interpretive essays on Jean Piaget*. New York: Oxford University Press.

Entwistle, D., Forsyth, D., and Muuss, R. (1964). The syntactic-paradigmatic shift in children's word association. *Journal of Verbal Learning and Verbal Behavior*, **3**, 19–29.

Ervin-Tripp, S. (1961). Changes with age in the verbal determinants of word-association. In A.S. Dil (Ed.), *Language acquisition and communicative choice*. Stanford: Stanford University Press.

Ervin-Tripp, S. (1970). Discourse agreement: How children answer questions. In J.R. Hayes (Ed.), *Cognition and the development of language*. New York: Wiley.

Ervin, S., and Foster, G. (1960). The development of meaning in children's descriptive terms. *Journal of Abnormal and Social Psychology*, **61**, 271–275.

Escalona, S. (1973). Basic modes of social interaction: Their emergence and patterning during the first two years of life. *Merrill Palmer Quarterly*, **19**, 205–232.

Fantini, A.E. (1976). *Language acquisition of a bilingual child*. Brattleboro, VT: The Experiment Press.

Feldman, C., and Shen, M. (1971). Some language-related cognitive advantages of bilingual five-year-olds. *Journal of Genetic Psychology*, **118**, 235–244.

Feldman, H., Goldin-Meadow, S., and Gleitman, L.R. (1978). Beyond Herodotus: The creation of language by linguistically deprived deaf children. In A. Lock (Ed.), *Action, gesture, and symbol: The emergence of language*. London: Academic Press.

Ferguson, C.A. (1964). Baby talk in six languages. *American Anthropologist*, **66**, 103–114.

Ferguson, C.A. (1977). Baby talk as a simplified register. In C. Snow and C. Ferguson (Eds.), *Talking to children: Language input and acquisition*. Cambridge, MA: Cambridge University Press.

Ferguson, C.A., and Farwell, C.B. (1975). Words and sounds in early language acquisition. *Language*, **51**, 419–439.

Ferguson, G. (1966). *Statistical analysis in psychology and education*, 2nd ed. New York: McGraw-Hill.

Ferguson, L.R. (1971). Origins of social development in infancy. *Merrill-Palmer Quarterly*, **17**, 119–139.

Fernald, A. (1984). The perceptual and affective salience of mothers' speech to infants. In L. Geagans, C. Garvey, and R. Golinkoff (Eds.), *The origins and growth of communication*. Norwood, NJ: Ablex.

Fernandez, J. (1972). Persuasions and performances: Of the beast in everybody and the metaphors in everyman. *Daedalus*, **101**, 39–60.

Ferreiro, E., and Sinclair, H. (1971). Temporal relationships in language. *Journal of Psycholinguistic Research*, **6**, 39–47.

Fillmore, C.J. (1968). The case for case. In E. Bach and R.T. Harms (Eds.), *Universals in linguistic theory*. New York: Holt, Rinehart & Winston.

Fillmore, C.J. (1977). The case for case reopened. In P. Cole and J.M. Saddock (Eds.), *Syntax and semantics*, Vol. 8. New York: Academic Press.

Fillmore, C.J. (1978). On the organization of semantic information in the lexicon. In D. Farkas, W.M. Jacobsen, and K.W. Todrys (Eds.), *Papers from the parasession on the lexicon*. Chicago Linguistic Society. Chicago: University of Chicago Press.

Fine, J. (1977). Text in context: Systematic grammar and conversational analysis in the study of children's dialogues. Unpublished doctoral disseration. Ithaca, NY: Cornell University.

Five to nine: Aspects of function and structure in the spoken language of elementary school children. (1972). Final report to the Ministry of Education. Ontario, Toronto: York University: Board of Education for the Borough of North York.

Flavell, J.H. (1981). Cognitive monitoring. In W.P. Dickson (Ed.), *Children's oral communication skills.* New York: Academic Press.

Flavell, J.H., Botkin, P.T., Fry, C.L., Wright, J.W., and Jarvis, P.E. (1968). *The development of role-taking and communication skills in children.* New York: Wiley.

Flavell, J.H., Speer, J.R., Green, F.L., and August, D.L. (1981). The development of comprehension monitoring and knowledge about communication. *Monographs of the Society for Research in Child Development,* **46** (Serial No. 192).

Fowler, A. (1981). Language learning in Downs Syndrome children. Unpublished manuscript. Philadelphia, PA: University of Pennsylvania.

Fowles, L., and Glanz, M.E. (1977). Competence and talent in verbal riddle comprehension. *Journal of Child Language,* **4,** 433–452.

Fraser, C., Bellugi, U., and Brown, R. (1963). Control of grammar in imitation, comprehension, and production. *Journal of Verbal Learning and Verbal Behavior,* **2,** 121–135.

Friedlander, B. (1968). The effect of speaker identity, voice inflection, vocabulary, and message redundancy on infants' selection of vocal reinforcement. *Journal of Experimental Child Psychology,* **6,** 443–459.

Fromkin, V. (Ed.) (1973). *Speech errors as linguistic evidence.* The Hague: Mouton.

Furrow, D., Nelson, K., and Benedict, H. (1979). Mothers' speech to children and syntactic development: Some simple relationships. *Journal of Child Language,* **6,** 423–442.

Fuson, K. (1979). The development of self-regulating aspects of speech: A review. In G. Zivin (Ed.), *The development of self-regulation through speech.* New York: Wiley.

Gardner, H. (1973). *The arts and human development.* New York: Wiley.

Gardner, H. (1974). Metaphors and modalities: How children project polar adjectives onto diverse domains. *Child Development,* **45,** 84–91.

Gardner, H., Kircher, M., Winner, E., and Perkins, D. (1975). Children's metaphoric productions and preferences. *Journal of Child Language,* **2,** 125–141.

Gardner, H., Winner, E., Bechhofer, R., and Wolf, D. (1978). The development of figurative language. In K. Nelson (Ed.), *Children's language.* New York: Gardner.

Garnica, O. (1977). Some characteristics of prosodic input to young children. In C. Snow and C. Ferguson (Eds.), *Talking to children: Language input and acquisition.* Cambridge, MA: Cambridge University Press.

Garvey, C. (1974). Interaction structures in social play. Paper presented at the New Orleans Symposium on Current Research in Children's Play. (Not published.)

Garvey, C. (1975). Requests and responses in children's speech. *Journal of Child Language,* **2,** 41–63.

Garvey, C. (1979). Contingent queries and their relations in discourse. In E. Ochs and B. Schieffelin (Eds.), *Development pragmatics.* New York: Academic Press.

Gelman, R. (1978). Cognitive development. *Annual Review of Psychology,* **29,** 297–332.

Gelman, R., and Baillargeon, R. (1983). A review of some Piagetian concepts. In J.H. Flavell and E.M. Markman (Eds.), *Cognitive development,* Vol. 3 of P.H. Mussen (General Ed.), *Handbook of child psychology.* New York: Wiley.

Gentner, D. (1977). Children's performance on a spatial analogies task. *Child Development*, **48**, 1034–1039.

Gentner, D. (1978). Testing the psychological reality of a representational model. In D.L. Waltz (Ed.), *Theoretical issues in natural language processing*, Vol. 2. New York: Association of Computing Machinery.

Gentner, D. (1982). Why nouns are learned before verbs: Linguistic relativity vs. natural partitioning. In S. Kuczaj (Ed.), *Language development: Language culture and cognition*. Hillsdale, NJ: Erlbaum.

Gleason, J.B. (1973). Code switching in children's language. In T.E. Moore (Ed.), *Cognitive development and the acquisition of language*. New York: Academic Press.

Gibson, E.J., and Spelke, E.S. (1983). The development of perception. In J.H. Flavell and E.M. Markman (Eds.), *Cognitive development*, Vol. 3 of P.H. Mussen (General Ed.), *Handbook of child psychology*. New York: Wiley.

Gleitman, L.R. (1965). Coordinating conjunctions in English. *Language*, **41**, 260–294.

Gleitman, L.R., and Gleitman, H. (1970). *Phrase and paraphrase*. New York: Norton.

Gleitman, L.R., and Wanner, E. (1982). Language acquisition: The state of the state of the art. In E. Wanner and L.R. Gleitman (Eds.), *Language acquisition: The state of the art*. New York: Cambridge University Press.

Gleitman, L.R., and Wanner, E. (1984a). Current issues in language learning. In M. Bornstein and M.E. Lamb (Eds.) *Developmental psychology*. Hillsdale, NJ: Erlbaum.

Gleitman, L.R., and Wanner, E. (1984b). Richly specific input to language learning. In O. Selfridge, E.L. Rissland, and M. Arbib (Eds.), *Adaptive control of ill-defined systems*. NY: Plenum.

Gleitman, L.R., Gleitman, H., and Shipley, E. (1972). The emergence of the child as grammarian. *Cognition*, **1**, 137–163.

Gleitman, L.R., Newport, E.L., and Gleitman, H. (1984). The current status of the motherese hypothesis. *Journal of Child Language*, **11**, 43–79.

Glucksberg, S., Krauss, R.M., and Higgins, E.T. (1975). The development of referential communication skills. In F.D. Horowitz (Ed.), *Review of child development research*, Vol. 4. Chicago: University of Chicago Press.

Goffman, E. (1963). *Behavior in public places*. New York: Free Press.

Gold, E.M. (1967). Language identification in the limit. *Information and Control*, **10**, 447–474.

Goldstein, K. (1927). Ueber Aphasie. *Abh. aus der Schw. Arch. f. Neurol. u. Psychiat.* Heft 6.

Goldstein, K. (1932). Die pathologischen Tatsachen und ihrer Bedeutung fuer das Problem der Sprache. *Kongr. D. Ges. Psychol.*, **12**.

Goodman, N. (1968). *Languages of art*. Indianapolis: Bobbs-Merrill.

Goodman, S. (1981). The integration of verbal and motor behavior in preschool children. *Child Development*, **52**, 280–289.

Gopnik, A. (1981). The development of non-nominal expressions in 12–42 month olds. In P. Dale and D. Ingram (Eds.), *Child language: An international perspective*. Baltimore, MD: University Park Press.

Gopnik, A. (1982). Words and plans: Early language and the development of intelligent action. *Journal of Child Language*, **9**, 617–633.

Gopnik, A. (1984). The acquisition of *gone* and the development of the object concept. *Journal of Child Language*, 11, 273–292.

Gopnik, A., and Meltzoff, A.N. (1984). Semantic and cognitive development in 15 to 21-month-old children. *Journal of Child Language*, 11, 495–515.

Greenfield, P.M., and Smith, J.H. (1976). *The structure of communication in early language development*. New York: Academic Press.

Gregory, M. (1967). Aspects of varieties differentiation. *Journal of Linguistics*, 3, 177–198.

Grice, H.P. (1975). Logic and conversation. In P. Cole and J.L. Morgan (Eds.), *Syntax and semantics*, Vol. 3. New York: Academic Press.

Grieve, R., and Hoogenraad, R. (1979). First words. In P. Fletcher and M. Garman (Eds.), *Language acquisition*. Cambridge, England: Cambridge University Press.

Halliday, M.A.K. (1970). Language structure and language function. In J. Lyons, (Ed.), *New horizons in linguistics*. Hammondworth, England: Penguin.

Halliday, M.A.K. (1973). *Exploration in the functions of language*. London: Edward Arnold.

Halliday, M.A.K. (1975). *Learning how to mean: Explorations in the development of language*. London: Edward Arnold.

Halliday, M.A.K. (1977). Test as semantic choice in social contexts. In A. van Dijk and J. Petofi (Eds.), *Grammar and descriptions*. Berlin: de Gruyter.

Halliday, M.A.K., and Hasan, R. (1976). *Cohesion in English*. London: Longmans' Linguistics Library.

Halliday, M.A.K., McIntosh, A., and Stevens, P. (1964). *The linguistic sciences and language teaching*. London: Longmans' Linguistics Library.

Handscombe, R. (1969). Linguistics and children's interests. In H. Fraser and W.R. O'Donnell (Eds.), *Applied linguistics and the teaching of English*. London: Longmans' Linguistics Library.

Harris, P. (1975). Inferences and semantic development. *Journal of Child Language*, 2, 143–152.

Harris, P.L. (1982). Cognitive prerequisites to language? *British Journal of Psychology*, 73, 187–195.

Harris, Z. (1957). Cooccurrence and transformations in linguistic structure. *Language*, 33, 283–240.

Harrison, B. (1972). *Meaning and structure*. New York and London: Harper & Row.

Henle, P. (1966). Metaphor. In P. Henle (Ed.), *Language, thought and culture*. Ann Arbor, MI: University of Michigan Press.

Holzman, M. (1972). The use of interrogative forms in the verbal interaction of three mothers and their children. *Journal of Psycholinguistic Research*, 1, 311–336.

Honeck, R.P., Sowry, B.M., and Voegtle, K. (1978). Proverbial understanding in a pictorial context. *Child Development*, 49, 327–331.

Hood, L., and Bloom, L. (1979). What, when, and how about why: A longitudinal study of early expressions of causality. *Monographs of the Society for Research in Child Development*, 44 (Serial No. 181).

Hood, L., Lahey, M., Lifter, K., and Bloom, L. (1978). Observational descriptive methodology in studying child language: Preliminary results on the development of complex sentences. In G.P. Sackett (Ed.), *Observing behavior*, Vol. 1: *Theory and applications in mental retardation*. Baltimore: University Park Press.

Horgan, D. (1980). Nouns: Love'em or leave'em. *Annals of the New York Academy of Sciences*, **345**, 5–26.

Huttenlocher, J. (1974). The origins of language comprehension. In R.L. Solso (Ed.), *Theories in cognitive psychology: The Loyola symposium*. Hillsdale, NJ: Erlbaum.

Huttenlocher, J., Smiley, P., and Charney, R. (1983). The emergence of action categories in the child: Evidence from verb meanings. *Psychological Review*, **90**, 72–93.

Hymes, D. (1972). Models of the interaction of language and social life. In J.J. Gumperz and D. Hymes (Eds.), *Directions in sociolinguistics*, New York: Holt, Rinehart & Winston.

Ianco-Worrall, A.D. (1972). Bilingualism and cognitive development. *Child Development*, **43**, 1390–1400.

Inhelder, B., and Piaget, J. (1958). *The growth of logical thinking from childhood to adolescence*. New York: Basic Books.

Inhelder, B., and Piaget, J. (1964). *The early growth of logic in the child*. London: Routledge & Kegan Paul.

Jackendorff, R. (1984). *Semantics and cognition*. Cambridge, MA: M.I.T. Press.

Jaffe, J., Stern, D., and Perry, J. (1973). "Conversational" coupling of gaze behavior in prelinguistic human development. *Journal of Psycholinguistic Research*, **2**, 321–330.

Jakobson, R. (1960). Linguistics and poetics. In T. Sebeok (Ed.), *Style in language*. Cambridge, MA: M.I.T. Press.

Jakobson, R. (1968). *Child language, aphasia and phonological universals*. The Hague: Mouton.

Jakobson, R., and Halle, M. (1971). *Fundamentals of language*. The Hague: Mouton.

Jones, E. (1950). On symbolism. *Papers on psychoanalysis*. London: Balliere, Tindell & Cox.

Kaila, E. (1932). Die Reaktionen des Sauglings auf des menschliche Gesicht. *Annales Universitatis Aboensis, B.*, **17**, 1–114.

Kaplan, E., and Kaplan, G. (1971). The prelinguistic child. In J. Eliot (Ed.), *Human development and cognitive processes*. New York: Holt, Rinehart and Winston.

Karmiloff-Smith, A. (1981). Language: A formal problem space for children. In W. Deutsch (Ed.), *The child's construction of language*. New York: Academic Press.

Katz, J.J. (1972). *Semantic theory*. New York: Harper & Row.

Katz, J.J., and Langendoen, D.T. (1976). Pragmatics and presupposition. *Language*, **52**, 1–19.

Katz, N., Baker, E., and Macnamara, J. (1974). On the child's acquisition of proper and common nouns. *Child Development*, **45**, 469–473.

Kay, D.A., and Anglin, J.M. (1982). Overextension and underextension in the child's receptive and expressive speech. *Journal of Child Language*, **9**, 83–98.

Keenan, E. (1974). Conversational competence in children. *Journal of Child Language*, **1**, 163–184.

Keenan, E.O. (1977). Making it last: Repetition in children's discourse. In S. Ervin-Tripp and C. Mitchell-Kernan (Eds.), *Child discourse*. New York: Academic Press.

Keenan, E.O., and Schieffelin, B.B. (1976). Topic as discourse notion: A study of topic in the conversations of children and adults. In C. Li (Ed.), *Subject and topic*. New York: Academic Press.

Kintsch, W. (1977). On comprehending stories. In P. Carpenter and M. Just (Eds.), *Cognitive processes in comprehension*. Hillsdale, NJ: Erlbaum.

Kogan, N., Connor, K., Gross, A., and Fava, D. (1980). Understanding visual metaphor: Developmental and individual differences. *Monographs of the Society for Research in Child Development*, **45** (Serial No. 183).

Kohlberg, L., Yeager, J., and Hjertholm, E. (1968). Private speech: Four studies and a review of theories. *Child Development*, **39**, 691–736.

Kozhevnikov, V., and Chistovich, L. (1965). *Speech, articulation and perception*. U.S. Department of Commerce: Joint Publication Research Service.

Kuczaj, S., and Daly, M. (1979). The development of hypothetical reference in the speech of young children. *Journal of Child Language*, **6**, 563–579.

Labov, W. (1970). The study of language in its social context. *Studium Generale*, **23**, 30–87.

Labov, W. (1973). The boundaries of words and their meanings. In C.J.N. Baily and R.W. Shuy (Eds.), *New ways of analyzing variation in English*. Washington, D.C.: Georgetown University Press.

Lackner, J.R. (1976). A developmental study of language behavior in retarded children. In D.M. Morehead and A.E. Morehead (Eds.), *Normal and deficient child language*. Baltimore: University Park Press.

Landau, B. (1982). Language learning in blind children. Unpublished Ph.D. dissertation. Philadelphia: University of Pennsylvania.

Landau, B., and Gleitman, L.R. (1985). *Language and experience*. Cambridge, MA: Harvard University Press.

Langer, S. (1948). *Philosophy in a new key*. New York: Mentor.

Lees, R. (1964). Formal discussion. In U. Bellugi and R. Brown (Eds.), The acquisition of language. *Monographs of the Society for Research in Child Development*, **29** (Serial No. 92).

Lehrer, A. (1970). Notes on lexicon gaps. *Journal of Linguistics*, **6**, 257–261.

Lenneberg, E.H. (1967). *Biological foundations of language*. New York: Wiley.

Leopold, W.F. (1939–1949). *Speech development of a bilingual child*, Volumes 1–4. Evanston, IL: Northwestern University Press.

Lewis, D. (1972). General semantics. In I.D. Davidson and G. Herman, (Eds.), *Semantics of natural language*. Dordrecht: Reidel.

Lewis, M. (1936). *Infant speech: A study of the beginnings of language*. London: Routledge & Kegan Paul.

Lewis, M., and Freedle, R. (1973). Mother–infant dyad: The cradle of meaning. In T. Pliner, L. Krames, and T. Alloway (Eds.), *Communication and affect: Language and thought*. New York: Academic Press.

Lieven, E. (1978). Conversations between mothers and young children: Individual differences and their implications for the study of language learning. In N. Waterson and C. Snow (Eds.), *The development of communication: Social and pragmatic factors in language acquisition*. London: Wiley.

Limber, J. (1973). The genesis of complex sentences. In T. Moore (Ed.), *Cognitive development and the acquisition of language*. New York: Academic Press.

Litowitz, B. (1975). Language: Waking and sleeping. *Psychoanalysis and contemporary science*, Vol. 4. New York: International Universities Press.

Lock, A. (1978). *Action, gesture and symbol: The emergence of language*. London: Academic Press.

Lock, A. (1980). *The guided reinvention of language*. London: Academic Press.

Lovell, K., and Dixon, E.M. (1965). The growth of grammar in imitation, comprehension, and production. *Journal of Child Psychology and Psychiatry*, **5**, 1–9.

Luria, A.R.L., and Vinogradova, O.S. (1959). An objective investigation of the dynamics of semantic systems. *British Journal of Psychology*, **50**, 89–105.

Luria, A., and Yudovich, R. (1971). *Speech and the development of mental processes in the child*. Harmondworth, England: Penguin.

Lust, B., and Mervis, C.A. (1980). Development of coordination in the natural speech of young children. *Journal of Child Language*, **7**, 279–304.

Lyons, J. (1977). *Semantics*. Cambridge, England: Cambridge University Press.

Mackay, D., and Thompson, B. (1968). *The initial teaching of reading and writing*, Programme in Linguistics and English Teaching, Paper 3. London: Longmans' Linguistics Library.

Macnamara, J. (1972). Cognitive basis of language learning in infants. *Psychology Review*, **79**, 1–13.

Macnamara, J. (1982). *Names for things*. Cambridge, MA: M.I.T. Press.

Malgady, R.G. (1977). Children's interpretation and appreciation of similes. *Child Development*, **48**, 1734–1738.

Mandler, J.M. (1979). Categorical and schematic organization in memory. In C.R. Puff (Ed.), *Memory organization and structure*. New York: Academic Press.

Mandler, J.M. (1982). Representation. In J.H. Flavell and E.M. Markman (Eds.), *Cognitive development*, Vol. 3 of P.H. Mussen (General Ed.), *Handbook of child psychology*. New York: Wiley.

Mandler, J.M. (1984). *Stories, scripts, scenes: Aspects of schema theory*. Hillsdale, NJ: Erlbaum.

Mandler, J.M., and Johnson, N.S. (1977). Remembrance of things parsed: Story structure and recall. *Cognitive Psychology*, **9**, 111–151.

Mandler, J.M., Scribner, S., Cole, M., and De Forest, M. (1980). Cross-cultural invariance in story recall. *Child Development*, **51**, 19–26.

Markman, E.M. (1976). Children's difficulty with word-referent differentiation. *Child Development*, **47**, 742–749.

Markman, E.M. (1977). Realizing that you don't understand: A preliminary investigation. *Child Development*, **48**, 986–992.

Markman, E.M. (1981). Two different principles of conceptual organization. In M.E. Lamb and A.L. Brown, (Eds.), *Advances in developmental psychology*, Vol. 1. Hillsdale, NJ: Erlbaum.

Markman, E.M., and Callanan, M.A. (1983). An analysis of hierarchical classification. In R. Sternberg (Ed.), *Advances in the psychology of human intelligence*, Vol. 2. Hillsdale, NJ: Erlbaum.

Markman, E.M., and Siebert, J. (1976). Classes and collections: Internal organization and resulting holistic properties. *Cognitive Psychology*, **8**, 561–577.

Masters, J.C., Mesibov, G.B., and Anderson, G.W. (1970). Word association type and the temporal stacking of responses. *Journal of Verbal Learning and Verbal Behavior*, **9**, 207–211.

Matter, G., and Davis, L. (1975). A reply to metaphor and linguistic theory. *Quarterly Journal of Speech*, **61**, 322–327.

McCarthy, D. (1954). Language development in children. In L. Carmichael (Ed.), *Manual of child psychology*, 2nd Ed. New York: Wiley.

McCune-Nicolich, L. (1981). The cognitive bases of relational words in the single-word period. *Journal of Child Language*, 8, 15–34.

McGhee, P. (1979). *Humor: Its origin and development*. San Francisco: Freeman.

McLaughlin, B. (1978). *Second language acquisition in childhood*. Hillsdale, NJ: Erlbaum.

McNeill, D. (1975). Semiotic extension. In R.L. Solso (Ed.), *Information processing and cognition: The Loyola Symposium*. Hillsdale, NJ: Erlbaum.

McShane, J. (1979). The development of naming. *Linguisitics*, 17, 879–905.

Menyuk, P. (1969). *Sentences children use*. Cambridge, MA: M.I.T. Press.

Mervis, C.B., and Rosch, E. (1981). Categorization of natural objects. In *Annual review of psychology*, Vol. 32. Palto Alto, CA: Annual Reviews.

Miller, G. (1977). *Spontaneous apprentices*. New York: Seabury Press.

Miller, G., and Johnson-Laird, P. (1976). *Language and perception*. Cambridge, MA: Harvard University Press.

Miller, W., and Ervin, S. (1964). The development of grammar in child language. In U. Bellugi and R. Brown (Eds.), *The acquisition of language. Monographs of the Society for Research in Child Development*, 29, 9–34.

Mueller, E. (1972). The maintenance of verbal exchanges between young children. *Child Development*, 43, 930–938.

Nelson, K. (1973). Structure and strategy in learning to talk. *Monographs of the Society for Research in Child Development*, 38 (Serial No. 149).

Nelson, K. (1974). Concept, word and sentence: Interrelations in acquisition and development. *Psychological Review*, 81, 267–285.

Nelson, K. (1975). Individual differences in early semantic and syntactic development. *Annals of the New York Academy of Science*, 263, 132–139.

Nelson, K. (1977a). Cognitive development and the acquisition of concepts. In R.C. Anderson, R.J. Spiro, and W.E. Montague (Eds.), *Schooling and the acquisition of knowledge*. Hillsdale, NJ: Erlbaum.

Nelson, K. (1977b). The syntagmatic–paradigmatic shift revisited: A review of research and theory. *Psychological Bulletin*, 84, 93–116.

Nelson, K. (1978a). Explorations in the development of a functional semantic system. In W. Collins (Ed.), *Children's language and communication*, Vol. 12. Hillsdale, NJ: Erlbaum.

Nelson, K. (1978b). How young children represent knowledge of their world in and out of language. In R.S. Siegler (Ed.), *Children's thinking: What develops?* Hillsdale, NJ: Erlbaum.

Nelson, K. (1980). The conceptual basis for language. Paper presented at the British Psychological Society Meeting, Edinburgh, Scotland, September 5–7.

Nelson, K. (1981). Individual differences in language development: Implications for development and language. *Developmental Psychology*, 17(2), 170–187.

Nelson, K., Rescorla, L., Gruendel, J., and Benedict, H. (1978). Early lexicons: What do they mean? *Child Development*, 49, 960–968.

Newport, E. (1977). Motherese: the speech of mothers to young children. In N. Castellan, D. Pisoni, and G. Potts (Eds.), *Cognitive theory*, 2nd Ed. Hillsdale, NJ: Erlbaum.

Newport, E. (1979). Constraints on structure: Evidence from American Sign Language. In W.A. Collins (Ed.), *Minnesota symposium on child psychology*, Vol. 14. Hillsdale, NJ: Erlbaum.

Newport, E., Gleitman, L., and Gleitman, H. (1977). Mother, I'd rather do it myself:

Some effects and non-effects of maternal speech style. In C. Snow and C. Ferguson (Eds.), *Talking to children: Language input and acquisition*. Cambridge, England: Cambridge University Press.

Nicolich, L.M. (1980). The cognitive bases of relational words in the single word period. Unpublished manuscript. New Brunswick, NJ: Rutgers University.

Ninio, A., and Bruner, J. (1978). The achievement and antecedents of labelling. *Journal of Child Language*, **5**, 1–16.

Norman, D.A. (1973). Memory, knowledge and the answering of questions. In R.L. Solso (Ed.), *Contemporary issues in cognitive psychology: The Loyola symposium*. New York: Wiley.

Olson, D. (1970). Language and thought: Aspects of a cognitive theory of semantics. *Psychological Review*, **77**, 257–273.

Ortony, A., Reynolds, R., and Arter, J. (1978). Metaphor: Theoretical and empirical research. *Psychological Bulletin*, **85**, 919–943.

Osgood, C. (1953). *Method and theory in experimental psychology*. New York: Oxford University Press.

Osherson, D., and Markman, E.M. (1975). Language and the ability to evaluate contradictions and tautologies. *Cognition*, **3**, 213–226.

Paivio, A. (1979). Psychological processes in the comprehension of metaphor. In A. Ortony (Ed.), *Metaphor and thought*. Cambridge: Cambridge University Press.

Paris, S.G., and Lindauer, B.K. (1976). The role of inference in children's comprehension and memory for sentences. *Cognitive Psychology*, 8, 217–227.

Pea, R. (1980). The development of negation in early child language. In D. Olson (Ed.), *The social foundations of language and thought*. New York: Norton.

Pelsma, R. (1910). A child's vocabulary and its development. *Pedagogical Seminary*, **17**, 328–369.

Peters, A.M. (1980). The units of language acquisition. *University of Hawaii Working Papers on Linguistics*, **12**.

Peterson, C.L., Danner, F.W., and Flavell, J.H. (1972). Developmental changes in children's responses to three indications of communicative failure. *Child Development*, **43**, 1463–1468.

Phillips, J. (1973). Syntax and vocabulary of mothers' speech to young children: Age and sex comparisons. *Child Development*, **44**, 182–185.

Piaget, J. (1929). *The child's conception of the world*. London: Kegan Paul, Trench, Trubner.

Piaget, J. (1926). *The language and thought of the child*. New York: Harcourt, Brace.

Piaget, J. (1932). *The moral judgment of the child*. London: Kegan Paul, Trench, Trubner.

Piaget, J. (1952). *The origins of intelligence in children*. New York: Norton.

Piaget, J. (1962). *Play, dreams and imitation in childhood*. New York: Norton.

Piaget, J., and Inhelder, B. (1971). *Mental imagery in the child*. London: Routledge & Kegan Paul.

Pinker, S.M. (1979a). Bilingual and monolingual children's awareness of words. Unpublished bachelor's thesis. Montreal: McGill University.

Pinker, S.M. (1979b). Formal models of language learning. *Cognition*, **7**, 217–283.

Pinker, S.M. (1982). A theory of the acquisition of lexical interpretive grammars. In J. Bresnan (Ed.), *The mental representation of grammatical relations*. Cambridge, MA: M.I.T. Press.

Pollio, M., and Pollio, H. (1974). The development of figurative language in children. *Journal of Psycholinguistic Research*, **3**, 185–201.

Premack, D. (1970). A functional analysis of language. *Journal of Experimental Animal Behavior*, **14**, 107–125.

Premack, D., and Premack, A.J. (1983). *The mind of an ape*. NY: Norton.

Propp, V. (1968). *Morphology of the folktale*. Austin, TX: University of Texas Press. (Originally published, 1928.)

Quine, W.V.O. (1960). *Word and object*. Cambridge, MA: M.I.T. Press.

Ramer, A.L.H. (1974). Syntactic styles and universal aspects of language emergence. Unpublished doctoral dissertation. New York: City University of New York.

Rees, N. (1978). Pragmatics of language: Applications to normal and disordered language development. In R. Schiefelbusch (Ed.), *Bases of language intervention*. Baltimore: University Park Press.

Remick, H. (1975). Maternal speech to children during language acquisition. In W. von Raffler-Engel and Y. Lebrun (Eds.), *Baby talk and infant speech*. Lisse: Swets & Zeitlinger.

Rescorla, L. (1976). Concept formation in word learning. Unpublished doctoral dissertation. New Haven: Yale University.

Reynolds, R.E., and Ortony, A. (1980). Some issues in the measurement of children's comprehension of metaphorical language. *Child Development*, **51**, 1110–1119.

Richards, I.A. (1965). *The philosophy of rhetoric*. Oxford, England: Oxford University Press.

Riegel, K.F. (1970). The language acquisition process: A reinterpretation of selected research findings. In R. Goulet and P.B. Baltes (Eds.), *Life-span development psychology research and theory*. New York: Academic Press.

Robinson, E.J. (1981a). The child's understanding of inadequate messages and communication failure: A problem of ignorance or egocentrism? In W.P. Dickson (Ed.), *Children's oral communication skills*. New York: Academic Press.

Robinson, E.J. (1981b). Conversational tactics and the advancement of the child's understanding about referential communication. In W.P. Robinson (Ed.), *Communication in development*. London: Academic Press.

Robinson, E.J., and Robinson, W.P. (1977). Development in the understanding of causes of success and failure in verbal communication. *Cognition*, **5**, 363–378.

Rodger, R. (1975). Number of non-zero, post-hoc contrasts from ANOVA and error-rate 1. *British Journal of Mathematical and Statistical Psychology*, **28**, 71–78.

Rommetveit, P. (1974). *On message structure*. New York: Wiley.

Rosch, E.H. (1978). Principles of categorization. In E.H. Rosch and B.B. Lloyd (Eds.), *Cognition and categorization*. Hillsdale, NJ: Erlbaum.

Rosch, E.H., and Mervis, C.B. (1975). Family resemblances: Studies in the internal structure of categories. *Cognitive Psychology*, **7**, 573–605.

Rosch, E.H., Mervis, C., Gray, W.D., Johnson, D.M., and Boyes-Braem, P. (1976). Basic objects in natural categories. *Cognitive Psychology*, **8**, 382–439.

Rosenbaum, P.S. (1967). *The grammar of English predicate complement constructions*. Research Monograph 47, Cambridge, MA: M.I.T. Press.

Rubenstein, B. (1972). On metaphor and related phenomena. In R.R. Holt and E. Peterfreund (Eds.), *Psychoanalysis and contemporary science*. New York: Macmillan.

Rubin, K. (1979). The impact of the natural setting on private speech. In G. Zivin (Ed.), *The development of self-regulation through speech.* New York: Wiley.

Rubin, K., and Dyck, L. (1980). Preschoolers' private speech in a play setting. *Merrill Palmer Quarterly,* **26,** 219–220.

Rumelhart, D.E. (1975). Notes on a schema for stories. In D.G. Bobrow and A. Collins (Eds.), *Representation and understanding: Studies in cognitive science.* New York: Academic Press.

Rumelhart, D.E. (1977a). Understanding and summarizing brief stories. In D. LaBerge and S.J. Samuels (Eds.), *Basic processing in reading: Perception and comprehension.* Hillsdale, NJ: Erlbaum.

Rumelhart, D.E. (1977b). Toward an interactive model of reading. In S. Dornic (Ed.), *Attention and performance,* Vol. 6. Hillsdale, NJ: Erlbaum.

Ryan, J. (1974). Early language development: Towards a communicational analysis. In M. Richards (Ed.), *The integration of a child into a social world.* London: Cambridge University Press.

Sachs, J., and Devin, J. (1976). Young children's use of age appropriate speech styles in social interaction and role-playing. *Journal of Child Language,* **3,** 81–98.

Sachs, J., Brown, R., and Salerno, R. (1972). Adults' speech to children. In W. von Raffler-Engel and Y. Lebrun (Eds.). *Baby talk and infant speech.* Lisse: Swets & Zeitlinger.

Sacks, H., Schegloff, E., and Jefferson, G. (1974). A simplest systematics for the organization of turn-taking for conversation. *Language,* **50,** 696–735.

Sarbin, T.R., and Allen, V.L. (1968). Role theory. In G. Lindzey and E. Aronson (Eds.), *Handbook of social psychology,* Vol. 1. Reading, MA: Addison-Wesley.

Schacter, F.F., Kirshner, K., Klips, B., Friedricks, M., and Sanders, K. (1974). Everyday preschool interpersonal speech usage: Methodological developmental, and sociolinguistic studies. *Monographs of the Society for Research in Child Development,* **39** (Serial No. 156).

Schaffer, H.R. (1978). Acquiring the concept of dialogue. In M.H. Bornstein and W. Kessen (Eds.), *Psychological development in infancy: From image to intention.* Hillsdale, NJ: Erlbaum.

Schaffer, L.F. (1930). Children's interpretations of cartoons. Columbia Teachers College, *Contributions to Education,* **429.**

Schank, R.C., and Abelson, R.P. (1977). *Scripts, plans, goals and understanding.* Hillsdale, NJ: Erlbaum.

Schegloff, E.A. (1968). Sequencing in conversational openings. *American Anthropologist,* **70,** 1075–1095.

Schlesinger, I. (1971). Productions of utterances and language acquisition. In D. Slobin (Ed.), *The ontogenesis of grammar.* New York: Academic Press.

Searle, J. (1969). *Speech acts: An essay in the philosophy of language.* London: Cambridge University Press.

Searles, H. (1965). The differentiation between concrete and metaphorical thinking in recovering schizophrenic patients. In H. Searles, *Collected papers on schizophrenia and related subjects.* New York: International Universities Press.

Sharpe, E. (1968). Psycho-physical problems revealed in language: An investigation of metaphor. In E. Sharpe (Ed.), *Collected papers on psychoanalysis.* London: Hogarth.

Shatz, M., and Gelman, R. (1973). The development of communication skills: Modifications in the speech of young children as a function of listener. *Monographs of the Society for Research in Child Development*, **38** (Serial No. 152).

Shibatani, M. (1976). The grammar of causative constructions: A conspectus. In M. Shibatani (Ed.), *Syntax and semantics*, Vol. 6. New York: Academic Press.

Schultz, T. (1976). A cognitive-developmental analysis of humor. In A.J. Chapman and H.C. Foot (Eds.), *Humor and laughter: Theory, research and applications*. New York: Wiley.

Siegel, L. (1978). Is the young child really preoperational? In L.S. Siegel and C.J. Brainerd (Eds.), *Alternatives to Piaget: Critical essays on the theory*. New York: Academic Press.

Sinclair, H. (1970). The transition from sensorimotor behavior to symbolic activity. *Interchange*, **1**, 119–126.

Singer, J.B., and Flavell, J.H. (1981). Development of knowledge about communication: Children's evaluations of explicitly ambiguous messages. *Child Development*, **52**, 1211–1215.

Skinner, B.F. (1953). *Science and human behavior*. New York: Macmillan.

Slobin, D.I. (1971). Developmental psycholinguistics. In W.O. Dingwall (Ed.), *A survey of linguistic science*. College Park, MD: Linguistic Program, University of Maryland.

Slobin, D.I. (1973). Cognitive prerequisites for the development of grammar. In C.A. Ferguson and D.I. Slobin (Eds.), *Studies of child language development*. New York: Holt, Rinehart & Winston.

Slobin, D.I. (1978). A case study of early language awareness. In A. Sinclair, R.J. Jarvella, and W.J.M. Levelt (Eds.), *The child's conception of language*. New York: Springer-Verlag.

Slobin, D.I., and Bever, T.G. (1982). Children use canonical sentence schemas: A cross-linguistic study of word order and inflections. *Cognition*, **12**, 229–266.

Slobin, D.I., and Welsh, C. (1973). Elicited imitation as a research tool in developmental psycholinguistics. In C.A. Ferguson and D.I. Slobin (Eds.), *Readings in child language acquisition*. New York: Holt, Rinehart & Winston.

Smiley, S.S., and Brown, A.L. (1979). Conceptual preference for thematic or taxonomic relations: A nonmonotonic age trend from preschool to old age. *Journal of Experimental Child Psychology*, **28**, 249–257.

Snow, C. (1972). Mother's speech to children learning language. *Child Development*, **43**, 549–565.

Snow, C.E. (1976). The development of conversation between mothers and babies. *Pragmatics Microfiche*, **I.6**, A2.

Snow, C.E. (1977). Mother's speech research: From input to interaction. In C.E. Snow and C. Ferguson (Eds.), *Talking to children: Language input and acquisition*. Cambridge, England: Cambridge University Press.

Snow, C.E., and Ferguson, C.A. (Eds.) (1977). *Talking to children: Language input and acquisition*. Cambridge, England: Cambridge University Press.

Snow, C.E., Arlman-Rupp, A., Hassing, Y., Jobse, J., Joosten, J., and Vorster, J. (1976). Mothers' speech in three social classes. *Journal of Psycholinguistic Research*, **5**, 1–20.

Spiro, R.J. (1977). Inferential reconstruction in memory for connected discourse. In R.C.

Anderson, R.J. Spiro, and W.E. Montague (Eds.), *Schooling and the acquisition of knowledge*. Hillsdale, NJ: Erlbaum.

Spitz, R., and Wolf, K. (1946). The smiling response. *Genetic Psychology Monographs*, **34**, 57–125.

Stalnaker, R. (1972). Pragmatics. In D. Davidson and G. Harman (Eds.), *Semantics of natural language*. Dordrecht: Reidel.

Stayton, D., Hogan, R., and Ainsworth, M.D.S. (1971). Infant obedience and maternal behavior: The origins of socialization reconsidered. *Child Development*, **42**, 1057–1069.

Stein, N.L. (1982). The definition of a story. *Pragmatics*, **6**, 487–507.

Stein, N.L. (1983). On the goals, functions, and knowledge of reading and writing. *Contemporary Educational Psychology*, **8**, 261–292.

Stein, N.L. (1986). Knowledge and process in the acquisition of writing skills. *Review of Research in Education*, Special Issue on Writing.

Stein, N.L., and Glenn, C.G. (1979). An analysis of story comprehension in elementary school children. In R.O. Freedle (Ed.), *New directions in discourse processing* (Vol. 2): *Advances in discourse processing*. Norwood, NJ: Ablex.

Stein, N.L., and Glenn, C.G. (1982). Children's concept of time: The development of a story schema. In W.J. Friedman (Ed.), *The developmental psychology of time*. New York: Academic Press.

Stein, N.L., and Kilgore, K. (1985). The development of a story concept. Unpublished manuscript. Chicago: University of Chicago.

Stein, N.L., and Levine, L. (1986). Thinking about feelings: The development and use of emotional knowledge. In R.E. Snow and M. Farr (Eds.), *Aptitude, learning, and instruction* (Vol. 3): *Cognition, conation, and affect*. Hillsdale, NJ: Erlbaum.

Stein, N.L., and Policastro, M. (1984). The concept of a story: A comparison between children's and teacher's perspectives. In H. Mandl, N.L. Stein, and T. Trabasso (Eds.), *Learning and comprehension of text*. Hillsdale, NJ: Erlbaum.

Stein, N.L., and Salgo, D. (1984). The relationship between storytelling skills and the concept of a story. Paper presented at the Psychonomics Society Meetings, San Antonio, Texas.

Stein, N.L., and Trabasso, T. (1982). What's in a story: An approach to comprehension and instruction. In R. Glaser (Ed.), *Advances in instructional psychology*, Vol. 2. Hillsdale, NJ: Erlbaum.

Stern, D.N. (1974). Mother and infant at play: The dyadic interaction involving facial, vocal, and gaze behavior. In M. Lewis and L. Rosenblum (Eds.), *The effect of the infant on its caretaker*. New York: Wiley.

Stern, D.N. (1975). The infant's stimulus "world" during social interaction. Paper presented at the Loch Lomond Symposium, University of Strathclyde.

Stern, W., and Stern, C. (1928). *Die Kindersprache*. Leipzig: Barth.

Stern, W. (1930). *Psychology of early childhood*. New York: Holt.

Stockwell, R., Schacter, P., and Partee, B. (1973). *The major syntactic structures of English*. New York: Holt, Rinehart & Winston.

Sutton-Smith, B. (1975). The importance of the storytaker: An investigation of the imaginative life. *The Urban Review*, **8**.

Talmy, L. (1976a). Communicative aims and means. In *Working papers on language universals*, Vol. 20. Stanford, CA: Stanford University Press.

Talmy, L. (1976b). Semantic causative types. In M. Shibatani (Ed.), *Syntax and semantics*, Vol. 6. New York: Academic Press.

Thompson, J.R., and Chapman, R.S. (1975). Who is "daddy"? *Papers and Reports in Child Language Development*, **10**, 59–68.

Thorndyke, P.W. (1977). Cognitive structures in comprehension and memory of narrative discourse. *Cognitive Psychology*, **9**, 77–110.

Tomasello, M., and Farrar, M. (1984). Cognitive bases of lexical development: Object permanence and relational words. *Journal of Child Language*, **11**, 477–495.

Trabasso, T., Stein, N.L., and Johnson, L.R. (1981). Children's knowledge of events: A causal analysis of story structure. In G. Bower (Ed.), *Learning and motivation*, Vol. 15. New York: Academic Press.

Trevarthen, C. (1974). Conversations with a two-month-old. *New Scientist*, **62**, 230–235.

Trevarthen, C., and Hubley, P. (1978). Secondary intersubjectivity: Confidence, confiding and acts of meaning in the first year. In A. Lock (Ed.), *Action, gesture and symbol: The emergence of language*. London: Academic Press.

Verbrugge, R.R. (1979). The primacy of metaphor in development. *New Directions in Child Development*, **6**, 77–84.

Vihman, M.M. (1979). Formulas in first and second language acquisition. *Papers and Reports in Child Language Development*, **18**, 75–92.

Vosniadou, S., and Ortony, A. (1983). The emergence of the literal-metaphorical-anomalous distinction in young children. *Child Development*, **54**, 154–161.

Vygotsky, L. (1962). *Thought and language*. Cambridge, MA: M.I.T. Press.

Vygotsky, L., and Luria, A. (1930). The function and fate of egocentric speech. Proceedings of the Ninth International Congress of Psychology, New Haven.

Wechsler, D. (1963). *Manual for the Wechsler Preschool and Primary Scale of Intelligence*. New York: Psychological Corporation.

Weeks, T.E. (1971). Speech registers in young children. *Child Development*, **42**, 1119–1131.

Weir, R. (1962). *Language in the crib*. The Hague: Mouton.

Wellek, R., and Warren, A. (1969). *A theory of literature*. New York: Harvest Books.

Wellman, H.M., and Lempers, J.D. (1977). The naturalistic communicative abilities of two-year-olds. *Child Development*, **48**, 1052–1057.

Werner, H. (1978). *Developmental processes: Selected writings of Heinz Werner, Vol. 1 & 2* (S.S. Barten and M.B. Franklin, Eds). New York: International Universities Press.

Werner, H., and Kaplan, E. (1950). The acquisition of word meanings: A developmental study. *Monographs of the Society for Research in Child Development*, **15** (Serial No. 15).

Werner, H., and Kaplan, B. (1963). *Symbol Formation*. New York: Wiley. (Reissued, 1983, Hillsdale, NJ: Erlbaum).

Werner, O., Levis-Matichekm, G., Evens, M., and Litowitz, B. (1975). An ethnoscience view of schizophrenic speech. In M. Sanches and B. Blount (Eds.), *Sociocultural dimensions of language use*. New York: Academic Press.

Wexler, K. (1982). A principle theory for language acquisition. In E. Wanner and L.R. Gleitman (Eds.), *Language acquisition: State of the art*. Cambridge, MA: Cambridge University Press.

Wexler, K., and Culicover, P.W. (1980). *Formal principles of language acquisition*. Cambridge, MA: M.I.T. Press.

Whorf, B.L. (1956). *Language, thought and reality*. Cambridge, MA: M.I.T. Press.

Wilcox, M.J., and Webster, J. (1980). Early discourse behavior: An analysis of children's responses to listener feedback. *Child Development*, **51**, 1120–1125.

Williams, C.E., and Legum, S.E. (1970). On recording samples of informal speech from elementary school children. Southwest Regional Educational Laboratory, Technical Report No. 25.

Winch, P. (1958). *The idea of a social science*. London: Routledge & Kegan Paul.

Winner, E. (1979). New names for old things: The emergence of metaphoric language. *Journal of Child Language*, **6**, 469–492.

Winner, E., Rosenstiel, A.K., and Gardner, H. (1976). The development of metaphoric understanding. *Developmental Psychology*, **12**, 289–297.

Winner, E., Wapner, W., Cicone, M., and Gardner, H. (1979). Measures of metaphor. *New Directions in Child Development: Fact, Fiction and Fantasy in Childhood*, **6**, 67–75.

Winner, E., Engel, M., and Gardner, H. (1980a). Misunderstanding metaphor: What's the problem? *Journal of Experimental Child Psychology*, **30**, 22–32.

Winner, E., McCarthy, M., and Gardner, H. (1980b). The ontogenesis of metaphor. In R.T. Honeck and R.R. Hoffman (Eds.), *Cognition and figurative language*. Hillsdale, NJ: Erlbaum.

Wittgenstein, L. (1953). *Philosophical investigations*. New York: Macmillan.

Wittgenstein, L. (1958). *The blue and brown books*. New York: Harper.

Wolman, R.N., and Barker, E.N. (1965). A developmental study of word definitions. *Journal of Genetic Psychology*, **107**, 159–166.

Wootten, J., Merkin, S., Hood, L., and Bloom, L. (1979). Wh-questions: linguistic evidence to explain the sequence of acquisition. Paper presented at the Biennial Meeting of the Society for Research in Child Development, San Francisco.

Subject Index

Babbling, 10, 30–31, 32, 45–46
Bilingualism
 and lexical innovation, 121
 and understanding of word-object relationship, 349–58
Biological predispositions in language learning,
 73, 87–88, 156–57, 158–75
Blindness and language learning, 172–73

Category boundaries
 and hypothetical reference, 130–36
 and joking, 343–44
 and metaphor, 300, 304, 343–45
Category formation
 and word meaning, 137–57
Code switching. See Speech styles
Cognitive development, 3, 4
 and jokes, 342–48
 and learning of relational terms, 62, 67
 and linguistic development, 68–69, 81, 158,
  164–65
 and metaphor, 314, 324, 338–39
 and speech styles, 228
Cohesion, in discourse, 251–62, 89–91, 100–
 105
Communication, adequacy of, 230–37
Communicative intentions, 3, 239, 245–46
 prelinguistic, 4, 28, 37
Comprehension, evaluation of, 179, 230–41
Comprehension vs. production, 5, 56
 of metaphor, 299, 304, 313

Concepts, 51–53, 58, 62
 acquisition and language, 155–56
 basic/superordinate and word learning, 137–
  57
 and word learning, 50–59
Contexts of language acquisition
 book reading, 36–49
 linguistic and situational, 52–53, 59
Conversation, 20–35, 239–40, 251–62, 263–
 77. See also Dialogue
 adjacency pairs in, 26, 27, 30, 35
 repairs in, 28, 35
 turn-taking in, 26–35
Conversation model, 25–35
Conversational routines, 202–204. See also
 Turn-taking
Critical periods in language learning, 88, 161
Cross-linguistic perspectives, 75–76, 107–108,
 160–61

Deafness and language learning, 169–70
Deixis, 61, 63
Dialogue. See also Conversation
 child-child, 251–62, 263–77
 mother-child, 4, 20–35, 36–49
 scriptal view of, 263–77
 teacher-child, 251–62
Downs Syndrome and language learning, 161,
 173–74

389

Author Index